D1091314

Praise for *Challenge for the Pacific*

"[Leckie] has succeeded in compressing numerous tales into a readable story, but his greatest contribution is a unique feeling for combat. . . . His marines are living, brawling, obscene, blasphemous—and utterly believable. He has caught their gallows humor, their cockiness and their savagery in the business of battle." —**John Toland**, *New York Times Books Review*

"[A] true winner. . . . Excitement, action, fast narrative pace, and a deep respect for the rudiments of genuine patriotism mark the story. . . . [Leckie] presents the Allies and the Japanese as separate people, giving them the stature of human beings involved in desperate battle." —*Nashville Banner* (Tennessee)

"[A] stirring story of America's survival in its grimmest hour. . . . As readable and gripping as a novel."
—*Patriot Ledger* (Massachusetts)

"Despite its scope, the story is told in individual terms—Japanese and American. Characters are very much alive on the printed page. *Challenge for the Pacific* is fast-paced and informative." —*Navy Times*

"Detailed and dramatic. . . . In these pages one can feel the frustration, despair and confusion experienced by both sides in the savage see-saw struggle." —*Tulsa World* (Oklahoma)

"[An] epic tale ably told. . . . To those who were there this book will bring back vivid memories of when Japanese suicidal charges came screaming out of the darkness, or when the surrounding waters flamed with naval gunfire. To those who were not there this book should bring some small realization of what it was like." —*El Paso Times* (Texas)

"Here is a book to wrench the heart. It is a driving, relentless narrative that summons up all of the hideous color and clamor of battle. But, more than that, it is a timely evocation of what a nation must do in wars to preserve its freedom. . . . [This] book is a splendid weld of the strategies, views and experiences of soldiers, sailors and airmen." —*Newark News* (New Jersey)

"*Challenge for the Pacific* is more than the battle of Guadalcanal. It is the living and dying of Americans and Japanese. . . . [Leckie] knows how a ground-pounding Marine thinks, talks and reacts." —*Leatherneck Magazine*

"[A] stirring blow-by-blow account. . . . [The author's] style insinuates itself into the blood of the reader and quickens the heartbeat. . . . In vivid, human terms [he] tells the full story." —*Greensboro Daily News* (North Carolina)

"Leckie puts flesh on the bones of history. . . . The book has the ring of authenticity. . . . It is intensely dramatic, vivid, broad, and yet intimate in detail, deeply moving in its portrayal of the human side of war. In the best sense, it is history made alive." —*Pasadena Star-News* (California)

"A vivid portrayal. . . . [This] well-rounded picture of what war is like from both sides of the front [is] worthy of attention." —*Buffalo Courier-Express* (New York)

"Leckie is a brilliant war writer." —*New Orleans Time Picayune*

Pacific

MUSSAU

MANUS

NEW HANOVER

Kavieng

NEW IRELAND

BISMARCK ARCHIPELAGO

Rabaul

5°s.

Cape Gloucester

St. George Channel

Dampier Strait

Gasmata

NEW BRITAIN

Lae

Salamaua

NEW GUINEA

Buna

Solomon

WOODLARK Is.

D'ENTRECASTEAUX ISLANDS

Port Moresby

10°s.

Milne Bay

LOUISIADE ARCHIPELAGO

Coral

150°E.

Liam Dunne

Ocean

AREA of ACTION in the SOLOMONS

MILES

0   100   200   300   400

160°E.

5°S.

KA

Kieta
BOUGAINVILLE

SOLOMON
ISLANDS

TLAND
IS.

CHOISEUL

Treasury
IS.
VELLA LAVELLA

SANTA
ISABEL

The

Sea

NEW
GEORGIA

Slot

KOLOMBANGARA

RENDOVA

VANGUNU

Tulagi

FLORIDA

MALAITA

RUSSELL IS.

Savo.

GAVUTU
TANAMBOGO

GUADALCANAL

10°S.

SAN CRISTOBAL

SANTA CRUZ
375 MILES

NEW HEBRIDES
525 MILES

NEW CALEDONIA
750 MILES

Sea

160°E.

CHALLENGE FOR THE PACIFIC

The Bloody Six-Month Battle of Guadalcanal

ROBERT LECKIE

DA CAPO PRESS • NEW YORK

Grateful acknowledgment is made for permission to include the following copyrighted material in this book:

Excerpts from *A Coastwatcher's Diary* by Martin Clemens. Reprinted by permission of the author.

Excerpts from *The Battle for Guadalcanal* by Brigadier General Samuel B. Griffith, II, copyright © 1963 by Samuel B. Griffith, II. Published by J. B. Lippincott Company. Reprinted by permission of the publisher.

Excerpts from *Strong Men Armed* by Robert Leckie, copyright © 1962 by Robert Leckie; *Helmet for My Pillow* by Robert Leckie, copyright 1957 by Robert Hugh Leckie. Reprinted by permission of Random House, Inc. and the author.

Excerpts from *Once a Marine: The Memoirs of General A. A. Vandegrift, U.S.M.C.,* as told to Robert B. Asprey, copyright © 1964 by A. A. Vandegrift and R. B. Asprey. Reprinted by permission of W. W. Norton & Company, Inc.

Excerpts from *Japanese Destroyer Captain* by Commander Tameichi Hara, with Fred Saito and Roger Pineau, copyright © 1961, by Captain Tameichi Hara, Fred Saito and Roger Pineau. Reprinted by permission of Ballantine Books, Inc.

Library of Congress Cataloging-in-Publication Data

Leckie, Robert.
Challenge for the Pacific: the bloody six-month Battle of Guadalcanal / Robert Leckie.—1st Da Capo Press ed.
p.   cm.
Originally published: Garden City, N.Y.: Doubleday, 1965, in series: The crossroads of world history series.
Includes bibliographical references (p.) and index.
ISBN 0-306-80911-7 (alk. paper)
1. World War, 1939–1945—Campaigns—Solomon Islands—Guadalcanal. I. Title.
D760.8.L4L43   1999
940.54′26—dc21   98-47407
                                                                                    CIP

First Da Capo Press edition 1999

This Da Capo Press paperback edition of *Challenge for the Pacific* is an unabridged republication of the edition first published in New York in 1965. It is reprinted by arrangement with the author.

Published by Da Capo Press, Inc.
A Member of Perseus Books Group
233 Spring Street, New York, N.Y. 10013

Manufactured in the United States of America

To Bud Conley, Lew Juergens, and Bill Smith
My Buddies on Guadalcanal

PREFACE

ON AUGUST 7, 1962—the twentieth anniversary of the landings at Guadalcanal—men of the First Marine Division Association received a message from Sergeant Major Vouza of the British Solomon Islands Police. Vouza said: "Tell them I love them all. Me old man now, and me no look good no more. But me never forget."

Neither would anyone else who had been on Guadalcanal, not the Japanese who tortured Vouza, and from whom this proud and fierce Solomon Islander exacted a fearsome vengeance, not the Americans who ultimately conquered. For Guadalcanal, as the historian Samuel Eliot Morison has said, is not a name but an emotion. It is a word evocative, even, of sense perception; of the putrescent reek of the jungle, the sharp ache of hunger or the pulpy feel of water-logged flesh, as well as of all those clanging, bellowing, stuttering battles—land, sea, and air—which were fought, night and day, to determine whether America or Japan would possess a ramshackle airfield set in the middle of 2500 square miles of malarial wilderness.

More important, historically, Guadalcanal was the place at which the tide in the Pacific War turned against Japan. Although this distinction has often been conferred upon Midway, the fact remains that the naval air battles fought at Midway did not turn the tide, but rather gave the first check to Japanese expansion while restoring, through the loss of four big Japanese aircraft carriers as against only one American, parity in carrier power.

After Midway the Japanese were still on the offensive. They thought that way and they acted that way. "After Coral Sea and Midway, I still had hope," said Captain Toshikazu Ohmae, operations officer for the Japanese Eighth Fleet, "but after Guadalcanal I felt that we could not win." Rear Admiral Raizo Tanaka, commander of the Guadalcanal Reinforcement Force, goes even further, declaring: "There is no question that Japan's doom was sealed with the closing of the struggle for Guadalcanal." Captain Tameichi Hara, a destroyer commander who fought under Tanaka at both Midway and Guadalcanal, shares his chief's opinion, writing: "What really spelled the downfall of the Imperial Navy, in my estimation, was the series of strategic and tactical blunders by (Admiral) Yamamoto after Midway, the Operations that started with the American landing at Guadalcanal in early August, 1942." And from the Japanese Army, as represented by Major General Kiyotake Kawaguchi, commander of Japan's first major attempt to recapture the island, comes this categorical statement: "Guadalcanal is no longer merely a name of an island in Japanese military history. It is the name of the graveyard of the Japanese Army."

Guadalcanal was also the graveyard for Japan's air force. Upwards of 800 aircraft, with 2362 of her finest pilots and crewmen, were lost there. Perhaps even more important, the habit of victory deserted the heretofore invincible Japanese pilots there, and before the battle was over Japanese carrier power ceased to be a factor in the Pacific until, nearly two years later, the invasion of Saipan lured it to its effective destruction. Japanese naval losses were also high. Even though Japan's loss of 24 warships totaling 134,389 tons was hardly greater than the American loss of 24 warships totaling 126,240 tons, Japan could not come close to matching the American replacement capacity. Finally, the total American dead was, at the utmost, only about one tenth of the Japanese probable total of fifty thousand men.

However, neither comparative statistics nor the number of men and arms engaged can measure a battle's importance in history. Only a few hundred fell when Joan of Arc raised the siege of Orléans and changed the course of events in the west, while Marathon, Valmy, Saratoga and Waterloo—to name a few other decisive battles—would not, in combined casualties, equal the number of those whose blood stained one of Genghis Khan's forgotten battlefields. A battle is only great because after it has been fought things are never the same. The war has been changed in its direction, its mood, its attitudes, its men, and sometimes its very tactics. Finally, in changing a war, a great battle alters the course of world events.

This condition and its corollaries are fulfilled by Guadalcanal.

After Guadalcanal the Pacific War that had been moving south toward Australasia-Fijis-Samoa turned north toward Japan, and the United States, having been starved for victory, never again tasted defeat. More simply, after Guadalcanal the Americans were on the offensive and the Japanese were on the defensive.

It was at Guadalcanal that such myths as the invincibility of the Japanese soldier or Zero fighter-plane were destroyed, that such devices as radar-controlled naval gunfire were introduced, and that such reputations as those of Chuichi Nagumo, the hero of Pearl Harbor, or the idolized Isoroku Yamamoto were either ruined or tarnished while those of such Americans as Halsey, Kinkaid, and Richmond Kelly Turner among the admirals, Alexander Patch and Lightning Joe Collins among the Army generals, and Archer Vandegrift and Roy Geiger among the Marines, were being made. From Guadalcanal came the tactics—land, sea, and air —which were to become American battle doctrine throughout World War II, and out of this struggle emerged the seasoned young leaders who were to command the ships and regiments and squadrons which were to strike the Axis enemy everywhere.

Guadalcanal wrecked Japan's grand strategy. Imperial General Headquarters had deliberately hurled the surprise attack at Pearl Harbor to prevent the United States Navy from interfering with the Japanese timetable of conquest in the Pacific. By the time America had recovered from Pearl Harbor, it was believed, Japan would have built a chain of impregnable island forts around her stolen empire. America, tiring of a costly and bloody war, would then be willing to negotiate a peace favorable to Japan. But Guadalcanal shattered this dream. There, barely a year after Pearl Harbor, the Americans stood in triumph with their faces turned toward Japan.

And once it was clear that Guadalcanal was lost, the sober heads at Imperial General Headquarters knew that all was lost. The countries of Southeast Asia, the lush, rich islands of the Southern Seas—all of these "lands of everlasting summer"—were to be taken away from them.

After Guadalcanal, as the Japanese knew in their despair, as the Americans realized with rising jubilation, the Pacific War could never be the same.

ROBERT LECKIE

Mountain Lakes, New Jersey
September 10, 1964

Contents

Maps

Part 1

THE CHALLENGE

Chapter 1

THE ADMIRAL was tall, hard, and humorless. His face was of flint and his will was of adamant. In the United States Navy which he commanded it was sometimes said, "He's so tough he shaves with a blowtorch." President Roosevelt was fond of repeating this quip in the admiral's presence, hoping to produce, if there had been no reports of fresh disaster in the past twenty-four hours, that fleeting cold spasm of mirth—like an iceberg tick—which the President, the Prime Minister of England, and the admiral's colleagues on the Anglo-American Combined Chiefs of Staff were able to identify as a smile.

If levity was rare in Admiral Ernest King, self-doubts or delusions were nonexistent. He was aware that he was respected rather than beloved by the Navy, and he knew that he was hated by roughly half of the chiefs of the Anglo-American alliance. Mr. Stimson, the U. S. Secretary of War, hated him; so did Winston Churchill and Field-Marshal Sir Alan Brooke and Admiral Sir Andrew Cunningham.[1] Nevertheless, Admiral King continued to express the wish that was anathema in the ears of these men, as it was also irritating or at least unwelcome in the ears of General George Marshall, the U. S. Army Chief of Staff, and General H. H. Arnold, chief of the Army Air Force.

Admiral King wanted Japan checked.

He wanted this even though he was bound to adhere to the grand strategy approved by Roosevelt and Churchill: concentrate on Hitler first while containing the Japanese.

But what was *containment?*

Containing the Japanese during the three months beginning with Pearl Harbor had been as easy as cornering a tornado. The Japanese had crippled the U. S. Pacific Fleet and all but driven Britain from the Indian Ocean by sinking *Prince of Wales* and

Repulse. Except for scattered American carrier strikes against the Gilberts and Marshalls the vast Pacific from Formosa to Hawaii was in danger of becoming a Japanese lake. Wake had fallen; Guam as well; the Philippines were on their way. Japan's "Greater East Asia Co-Prosperity Sphere" had already absorbed the Dutch East Indies with all their vast and precious deposits of oil and minerals, it had supplanted the French in Indochina and evicted the British from Singapore. Burma, Malaya, and Thailand were also Japanese. The unbreachable Malay Barrier had been broken almost as easily as the invincible Maginot Line had been turned. Japan now looked west toward India with her hundreds of millions; and if Rommel should beat the British in North Africa, a German-Japanese juncture in the Middle East would become a dreadful probability. Meanwhile, great China was cut off and Australia—to which General Douglas MacArthur had been ordered should he succeed in escaping from Corregidor—was threatened by a Japanese invasion of New Guinea. At that moment in early March, as Admiral King knew, the necessary invasion force was being gathered at Rabaul, the bastion which the Japanese were building on the eastern tip of New Britain.

All this—all this ferocious speed and precision, all this lightning conquest, this sweeping of the seas and seizure of the skies —all this was containment?

Admiral King did not think so. He thought it was rather creeping catastrophe. He thought that the Japanese, unchecked, would reach out again. They would try to cut off Australia, drive deeper eastward toward Hawaii; and build an island barrier behind which they could drain off the resources of their huge new stolen empire. It was because King feared this eventuality that he had, as early as January 1942, when the drum roll of Japanese victories was beating loudest, moved to put a garrison of American troops on Fiji. Already forging an island chain to Australia, he was still not satisfied: in mid-February he wrote to General Marshall urging that it was essential to occupy additional islands "as rapidly as possible." The Chief of Staff did not reply for some time. When he did, he asked what King's purpose might be. The Navy Commander-in-Chief, Cominch as he was called, answered that he hoped to build a series of strongpoints from which a "step-by-step" advance might be made through the Solomon Islands against Rabaul.

That was on March 2. Three days later, Admiral King addressed a memorandum to President Roosevelt. He outlined his plan of operations against the Japanese. He summarized them in three phrases:

Hold Hawaii;

Support Australasia;

Drive northwestward from New Hebrides.

Admiral Ernest King was not then aware of it, but he had at that moment put a tentative finger on an island named Guadalcanal.

Japan *was* preparing to reach out again.

At Imperial General Headquarters in Tokyo the faces of the planners were bright with victory fever.[2] Who could blame them, really? Who else might bask so long in such a sun of success without becoming slightly giddy? Of course, some of the officers of the Naval General Staff had passed from fever into delirium. Some of them—conscious that it was the Navy which had brought off the great stroke at Pearl Harbor, which had played the greater role in the other victories, which had shot the enemy aviators from the skies—some of them were proposing that Australia be invaded.

The Navy's cooler heads found the proposal ridiculous.

The men of the Army General Staff thought it was impossible.

The Army, they explained, could never scrape together the ten divisions or more required for such an operation. The Navy officers nodded reflectively, saying nothing of their underlying suspicion that the Army, optimistic about Germany's chances against Russia that spring, was secretly hoarding its forces for use on the continent. The Army, as they knew, regarded the Soviet Union as the number one potential enemy.[3] Therefore, the Army, looking northwestward, could not be expected to be enthusiastic about committing troops in the southeast.

So the Naval General Staff decided that instead of invading Australia it would be more feasible to isolate Australia. The flow of American war matériel to the island continent could be blocked by seizing eastern New Guinea and driving through the Solomons into the New Caledonia-Fijis area. What did the Army think of this?

The Army approved. It promised to furnish its South Seas Detachment for the operation. These decisions also were reached in March. On the eighth day of that month, Lae and Salamaua in

New Guinea were invaded. Two days later Finschhafen was occupied.

Unknowingly, Imperial General Headquarters had pointed its baton at the island called Guadalcanal.

Among the forces gathering for the operation to isolate Australia was the Japanese Navy's 25th Air Flotilla. Its mission was to hammer at Port Moresby, the big Allied base on New Guinea which lay only a few hundred miles north of the Australian continent.

But in early March the 25th Air Flotilla was understrength. One of its three components, and perhaps the best in quality, the Tainan Fighter Wing, was still far away on the fabled island of Bali in the East Indies. Orders were dispatched to Bali alerting the Tainan Wing for movement.

Saburo Sakai was the crack pilot of the crack Tainan Fighter Wing. Saburo was not only a born fighter, he was born into a fighting caste. He was a *samurai*, the scion of professional soldiers, and he could trace his ancestry to those samurai who had invaded Korea in the sixteenth century. Saburo regarded himself as a samurai even though that caste had been abolished by the great Emperor Meiji at the end of the last century. Saburo was proud that his ancestors were among those haughty warriors of the city of Saga who had refused to give up their twin swords and had risen in revolt. And if, because of Imperial rescript, the proud and cruel samurai could no longer be cruel, no longer swing their heavy two-handed sabers to sever, at a single slash, the body of some poor defenseless *Eta* or pariah who had offended them,[4] they could always remain proud. Saburo Sakai's people had remained proud, scratching out a bare subsistence on a tiny farm near Saga, still scorning money, still wearing the emblem of the two sabers symbolic of their caste, and still priding themselves on their stoic indifference to pain and the strength of their sword hands.

Then, in the 1930s, the military adventurers seized power in Japan. The samurai was again in favor; his knightly code of *bushido*—a mixture of chivalry and cruelty—was adopted as the standard for all the young men of Japan. In 1933, at the age of sixteen, Saburo enlisted in the Navy. He endured the purposeful

torture called "recruit training" in the Japanese Navy, went to sea
on the battleships *Kirishima* and *Haruna,* applied for the Navy
Flier's School, and was accepted.

Saburo, a youth of normal Japanese height, which is about a
half foot shorter than that of the normal American, possessed an
iron body. Though his nature was warm and good-humored, his
will was of the same unbending metal. He became the outstanding student pilot of the year. He could hang by one arm from the
top of a pole for half an hour, swim fifty meters in well under
thirty seconds, stay underwater for two and a half minutes, and
because a fighter pilot's movements need to be quick, he had so
conditioned his reflexes that he could catch a fly in a single lightning lunge.

At the end of 1937 Saburo was graduated as the outstanding
student of the Thirty-eighth Non-Commissioned Officers Class.
Of seventy-five hand-picked candidates for that class, only twenty-
five had survived. One day Japan would rue this policy of training
only an elite of an elite, of providing itself with no reserve of
skilled pilots to offset combat losses, but in the Sino-Japanese War
of the mid-1930s the Japanese pilots fought with such clear superiority as to indicate that they would have a long combat life
indeed.

Saburo Sakai fought in that war. He became famous for his
ardor and daring. Wounded once during a surprise enemy air
raid, he ran for his plane streaming blood, taking off to pursue
the Chinese bombers and to cripple one of them before he was
forced to return to base. By December 7, 1941, Saburo Sakai was
already an ace. He flew from Formosa in the first strikes against
Clark Field in the Philippines. He was the first Japanese pilot to
shoot down an American fighter over those islands. He was the
first to flame a Flying Fortress, the very bomber piloted by Captain Colin Kelly, America's first war hero. By March of 1942,
Saburo Sakai had shot down thirteen aircraft: Chinese, Russian,
British, Dutch, and American. By that time also he and his comrades had reassembled at Bali. They were there to rest, but inac-
tivity only made them restless. They became irritable. They fought
with the soldiers who guarded their base. They drank or visited
those brothels without which no Japanese military force can long
endure. Saburo Sakai did neither, for he was a fighter pilot and a

samurai who stuck to his code. Nevertheless, he also fretted, wondering if he would ever get home to see his family.

On March 12 came the great news. Rotation! The men with the longest time overseas were being relieved to go home, and Saburo had more time out than any of them.

But the new leader of the Wing, Lieutenant Commander Tadashi Nakajima, did not call Saburo's name. Crushed, Saburo asked him if there had been a mistake.

"No, you do not go home with the other men," Nakajima said. "I need you, Sakai, to go with me. We are advancing to a new air base. It's Rabaul—on the island of New Britain—the foremost post against the enemy. You're the best pilot in the squadron, Sakai, and I want you to fly with me."[5]

There was no appeal, not for an enlisted man in the Japanese Navy. Heartbroken, Saburo Sakai became one of eighty pilots who were herded aboard a tiny, stinking, decrepit freighter for the 2500-mile voyage to Rabaul. Only a 1000-ton subchaser escorted them. Indifferent to human suffering, and therefore blind to human value, Japan had placed a good portion of her finest naval fliers aboard a rusty old derelict and exposed them to the very real peril of a single torpedo or 500-pound bomb.

But the rattler made Rabaul. It entered spacious, horseshoe-shaped Simpson Harbor and discharged its passengers. The pilots were appalled. Vunakanau Airfield was little more than a narrow, dusty airstrip set in the shadow of a live volcano. From time to time a deep rumbling shook the field and smoke and stones spouted from the crater's mouth. Nevertheless the men took heart when a seaplane tender delivered twenty of the latest models of the Zero fighter. They went back into action, and Saburo Sakai was again the scourge of the enemy. He flew on fighter sweeps to Port Moresby or escorted twin-engine "Betty" bombers on raiding forays over the big Allied base, and he shot down enemy planes with astonishing ease. The American P-39s and P-40s—Bell Airacobras and Curtiss Warhawks—were no match for the Japanese Zeros. The Zero was faster and much more maneuverable; and no one could cut inside an enemy fighter's turn so sharply as Saburo Sakai, bringing the American or Australian pilot under the full aimed fire of twin 20-mm. cannon and a pair of light machine guns.

Saburo's squadron always flew west toward New Guinea. But

there were other planes of the 25th Air Flotilla which flew southeast to the Solomon Islands. Beginning with big Bougainville about two hundred miles southeast of Rabaul, the Solomons run on a southeast tangent for roughly another four hundred miles. They form a double chain of islands—actually the peaks of a great drowned mountain range—facing each other at near-regular intervals across a straight blue channel from twenty to one hundred miles wide.

The objective of the Japanese bombers was the tiny island of Tulagi, the site of the headquarters of the British Resident Commissioner—for Britain held the Southern Solomons—and now used by the Royal Australian Air Force as a seaplane base. There was also a radio station on Tulagi. The Japanese bombed it regularly. They could not know that their explosives were merely convulsing the rubble of ancient and inadequate radio equipment. The operator, a retired Australian seaman named Sexton, had continually complained to headquarters: "If the Japs come here and ask me where the radio station is, and I show them *this,* they'll shoot me for concealing the real one."[6]

Tulagi had an excellent anchorage, formed between the island's northern shore and the bigger bulk of Florida Island to the north. Sometimes, after the Japanese pilots had watched their bomb-hits making yellow mushrooms on the radio station, or their misses forming white rings in the black of the bay, they banked lazily to fly low over a large long island twenty miles directly across the channel behind or to the south of Tulagi-Florida.

Seen from the sky, it was a beautiful island; about ninety miles in length and twenty-five at its wide waist, and traversed end to end by lofty mountains, some as high as 8000 feet. The mountains crowded steeply down to the sea on Guadalcanal's southern or weather coast, abruptly joining reefs and rocks where a thunderous tall surf pounded eternally: no boats could land on that coast, and very few could hold at anchor there. But the northern coast, ah!, there was a long and gentle shore upon which the smallest boats might beach. Here, groves of seaward-leaning coconut palms threw star-shaped shadows upon white beaches scoured by murmuring wavelets; here the island's numerous swift and narrow rivers came tumbling down to the sea or were penned by impassable sandbars into deep lagoons; and here the sun sparkled on water, glinted off the brilliant plumage of jeweled birds, glittered on sand and beamed upon mountainsides dappled by broad patches of tall tan grass.

At night—on one of those high, soft, star-dusted southern nights when a white wand of a moon enchanted all in violet and silver—it broke the pilots' hearts.

It was a lovely island, as exotic as its Spanish name; a word which contained two of those outlandish L-sounds which, on Japanese lips, usually come forth as R. And so the Flotilla's pilots referred to their enchanted island as *"Katakana."*

And that, of course, is Japanese for Guadalcanal.

Martin Clemens was on Guadalcanal. He was the British District Officer. He was as British as a young and charming and ambitious civil servant can be. In his late twenties, Martin was a dashing figure: tall, blond, and handsome in his slouch hat and khaki shorts, a small pistol at his hip, a fine military mustache upon his lips and a radiant golden beard beginning to burgeon upon his chin.

Martin Clemens had been three years in the Southern Solomons, having trained there as a cadet and served as a District Officer on San Cristoval, southernmost of the chain, and Malaita on the opposite side of the channel. Clemens knew the loneliness of these sparsely inhabited islands. He had spent days in the wilderness of the jungles, seeing only his native scouts and carriers; coming suddenly upon those tiny "villages" which were often only clusters of thatched huts set upon the cliff of some abyss or the bank of some wild river. There the District Officer was respected because British law was feared; but there also no able-bodied male was ever without his tomahawk or spear.

Clemens also thought that Guadalcanal was beautiful. On the outside.

On the inside, he knew, she was a poisonous morass. Crocodiles hid in her creeks or patrolled her turgid backwaters. Her jungles were alive with slithering, crawling, scuttling things; with giant lizards that barked like dogs, with huge red furry spiders, with centipedes and leeches and scorpions, with rats and bats and fiddler crabs and one big species of landcrab which moved through the bush with all the stealth of a steamroller. Beautiful butterflies abounded on Guadalcanal, but there were also devouring myriads of sucking, biting, burrowing insects that found sustenance in hu-

man blood: armies of fiery white ants, swarms upon swarms of
filthy black flies that fed upon open cuts and made festering ulcers
of them, and clouds of malaria-bearing mosquitoes. When it was
hot, Guadalcanal was humid; when the rains came she was sodden and chill, and all her reeking vegetation was soft and squishy
to the touch. No, she was neither enchanting nor lovable; and
Martin Clemens had not liked her since he came to Aola Bay on
Guadalcanal's northeast coast at the end of January.

Now, at the end of March, he was in charge of the entire island
and faced with the problem of what to do with a native popula-
tion whose loyalty seemed to be wavering. Three months ago there
had been peace and order. But then, with the Japanese occupation of Rabaul, all had changed to chaos. Most of the Europeans
had fled and many of their habitations had been wrecked by natives either resentful or parading resentment as an excuse for loot-
ing. Some of the older natives could remember that the Germans
had been ousted from Bougainville in World War I. Some of them
were wondering aloud if the detested Japanese—those short tan
men who plundered the pearl shell on the natives' reefs—were
actually tough enough to do the same to the British. Were men
like Ishimoto to replace the District Officers? Mr. Ishimoto, the
surly little carpenter who had worked for the Lever Brothers
Plantation on Tulagi, would he be back with his conquering
countrymen? What would happen to them all then? What would
the Japanese do to them?

Up north, they had heard, the Japanese had slaughtered cattle
and requisitioned food. They had forced the natives to work for
them. They had killed missionaries and closed the mission schools,
opening their own where the only thing they taught was how to
bow low. And the Japanese *were* coming. This they knew. Their
minds were not so simple as to mistake the meaning of the bombing raids on Tulagi.

So they came crowding around Clemens, these headmen, their
dark bodies glistening with sweat, their strong white teeth stained
red with betel-nut juice, their huge fuzzy heads bleached pink
with lime and fire-ash, their broad, seamed faces alive with anxiety
and doubt.

"Japan he come, Massa," they said. "You stop along us?"

Clemens nodded gravely.

"No matter altogether Japan he come," he said. "Me stop along you-fellow." Their tense faces relaxed, and Clemens continued: "Business belong you-fellow all the same follow me. All the way. By an' by, altogether man belong me-fellow come save you-me. Me no savvy who, me no savvy when, but by an' by everything he all right."[7]

It was not a very spectacular promise, especially on the lips of a stranger most of them had never met before; but it was all that Clemens could say: stick with me and you won't be hurt.

The headmen left with quiet murmurs. Clemens could only hope they would stick. Meanwhile, he thought with gentle irony, my orders remain: "Deny the resources of the district to the enemy." How? With whom? He was alone, but for a few gold-miners up on Gold Ridge. D. S. MacFarlan, the Australian naval officer who had taught him how to use the teleradio, had already "upsticked and away," taking with him Ken Hay, the manager of Berande Plantation. Clemens smiled at the thought of the two of them back in the bush: MacFarlan in his immaculate whites, Hay —one of the fattest men he had ever seen—puffing up a jungle track. Then there was Snowy Rhoades. Snowy was at the northwest end of the island. Snowy, with his bushy hair and cold eyes and prize-fighter's stance; he was tough enough, too tough in fact. He liked the idea of the Japanese coming, so that he could kill a few of them. The difficulty with Snowy would be to keep him and his police boys quiet. If they were going to be of any use as coastwatchers, they had to lie low.

Martin Clemens looked at the teleradio MacFarlan had brought him. This and his police scouts would be about all he had, not to "deny the enemy," but to spy on the enemy—once they came.

For Martin Clemens, besides being a British District Officer, was also a coastwatcher for the Royal Australian Navy.

Lieutenant Commander Eric Feldt of the Royal Australian Navy directed the coastwatchers, that unique organization of brave and resourceful men who operated inside Japanese-occupied territory to report on enemy movements. It was Commander Feldt who had sent MacFarlan south to instruct Clemens and the others in the use of the teleradio and to teach them code. They were not of much use at the moment, but they would be, for the enemy operation obviously preparing in Rabaul would most certainly engulf the Southern Solomons.

Coastwatchers of the Northern Solomons, and on the tiny is-
lands off-lying Rabaul and her sister base of Kavieng on New
Ireland, were already operating. It was they who had reported the
Japanese invasion build-up, and their signals describing enemy
aerial formations had been invaluable in alerting bases such as
Port Moresby to the danger of air raids.

In choosing his coastwatchers, Feldt had generally selected "islanders"—mostly Australians—who scorned to wear any man's
collar and had found the independence they prized in the un-
tamed islands of Melanesia. They were planters, ship captains,
goldminers, or unmitigated scamps, with here and there a black-
birder or slave-trader. They drank very, very hard, loved widely
and freely, looked down upon the natives with a protective pa-
ternalism—and spoke a language which, bristling with "bleddy"
this and "baaastid" that, was unprintable in the extreme, especially when it relied upon a famous four-letter word which was
used to modify everything except the sexual act that it described.
Missionaries were always shocked to discover that the pidgin
English they were expected to use was studded with these words.
Ashes, for example, were described as "shit-belong-fire" and an
enemy bombing raid reported as, "Japan he shit along sky."

However their shortcomings, the islanders were intensely loyal.
They could be relied upon to hate the Japanese with the fine and
fruitful ferocity of the free man who has his back to the wall.
Because of this, they were chosen by Feldt; and it was a wise
choice.

By the end of March a coastwatching chain extending from
New Ireland down to San Cristoval at the southern end of the
Solomons was complete. The men in the perilous northern stations, absolutely dependent upon the fidelity of their native scouts
—none of whom would ever betray them—skillfully eluded
Japanese patrols while continuing to feed precious information into
the Allied Intelligence network functioning in Australia under the
command of General MacArthur.

A few days before General Douglas MacArthur made his dramatic escape by torpedo boat from Corregidor, the big carrier
Enterprise dropped anchor in Pearl Harbor after a successful
bombing raid on Japanese-held Marcus Island. On her bridge
was a pugnacious admiral with a huge commanding head and a

craggy bristling face. He was William F. (Bull) Halsey, perhaps the most aggressive admiral in the American Navy. Bull Halsey had already led the strikes on Wake and the Marshalls, and was already famous at home for his hatred of the enemy and his salty contempt for fainthearted sailors. The day Admiral Halsey had sailed into Pearl Harbor and seen the horrible wreckage of the fleet in Battleship Row, he had snarled through clenched teeth: "Before we're through with 'em the Japanese language will be spoken only in hell!" A few days later, at sea again and infuriated by a bad case of jitters developing in his task force, he signaled his ships:

WE ARE WASTING TOO MANY DEPTH CHARGES ON NEUTRAL FISH.

Halsey and the *Enterprise* were not to remain long in Pearl, for Admiral Chester Nimitz, Commander of the Pacific Ocean Area, had an assignment for him. The white-haired Nimitz explained it briskly to his most valued commander: in January of 1942, Admiral King had conceived the idea of staging a spectacular diversionary raid on Japan. King's proposal had received the enthusiastic support of General Arnold of the Army Air Force. Arnold had agreed to provide sixteen long-range Mitchell medium bombers under command of Lieutenant Colonel James Doolittle. They were to be trained to take off from Navy carriers. That force was now ready.

Nimitz asked Halsey, "Do you believe it would work, Bill?"

"They'll need a lot of luck."

"Are you willing to take them out there?"

"Yes, I am."

"Good!" Nimitz said. "It's all yours!"[8]

Bull Halsey left Nimitz's headquarters to confer with Doolittle. They agreed that they would try to sneak to within 400 miles of Japan, but that they would launch the planes from farther out if they were discovered. They agreed also, gleefully, that the attack would rattle the enemy's front teeth, even though it was far from making a real war of it with Japan.

War with Japan, the United States Marine Corps had maintained for three decades, would be a naval war, an island war, an amphibious war. In 1921, one of the Marines' most thoughtful officers, Lieutenant Colonel Earl ("Pete") Ellis, wrote a prescient essay which began with the words:

"Japan is a World Power and her army and navy will doubtless be up to date as to training and materiel. Considering our consistent policy of non-aggression, she will probably initiate the war; which will indicate that, in her own mind, she believes that, considering her natural defensive position, she has sufficient military strength to defeat our fleet."

From this, Ellis concluded:

"In order to impose our will upon Japan, it will be necessary for us to project our fleet and land forces across the Pacific and wage war in Japanese waters. To effect this requires that we have sufficient bases to support the fleet, both during its projection and afterwards."[9]

Bases meant islands, Ellis argued, and many of these would be defended. No matter, they would have to be seized; and Ellis went on to forecast, with remarkable accuracy, the kind and size of force that would be needed to do it. Unfortunately, Ellis lost his life while on an espionage mission in the Pacific, murdered, some investigators suggest, by the Japanese within their Caroline Islands bastion.[10] But Ellis's conclusions were not forgotten by the officers who were to command the Marine Corps in the years between the wars.

Chief of all, these men refused to accept the dreary dictum which the British debacle at Gallipoli in World War I seemed to have laid down: that hostile and defended shores cannot be seized from the sea. The Marines argued that they could; moreover that it was not necessary to capture ports with all their ship facilities but that invasions could be made across open beaches. Most brass ears were deaf to this doctrine. Many generals, and some admirals, regarded Marines as nothing but beach-jumpers[11] who were unfit to command more than a platoon,[12] let alone evolve and develop new military doctrine. After all, the Marine Corps was a mere auxiliary force of scarcely twenty thousand men; it was only, in the favorite phrase of its detractors—one which President Harry Truman was to make notoriously erroneous in the Korean War—"the Navy's police force."

But the Marines persevered. They had to. Without amphibious warfare they had no reason to be regarded as anything else but naval police. Fighting for their existence, they developed amphibious tactics and equipment. The New Orleans boatbuilder, Andrew Higgins, was encouraged to continue experimenting—sometimes at his own expense—with better and better types of landing craft; and from the inventor Donald Roebling came the Alligator, a tracked boat able to crawl over land obstacles, which was to be the forerunner of the famous "amtrack." Practice landings were made whenever the Navy could be persuaded to make a few ships available. And anything that was done had to be done on a shoestring, for American Congresses between world wars were as bellicosely pacifist as the Cold War Congresses have been meekly militarist. Military budgets were gleefully meat-axed to the starry-eyed approval of a nation naively convinced that if you turn your back on war it will go away. Foremost in this American between-wars custom of "making mock of uniforms that guard you while you sleep" was the Senate Armed Forces Committee that sought to embarrass the Army Chief of Staff, General Douglas MacArthur, by inquiring if the Army really needed all of that toilet paper it had ordered. In such surroundings, caught between two fires, as it were, the Marines worked out their ideas on amphibious warfare.

Meanwhile, the Marines—unlike other branches of the service—were consistently in action between the wars. They were fighting the "Banana Wars," learning, in the jungles of Haiti and Nicaragua, all the lessons of jungle warfare that would be applied on a much larger and more vital scale in the wildernesses of Oceania. Service on the Navy's capital ships taught them to appreciate the importance of seapower, as well as of ship-based air power, and duty at troublesome China stations enabled them to study the Japanese at first hand and to learn—most valuable lesson of all—not to underestimate them.

It was a hard school, but out of it came a stream of tough and seasoned professionals fired with a sense of mission. One of them was Major General Alexander Archer Vandegrift.

Tall, strong, hard-jawed, and extremely courteous, Archer Vandegrift was of old Virginia stock, the grandson of Confederate soldiers. He had spent his boyhood listening to their stories, and he could never forget the grandfather who had prayed to "the God of Abraham, Isaac, Jacob, Robert E. Lee and Stonewall Jackson."[13] Archer Vandegrift was in the mold of Stonewall Jackson. He was both wary and audacious, seldom without a plan.

He had been a Marine officer for thirty-three years, having spent some of his most instructive ones under General Smedley D. Butler, the celebrated and legendary "Old Gimlet Eye" of the Banana Wars. Butler had given him the passing nickname of "Sunny Jim" because Vandegrift had ridden the cowcatcher of a rickety old Nicaraguan locomotive, "to look for mines" as Butler had ordered, and had come back to report with a grin on his face.

Two decades later, on March 23, 1942, at New River, North Carolina, General Vandegrift received both his second star and the command of the First Marine Division. He had already been its assistant commander, having helped plan and conduct practice landings, one of which was an oddly prophetical exercise at Solomons Island on Chesapeake Bay. But now he had full charge and he poured all his energies into raising it from about 11,000 men to its full strength of 19,000. Each of the four regiments—First, Fifth, and Seventh rifle regiments, the Eleventh of artillery—was understrength.

From all over the Marine Corps the old salts and China hands came pouring into New River. There were NCOs yanked off soft "planks" at the Navy yards. There were grizzled old gunnery sergeants who had fought in France or chased "Cacos" in Haiti or "bandidos" in Nicaragua. There were inveterate privates who had spent as much time in the brig as in barracks. Gamblers, drinkers and connivers, brawlers who had fought soldiers and sailors of every nationality in every bar from Brooklyn to Bangkok, blasphemous and profane with a fine fluency that would astound an Australian coastwatcher, they were nevertheless professional soldiers who knew their hard calling in every detail from stripping a machine gun blindfolded to tying a tourniquet with their teeth. They were tough and they knew it, and they exulted in that knowledge. No one has described them better than Colonel John W. Thomason: ". . . They were the Leathernecks, the old breed of American regular, regarding the service as home and war as occupation, and they transmitted their temper and character and viewpoint to the high-hearted volunteer mass."

And those high-hearted volunteers, the new breed, were also streaming into New River, to flesh out the division and to transmit to the old breed something of their own temper: their gaiety and their zest.

These were the youths fresh from boot training at Parris Island. They knew almost nothing about war, but they knew why they had gone to one. In their late teens and early twenties, they had stormed the recruiting centers after the news of Pearl Harbor had been broadcast. Some of them had come straight from basketball games and bowling matches, still clutching the little canvas bags containing their uniforms or bowling balls. They were angry. Their country had been attacked without warning. Standing in line to be examined by the doctors, they had muttered over and over, "The little yellow bastards, The little yellow bastards."[14] They wanted to kill Japs, they told the officers who questioned them. These were not refined or oblique or delicate young men, these youths who were filling the ranks of the First Marine Division that spring; no, they were mostly "tough guys"—some of whom could be fairly described as juvenile delinquents—whose primitive instincts had been aroused by the infamy of the enemy.

Yet, they were idealistic, too. They felt vaguely that they were being noble by volunteering to fight their country's battles on the very day of disaster. Unfortunately, they had no battle cry to express their inmost feelings. They were not able to shout, like the enemy they would meet, "Blood for the Emperor!" Few of them had heard of the Four Freedoms, and those who had were not likely to proclaim them in combat—instinctively aware that conclusions, however accurate and humane, can never rally men to battle—and so they had to substitute the next best, or perhaps even a better thing: their sardonic sense of humor.

And this was well expressed by the youth who came to the Federal Building in New York on the night of December 7, 1941, only to be told by the doctor that he could not be accepted by the Marines, unless, to conform to certain health standards, he had himself circumcised.

"Circumcised!" the startled youth burst out. "What in hell do you think I'm gonna do to the enemy?"[15]

Nevertheless, the doctor was adamant, and the youth departed to have the operation performed. A month later he was in Parris Island, where he was given the nickname of "Lucky," and in March of 1942 he had joined the flood of Marines flowing to New River.* With such men, old breed and new, with his veteran bat-

* Ed. note: Lucky is the author.

talion and regimental commanders, Archer Vandegrift hoped to forge a fine amphibious striking force.

They should be ready to go, he thought, at about the end of the year.

Chapter 2

ADMIRAL YAMAMOTO had dropped a blockbuster. The Commander-in-Chief of Japan's Combined Fleet had proposed the capture of Midway Island only 1130 miles from Hawaii, and he was demanding approval of this daring plan over Naval General Staff's own modest operation to isolate Australia.

Staff was both appalled and disconcerted; appalled because the dangers of this long thrust into American waters seemed so obvious, disconcerted because, even though Staff was superior to Fleet and could veto the Midway plan, in those days of Japan's victory fever it would be a bold admiral indeed who would challenge Isoroku Yamamoto.

His popularity and prestige were enormous. He was the idol of the fleet, this iron admiral of the shaven head and square fighting face; he was revered as a combat sailor who had lost two fingers of his left hand serving under Admiral Togo at Port Arthur, and admired as a strategist and planner who was beginning to rival even that immortal of Japanese history.

Moreover, Yamamoto's reputation for integrity was invincible. All of the generals and admirals of Imperial General Headquarters were aware that Yamamoto, almost alone among ranking officers, had warned Japan against going to war with America. In 1940 the fire-breathing young Army officers of Tojo's War Party so hated Yamamoto that he was deliberately relieved as Navy Vice-Minister and sent to sea as chief of Combined Fleet because, in the words of a member of the Supreme War Council: ". . . he would have been assassinated if he had stayed in Tokyo, and that would have been a great loss to our country."[1] In that same year Yamamoto was asked by former Premier Prince Konoye if Japan had a chance against the United States, and he replied: "I can raise havoc with them for one year, but after that I can give no guarantee."[2] Yamamoto knew America, the character of its people and its incredible industrial potential, for he had served as a Naval attaché in Washington where his renown as a cool and daring poker player was rivaled only by his obvious hatred for his hosts. Nevertheless, in a letter that the Americans were even then misquoting and misinterpreting, Yamamoto had written to a friend: "If we should go to war against the United States we must recognize the fact that the armistice will have to be dictated from the White House."[3] By this he meant merely that Japan had no hope of victory, and not, as the American press was then proclaiming, that this "arrogant little monkey-man" expected to coil his tail in the White House. Yet, once the decision for war was made, Isoroku Yamamoto served his Emperor with single-minded devotion. More than any man, he had been responsible for the strategy of striking America suddenly and hard, of pushing her so far back in the Pacific and so crippling her power to retaliate, that by the time she recovered she would be faced with a long and costly war— one that she would be eager to terminate by negotiation. Thus, Yamamoto had pursued what was virtually his own policy, when, directing Combined Fleet from his flagship, the mighty battleship *Yamato*, he had delivered those "First Phase" sledgehammer blows. And now the time for the Second Phase was at hand, and Isoroku Yamamoto was reaching out again.

On April 2 Commander Yasuji Watanabe, operations officer of Combined Fleet, came to Tokyo to present Yamamoto's plan. He met Commander Tatsukichi Miyo, representing Navy General Staff. Like most Staff officers consulting the victory-men of Fleet, Miyo was carefully courteous. He did not decry but plead. He was almost in tears as he tried to warn Watanabe of the dangers of the Midway operation.[4] But Watanabe was obdurate, and the debate continued for three more days. On April 5, as though weary of the wrangle, Watanabe arose from the conference table to place a direct call with Admiral Yamamoto aboard *Yamato*. He returned to state Yamamoto's uncompromising position:

"In the last analysis, the success or failure of our entire strategy in the Pacific will be determined by whether or not we succeed in destroying the United States Fleet, more particularly its carrier task forces. The Naval General Staff advocates severing the supply line between the United States and Australia. It would seek to do this by placing certain areas under Japanese control, but the most direct and effective way to achieve this objective is to destroy the enemy's carrier forces, without which the supply line could not in any case be maintained. We believe that by launching the proposed operations against Midway, we can succeed in drawing out the enemy's carrier strength and destroying it in decisive battle. If, on the other hand, the enemy should avoid our challenge, we shall still realize an important gain by advancing our defensive perimeter to Midway . . . without obstruction."[5]

It was obvious that Isoroku Yamamoto was determined that his plan should carry. With great reluctance Rear Admiral Shigeru Fukudome turned to Vice-Admiral Seiichi Ito to ask in a low voice: "Shall we agree?"

Ito nodded silently, and Watanabe left the conference room beaming.

Nevertheless, Naval General Staff's approval was not wholehearted. Bickering over the date began. Fleet wanted Midway to take place in early June, Staff rather more like early July. And this may have been because the Naval General Staff's operation against Australia was already begun.

The Japanese aerial onslaught against Port Moresby and Tulagi was mounting. To help press it, Saburo Sakai's squadron had been transferred on April 8 to the new base at Lae on New Guinea. Lae was closer to Port Moresby. It was also a pesthole. Its airfield was even smaller and bumpier than Vunakanau at Rabaul and the food was abominable.

Each morning the pilots arose at three-thirty to gulp down an unpalatable breakfast of rice, soybean-paste soup, dried vegetables, and pickles. Then, at eight o'clock, they flew either patrol or fighter missions. Back for lunch of rice and canned fish or meat, which was repeated for dinner, the pilots either went on standby duty, or roared aloft to intercept sudden enemy attacks, until, at five o'clock, they assembled for calisthenics. After supper they read or wrote letters home or held impromptu concerts with accordions and harmonicas and guitars.

It would have been a dull and deadly routine but for the constant thrill of aerial combat. Day after day, for four months, Saburo Sakai gunned his mud-brown Zero aloft from the strip at Lae, climbing high into the sky to go winging over the towering 15,000-foot Owen Stanley Mountains standing between Lae and

Port Moresby, and to fall upon the enemy with flaming guns. Steadily his score of kills mounted: twenty . . . thirty . . . forty . . . fifty . . . It seemed incredible. Saburo was easily Japan's greatest ace, and his fame went far and wide through the homeland and the South Seas.

One day a rookie pilot named Hiroyoshi Nishizawa joined the squadron. Saburo was astonished to see with what skill Nishizawa shot down an enemy Airacobra on his first flight. Nishizawa was a natural, and Saburo wondered if he was not also better than he was. One thing Saburo did know: neither he nor his comrades were very fond of Nishizawa. Silent and surly, this skinny youth of twenty-three years kept to himself. He was rarely seen smiling, unless it was the bloodless grimace with which he reported a fresh kill. "The Devil," they called him.

Another accomplished rookie pilot was Toshio Ota, who was even a year younger than the Devil. Sakai, Nishizawa, and Ota, Japan's three top aces in that order, they were soon to become the scourge of New Guinea, kings of the air above the bright blue Coral Sea, and the squadron in which they flew was by far the most outstanding in the war.

Lieutenant (j.g.) Junichi Sasai commanded the squadron. The men loved him. Unlike most graduates of Eta Jima, the Japanese Annapolis, he had compassion for the enlisted men. He haggled with the quartermaster for the candy they needed to replace energy sapped by ceaseless combat, or he "procured" cigarettes for them. They called Lieutenant Sasai "The Flying Tiger," not in allusion to the American Volunteer Group of pilots whom Saburo had met in China, but because of the roaring tiger carved on the big silver belt buckle he wore. In Japanese legend, a tiger prowls a thousand miles and always returns from his hunt. That was the meaning of the buckle. Sasai's father, a retired Navy captain, had made three of them, giving one to his son and the other two to his sons-in-law.

One of these sons-in-law, Lieutenant Commander Yoshio Tashiro, was the pilot of a four-engined Kawanishi flying boat. He was, that April, based at Rabaul—flying bombing missions south to Tulagi.

Martin Clemens was sure that the big Kawanishis turning from their bombing runs at Tulagi could not possibly spot the red tiles of his roof. Still, they gave him the shivers when they thundered low over Aola Bay on Guadalcanal. It was not so much that there seemed to be more of them every day, it was that they had absolute control of the air. Clemens didn't even bother to look up when he heard airplane motors. He knew that they would be Japanese. The Australian seaplanes, being much smaller than the Kawanishis, generally went and hid when they had wind of an air raid.

Clemens felt very lonely and exposed. He was not heartened by the fact that the Australians had already informed him of the code signal that would signify their departure. It was "Steak and eggs," or, as the Aussies with their cockney accents pronounced it, "Styke 'n ayggs."

It only served to remind Clemens that his food was running low.

Out in the "boondocks" at Onslow Beach in North Carolina the only eggs served were powdered—much to the disgust of Archer Vandegrift, who had never forgotten the reek of a Chinese powdered-egg factory—and the only steak was a soggy counterfeit which the cooks coyly called "Swiss steak" and for which the troops had coined more colorful names, the only printable one of which was "boiled boondocker," boondockers being the crepe-soled buckskin boots which Marines wore while tramping the boondocks, or wild country.

In early April, Vandegrift's division was beginning to coalesce. The boots had lost their frightened look and no longer said "Sir" to corporals or saluted anyone whose clothes seemed to fit. They had begun to swagger a bit. They were getting salty enough to speak of the floor or ground as "the deck," to "shove off" rather than depart, to "go ashore" when they went into town, and to ask, whenever they were out rumor-mongering—the favorite pastime of all good armies since Agamemnon's—"Hey, what's the scuttlebutt?"

Even old-timers such as Master Gunnery Sergeant Lew Diamond, a white-haired Marine brahmin with a goatish goateed face and a bearish body, would concede grudgingly, "Them knotheads may not be so bad, after all," and Sergeant Manila John Basilone had ceased to "snow" his machine-gun section with lurid tales of life on Dewey Boulevard in Manila and had granted that all of them had not been found under flat stones and might possibly have had an earlier and human existence elsewhere. These young Marines thought of themselves as the best fighters in the world, although the only fighting they had done had been with an occasional soldier or sailor unfortunate enough to come home on leave to New River or nearby Jacksonville, or with each other in the unpainted shacks which followed them to the boondocks and sold them beer at fifteen cents a bottle and canned patriotic ballads such as "Goodby Mama, I'm Off to Yokohama," at five cents per sentimental song. Sometimes moonshiners visited the pine woods where the First Marine Division lived in pup tents and slept on the ground. The moonshiners sold the Marines jugs of that potent corn whisky called "white lightning." Navy medical corpsmen and physicians who operated the battalion aid stations known as "sick bays" always could tell when the moonshiners had been around: there were twice as many men on sick call and the gentian violet had to be spread thin to cover all that bruised and battered flesh.

Even so, the interfamilial brawling was a good sign. The men were developing an *esprit*. Each squad thought itself the best in the platoon, each platoon the best in the company and so on up through battalions and regiments. Riflemen regarded machine gunners as second-wave softies, the gunners looked down upon mortarmen as "rear-echelon bastards," while the sight of clerks and technicians—to say nothing of artillerymen, about as common as a colonel in a pup tent—filled them all with stuttering rage. This is what is called the mystique of the Marine: the one man who might possibly have been the point in a battalion attack contemplates everyone else not so engaged with withering contempt. A man perhaps as much as five yards behind the lines is asked, "Where were you when the stuff hit the fan?"

All of this, nevertheless, was mere training; it was all very lighthearted, and the real thing, the fiery crucible of combat, seemed far away.

It seemed to General Vandegrift to be very far away, for he still considered his division many months short of combat-readiness. None of the new arrivals—and few of the battalion commanders—had been through a full-dress ship-to-shore landing maneuver. They had to be content with a wooden mock-up of a ship built beside Onslow Beach. Cargo nets were thrown over the side of this ungainly Trojan seahorse and the men clambered down them in full gear. Worse than this, far worse, were the mid-April levees on the division.

Lieutenant Colonel Merritt ("Red Mike") Edson had arrived from Washington with authority to comb Vandegrift's division for the best officers and men to fill his First Raider Battalion. Vandegrift could only fume—silently. He knew that President Roosevelt fancied having an American counterpart of the British commandos, although the Marine Corps Commandant, General Thomas Holcomb, shared Vandegrift's aversion to making an elite out of an elite. Unfortunately, FDR had become infected by Winston Churchill's penchant for military novelty, and because Roosevelt was actually very fond of the Marine Corps—he sometimes said "We Marines" in conversations with Holcomb[6]—he conferred this unwelcome enthusiasm on his favorite service. FDR's oldest son, James, was to be executive officer of the Second Raiders under the famous Lieutenant Colonel Evans Carlson.

After Edson departed from New River, leaving the Fifth Marines* slightly skeletonized, the worst blow fell. Vandegrift was ordered to beef up the Seventh Regiment with his best men, weapons and equipment and to send it to the Samoan Islands. The general despaired. Into the Seventh had gone many of his finest battalion commanders, tough and aggressive patrol officers from Haiti and Nicaragua, Marines such as Chesty Puller and Herman Henry Hanneken who knew how to handle troops in jungle warfare. Now Vandegrift had to build again. For what? More raids? Was he to spend the war training troops for other men to command?

On April 15—five days after the Seventh shipped out—Vandegrift's gloomy doubts were joyously dispelled. He was notified that he was to take the rest of his division to New Zealand. He was to train there preparatory to going into action as the Landing Force of the newly established South Pacific Amphibious Force.

The South Pacific Area and Force had only just been established. The Joint Chiefs of Staff had already divided the Pacific Theater into the Southwest Pacific Area, commanded by General Douglas MacArthur from Australia, and the Pacific Ocean Area,

---

* The word "Marines" is interchangeable with "regiment." It never denotes a division. Thus, to say First Marines is to mean First Marine Regiment, never First Marine Division.

commanded by Admiral Chester Nimitz from Hawaii. But because Nimitz's area was so vast, it was decided to subdivide it. The South Pacific Area was therefore created, with its commander responsible to Nimitz. This commander was to be Vice-Admiral Robert L. Ghormley. On April 17, Ghormley received this vague and hardly inspiring message from Admiral King.

"You have been selected to command the South Pacific Force and South Pacific Area. You will have a large area under your command and a most difficult task. I do not have the tools to give you to carry out that task as it should be. You will establish your headquarters in Auckland, New Zealand, with an advanced base at Tongatabu. In time, possibly this fall, we hope to start an offensive from the South Pacific. You will then probably find it necessary to shift the advanced base as the situation demands and move your headquarters to meet special situations."

For a striking force a single untrained and understrength Marine division, for support a shortage of ships and airplanes and hundreds of other invaluable items such as bulldozers and runway matting—and yet, Admiral Ernest King was already preparing the Pacific counteroffensive. He was adhering to his own admonition, "Do the best with what you have," and he was waiting for the Japanese to overreach.

Unknown to King, he had already set in motion the operation that was to force the Japanese hand next day.

The lookout on the Japanese picket boat sighted airplanes overhead. He could not make out their identity, but surely, only 700 miles from Tokyo they could not be enemy. Nevertheless, he went below to wake the captain.

"Planes above, sir," he shouted.

The skipper was not interested. He stayed in his bunk. The lookout went topside. An hour or so later he stiffened. He saw a pair of carriers on the horizon. Strange. He went below to wake the skipper again.

"Two of our beautiful carriers ahead, sir."

The captain came on deck and studied the ships through his glass. Color drained from his face. "They're beautiful," he said. "But they're not ours." He went below and shot himself in the head, for he had failed in his duty to protect the homeland and the Emperor.[7]

The carriers he had seen were *Enterprise* and *Hornet,* under command of Admiral Bull Halsey, and the planes were Jimmy Doolittle's Mitchell bombers speeding for Tokyo and other Japanese cities. Once they had dropped their bombs, they would fly on to Chinese airfields. Meanwhile, *Enterprise* and *Hornet* were streaking for home at top speed.

A few hours later, the American ships tuned their radios to Tokyo. An English-speaking propagandist came on the air. He explained that of all the countries then at war, only Japan was free from attack. Admiral Yamamoto and the invincible Combined Fleet would utterly destroy anyone foolish enough to approach the shores of the sacred homeland. How fortunate the sons and daughters of Nippon, enjoying today not only the Festival of the Cherry Blossoms, but two fine baseball games as well.

It was then that Bull Halsey heard the air-raid siren.

Japan was stunned. Not only Bull Halsey heard the sirens, but the haggling officers of Naval General Staff and Combined Fleet as well. Admiral Isoroku Yamamoto burned with shame. He put on dress whites and called on Emperor Hirohito to apologize. And he came into Naval General Staff headquarters with his sword in his hand.

The Midway operation *must* be executed.[8] Obviously, the threat from the east was more urgent than the operation to isolate Australia. The Americans must be pushed back so far that the possibility of another such insult to the Emperor and the Navy would be ended forever. This time Staff agreed without reserve. Its pride had been wounded and its chief, Admiral Osami Nagano, was also full of remorse.

With all obstacles removed, the Midway invasion was set for early June. But then, with a characteristic inflexibility so baffling to westerners, acting upon the national conviction that a course undertaken must be followed, Naval General Staff blandly continued its own operation against Australia.

Port Moresby and Tulagi were to be invaded and captured in early May. Once again, without being aware of it, Japan's Naval General Staff was drawing closer to the island named Guadalcanal.

Chapter 3

"STYKE 'N AYGGS, dammit, styke 'n ayggs!"

It came crackling over the teleradio in shrill and nasal urgency, this signal of imminent Australian departure, and it chilled the heart of Martin Clemens seated in his radio shack and watching the gray dawn of May 2 creep down the coast toward Snowy Rhoades on Cape Esperance at the western tip of Guadalcanal.

Though dismayed, Clemens was not entirely surprised. The day before the Japanese had hurled their most savage attack on the twin islets of Gavutu-Tanambogo in Tulagi Harbor. One of the RAAF's remaining two flying boats had lumbered aloft with a huge hole in one wing, to disappear forever. The other had been caught on the water and smashed. It was later towed across the channel to Aola, where natives had dragged it out of sight and destroyed it.

So now the Japanese were truly coming and the Australians were leaving. Clemens and his handful of Europeans were all alone. How would the natives react to the Japanese?

Only last month a European had been murdered up in the Goldfields. One of the "bleddy boongs," as most Australian planters described the natives, had done for Billy Wilmot with a long-handled ax. The interior of the poor old beachcomber's hut had been spattered with blood, and the body, which Clemens had ordered exhumed, was a horrible, sickening sight. Luckily for most of the natives—the Christians—they had been at Good Friday services when the murder occurred. Of two pagan suspects, one of them owned just the ax to do the job; and on such flimsy evidence Clemens had taken the man into custody. But Clemens could not be sure. Moreover, the identity of the killer troubled him not so much as the fact of a European murdered at a time when plantations were being looted by rebellious natives and the Japanese were on their way. Through Clemens's mind there flitted a phrase from one of the books on the Solomon Islanders: ". . . these people are primarily and emphatically savages, with some good points certainly, but in their nature reigns unchecked the instinct of destruction."[1]

Clemens was also having difficulty of a lesser though perhaps more irritating nature with the Catholic fathers at the Ruavatu Mission a few miles west of Aola. He had advised them to take refuge inland. But Father Henry Oude-Engberink, the Dutch priest in charge, replied that he and the American Father Arthur Duhamel and the three European nuns at the mission would remain with their flock. They were neutral. The war was not their concern. Clemens tried to explain that the Japanese would certainly not be "neutral" toward the nuns, that to remain on the coast was dangerous and foolhardy when the mission party might maintain its neutrality in the safety of the bush, but Father Engberink was obdurate: his place was with his flock. Bishop Aubin at the mission headquarters in Visale on the western end of the island had already decided to follow a policy of neutrality. To take sides, that was the charge always raised against missionaries: that they served a foreign power. It was the age-old excuse for persecutions. No, the fathers and the nuns would give the Japanese no grounds for such false accusations. They served no power but God.

That was that, and the interview had ended on a note of cool cordiality.

And now, the Japanese were coming south. Now the time of preparation and of worry was coming to an end. Soon he would find out if the natives were really to be trusted, if a policy of "neutrality" would really impress the bloodthirsty Knights of Bushido, and if he, Martin Clemens, would be clever enough to keep his life. Now, he thought, mentally quoting from his constant companion, his only book, Shakespeare's *Henry V,* now:

"We are in God's hands, brother."

Next morning the Japanese invasion force under Rear Admiral Aritomo Goto glided into empty Tulagi Harbor. Goto put ashore troops of the Kure and Sasebo Special Naval Landing Forces—so-called Japanese "Marines"—as well as aviation and communications personnel to staff a seaplane base and radio station. Unhurried because unharried, Goto unloaded at his leisure; stocking the Emperor's latest acquisitions with great quantities of oil and gasoline and an inordinately large supply of beer and sake,* hard candy for the fliers, and cases of canned beef, pineapple, and crab meat.

Later there arrived the first of twelve float Zero fighter-planes and twelve Kawanishi flying boats, one of which was piloted by Lieutenant Commander Yoshio Tashiro, the brother-in-law of Saburo Sakai's squadron commander. Another arrival was Mr. Ishimoto, the former Lever Brothers carpenter who was now returning to Tulagi as a conqueror. Ishimoto wore the uniform of a petty officer in the Japanese Navy, but he was nevertheless identified and reported by Martin Clemens's scouts. The presence of the entire invasion force—the southern arm of the operation to cut the Australian-American lifeline—was also reported to the American carrier force to the south under Rear Admiral Frank Jack Fletcher.

Leaving the *Lexington* group to continue refueling, Fletcher hurried north with *Yorktown* and her group of screening ships. At dawn next morning, Fletcher swung *Yorktown* into the wind and flew off his strikes against Goto.

The Japanese in Tulagi were caught completely by surprise. "Massa, massa!" one of Clemens's scouts shouted, waking him. "Altogether Japan he catchem trouble!"[2]

Clemens rushed to the shores of Aola Bay. Surrounded by delighted natives, he saw the American dive-bombers come plummeting out of the sun in long straight dives. Explosions rolled over the water. Pillars of smoke rose into the sky. Cheers and cries of derision rose from the throats of the scouts. They shook their fists and howled, "Japan he die-finish!" And of course, the reports of enemy destruction were exaggerated. It was claimed that nine ships were sunk. Actually, *Yorktown's* airplanes had put only a destroyer, two mine sweepers and a destroyer-transport on the bottom of those waters which, because of the scores of ships that were to perish in them, were to be known henceforth as Iron Bottom Bay. More important, Goto's cocksure force had been

* Rice wine, pronounced to rhyme with rocky.

sent racing north up the long straight Solomons sea corridor which was to enter history as The Slot.

Admiral Fletcher's pilots had dropped the opening bombs in the Battle of the Coral Sea.

That night, while Admiral Goto streaked homeward through The Slot, the more powerful northern force steamed out of Rabaul. It was bound for Port Moresby. It sailed south, hoping to circle the tip of northeastern New Guinea and come up suddenly upon the big Allied base.

The light carrier *Shoho* and her screen accompanied the landing force. But a far more potent group built around the big carriers *Shokaku* and *Zuikaku* was slipping around the top of the Solomon Islands and racing south to catch the American force which had struck at Goto.

The next day, May 5, was uneventful. On the following day, May 6, Admiral Fletcher reunited his forces and headed *Enterprise* and *Yorktown* toward the tip of New Guinea. On May 7, the Battle of the Coral Sea was fully joined. In the first American attack ever launched upon an enemy carrier, Fletcher's pilots pounced upon *Shoho* in a shower of bombs and torpedoes and sunk her in a matter of minutes. Because of this, the Port Moresby invasion was called off, and the troops sent back to Rabaul.

Next day Japan's big carriers retaliated. They sank *Lexington*. But *Shokaku* was damaged and *Zuikaku* suffered severe losses in planes and pilots.

Thus the first seafight in history during which the contending ships did not exchange a shot, and it had been a Japanese tactical victory. The American loss of 30,000-ton *Lexington,* with oiler *Neosho* and destroyer *Sims,* far outweighed Japan's loss of 12,000-ton *Shoho* and the ships sunk at Tulagi. Nevertheless, the strategic victory was American. Big *Shokaku* and *Zuikaku* had to be counted out of Admiral Yamamoto's plans for Midway, and Port Moresby had been saved.

Japan had suffered her first reverse.

In Tokyo, the cancellation of the Port Moresby invasion was regarded as a temporary setback to the operation to isolate Australia. It was decided that Port Moresby could be taken in the rear. Troops would be ferried the short safe distance from Rabaul to Buna and would then march over the lofty Owen Stanleys to occupy the Allied base.

On May 18, Imperial General Headquarters activated the 17th Army with orders to carry out these operations. Command was given to Lieutenant General Haruyoshi Hyakutake.

Thin, testy, and tenacious, Haruyoshi Hyakutake was regarded as one of Japan's most promising "younger" generals. Like Alexander Archer Vandegrift of the American Marines, he was fifty-five and a veteran of thirty-three years of service. Although equal in rank,* Hyakutake commanded a much larger body of troops; but these, like Vandegrift's own, were widely scattered.

On the very day that Hyakutake took command of the 17th Army, he was—again like Vandegrift—deprived of one of his finest units, and commanders. The fierce Colonel Kiyono Ichiki was selected to lead his crack regiment of landing troops ashore on Midway. While Hyakutake prepared to fly down to his new headquarters at Rabaul, Colonel Ichiki and his staff boarded battleship *Yamato* to be briefed on their part in Admiral Yamamoto's grand design.

Undismayed—for Haruyoshi Hyakutake was a man of optimism and a supreme confidence bordering on arrogance—17th Army's commander busied himself assembling forces spread throughout China and the Dutch East Indies. He had not the slightest doubt that he would make short work of Moresby, and his only thought for Tulagi was that it would cover his exposed left flank.

And he paid absolutely no attention to the big island with the strange name on the other side of Iron Bottom Bay.

Two days later, not nearly so free of doubt or dismay, Major General Archer Vandegrift sailed from Norfolk, Virginia, for Wellington, New Zealand. With him aboard big *Wakefield*—the converted passenger liner *Manhattan*—were the Fifth Marines and most of the Eleventh's artillery. They sailed under destroyer escort down the perilous Atlantic Coast, silhouetted for German submarines, like so many doomed tankers and merchantmen before them, by the pleasure-as-usual lights of the seashore resorts. They entered the Panama Canal and debouched into the Pacific, where the destroyers left them and later their long-range plane escort.

* There were no brigadier generals in the Japanese Army. A Japanese lieutenant general was only equal to an American major general.

With only their own speed and a zigzag course to protect them against Japanese submarines, they sailed the vast Pacific in solitude. Only Vandegrift and a few others knew that *Wakefield* carried enough life jackets and lifeboats for only half the men. But the men were irrepressible. In the only moment of crisis—when *Wakefield* plowed into an enormous swell and waves of water plunged down open hatches—a lighthearted Marine averted panic with the cry:

"Women and children first!"

It was May 27—Japan's Navy Day, the date upon which the immortal Admiral Heihachiro Togo had annihilated the Russian Fleet at Tsushima—and today, thirty-seven years later, Admiral Yamamoto was leading Combined Fleet to Midway.

Yamamoto himself was aboard *Yamato,* the 64,000-ton battleship which was easily the mightiest ship afloat. *Yamato* mounted nine 18.1-inch* guns firing 3200-pound shells, 500 pounds heavier than the 16-inch projectiles fired by the best of the American battleships. One of her turrets weighed as much as a big destroyer and her sides were armored with steel sixteen inches thick. She was the symbol of Japan's naval strength, this monster battleship, and Yamamoto gloried in her power. Here, as she lay at anchor at Hashirajima in the Inland Sea, the admiral had worked out the final details of the operation which was to destroy American seapower in the Pacific.

First he had attended to the possibility of any repetition of the Doolittle raid. A northern invasion force built around three light carriers was already enroute to the western Aleutians in the North Pacific. Its mission was to seize Kiska and Attu, thus pushing American airbases back eastward, and also to draw American carrier strength away from Midway.

It was at Midway that the knockout blow was to be delivered. Most of the vast armada of 162 ships which Yamamoto had assembled were to sail to that island. The striking force consisted of four big, fast carriers under Chuichi Nagumo, the hero of Pearl Harbor, supported by one light carrier and four seaplane carriers, and backed up by no less than eleven battleships and a host of cruisers and destroyers and submarines. Once all these fighting

---

* Naval artillery is measured by the diameter of the shells fired.

ships had done their work, Colonel Kiyono Ichiki's shock troops would storm ashore at Midway.

At eight o'clock in the morning of that momentous Navy Day, Nagumo's flagship, *Akagi,* hoisted the signal:

"Sortie as scheduled!"

With cheering crews lining the rails, the carriers slipped past the battleships that were to follow. Destroyers and cruisers of the protecting screens took up their stations, white bow waves curling away from their prows. Steadily and with great majesty, Striking Force made for Bungo Strait. The ships passed through these narrow waters with all hands at battle station, until they had entered the Pacific and the bullhorns blared:

"Passage through strait completed. Stow gear. Restore normal condition of readiness."

Aboard the carriers, men in undress whites and green work uniforms began to drift up to the flight decks to smoke. Some took off their shirts to do calisthenics in the waning sun. Officers sitting in canvas deck chairs chatted guardedly about the operation.

In a few more minutes, all of Striking Force would be at sea.

Landing Force was already underway.

It had sailed from Saipan under Rear Admiral Raizo Tanaka. Tanaka, a veteran destroyer leader who had participated in Japanese landings on the Philippines and the Dutch East Indies, had his doubts about the Midway operation. So did Commander Tameichi Hara, one of Tanaka's ablest destroyer captains. After Tanaka had whispered details of the plan to Hara early last spring, the commander had blurted out his conviction that high command had lost its mind.[3]

"Shhhhh!" Tanaka said warningly. "As a matter of fact, I'm not sure about it. I hope it's not true."[4]

But it was, and Tanaka's squadron consisting of flag cruiser *Jintsu* and ten destroyers, including Hara's *Amatsukaze,* was ordered to escort Colonel Ichiki's transports from Saipan to Midway. The day before Striking Force sortied from Japan, they put to sea.

Colonel Ichiki, as always, was supremely confident. Tanaka was not. Nor was Hara, who stood on *Amatsukaze's* bridge, sunk in misgivings.[5]

Admiral Chester Nimitz knew of the Japanese approach. Excellent intelligence work, notably assisted by the breaking of the Japanese code, had alerted Nimitz to Japanese Combined Fleet's intention to sail to battle again. Nimitz became convinced that the strike was aimed at either Hawaii or Midway, probably Midway, and he conveyed this belief to Admiral King.

King agreed. He directed Nimitz to take the risk of deploying his carriers from the South Pacific to the defense of Midway and Hawaii. Nimitz got off an urgent message to Bull Halsey with *Enterprise* and *Hornet*.

"Expedite return."

Halsey's ships bent it on for Hawaii. They sailed into Pearl Harbor on May 26. But their commander, Nimitz's most aggressive flag officer, was unfit to fight.

Six months on the bridge under the tropic sun, six months of tension, had afflicted Halsey with an unbearable skin eruption. He could not keep from scratching, and the disease spread. By the time he had returned to Hawaii, he had exhausted every home-made remedy, including oatmeal baths, and had lost twenty pounds.

Halsey went into the hospital, while Nimitz placed command of the defense of Midway under both Admiral Fletcher and Vice-Admiral Raymond Spruance.

They would have a fleet of seventy-six ships built around *Enterprise, Hornet,* and *Yorktown,* without, however, a single battleship to protect them. The carriers would depend on cruisers and destroyers for their screens, a garrison of Marines would provide Midway's land defenses, while land-based Marine and Army air would also be deployed against the enemy. Finally, there was the calm and canny Nimitz, who refused to take the enemy's Aleutians bait, and sent Fletcher and Spruance into the battle with these instructions:

". . . you will be governed by the principle of calculated risk, which you shall interpret to mean the avoidance of exposure of your force to attack by superior enemy forces without good prospect of inflicting, as a result of such exposure, greater damage on the enemy."

Meanwhile, the American pilots were searching the Pacific. On June 3, Ensign Jack Reid lifted a Catalina flying boat off Midway and headed for the very sector at which Nimitz expected the enemy forces to converge. Seven hundred miles out he saw a cluster of specks come crawling over the rim of the horizon.

"Do you see what I see?" Reid yelled to his co-pilot.

"You're damned right I do!" the co-pilot shouted, and Reid ducked into a cloud.[6]

Someone besides Snowy Rhoades to the west and Martin Clemens to the east, and all the missionaries and Melanesians between them, had at last taken notice of Guadalcanal.

The Japanese had come.

On May 28 a scouting party arrived from Tulagi, landing at Lunga midway on the northern coast. In the early days of June they paid more visits, accompanied by Mr. Ishimoto. They slaughtered plantation cattle with machine guns and butchered them with great waste. At other times Ishimoto asked the natives the whereabouts of the District Officer, for Clemens had withdrawn from Aola Bay to the bush village of Paripao.

"Him he gone," the natives replied. "Him no more."[7]

Such evasive replies infuriated Ishimoto. He lectured the natives on their duty to the Greater East Asia Co-Prosperity Sphere, and he was encouraged by some of the men in the front rank who nodded their heads vigorously. Ishimoto's claque, of course, was composed of Martin Clemens's "plain-clothes men."

The District Officer had stripped his scouts of all distinguishing badges. They wore ordinary lap-laps like the other natives and their instructions were to mingle with the Japanese, to work for them, and to spy on them. They had become proficient in reporting enemy ships. It was no longer, "One big-fellow war he stop," but "One fellow cruiser gottem gun 'long six inch." There had been difficulty in identifying the caliber of the antiaircraft guns on Tulagi, until Clemens hit upon the idea of keeping small logs of varying diameter in his hut at Paripao.

The scouts would paddle over to Tulagi in their graceful gondolas and climb the enemy guns at night, carefully grasping the barrels in their hands or hefting the shells. Back at Paripao they would squat with closed eyes and expressions of pained concentration on their faces while Clemens placed log after log in their hands. Then, with faces brightening and the exclamation, "Him no more, massa!," one or another of them would burst out: "Gottem shell like small fellow beerbottle."

"A three-incher!" Clemens would exclaim, and the information would go off to Australia.

One day in June, Clemens received an ominous message from Snowy Rhoades, which went:

"Japs at Savo (Island) with one machine gun and tin hats, enquiring for whereabouts of white men on Guadalcanal. Said they would go there in about two weeks time."[8]

In other words, they were coming to Clemens's island to stay.

The First Marines were leaving New River.

With the Seventh Marines still on detached duty in Samoa, with the Fifth Marines and most of the artillery still sailing toward New Zealand, the last of Vandegrift's echelons was heading for the West Coast under Brigadier General William Rupertus, the division's assistant commander. The night before the departure by rail, the men gave themselves a farewell party. They went down to the "slop chute" and bought cases of canned beer and carried them back to those rickety, stifling, mosquito-ridden squad huts that they detested. They began to drink, and then, to sing. They sang songs like "I've Been Working on the Railroad" or "Merrily We Roll Along" or other favorites such as "The Old Mill Stream" or "A Tavern in the Town" before turning to the serviceman's repertoire of regional songs, "Dixie," "The Wabash Cannonball":

Listen to the jingle, the rumble and the roar
Ridin' through the woodlands and the ocean by the shore.

"Birmingham Jail," "Red River Valley," after which, as an inevitable sign of insobriety they began bawling out bawdies and dirty songs, but then, because only a few lewdly dedicated minds among them actually knew all the words, they had to fall back on the college ballads which everyone knew, ending with the sentimental "Sweetheart of Sigma Chi," and being, by that time, so sentimentally drunk, there was nothing left to do but blubber about "My Mom" and "M Is for the Million Things She Gave Me," until, at the conclusion of "I'll Be Home for Christmas," some of them were weeping openly and others so outraged by the realization that they would *not* be home for Christmas that they had begun to wrestle on the floor or duel each other with sheathed bayonets—"grab-assing," as the Marines call it—while others had wandered outside to pick fights with other squads.

Up at the Second Battalion, one of the machine gunners had

begun to punch holes in the huts' wallboard sides. The man was Indian Johnny Rivers, a powerfully built youth of about medium height, half Indian and half English, who had been raised in the Pennsylvania Dutch country. He had been a professional prize-fighter before the war, and he was, with his keen good humor and laughing black eyes, a great favorite with both men and officers. The gunners cheered and whooped as Johnny staggered from hut to hut, crouching and unleashing his famous right, yelling "Here's another one for the goddamed mosquitoes to come in!"[9]

It was a marvelous method of letting off the steam which months of boredom and frustration can generate in such exuberant spirits. Soon other gunners joined Rivers in ventilating the despised shacks, symbols of all that they had hated during those weeks upon weeks of marching, marching, marching, of sleeping in the rain or eating a sodden slop for chow, of sitting for monotonous hours in wallowing Higgins boats while seasick men threw up to windward, or of repeatedly jumping into the surf and running up the beach with heavy, squish-booted step to fall on the sand and crawl forward with cradled rifle and become coated in grit like a fish in flour. Punching holes in flimsy walls should square away those "chicken" captains and corporals and every other regulation martinet who insisted upon doing things by the book—like the enraged Gunny Jim Blalock who at that very moment was bawling "Knock if awff!" and promising them that they would all "see the man" in the morning.

They did. But Lieutenant Colonel Al Pollock, Rivers' battalion commander, was helpless, on the day of departure, to do more than give the men a tongue-lashing and put them on restriction. This was merely a disciplinary tautology, because as Rivers' buddy, Private Al Schmid, a short, stocky brashness with an irrepressible blond cowlick, explained the situation: "We were on restriction already!"

"Yah-vo!" said Johnny, and 'that afternoon he and Smitty and the rest of the First Marines went aboard their train.[10]

They were astonished. Here was no grimy, crowded troop train but a line of Pullman cars with a separate berth for each man, with porters and a luxurious dining car in which waiters in white jackets served their individual tastes on clean plates and starched linen. Very few twenty-one-dollar-a-month privates have gone so opulently to war.

Five days later—having traversed that vast and gloriously varied country which most of them had never seen before—having been charmed by gophers gaping at them from prairie holes, having marveled at the primitive pure beauty of the Ozarks or the myriad million fireflies that seemed to set the Kansas wheatfields blazing, having missed the Mississippi by a night crossing but having caught their breath at the grandeur of the Rockies, they climbed the Sierra Nevadas like a long slow roller-coaster and went racing down the reverse grades to San Francisco and the sea.

As they disembarked from the trains to board waiting ships, newsboys went among them hawking newspapers with great black headlines announcing that a vast air-sea battle was being fought at a place called Midway Island.

The Japanese struck first.

Confident that no American carriers could possibly reach the Midway area for two more days, Admiral Chuichi Nagumo launched his opening strike at Midway Island itself while flying off a merely routine search for enemy ships.

On June 4, just before sunrise, 108 fighters, dive-bombers and torpedo-bombers roared aloft from the decks of Admiral Nagumo's four big carriers. Marine pilots at Midway rose to intercept them. They were slaughtered. Marines flying the near-useless Brewster Buffaloes had no chance against the superior Zero. Only pilots such as Captain Marion Carl flying the new Grumman Wildcats were able to battle the Zero on anything like even terms. In all, fifteen American fighters were shot down. But superb American antiaircraft fire prevented the enemy from damaging Midway's runways, while downing or damaging dozens of enemy aircraft.

One third of the Japanese attacking force was either shot down or badly damaged, and the formation leader radioed Admiral Nagumo that a second strike against Midway was required. Even as the report was being received, Midway's land-based bombers came winging over Nagumo's ships. They were driven off with heavy losses, the Japanese ships were not scratched, but the very appearance of the Americans served to underscore the report that Midway's airfields were far from being knocked out.

Nagumo ordered ninety-three planes, then armed for possible strikes against enemy ships, to be rearmed with fragmentation and incendiary bombs for use against Midway. As the armorers rushed to comply, a search plane reported ten American ships to the northeast.

Chuichi Nagumo was thunderstruck. No American ships were supposed to be within a thousand miles of Midway! Shaken, pacing *Akagi's* bridge with his white-gloved hands locked behind his back, Nagumo took a full quarter-hour to decide to order the ninety-three planes changed back to ship-bombs. By then, it was too late—the formations which had attacked Midway were returning and all flight decks had to be cleared to receive them. Still sailing toward Midway in box formation, the four big carriers—*Akagi, Hiryu, Soryu,* and *Kaga*—began taking planes aboard.

An hour later all decks were cleared. Nagumo ordered the second strike launched against the American task force.

And in so doing he did exactly what the Americans expected him to do.

Captain Miles Browning, Bull Halsey's chief of staff on loan to Admiral Spruance, had calculated that Nagumo would keep steaming toward Midway and would launch a second strike at the island. He decided that the time to hit the Japanese would be while they were refueling planes on deck.

At seven that morning, 175 miles from the enemy's calculated position, Spruance ordered *Enterprise* and *Hornet* to launch planes. Twenty Wildcats, sixty-seven Dauntless dive-bombers, and twenty-nine Devastator dive-bombers—116 planes in all—went hurtling aloft. Admiral Fletcher delayed *Yorktown's* launching on the chance that other targets might be discovered. Even so, by nine o'clock, just as the last of the warbirds from *Enterprise* and *Hornet* were airborne, *Yorktown* had thirty-five planes—six Wildcats, seventeen Dauntlesses, and twelve Devastators—in the skies.

Most of them caught Nagumo. They found his four big carriers as expected, rearming and refueling.

Hornet's torpedo-bombers—her fighters and dive-bombers missed the enemy entirely—attacked first. They were annihilated. Of fifteen Devastators that struck, every one was shot down and only one pilot survived. *Enterprise's* torpedo squadron skimmed in next, and was also slaughtered: ten out of fourteen destroyed. Then came *Yorktown's* dozen Devastators, and only four survived.

Not a single Japanese ship was touched.

In about a hundred glittering seconds it seemed to Chuichi Nagumo that the war was won.

And then the matchless American dive-bombers also found the Japanese.

There were thirty-seven Dauntlesses from *Enterprise* under Lieutenant Commander Clarence McCluskey. McCluskey took half of them down on *Kaga,* while Lieutenant Earl Gallaher led the rest against *Akagi.*

They sank them both.

Next, seventeen Dauntlesses from *Yorktown* under Lieutenant Commander Max Leslie fell upon *Soryu* and left her a crippled wreck to be broken in two by the torpedoes of U.S. submarine *Nautilus.*

In six minutes, Nagumo had lost his own flagship—having to transfer to the cruiser *Nagara*—and two other carriers. But he retaliated by ending the career of *Yorktown.* And while the bold Japanese Kates were breaking through *Yorktown's* antiaircraft screen to put three torpedoes into the great ship's hull, twenty-four Dauntlesses led by the formidable Gallaher found *Hiryu,* fell upon her, and put her on the bottom.

Well to the rear with *Yamato* and the Main Body, Isoroku Yamamoto read reports of the battle in stunned silence. His entire fast carrier group—four big flattops—had been lost, against only one American carrier sunk. With them went their complement of 250 planes, and 2200 officers and men. Although the smaller northern force had seized bases in the Aleutians, it had failed in its chief mission: to lure the Americans away from Midway.

Yamamoto recognized disaster when he saw it, and he ordered a general retirement. For the first time in 350 years Japan had suffered a naval defeat. At one blow—in a single day's fighting— the advantage gained at Pearl Harbor had been lost and parity in carrier power was restored in the Pacific.

All of the Japanese ships reversed course. Isoroku Yamamoto went to his cabin and stayed there for the remainder of the voyage. Tight-lipped and sorrowing, Admiral Tanaka and Commander Hara escorted a bewildered Colonel Ichiki back to Guam.

Never again was the word Midway mentioned in the Japanese Navy.

Ernest King saw his chance.

The Japanese had been checked at Midway and it was now time for the Americans to seize the offensive. The question was:

Where? By the middle of the month King had decided that Tulagi-Guadalcanal in the Solomons was the proper place. He proposed the operation to the Joint Chiefs of Staff.

But General Marshall and General Arnold were firmly committed to the build-up of the U.S. forces in England—OPERATION BOLERO, as it was called. On May 6, President Roosevelt had told them: "I do not want BOLERO slowed down." They were cool to King's proposal, even though Cominch backed it up with intelligence reports that the Japanese were moving into Guadalcanal. After much debate, with some reluctance, they agreed.

But who would command?

Marshall wanted General MacArthur and King wanted Admiral Nimitz. It would be a Navy show with the Navy's Marines, King argued, even though the Solomons did lie within MacArthur's Southwest Pacific Area. Finally, again after debate, the Solomons were included in the South Pacific Area which Admiral Ghormley was developing under Nimitz's control.

On June 25 the Joint Chiefs notified Ghormley to confer with MacArthur on the operation.

Next day Ghormley, in Auckland, telephoned General Vandegrift in Wellington.

Wakefield had entered Wellington's beautiful harbor on a Sunday, June 21. Marines crowding the rails saw a great round of deep blue water girdled by an amphitheater of sloping green hills dotted by white houses with red-tile roofs.

But there was bad news in Wellington.

Lieutenant Colonel William Twining, chief of Vandegrift's advance party, came aboard with the report that the unloading of the cargo ships which had preceded them was far behind schedule.

"What in hell is wrong?" Vandegrift exploded.

"They work differently from us," Twining replied. "They stop for morning tea, lunch, afternoon tea. If it's raining they don't work at all."[11]

Vandegrift met the impasse with characteristic directness. Heedless of the sensitivities of socialist unions basking in the favor of a Labor Government, he ordered his Marines to form working parties and unload the ships themselves. It was fortunate that he had acted thus and so quickly, for five days later he received Ghormley's telephone call, and on the next day he and his staff were flying to Auckland.

Vandegrift was astounded when he entered Ghormley's office. He had known the admiral as a suave and gracious diplomat. But Ghormley appeared harassed. His manner was brusque.

"Vandegrift," the admiral said, "I have some very disconcerting news."

"I'm sorry to hear that, Admiral," the general said.

But the admiral merely handed the general a top-secret dispatch and grunted, "You will be more sorry when you read this."[12]

Archer Vandegrift could not believe what he read. It was the Joint Chiefs' directive and it specified that the First Marine Division—his, Vandegrift's—would seize Tulagi and Guadalcanal. They were to land August 1. Five weeks away!

Vandegrift read the dispatch again, slowly, in a tense silence broken by the drumming of Ghormley's slender fingers on the table.

At last Vandegrift looked up and expostulated: his division was fragmented, one third in Samoa, one third in Wellington, one third at sea; most of his men had not been in uniform six months; most of his equipment was new and needed to be broken in; his supplies would now need to be unloaded, sorted, and combat loaded; he knew nothing of Guadalcanal, not even its location. He concluded:

"I just don't see how we can land anywhere by August first."

Ghormley nodded. "I don't see how we can land at all, and I am going to take it up with MacArthur. Meanwhile, we'll have to go ahead as best as we can."[13]

Archer Vandegrift began going ahead immediately. He summoned his staff to Ghormley's headquarters, learning that he would be able to replace the missing Seventh Regiment with the Second Marine Regiment, that he would also have Edson's Raiders—reclaimed rather than received, he thought dryly—as well as the Third Defense Battalion. These units, of course, were widely scattered: the Second Marines were aboard ship in San Diego, Edson was in Samoa, and the defense unit was in Hawaii. Nevertheless, they could rendezvous at sea. The most pressing matter at the moment, even moreso than licking in weeks a logistics problem that normally required months, was to find out something—anything—about Guadalcanal Island.

Chapter 4

ON GUADALCANAL the month of June had come to an end in a howling midnight rainstorm. At first light of the first day of July, young Constable Dovu came slogging up the slime-slick trail to Paripao, slipping and catching at bushes to keep his balance, calling out breathlessly:

"Massa, massa! Japan he come along Guadalcanal!"

Clemens burst from his hut, his beard dripping like a blond teardrop, and Dovu rushed on:

"One thousand Japan-man come ashore along Lunga. Gottem big fella machine gun." Dovu paused for breath, and Clemens cut in sharply.

"Which way you savvy one thousand he stop along Lunga?"

Stung, Dovu explained: "Me sit down along scrub. Catchem ten fella stone along hand, and me countem Japan-man come ashore."[1]

Annoyed, suddenly realizing that the Japanese had probably landed from the cruiser he had seen in the Bay only two days ago, Clemens snapped out an order for Dovu to return to Lunga to observe the Japanese there.

Dovu spun and went sliding down the track, his dark arms outstretched for balance, the mud spurting between his big prehensile toes. He and the other scouts would be back repeatedly within the next week. On July 5, they reported that the Japanese had begun to burn off the tall kunai grass in the plains behind the Lunga coconut groves. Clemens instantly divined that the enemy was building an airfield. He radioed the news to Commander Feldt, unaware that this information, relayed to Washington, had electrified the U. S. Joint Chiefs of Staff.

Meanwhile, Clemens decided to move farther back into the bush. He withdrew to Vungano about halfway across the island.

In streaming rain, fording rivers in flood, tightrope-walking over razorbacked ridges, and plastered with mud that worked itself into the eyes and nose and mouth or got into his boots and lay between his toes in coarse cold clots, Clemens plodded dismally along in the track of about a dozen carriers balancing boxed components of his teleradio on their powerful shoulders. Glum though he was, Clemens could at least take consolation from the fact that Sergeant Major Vouza was with him.

Vouza was a real acquisition. He had been in the police service for twenty-five years and had only just retired. He had volunteered to help Clemens. In his forties—close to old age for a Melanesian —Vouza was still a splendid human being, with his broad, deep, muscular torso, his keen, piercing eyes, and a face which shone with loyalty and courage. Clemens put Vouza in charge of all the scouts.

Meanwhile, the Japanese were relieving Clemens of his greatest concern: whether or not the natives would go over to the new masters of the Solomons. Eager to obtain laborers for the new airfield, the Japanese recruited them at bayonet point. They plundered the natives' vegetable gardens and they strutted. Mr. Ishimoto arrived at Aola Bay and proclaimed himself, in effect, the new District Officer. He had orders typed up and issued in all coastal villages. They said:

JAPANESE OFFICIAL issued in 16th July, 1942, to inhabitants of Guadalcanal.
Notice No. 1. All of the inhabitants of this island must be ordered by Japanese Government to co-operate for Japan. Any inhabitants against it should be severely punished by Japanese martial law.
Order no: 2. Men only of 14 years of old or less than fifty years have to work for Japanese troops at some places on this island. During work for Japanese troops they will be given meals, etcetera.

Gradually, Mr. Ishimoto's "etcetera"—a euphemism for oppression—solved the native problem. The Japanese became hated. When Ishimoto went patrolling for Martin Clemens during the last few days of July, the natives sent him sloshing down the wrong track. Clemens wisely withdrew deeper into the bush—barefooted this time, to save his remaining pair of tattered boots—achieving the dubious distinction of becoming the first white man to enter the precincts of Vuchikoro, a community of about ten miserable thatched huts perched like a ragged eagle's nest on the edge of an abyss.

As July ended and August began, the rains came.

It should not have been raining, for the monsoons were not due until November. It was the time of the southeast trades, and there should have been little rain; yet, the rains were pouring down from New Zealand to Rabaul, marching up and down the Coral Sea in slanting gray sheets, making an utter mush of the First Marine Division's piles of supplies lying naked on the Wellington docks, and drumming out a tattoo of welcome to Vice-Admiral Gunichi Mikawa as he sailed into Simpson Harbor at Rabaul to occupy the headquarters of his newly activated Eighth Fleet.

Mikawa's command had been activated after the Midway debacle had forced cancellation of the invasion of New Caledonia and the Fijis. Japan was now going to concentrate on "the Outer South Seas," that is a huge area encompassing New Guinea, New Britain, and the Solomons, with headquarters at Rabaul. Mikawa's new Eighth Fleet would relieve the Fourth Fleet of responsibility in this theater, and Mikawa would thereafter support General Hyakutake's 17th Army in the paramount operation against Port Moresby.

Gunichi Mikawa was a combat veteran. He had been second in command at Pearl Harbor and had led a battleship division at Midway. He was gentle and soft-spoken, in appearance one of those "British admirals" in which the Japanese Navy abounded. Having taken the British Royal Navy as their model, many Japanese officers had also patterned themselves on the English gentleman[2]; often equating the gentlemanly with a kind of amiable reticence. Fortunately for Emperor Hirohito, Gunichi Mikawa was not one of them: his silken manner sheathed the sword of a samurai.

On July 14, Admiral Mikawa called Commander Toshikazu Ohmae to his modest home in Setagaya, an outlying ward of Tokyo. Ohmae, considered one of the Japanese Navy's outstanding planners, was to be the Eighth Fleet's operations officer. The two men sat among the bright leaves sipping tea. Mikawa expressed his delight in exercising independent command.

"I want you to go out to the forward areas for a first-hand look at the situation," he told Ohmae. "Survey local conditions at our bases."[3]

Ohmae departed two days later. On July 20 his flying boat taxied into the seaplane base at Rabaul. It was a clear day. A bright sun sparkled on the blue waters of Simpson Harbor, glinting off the red hull of a half-sunken freighter. Ohmae was impressed by this testimony to American bombing accuracy, but he was not impressed by Rabaul. Small vessels were bunched together with no thought for protection against air raids. Ashore there was inter-service bickering, and hostility toward Japan's new Eighth Fleet. Ohmae's request for headquarters was countered with the insinuation that any genuine naval commander should prefer to command afloat. He replied that Admiral Mikawa wanted to keep his forces safely to the rear—behind New Ireland to the north while directing operations ashore at Rabaul. Grudgingly, the base force set aside a ramshackle building without even toilet facilities.

Talks with officers of the 25th Air Flotilla also depressed Ohmae. This outfit—which included such famous pilots as Saburo Sakai, Nishizawa, and Ota—had been carrying on the gruelling air war against Port Moresby. It seemed to Ohmae that the 25th Air Flotilla was interested in nothing but relief.[4] Worse, no one —Army or Navy—seemed concerned about the southern Solomons. Ohmae was gratified, however, to learn that an airfield was under construction on Guadalcanal Island.

Leaving Rabaul, Captain Ohmae flew north to the great sea bastion at Truk. There, he was invited to a dinner in honor of Lieutenant General Haruyoshi Hyakutake. He was dismayed to find that Hyakutake had not the slightest interest in the southern Solomons. Hyakutake cared only for the Port Moresby operation. Even the Truk admirals joined the general in dismissing Ohmae's fears of an enemy invasion of the Solomons as the anxiety of a newcomer.

On July 25 Admiral Mikawa arrived at Truk. He was aboard his flagship, *Chokai,* a powerful cruiser disfigured, in American eyes, by her bizarre silhouette described by a fat forward stack canted sharply back and a skinny second stack sticking straight up. Ohmae reported to Mikawa. Disturbed by what he heard, Mikawa requested an immediate conference with Vice-Admiral Shigeyoshi Inoue, commander of the Fourth Fleet. They met that afternoon and Inoue also laughed at Mikawa's fears for the Solomons. The enemy, said Inoue, was still reeling from the shock of defeats from Pearl Harbor to Singapore. Neither admiral said a word about Midway, even though both of them knew all the details of that disaster. Inoue, it seemed to Mikawa, appeared anxious to have the new Eighth Fleet relieve Fourth Fleet of responsibility for that huge Outer South Seas Area centering at Rabaul. At midnight of the twenty-sixth the transfer was effected.

Next day Mikawa and Ohmae sailed south for Rabaul. Both sailors who loved the sea, they were happy to have the turbines of a ship turning beneath their feet again. They tried to take a more optimistic view of that exposed left flank in the Solomons. At least, as Ohmae had discovered, the new airfield suitable for sixty planes should lessen the danger of invasion there.

It should be ready by August 7.

August 7 was also the date for the American invasion.

Admiral King had set the new deadline. In early July the Joint Chiefs had received a report from Admiral Ghormley and General MacArthur, stating: "It is our joint opinion, arrived at independently and confirmed after discussion, that the initiation of this operation at this time, without reasonable assurance of an adequate air cover during each phase, would be attended with the gravest risk . . . It is recommended that this operation be deferred pending the further development of forces in the South Pacific and Southwest Pacific Areas . . ." King read the dispatch and snorted to General Marshall: "Three weeks ago MacArthur stated that, if he could be furnished amphibious forces and two carriers, he could push right through to Rabaul . . . He now feels that he not only cannot undertake this extended operation but also not even the Tulagi operations."[5] Unimpressed, Admiral King replied:

"Execute."[6]

But then, after General Vandegrift had made it clear that he could not possibly invade by August 1, King agreed to a three-day postponement. After Ghormley and Vandegrift protested anew, he added three more days of grace. But that was it: it *had* to be August 7. Coastwatcher reports and reconnaissance flights of Army B-17s indicated that the airfield on Guadalcanal was nearly completed. To invade in the face of land-based air would be far too dangerous.

And so Archer Vandegrift went grimly ahead with the invasion which his staff was already calling "Operation Shoestring."

The area Vandegrift hoped to seize centered around the airfield and ran about ten miles along the mid-northern coast and perhaps three miles inland. On its west, according to the details of an old marine chart, was the Lunga River and on the east was the Ilu River. Vandegrift had learned from Martin Clemens that this area was defended by from 2000 to 10,000 Japanese —a disturbingly loose estimate—and that there was a lesser force on Tulagi and Gavutu-Tanambogo. Clemens had also reported that there were enemy guns emplaced on the beaches west of the Lunga, and so Vandegrift decided to land on the unprotected beaches east of the Ilu. The landings on Tulagi were to be made on its open western end, while the twin islets of Gavutu-Tanambogo, being so small and well-fortified, would simply have to be stormed.

Guadalcanal, of course, was to require the bulk of Vandegrift's forces, and it was still the biggest worry. Information on the island's terrain consisted of that old marine chart, a few faded photographs made by missionaries five years before the Japanese landed, and a short story by Jack London, as well as London's personal anathema upon the entire group: "If I were a king, the worst punishment I could inflict on my enemies would be to banish them to the Solomons. On second thought, king or no king, I don't think I'd have the heart to do it." To supplement this unspectacular hoard, Vandegrift sent Lieutenant Colonel Frank Goettge flying to Australia. Goettge conferred with Commander Feldt and his hard-bitten islanders. He brought back some helpful information on the target area's terrain as well as eight islanders who had lived on Tulagi or Guadalcanal. The islanders —whose elephantine thirst made the purchase of Scotch whisky an acceptable military expense—were interrogated almost daily. Some of their information proved invaluable; some, just because it was thought to be invaluable, was to prove costly. One day General Vandegrift called for a plantation manager who had lived near Red Beach, the designated landing zone on Guadalcanal. Vandegrift pointed to the Ilu River on his chart, and inquired about the river's characteristics.

"Since this is the dry season," the islander said, "you will have no trouble in fording it."

"It won't be an obstacle?"

"No, it will not be an obstacle."[7]

It *would* be an obstacle, because it was raining this dry season and because the river was not the Ilu but the Tenaru. And because of this assurance, General Vandegrift would leave valuable bridging equipment behind.

Meanwhile, all other attempts to map Guadalcanal were meeting similar frustration. Although the Army's 648th Engineer Topographic Battalion had obligingly put on a "red-rush" aerial photo-mapping of the island, a naval transportation officer saw to it that the finished mosaic was carefully filed at the bottom of a mounting pile of boxes in an Auckland warehouse. Vandegrift never got it. Nor did he get much help from Lieutenant Colonel Twining, who, with Major William McKean, had boarded a Flying Fortress at Port Moresby and flown over Guadalcanal. The plane had been jumped by three float Zeros over Tulagi Harbor, and Twining and McKean had understandably been more engrossed in the ensuing air battle than in Guadalcanal. They remained thus preoccupied while the Fort's gunners sent two Zeros spinning down in flames and fought off the pursuit of the third. After the big bomber finally got back to Moresby, coming in with bone-dry tanks, all that Twining and McKean could tell Vandegrift was that the landing beaches he had selected seemed suitable. Still desperate for terrain intelligence, the general asked Admiral Ghormley to approve landing a scouting party by submarine, but Ghormley replied that this was "too dangerous." In the end, the opening of the American counteroffensive against Japan was to be based on a map so sketchy that Archer Vandegrift might have been landing on the moon.

During the landings, Vandegrift naturally expected the support of carrier-based aircraft. But after that who would fly from the airfield which Admiral King wanted so badly? The choice fell upon Marine Air Group 23—two squadrons of fighters and two of dive-bombers—commanded by Colonel William Wallace. But this outfit was then back in Hawaii checking out on carrier landings and takeoffs. No one seemed to know how such short-range aircraft were to cross thousands of miles of water to Guadalcanal.

Supply was another headache. The ships could be loaded only with "items actually required to live and fight." Seabags, bedrolls, tentage—hardly articles of luxury—had to be left behind. Considerable heavy equipment and motor transport was hauled off the ships and placed in storage. Bulk supply—fuel, lubricants, rations —was cut to sixty days. Ammunition was reduced from fifteen to ten days of fire. And so the work of unloading and sorting and combat-loading went forward in those cold drenching rains.

Wellington's spacious Aotea Quay was turned into an ankle-deep marsh of tons upon tons of cereal, cigarettes, candy, and little cans of C rations, whatever had spilled out of sodden and burst containers and had been churned into a pulpy mass by the feet of thousands of toiling Marines or the wheels of flat-bedded New Zealand lorries laboriously crawling through drifts of corn-flakes. Here was bedlam made more chaotic by the sense of urgency energizing all those scurrying men in tan helmets and brown ponchos, made more nightmarish by wharf lights glowing ghostly throughout mackerel day and streaming night, and more lunatic by the sound of rain striking steel decks to counterpoint, with the monotony of a monstrous metronome, the whining of winches, the shouting of bosun's mates, and the crying of Marines warning one another of huge hooks swinging free or of trucks, slung in cargo nets like toys, rising from the holds with dangerous rapidity and falling too quickly toward the dock. There were curses, too, yells of frustration whenever Marines stumbled over C-ration cans imbedded in the mess or sharp cries of pain uttered by men tearing their flesh on rolls of barbed wire.

"Goddlemighty damn! What'n hell we need barbed wire for? I thought we were going on maneuvers."[8]

That was what they had been told. It was a necessary security precaution, and might also preclude against any of the unvaliant missing the outgoing ships. No leave was granted, of course, but almost all of the men managed to slip into Wellington to promenade the city's quaint steep streets, to dance with New Zealand girls, to eat steak and eggs or to savor such exotic potions as rum-and-raspberry or gin-and-lemon. And as the rains continued, and order came marvelously out of chaos, General Vandegrift alerted the First Marines to stand by to transship upon arrival.

Clifton Cates commanded the First Marines. He was a man as trim as a whiplash, as suave as steel in his breeches and puttees and sun helmet, puffing calmly on a long cigarette holder with which he sometimes punctuated orders given in a pleasant Tennessee drawl. Colonel Cates was an Old China Hand who had fought in France in World War I. He had been wounded twice, gassed once, and had won seven medals for bravery. Having commanded a platoon, a company, and a battalion in battle, he now had this regiment—and he was both worried and enraged about it.

Colonel Cates was enraged because the ship *John Ericsson* carrying most of his men was little better than an African slaver. If Cates had had the power he would have put the ship's owner and her master in their own brig and let them rot on what they fed the troops: spoiled meat, rancid butter, and rotten eggs without an ounce of fresh food.

John Ericsson stank like a floating head. Hundreds of nauseated men thronged her leeward rails and those who could not retch over the side vomited into their steel battle helmets. The heads below decks reeked like open cesspools. Men devoured by dysentery waited outside the heads in long lines; men who could not get to them in time also used their helmets. The war was just beginning and the profiteer was already battening on American misery like a leech sucking blood.

The worries which nagged Colonel Cates were of a less infuriating nature. He was concerned that the men might be going stale. From San Francisco to Wellington was a voyage of about three weeks, and that was time enough to soften muscles only recently hardened by a few months of training. The men were idle and bored. Either they played cards or lounged on top of covered hatches, sunning themselves and "batting the breeze," or they lined the gunwales to watch the flying fish or stare vacantly into white wakes boiling off the fantails, their minds thousands of miles eastward among the scenes of childhood.

On some of the less crowded ships it was possible to organize calisthenics, and aboard the *George F. Elliott* the men of Cates's Second Battalion held boxing matches.

Indian Johnny Rivers was frequently in the ring. He sparred lightly with his opponents, careful not to hit them too hard. But one day, as the convoy and its escort of circling warships plowed through the blue Pacific, Johnny Rivers heard his friend Al Schmid yelling, "Your right, Johnny—use your right!"

Rivers swung his right.

His opponent stiffened and his eyes became glassy and his knees buckled.

Rivers came back to his corner, ruefully shaking his head. "What's the idea, Smitty? I didn't want to hit him with my right." Then the irrepressible Rivers grinned. "Boy, I sure hit him though, didn't I?"[9]

So the men of the First Marines sailed on toward New Zealand, and far behind them came the men of the Second Marines under the formidable protection of the aircraft carrier *Wasp*. This great ship which Winston Churchill had hailed as the savior of Malta had been rushed from the Atlantic to the Pacific to escort this borrowed regiment to the First Marine Division's rendezvous area in the Fijis.

Admiral Frank Jack Fletcher had sortied from Hawaii. His ships included carriers *Saratoga* and *Enterprise,* battleship *North Carolina,* one light and five heavy crusiers, sixteen destroyers and three oilers. After he had rendezvoused with *Wasp* and all the other warships and transports then at sea or in New Zealand, the force would number eighty-nine ships and 19,000 United States Marines. It would be the greatest invasion fleet yet assembled.

But Admiral Fletcher was not jubilant. He was thinking of the three carriers—all that America had in the Pacific—and how dangerous it would be to risk them in the narrow and uncharted waters of the Solomons. Admiral Fletcher did not like this operation at all. Back at Pearl Harbor he had openly predicted that it would "be a failure."[10] He had had nothing to do with planning it.

In such high hopes did Admiral Frank Jack Fletcher put out for the Fijis to take command of the entire Expeditionary Force.

Beneath Fletcher in the chain of command was Vice-Admiral Richmond Kelly Turner. He was a planner and perfectionist, Kelly Turner, a man of beetling brows and rimless glasses, of ferocious language and a tongue as caustic as a shaving stick; he was a leader so pedantic that he would not hesitate to tell a coxswain how to beach his boat. This was the admiral who was to command the Amphibious Force, and Major General Vandegrift who commanded only the Landing Force—that is, the 19,000 Marines who were to seize the objectives—soon found that this was also a sailor who often mistook his sextant for a soldier's baton.

Of this Vandegrift was made aware on July 18, when, a few days after the First Marines had arrived in Wellington, Turner's flagship *McCawley* sailed into the harbor and broke out the admiral's two-star flag. Turner quickly told Vandegrift that he was keeping all but one battalion of the Second Marines for the seizure of unoccupied Ndeni in the Santa Cruz Islands east of the Solomons. Vandegrift replied that this was to be only a later phase of the operation, and that he was counting on the Second Marines for his reserve. If he could not have them, he said, then he would have to change his plans. The meeting ended on a note of impasse.

Four days later—July 22—Vandegrift and his Marines stood majestically out to sea, bound for the Fiji Islands.

On July 26, the top American commanders met.

Turner and Vandegrift risked a heavy sea to transfer from *McCawley* to the destroyer *Dewey*. Already aboard *Dewey* were Rear Admiral John S. McCain, who commanded all of Admiral Ghormley's aircraft in the South Pacific, Lieutenant Colonel Twining, and Colonel Laverne ("Blondie") Saunders, commander of the Army Air Force's Flying Fortresses. *Dewey* made for *Saratoga*, Fletcher's flagship, and came about beneath its towering beam. Admiral McCain seized a Jacob's ladder and started up.

A garbage chute swung open and the little admiral was showered with milk.

It was an infuriating beginning foretelling an unfriendly conference.

Archer Vandegrift, who had once been startled to see the unruffled Ghormley acting like a drill sergeant, was now amazed to see that Fletcher looked tired and nervous, and he put it down to the admiral's recent battles of the Coral Sea and Midway.[11] Next, he was surprised to learn that Fletcher had neither knowledge of nor interest in the Guadalcanal operation.[12] Finally, he was thunderstruck to hear him saying frankly that it would not succeed.[13] Then, Admiral Fletcher turned on Admiral Turner and angrily accused him of "instigating" the Solomons invasion.[14] Unimpressed by Turner's indignant denial, Fletcher interrupted him to ask:

"How many days will it take to unload the troops?"

"Five," Turner replied.

Fletcher shook his head stubbornly. Two days, he said, were quite enough. He would not risk his carriers any longer.

Vandegrift struggled to control himself. He tried to explain that this was no mere "hit-and-run" operation. This was an expedition to take and to hold fortified enemy islands. He, Vandegrift, commanded a heavily reinforced division. There was going to be a fight. His Marines would need air cover. Even five days of air cover was scarcely sufficient. Two was suicidal.

Admiral Turner agreed, with heat and with force.

Admiral Frank Jack Fletcher shook his head. He was leaving with his carriers on the third day.

"The conference is dismissed," he said curtly.

The commanders arose. With them was Vice-Admiral Daniel Callaghan, chief of staff to Admiral Ghormley. He had been present at the entire conference and had taken notes on what was said.

But he represented the admiral who commanded the entire Area, as well as this first American counteroffensive, and he never said a word.

Two days later the First Marine Division attempted to practice landings on the beaches of Koro Island. In full battle gear, the men scrambled down the cargo nets into waiting Higgins boats to form in a circle, then to go monotonously circling, circling, circling, and to sail back to their ships and clamber back up the nets to return to their holds.

The maneuvers were a fiasco. Sharp offshore coral prevented many boats from landing on the designated beaches, other boats broke down, the naval gunfire was inaccurate and the dive-bombers missed their targets.

But Admiral Turner and General Vandegrift, who had begun to respect each other and who were both optimists in battle, agreed that at least the defects had shown up early and there would be time to rectify them. A poor rehearsal, they said, means a good show.

On the last day of July there was frustration of an entirely different order. Marine officers from Wellington had flown in and they brought with them copies of the July 4 edition of the *Wellington Dominion*, which said:

HOPE OF COMING U.S. THRUST
South Pacific Marines
INTENSIFIED RAIDS IN NORTH
(Received July 3, 7 P.M.)

New York, July 2.

Operations to seize Japanese-held bases, such as Rabaul, Wake Island and Tulagi, are advocated by the military writer of the *New York Herald Tribune,* Major Eliot. One of the signs which suggest that the [Allies] may be getting ready to capitalize on the naval advantage gained on the Coral Sea and Midway battles is the recent American bombing of Wake Island, he says. The other signs include the intensified raids on the Timor and New Guinea areas.

". . . What is needed is to drive the Japanese out of their positions and convert them to our own use. The only way to take positions such as Rabaul, Wake Island, and Tulagi, is to land troops to take physical possession of them."

The newspaper [*New York Times*] adds: "It may also be significant that the censor passed the news of the arrival of the completely equipped expeditionary force of American Marines at a South Pacific port recently, as Marines are not usually sent to bases where action is not expected."

Nor were Marines allowed to mention so much as a bathing suit in their letters home, so strict was their Division's security; and yet the chief of censors had presumed to permit newspapers to publish their whereabouts, and columnists had not scrupled to pinpoint their destination, for both the Japanese and the people down under found the name Tulagi synonymous with Solomon Islands. The disclosure was not treachery, of course, it was only stupidity—which is sometimes more destructive. Filled with futile fury, the Marines could only curse the caprice of the free press they would soon be defending.

That evening the sun sank into the sea ahead of them like a dull red disk.

"Looks like a Jap meatball," said Private Lew Juergens, one of the Marines aboard *Elliott.*

"It's symbolic," the young private called Lucky said sententiously. "It's the setting of the Rising Sun."

"Ah, shaddap," Juergens growled. "Trouble with you, Lucky, you read too many books."[15]

Then the ships upped anchor and sailed away.

Chapter 5

LIEUTENANT GENERAL HARUYOSHI HYAKUTAKE arrived at Rabaul on July 24, and was immediately greeted by good news from New Guinea. Troops landed at Buna had pressed into the Owen Stanleys to scout for passable mountain trails and had reported finding the Kokoda Track.

This little-known and little-used trail ran from Buna to Kokoda, a small mountain plateau on which the Allies had built an airfield, and from Kokoda to a 6000-foot mountain pass penetrating the otherwise impenetrable Owen Stanleys. On the very day of Hyakutake's arrival, his forward elements had invested Kokoda. Within the next few days they captured the airfield from an outnumbered force of Australians and on July 29 decisively defeated an enemy counterattack.

It seemed to Haruyoshi Hyakutake that he might try to invest Moresby from both sea and land. He would send more troops to strike along the Buna-Kokoda-Moresby axis, and mount a fresh seaborne invasion.

On July 30 Vice-Admiral Gunichi Mikawa sailed into Simpson Harbor aboard *Chokai,* and the next day he met with Hyakutake and agreed to the new plan. Ships from Mikawa's Eighth Fleet and planes of the 25th Air Flotilla would support the seaborne phase. Some air squadrons now based in New Guinea would be recalled to Rabaul.

Nothing was said of Guadalcanal. General Hyakutake—in fact, the entire Japanese Army—was ignorant of the fact that the Japanese Navy had begun to build an airfield there. General Hyakutake had absolutely no fear of any sizable American counterattack—in the Southern Solomons or anywhere else. For this, he could not be blamed. The Army did not know of the Navy's disastrous defeat at Midway. The generals believed the Navy's falsified claims of victory. Even General Hideki Tojo, the Prime Minister of Japan, though aware of the defeat, did not know the details.[1]

Admiral Mikawa did not inform General Hyakutake of the truth about Midway. The Navy could not lose face before the Army. So Hyakutake, Mikawa, and Admiral Nishizo Tsukahara, commander of Eleventh Air Fleet, signed an Army-Navy Central Agreement covering the outer South Seas Area. The Navy would continue to be responsible for the defense of the Solomons. General Hyakutake was now free to concentrate on Port Moresby.

It was August 2 and Saburo Sakai and eight of his comrades were flying over Buna at 12,000 feet when Saburo saw five moving specks against the seaward clouds. Flying Fortresses! Here was Saburo's chance, the chance of all of them to show that a direct, nose-on attack could destroy the American bomber that had become the Japanese fighter pilot's scourge.

Saburo flew his Zero alongside the plane of Lieutenant Sasai. He pointed to the Forts. Sasai nodded. He raised his right hand and rocked his wings. The nine Zeros broke V formation and formed in column. Nine emergency fuel tanks went tumbling through the air. Sakai, Nishizawa, Ota, Yonekawa, Hatori, Endo —all of Japan's leading aces—went into action behind their beloved Lieutenant Sasai.

One after another they made their passes. They selected individual targets, pushed their engines onto overboost, and went roaring at three hundred miles an hour toward the Fort's nose—triggering cannon shells at the enemy's wing tanks. Saburo could not believe his eyes. The great steel birds seemed to be disappearing in flames. One . . . two . . . three . . . Then, on his second pass, Saburo caught a Fort trying to race away. It was still encumbered by its bomb load. Saburo dove to gain speed. He came up beneath the bomber, angling on its big left wing. He watched his shells exploding, tearing off chunks of metal. Now they were moving toward the bomb bay . . .

The sky became a turbulent sea of blinding white light. Saburo's plane was hurled upward. It flipped over on its back. Saburo's ears rang and his nose began to bleed, and when he looked for the enemy plane he saw that it had vanished. Groggy but jubilant, Saburo decided that he had hit the enemy's bomb load.

Brushing the blood from his lips, he joined Nishizawa in attacking the fifth Fort. This, too, seemed to go up in flames.

His own plane crippled, a piece of shrapnel in his palm, Saburo flew back to Lae and a wild ovation from the ground crews. The mechanics whooped and shouted with glee while Saburo and the others related how they had shot down five Flying Fortresses in a single afternoon.

But they had not. They had shot down only one and damaged another, while losing one of their own pilots.[2] Nevertheless their elation seized them like a joyous fever, for they sincerely believed that the smoke and flames of American gunfire had been the enemy bombers' funeral pyres. They were irresistible, they thought, the best fighter pilots in the world, and they thirsted for a shot at the American naval pilots whom they had never fought.

Next day they were transferred to Rabaul.

On August 6 Martin Clemens came very close to despair. In the past few weeks he had seen the Japanese tightening their grasp on Guadalcanal and heard reports that all the natives had begun to loot the plantations. On August 4 his food gave out and all that his scroungers could bring to him at his new hideout at Matanga was seventy-five pounds of stringy yams and a few pumpkins. It was barely enough to warm the bellies of Clemens and his twenty-four scouts; nevertheless it would have to serve to keep them alive for days.

On August 5 the scouts had reported that the airfield was finished. There might be Japanese planes landing on it on Friday, the seventh. That, Clemens thought grimly, would just about tear it. It meant that he and Snowy and the others might soon be running for their lives, if not fighting for them.

Clemens felt a sudden hot rush of resentment. They had radioed information on every last blasted piece of equipment that the Japanese possessed. And what happened? Nothing. Nothing but a few Flying Fortresses laying a few desultory eggs and that was all. When would it end? Were they expected to carry on like this forever? Wasn't *anybody* going to have a go at the Japs? Sitting glumly on his bedroll, Clemens was roused from his gloom by the appearance in the hut of his cook, Michael. The man put the last of Clemens's ration—a plate of yams—before him.

"Massa," Michael said gently, "you sick too much. More better you *kai-kai*. You no *kai-kai* all day."

"Which way me *kai-kai*, Michael?" Clemens burst out. "Belly belong me all the same buggerup!"[3]

Instantly ashamed of his petulance, struggling against breakdown, Clemens pushed the food away. He turned his face down on his bedroll and let the clamor of a flooding river swell in his ears like the rising roar of doom.

The bombers which Clemens missed so bitterly over Guadalcanal were the Flying Fortresses of Colonel Blondie Saunders' 11th Bombardment Group. They were based on Espiritu Santo in the New Hebrides, about 600 miles to the southeast. If Clemens could have known what had kept these bombers away, he would have joyfully forgiven them: the Forts had been flying daily over 1600 miles of open water, searching for enemy ships—especially aircraft carriers—which might endanger the vast American convoy stealing up on the Solomons.

On the sixth of August bad weather had grounded both Japanese and American planes. On that day Brigadier General William Rose, Colonel Saunders, and all available hands worked for twenty hours in a driving rainstorm, forming a bucket brigade to put 25,-000 gallons of gasoline aboard the Forts that would fly tomorrow —rain or shine—to support the Guadalcanal invasion.

It was getting to be dusk of the sixth of August and a quiet was coming over the ships.

Throughout the day the men had been preparing for battle. The winches had been started and the hatches thrown open. On the artillery transports 75- or 105-mm howitzers were hauled aloft and trundled to the gunwales; coils of rope for towing them inland were looped about their stubby barrels. Winchmen on the assault transports brought boxes of ammunition, mortar shells, spare gun parts, and roll after roll of barbed wire on deck. Everywhere was the spluttering sound of landing-boat motors being tested. Their coxswains—many of them from the Coast Guard—stood at the throttle even as these low wooden craft were unlashed and swung out on davits.

The skies were overcast, the air moist and sticky. Sweat oozing from the bodies of men at work made dark patches on the Ma-

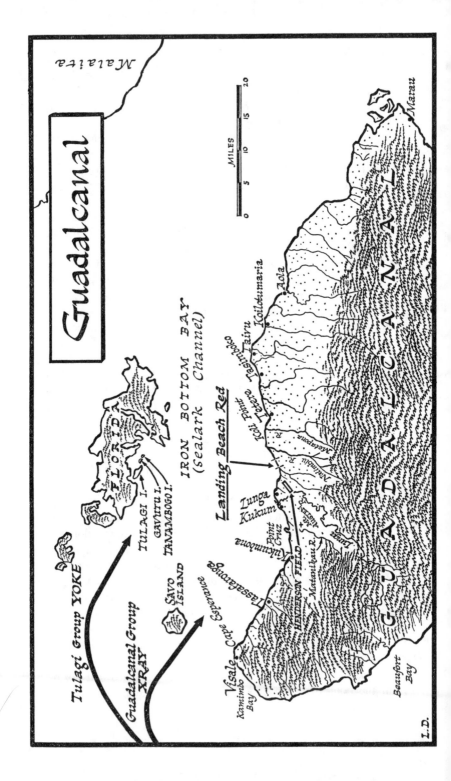

Guadalcanal

Malaita

Tulagi Group YOKE

Guadalcanal Group XRAY

FLORIDA

TULAGI I.
GAVUTU I.
TANAMBOGO I.

SAVO ISLAND

IRON BOTTOM BAY
(sealark Channel)

Landing Beach Red

Tenaru
Tagimbogo
Tenaru
Koli Point
Koilotumaria
Aola
Metapona R.
Metapona
Mbalasuna R.
Matanikau R.
Tetere

Lunga
Kukum
HENDERSON FIELD
Point Cruz
Lulumbona

GUADALCANAL

Tassafaronga
Cape Esperance
Visale
Kaminibo Bay

Beaufort Bay

Marau

MILES
0 5 10 15 20

I.D.

rines' pale green twill dungarees and blotched the sailors' light blue shirts. Tension made the sweat come faster, and the strain seemed more evident on the faces of the sailors. They had been inclined to belittle their passengers. They had scoffed at these "foot-sloggers" who lived like cattle in stifling holds, sleeping on five-tiered mats with their packs for pillows and their noses but a few inches beneath the bulkheads or the bunks above. Sailors accustomed to regular meals and quarters with individual bunks, clean linen, and fresh water could not help but feel superior to men who took salt-water showers and ate on their feet in steaming, pitching mess-halls where the decks were slippery with sweat and spilled coffee, and the food was a kind of tasteless though sanitary swill. But now, on the day before the battle, the sailors saw the Marines sharpening bayonets and knives, inspecting grenade pins and canteens, blacking rifle sights or applying a last light coat of oil to rifle bores; they saw machine gunners carefully folding long, 250-round belts of ammunition in oblong green boxes, or men of their own Navy —doctors and pharmacist's mates of the Medical Corps—checking the kits and medications with which they expected to bind wounds and perhaps save lives during the morning's fight. Seeing this, the sailors felt a sudden humility. They felt that they and their ships were secondary and that the true purpose of the war was to get these men to battle, to bring them to the beaches where the width of a shirt rather than of a ship's armor plate stood between them and the enemy's steel.

The Marines themselves were in a mood of sardonic gaiety. They listened for the last time to officers gravely informing them that the Japanese soldier was "the greatest jungle-fighter in the world," a strong, cruel stoic who tortured and killed in the name of an Emperor he believed to be divine, a superman able to subsist on a handful of rice while marching farther and enduring more than any other soldier in the world. Because these Marines had heard this hysterical hokum since it began after Pearl Harbor eight months ago and had finally tired of it, they began to crack jokes or to interrupt the speakers.

"Hey, Lieutenant," a freckled Southerner on the *Elliott* called, "ah nevah heard tell of Japs livin' in jungles. Ah thot most'v 'em was city-slickers like the Yanks heah."

"Yah-vo, Jawgia," Johnny Rivers boomed. "But we won't have

to coax them monkeys out of the trees with corn-pone like we did you."[4]

On *Elliott's* fantail a rifleman named Phil Chaffee stood among a circle of grinning Marines. He was talking in a Maine twang, shaking an empty Bull Durham tobacco sack with one hand and occasionally raising the other to twist the ends of a huge curling mustache. "Boys," he said, "I'm gonter make me a fortune in this here war. I hear all them Japs is got gold teeth. So," he grunted, pulling an object from his pocket, "I got me m' pliers, 'an"—he fished out another object—"I got me m' flashlight." The men burst out laughing, and Chaffee snapped: "Laugh, you yardbirds! But I'm goin' prospectin'. Mebbe they ain't no King Solomon's Mines on them Solomon Islands like they say, but I'm gonna get me a sackful of gold anyway." He grinned and shook the sack. *"Pure gold!"*

A fresh burst of laughter was silenced by the impersonal voice blaring from the ship's bullhorn:

"Darken ship. The smoking lamp is out on all weather decks. All troops below decks."

Aboard all the troopships the men went below. They descended to holds far below the water line, the Catholics to go to confession and the Protestants to chaplain's services, others to write the last letter home, and some to lie fully clad on their bunks (no one would undress that night) alone with their reveries or their forebodings. In the heads, where the air was blue with tobacco smoke and loathsome with the reek of human refuse, the "showdown" games were being held between the lucky—or skillful—hands into which most of the money had finally settled. Hundreds of dollars would be bet upon the flip of a single card, and when the games ended, the winners would either send the money home via the ships' post offices or stuff it into money belts bought in San Francisco against just such eventuality.

Up on *American Legion's* officers' deck Colonel Leroy Hunt entertained his officers with a stylish buck-and-wing, singing his own accompaniment in a deep bass voice. Hunt commanded the Fifth Marines. Like Colonel Cates, he was a distinguished veteran of the fighting in France in World War I, having also been wounded twice, gassed once, and been awarded a half-dozen medals. Hunt's Fifth Regiment would lead the assault on Guadalcanal next day, with Cates's First Marines coming in behind him.

It was almost dark now. Major General Vandegrift stood at the rail of *McCawley* peering into the gathering gloom. Vandegrift was relieved. They had been able to come up on the Solomons' back door undetected. Surprise should be his. He would need that advantage, Vandegrift thought, because he expected a hard battle. Nevertheless, he was in good spirits. He had done all that he could and now there was nothing more to be done. His conscience clear, Archer Vandegrift felt relieved. Suddenly he became aware of the darkness and of his own bad night vision. He called for an officer to assist him to his quarters, and sat down to finish a letter to his wife.

"Tomorrow morning at dawn we land in the first major offensive of this war. Our plans have been made and God grant that our judgment has been sound. We have rehearsed the plans. The officers and men are keen and ready to go. Way before you read this you will have heard of it. Whatever happens you'll know that I did my best. Let us hope that best will be enough . . ."[5]

Below decks the lights were out. All was silent save the throbbing of the ships' motors, the steady breathing of men relaxed in sleep, the quicker gasping of men tense and wide-eyed in the dark. Above, the lights began to go out in the wardrooms. Officers put away their cards and chessboards.

Steaming steadily at twelve knots, the invasion force slipped along Guadalcanal's southern coast. In the early hours of August 7, 1942, the ships were off Cape Esperance at the island's western tip. At two o'clock in the morning, by the light of a quarter moon just then emerging, lookouts on the weather decks could make out the round brooding bulk of Savo Island standing sentinel at the entrance to Iron Bottom Bay. Great gray shapes sliding toward an unsuspecting enemy, the ships entered. They split into two groups. The Tulagi force sailed on the northern side of Savo, the Guadalcanal force on the southern. And there was still not a sign from the foe.

One hundred miles to the south, Admiral Fletcher's aircraft carriers were turning slowly into the wind. Dauntlesses, Avengers, and Wildcats—the great warbirds of the American Navy—all were out on flight decks. No more the Devastator or Vindicator or Buffalo. The Japanese had annihilated them, seen to it that they were scrapped, and had inadvertently done a great favor for the young men smoking and drinking coffee in the pilots' ready rooms.

Outside, the motors were started. Props swung, caught and spun briefly, stopped and caught again, while the engines coughed blue smoke. Engines cleared and began idling. Blue halos encircled the cowlings. Each of the carriers—*Wasp, Saratoga,* and *Enterprise*—might have been marked from the air by those bright blue rings on their decks. But there was no enemy in the sky above them. One hour before sunrise, the great ships began launching.

Up at Iron Bottom Bay it was getting daylight and the ships were at their stations. The Japanese were still sleeping. They did not awake until, at 6:13 A.M., the first shells from the cruiser *Quincy's* turrets hurled America's reply to the nation which had contrived Pearl Harbor.

Aboard the ships, Marines were coming up on deck, their bellies full of Navy beans and their eyes blinking in the unaccustomed sunlight.

"F Company stand by to disembark! First platoon stand by to disembark!"

"All right, you men—down them cargo nets."[6]

They went over the side. Bandoliers slung crisscross over their breasts, cartridge belts bulging with bullets, carrying machine-gun and mortar parts weighing up to fifty pounds or loaded down with automatic rifles, with helmets bumping over their eyes and the muzzles of slung rifles digging into their necks or pistols flapping at their hips, heavy and awkward with the habiliments of war, they went clambering down the cargo nets. They clung to the coarse ropes with desperately clutching hands while the movement of the ships banged them mercilessly against steel hulls. They waited like patient armored ants while man after man let go and jumped into the Higgins boats wallowing below, until, at last, they were all embarked, bayonets were fixed, heads were ducked below the gunwales, and the boats taxied slowly toward the landing circles.

And now the iron voices of the bombardment ships were bellowing, now the six- and eight-inch muzzles spouted orange, now great gobbets and gouts of flame and splintering debris shot into the air from the shores of both Guadalcanal and Tulagi, and now columns of black smoke rose into the air while the Dauntlesses dove and dove relentlessly and the Avengers skimmed in low.

High up at Vungano, Sergeant Major Vouza saw it all and hastened downtrail to tell his master.

Below him at Matanga, Martin Clemens was on his feet shouting in exultant joy. He had bounded from his bedroll at the first crash of *Quincy's* guns, instinctively aware of its meaning, tired no longer, and crowing: "Calloo, callay, oh what a day!"[7] Vouza found the District Officer crouched gleefully beside a radio crackling with the voices of American pilots spotting targets for the gunfire ships, of others shouting to one another or begging their ships for new missions. One after another the scouts came down from Matanga. Grinning broadly, they related how favorite targets, ones that they had scouted for Clemens and his radio, had gone up in flames and smoke.

Out on the Bay the landing boats were fanning out into assault waves. Power was poured to the motors. Sterns dug deep into the waves. Hulls down, white wakes creaming out behind them, the Marines sped north and south toward palm-fringed shores.

Six hundred miles to the northwest, Vice-Admiral Gunichi Mikawa read a message from Guadalcanal, "Encountered American landing forces and are retreating into the jungle"; and one from Tulagi, "The enemy force is overwhelming. We will defend our positions to the death, praying for everlasting victory."[8] Reacting swiftly, Admiral Mikawa began collecting ships and men for a counterstroke.

Even as the Americans entered the Solomons, the Japanese began preparing to throw them out again.

Part 2

ALONE

Chapter 1

IT WAS at Tulagi that the American counteroffensive began.

Minutes after Tulagi radioed its last defiant message, shells from cruiser *San Juan* smashed the radio shack. Tulagi was never heard from again.

Out in the harbor men of the Yokohama Air Group frantically sought to save eight blazing Kawanishi flying boats caught on the surface like sitting ducks. A ninth, piloted by Lieutenant Commander Yoshio Tashiro, roared over the water and tried to flounder aloft, only to be tumbled back in flames by *San Juan's* guns. Commander Tashiro and his roaring tiger belt-buckle—triplet to the one worn by his brother-in-law Lieutenant Junichi Sasai—sank to the bottom of Iron Bottom Bay.

Off Tulagi's southern coast the men of the First Raider Battalion were debarking from destroyer-transports which had brought them from New Caledonia. Lieutenant Colonel Edson watched them going. Short, wiry, pale, and icy-eyed, his eyebrows mere wisps of that carroty red hair which had earned him the nickname of "Red Mike," Edson stood with his hands on the butt of the big six-shooter he wore, Western style, smiling his cold smile while making sure that the men were stripped down for battle.

"Don't worry about the food," he told a company commander fretting about the absence of rations. "There's plenty there. Japs eat, too. All you have to do is get it."[1]

Edson was not leading the attack personally. Lieutenant Colonel Sam Griffith would do that. Griffith was another hard professional, but with an intellectual side. He was a Chinese scholar, a Marine who could write as well as fight. Shortly before eight o'clock, with the British Residency and other buildings on the southeastern tip enshrouded in smoke, Griffith and the Raiders sped for the northwestern end of the little, boot-shaped island. At eight o'clock their Higgins boats grated to a halt on coral shoals and assault riflemen leaped into the surf.

They sank into waist-deep water. Many of them floundered beneath heavy loads and went under. Others slipped on slimy coral underfooting and also sank. Yanked to their feet by their buddies, they struggled shoreward. They emerged with blood streaming from hands and knees torn by cruel coral. Fortunately, no enemy fire spat from the jungle and they plunged into its murk. At 8:15 A.M. Griffith signaled:

"Landing successful, no opposition."

Now the Raiders moved swiftly. They were two thirds up the island. They scaled a steep grim cliff to their front and wheeled right. They drove southeastward along the cliff's spine and sloping sides. Behind them, the Second Battalion, Fifth Marines, under Lieutenant Colonel Harold Rosecrans crossed the same landing beaches and swung left. Rosecrans' men were to clear the northwestern third. They struck out quickly and found the territory undefended. They turned again and moved in behind Griffith in support.

Throughout the morning the Raiders moved over rough, jumbled ground, working through rocks and trees, keeping clear of shore trails covered by enemy cliffs. At noon they spilled into the former Chinese settlement on the island's north coast, and there the Japanese struck back.

Mortar shells began to fall. Marines toppled. Lieutenant (j.g.) Samuel Miles, a physician, rushed to help three badly wounded men and fell dead, the first casualty of the campaign. A company commander was wounded. The Marines moved more warily against these rickety Chinese shacks and the tempo of their advance slowed. Late in the afternoon, Edson, who had come ashore, called a halt.

The Marines held a line running roughly from Carpenter's Wharf on the north to a small clubhouse south of the Residency. It was not really a continuous line, rather a position held by Raiders in hastily scooped two- or three-man foxholes—sometimes connected with each other, more often not—with the Second Battalion, Fifth, backing them up.

Red Mike Edson calculated that there were about three hundred Japanese defenders in front of his men, and he expected that they would counterattack that night.

Rabaul's counterattack was already underway.

Upon receipt of the Tulagi message, Vice-Admiral Gunichi Mikawa had ordered the 25th Air Flotilla to send twenty-four Betty bombers bound for New Guinea to Tulagi-Guadalcanal instead. Then he called in the Tainan Group's fighter leader, Commander Tadashi Nakajima. He showed him the target area. Nakajima was thunderstruck. Six hundred miles to the target and six hundred back! Even if his Zeros could land at Buka on Bougainville on the way back, they would still be flying the longest fighter mission ever. Mikawa did not care.

"Take every Zero that will fly," he said.

Nakajima protested. "This is the longest fighter mission in history. Not all of my men are capable of making it. Let me take only my twelve best pilots."[2]

His eyes blazing, Mikawa shoved the Tulagi farewell over the table. Nakajima read it and stiffened. Very well, then: eighteen Zeros for Guadalcanal. Nakajima left the shack and told an orderly to recall the men waiting in cockpits for the New Guinea mission. They came back—Sakai, Nishizawa, Ota, Lieutenant Sasai—the best of Japan's aces, and they wondered at the anger on Nakajima's face. Handing out maps of the Solomons, he told them quickly of the American strike. Lieutenant Sasai's face blanched. He stared straight ahead and said softly: "My brother-in-law was assigned to Tulagi."[3] Nakajima ignored him and rapped out the distance to the target. The men gave low whistles of disbelief. Nakajima ignored them too and snapped: "We will take off at once for Guadalcanal."

The pilots broke up into trios. Saburo Sakai turned to his wingmen, Yonekawa and Hatori. "You'll meet the American Navy fliers for the first time today. They are going to have us at a distinct advantage because of the distance we have to fly. I want you both to use the greatest caution. Above all, never break away from me. No matter what happens, no matter what goes on around us, stick as close to my plane as you can. Remember that—don't break away."[4]

Yonekawa and Hatori nodded. Why break away anyway? Saburo Sakai had never lost a wingman.

Turning, the three pilots joined the others sprinting for their Zeros. They climbed into cockpits and watched two dozen Bettys go thundering down the runway ahead of them. At last Commander Nakajima lifted his hand over his head. Within ten minutes all of his fighters were airborne.

In Tokyo, reports of the American invasion did not unduly disturb Imperial General Headquarters. Army General Staff's chief reaction was one of surprise to find that the Navy had been building an airfield on "this insignificant island in the South Seas, inhabited only by natives."[5] An intelligence report from the Japanese Military Attaché in Moscow claimed that there were only 2000 Americans involved and that they intended to destroy the airfield and withdraw.[6] The enemy operation was nothing but a reconnaissance-in-force. The report was believed, although both Army and Navy agreed that the Americans should be ousted before they could put the airfield into operation.

General Gen Sugiyama, chief of Army General Staff, spent the morning hunting for a unit to do the job.

Admiral Osami Nagano, chief of Naval General Staff, passed a more active day. First, he had received Admiral Mikawa's radioed request for approval of his proposal to launch a night surface attack against the American fleet. Nagano had been appalled. A night attack in the narrow, uncharted water of The Slot seemed too risky. But his staff, arguing that this was a chance to hit the Americans hard, persuaded him to approve Mikawa's plan. He signaled:

"Execute."

Next, Nagano directed Combined Fleet to give first priority to the recapture of Guadalcanal. Admiral Yamamoto immediately set up a supreme Southeast Area Force and notified Vice-Admiral Nishizo Tsukahara on Saipan to take charge of it. Tsukahara, commander of the Eleventh Air Fleet, quickly made provisions to lead the cream of his command to Rabaul for action next day. Tsukahara now superseded Mikawa.

Admiral Yamamoto also began gathering all available ships and planes for a massive sortie. Characteristically, he considered the Solomons invasion as one more chance to destroy the enemy fleet. It was not Guadalcanal that was important to him; it was the fact that the American Navy was gathered there in force and could be annihilated in decisive battle.

Thus the importance of Guadalcanal to Japan's military leaders: General Sugiyama, echoed by General Hyakutake, thought it a mere nuisance which might interfere with the Port Moresby operation and must therefore be quickly squelched, Admirals Nagano and Yamamoto saw it as an opportunity to regain the naval edge lost at Midway.

Nevertheless, Nagano thought enough of the event to report it to Emperor Hirohito. Putting on dress whites, Nagano went to the Emperor's summer villa at Nikko. Alarmed, more prescient than his admirals, Hirohito said he would return to Tokyo.

"Your Majesty," Nagano protested, "it is nothing worthy of Your Majesty's attention."[7] Nagano showed the Emperor the report from Moscow, and Hirohito stayed in Nikko.

Gunichi Mikawa was overjoyed to receive Naval General Staff's order to attack. He had already ordered Rear Admiral Aritomo Goto to sortie from New Ireland with Eighth Fleet's big sluggers, heavy cruisers *Chokai, Aoba, Kinugasa, Kako,* and *Furutaka,* along with destroyer *Yunagi.* Mikawa intended to board *Chokai* to lead his force, plus light cruisers *Tenryu* and *Yubari* then in harbor at Rabaul, south to the Solomons.

Mikawa had also attended to reinforcements for the Solomons garrisons. Hyakutake had been of no help, as Mikawa had expected, insisting that he could not spare a man from the Port Moresby operation. So the admiral had had to scrape up 410 men from the Fifth Sasebo Special Naval Landing Force and from the 81st Garrison Unit. He put them under Lieutenant Endo with instructions to board transport *Meiyo Maru* and sail south for Guadalcanal next day.

Mikawa realized that this was not very many men, but he expected them to do some good; for he, too, believed that there were only about 2000 Americans to the south.

Japanese bombers flying to Guadalcanal from the airfield at Kavieng on New Ireland usually passed over Buka Passage in the northern Solomons—where they could be seen by the coastwatcher, Jack Read.

Bombers flying from Rabaul passed over Buin on Bougainville —and there they could be spotted by the coastwatcher, Paul Mason.

At half-past ten that morning of August 7 the bespectacled and benign Mason sat serenely within his palm-thatched hut on Malabite Hill and heard the thunder of motors overhead. He rushed outside and counted the Bettys preceding the Zeros down to Guadalcanal. He ran back inside and signaled:

"Twenty-four torpedo bombers headed yours."

Twenty-five minutes later, aboard the Australian cruiser *Canberra* down at Iron Bottom Bay, sailors heard the bullhorn announce:

"The ship will be attacked at noon by twenty-four torpedo bombers. All hands will pipe to dinner at eleven o'clock."

The "bonzer boys up north," as the Australians described their countrymen of the coastwatchers, had given the convoy's sailors time to line their bellies for battle, and Admiral Fletcher's fighter pilots time to climb high over Savo Island to await the oncoming enemy.

Commander Nakajima's fighters were flying at 13,000 feet. Sixty miles south of Rabaul they passed over Green Island. Saburo Sakai looked down in astonishment. He had never seen such incredibly green hills before. He noticed that the island was horseshoe-shaped and he filed the landmark in his brain.

Over Bougainville the sun beat so harshly upon the canopy of Saburo's airplane that it made him thirsty. He took a bottle of soda from his lunchbox. Forgetting the high-pressure altitude, Saburo slit the cork—and the soda came foaming into his cockpit, covering everything until it was dried by the cockpit draft. But there was a coating of dried sugar left on Saburo's goggles and his windscreen and controls. He had to rub them clean. As he did, his Zero wandered all over the formation, and he missed the beauty of The Slot as they winged southeastward over that broad, blue sea-corridor.

Over New Georgia the formation began climbing, crossing the Russells at 20,000 feet. Fifty miles ahead of them the pilots could see Guadalcanal. Next they saw Iron Bottom Bay and gasped at the spectacle of so many ships, such a vast armada cleaving white, crisscrossing wakes in the water. Then they saw the Wildcats. There were six of them, stubby, powerful craft painted olive but for the white underside of their wings. They came plunging down out of the sun. But they ignored Saburo and his comrades. They were diving on the torpedo bombers, heedless of the popping black bursts of antiaircraft fire which rose from the American ships and kept the Bettys respectfully high.

Some of the Zeros raced ahead, firing to distract the Americans. But the Wildcats rolled together and disappeared in dives. They forced the Bettys to bomb wildly, to make foolish attempts to hit moving ships from four miles up. Saburo ground his teeth and wondered why the bombers had not been carrying torpedoes. Perhaps it was because they had been loaded for land bombing against New Guinea. Whatever, it was a waste—and now the Wildcats were growling and spitting among the Bettys. Some of the Japanese planes fell blazing into the Bay.

Nakajima's Zeros formed up and escorted the bombers as far north as the Russells. Then they turned back to Guadalcanal. And the Wildcats jumped them. Time after time the Americans came plunging out of the sun, fired, rolled back and vanished far below. Each time they fired quick bursts from six .50-caliber machine guns mounted in the wings of each plane. After each pass, the Wildcats climbed into the sun to make their single, massed, slashing attack, and to bank and climb again. Such tactics astounded Nakajima's pilots. They cut his formation to pieces, and they forced him to flee for safety.

Saburo Sakai was also shaken. Japan's leading ace gaped at the spectacle of a single Wildcat taking on three Zeros in a wild left-spiraling dogfight. The American had come out on the tail of a Zero and was stitching its wings and tail with bullets when Saburo dove and drove him off. It was then that Saburo Sakai became engaged in the dogfight of his life. Spin for spin, roll for roll, spiral for spiral, the American matched the Japanese master. They fought each other and also those tremendous G pressures which pushed each pilot down in his seat, investing flying suits with the weight of lead and heads with the senseless density of iron. At last Saburo got the upper hand. Again and again he cut inside the American, he wounded him, and then, as the man flew on like a bleeding automaton, Saburo drove in for the kill with a stream of cannon shells that sent the Wildcat spinning seaward in flames and its pilot drifting limply toward Guadalcanal's beaches beneath a blossoming, billowing parachute.

It was Saburo Sakai's fifty-ninth kill and within a few minutes he had his sixtieth—a Dauntless dive-bomber.

His blood up, Saburo climbed to 13,000 feet to hunt for further game. He sighted eight aircraft over Guadalcanal. He gunned his motor to come up on them in surprise. He would take the Wildcats on the right and leave the others for three Zeros following him. But the American planes were not Wildcats. They were Avengers, heavy, sturdy torpedo-bombers; they had .50-caliber gunners in top and belly turrets; and they were waiting for Saburo Sakai.

Saburo saw the trap too late. He tried to fireball out of it with overboosted engine and flaming guns. The Americans opened fire.

From twenty yards away Saburo Sakai could see the stuttering muzzles of those massed guns, and then a terrible power smashed at his body, searing spikes went driving into his brain, and his Zero nosed over and fell toward the sea.

Before Tulagi had been assaulted it had been necessary to secure the island's left flank. This had been accomplished at 7:40 o'clock in the morning when B Company of the First Battalion, Second Marines, landed at Haleta Village on Florida Island. Private Russell Miller was the first Marine ashore, thus becoming the first American to tread Japanese-held soil in World War II.

Next it was required to protect the right flank of Gavutu-Tanambogo by occupying the tip of Halavo Peninsula on Florida. Other Marines of the same battalion carried out this mission. Both operations were unopposed.

It was different at Gavutu-Tanambogo. These Siamese-twin islets, joined by a narrow causeway, were both tiny; Gavutu barely 500 by 300 yards, Tanambogo even smaller. Both were steep, ringed by coral, pocked by armored caves, and defended by troops sworn to go down fighting. Marines of the First Parachute Battalion were to take these objectives, beginning with Gavutu. They had to sail around the island to get at the only landing place, a seaplane ramp and pier on the northeastern tip.

About noon of August 7, almost coincidental with the arrival of the Japanese airplanes, Major Robert Williams and his Paramarines sped toward the seaplane ramp.

Automatic fire struck them in the boats. They found that naval shelling had torn the ramp into jagged pieces. Swerving wildly, the boats made for the pier. Some men jumped onto it, getting inland. Most of them were pinned down beside the pier. A hail of fire came from three sides: from a Gavutu hill to the left, from trenches behind the pier and from Tanambogo on the right. Major Williams was hit and command passed to Major Charles Miller. Riddled, the Paramarines called desperately for naval gunfire to knock out the enemy positions. But the covering destroyers dared not run close in uncharted, shoal-filled waters.

A landing boat full of mortars roared to the rescue. Mortarmen vaulted over gunwales and bent swiftly to the task of setting up their unlovely stovepipe killers. Soon shells were *plop-plopping* from tubes to fall with a killing *crrrunch-whummp* in enemy trenches. Enemy fire fell off and the assault swept forward. Fresh units came in to join it. The Japanese fought doggedly from their trenches. Corporal George Grady charged eight of them, firing his Thompson submachine gun as he ran. Two fell dead and Grady's tommy gun jammed. He swung the weapon like a club and smashed an enemy soldier to the ground. He drew his sheath knife and stabbed two more. And then the others were upon him to exact his own life.

Gradually the Marines gained the upper hand. By midafternoon they held the highest land on the islet and the American flag was flung to the wind there. But the Marines stood atop a volcano. Beneath their very feet was a series of about two dozen impregnable coral caves, and around these a fierce battle began.

Improvising swiftly, the Marines strapped explosives to the end of long poles. They fitted them with five-second fuses and pushed or hurled them into cave mouths. Big blond Captain Harry Torgerson led the attack. His first charge sealed off an enemy position and blew his pants off. "Boy, that one was a pisser!"[8] Torgerson yelled, running back for more explosives.

"Goddam, Captain," an irreverent Marine called, "you done lost the seat of yer pants."

"Screw the pants," Torgerson bellowed, "get me more dynamite!"[9]

One by one the caves fell to Torgerson and his pole-chargers and Gavutu was conquered before nightfall.

A strong cold wind blowing through his shattered windshield restored Saburo Sakai to consciousness.

He felt his plane falling, plummeting like a stone. But he could see nothing, only red, only a world of scarlet. Flames? No. He felt no heat. He groped for the stick with his right hand. He pulled it back gently. Pressure pushed him back into his seat. The Zero was coming out of its dive.

But where was he? What was he to do?

He tried reaching for the throttle with his left hand. He could not. He worked his feet on the rudder bar. Only the right one moved, and the Zero skidded violently.

Saburo's left side was paralyzed.

He began to weep.

Tears flowed from the samurai's eyes and suddenly the red thinned and vanished and he saw sunlight again. He had wept away the blood that had gummed his vision.[10]

Even so he could see only dimly. Once he had lost sight of the water, and the great black shapes sliding by beneath his wings, he realized vaguely that he was lost. His instruments were sometimes clear, sometimes a blur—and he had to trust to touch. Fits of madness or a terrible overpowering desire to sleep seized him. But he flew on, thinking suddenly that the blood must have come from a wound. He raised his right hand to snap off his glove and felt his head. There was a slit in his helmet, there was a hole in his head. He could feel the thick sticky blood inside it, feel his skull, and he feared to feel deeper.

His Zero droned on and he discovered that he was flying at 200 miles an hour. The wind dried his face. Then his right eye flamed in pain. He put his hand before it, withdrew it, and discovered that his vision had not changed. He was blind in his right eye. Wave after wave of pain passed over him. He became conscious of loss of blood. With only one hand, he tried to use his four service bandages. The wind tore them away. He unwound his silk muffler. He pushed it beneath his helmet. Agonizing inch by agonizing inch he shoved it up and into his wound.

Saburo Sakai flew on. His vision and his thinking gradually clearing, he found himself on a 330-course bound for the middle of the Pacific. He corrected it and flew on, the samurai of the sky. He flew on, fighting drowsiness and despair, he flew on racked with pain and aware that he probably did not have enough gas to reach a Japanese-held island. Then he saw beneath him that strikingly green, horseshoe-shaped island.

Green Island!

He was only sixty miles south of Rabaul.

Saburo Sakai's hand trembled on the throttle. He could make

it! And there was a big island dead ahead. There was a mountain. Saburo cursed. He recognized the mountain. He was over New Ireland. He would have to cross this 2400-foot mountain peak to come down at Rabaul on the other side. He would have to climb and consume more gas. But he would have to, and he flew on— his Zero now rocked by the lash of a rain squall.

Saburo came down over St. George Channel between New Ireland and Rabaul and saw the great foaming wakes of two big ships blow beneath his wings. He saw the ships—heavy cruisers —steaming south at full speed.

But then he saw tiny Vunakunau beneath his wings. He saw the narrow runway and decided to try to ditch off the beach. He was only a few feet above the water when he changed his mind. The impact might knock him unconscious and he would drown. He had to climb again, he had to circle the field four times, in all, before he finally lowered down. A sharp jolt, a skid, an abrupt halt—and then a blessed blackness engulfed him.

Japan's greatest ace had come home on his iron will and his unrivaled flying skill, but he had lost the sight of one eye and would not fly again until the last days of the war. Attrition had begun in the invincible Tainan Air Group, in the 25th Flotilla. Although there was sudden joy in the faces of the men who lifted unconscious Saburo Sakai from his bloody and riddled cockpit, behind their eyes lay an older, deeper grief.

Of fifty-one aircraft that left Rabaul that August 7, thirty had not come back.

The Americans could not possibly take Tanambogo from Gavutu. Every so often bursts of daisy-cutting machine-gun fire came whistling over the causeway from this smaller of the twin islets. No one ventured near the causeway above ground.

Brigadier General William Rupertus, who commanded the operations in the harbor islands, decided to take Tanambogo from the sea. He called upon Company B of the Second Marines, the outfit which had seized Haleta on Florida Island without firing a shot.

Air strikes were called down on Tanambogo. Destroyers pounded its installations. A Japanese three-inch gun was blown into the air in full view of the Marines coming to the assault. Daylight was fading fast as the coxswains pointed their prows shoreward and gunned the motors.

From a hilltop crowning Tanambogo came a terrible, withering fire. Private Russell Miller, the first American to land on Japanese soil, fell dead at his Lewis gun. A destroyer shell fell short and exploded among the boats. A coxswain was wounded and torn from the wheel of his boat. The craft yawed wildly, swinging around and heading back to Gavutu. Others followed it. Only three boats dared the Japanese fire and only one got ashore. Its occupants were pinned down and chopped up by Japanese fire. Under cover of night, friendly boats slipped in to take off dazed American survivors.

Tanambogo was very tough, Rupertus admitted. He would have to have more men. He appealed to Vandegrift who in turn appealed to Admiral Turner. Another battalion of the Second Marines—one which Turner had been holding back for the Ndeni operation—was released to Rupertus. At dawn of August 8, the attack would be renewed.

The two cruisers seen by Saburo Sakai were *Aoba* and *Kinugasa*. They were part of the force of five heavy cruisers and one destroyer which Rear Admiral Aritomo Goto had brought south from Kavieng under Admiral Mikawa's orders. Before Saburo saw them they had also been sighted by an American B-17, which radioed the sighting back to Australia. After that Goto had detached *Chokai* and the destroyer *Yunagi* to pick up the Eighth Fleet commander while he continued on in *Aoba* with the others.

Chokai sailed into Simpson Harbor at two o'clock. Admiral Mikawa and his staff came aboard and Eighth Fleet commander's red-and-white striped flag was broken from the masthead. A half-hour later, with *Yunagi* and the two light cruisers, Mikawa's flagship stood out of the harbor.

It was a fine clear day. A sea as calm as a mirror lay glimmering in the sunlight. On *Chokai's* bridge the officers chatted in high spirits. The men were excited. Everyone knew that they were sailing to battle.

Gunichi Mikawa was confident, even though he was aware of the terrible risks that he ran. His returning pilots had already informed him of the vastness of the American fleet. They had seen no aircraft carriers but Mikawa knew that carriers had to be somewhere in the vicinity. Mikawa dreaded the carriers, and he hoped to avoid aerial attack.

Throughout the afternoon and night of August 7, Mikawa intended to steam toward Bougainville. Next day, August 8, would be spent marking time north of Bougainville, well out of range of carrier aircraft. With dusk the ships would enter The Slot. They would come up on the enemy under cover of darkness, destroy him, and then race north again to be out of carrier range by daylight of August 9.

Mikawa's eight ships were to strike like a wolfpack falling on a flock of sheep. First they would destroy the sheep dogs, the American warships, after which the sheep, the transports, could be devoured at leisure.

Three hours out of Rabaul, Mikawa's and Goto's ships made rendezvous. "Alert cruising disposition," was ordered for the night. As the ships swung into line an American submarine was sighted. It was the veteran *S-38* under Lieutenant Commander H. F. Munson. Mikawa ordered his ships to turn east to avoid it. Munson let them go. He had been so close to the enemy column that he could feel his vessel shuddering under their powerful wash. Nor could he, Munson, maneuver. Nevertheless he could see that something big was brewing. He decided to patrol St. George Channel, and meanwhile, he sent off the report: "Two destroyers and three larger ships of unknown type, heading 140 degrees True, at high speed, 8 miles west of Cape St. George." Although Munson had miscounted the number of ships, he had still given Guadalcanal a valuable warning.

Admiral Richmond Kelly Turner did not heed the warning, just as he had dismissed the earlier report of Goto's ships made by a Flying Fortress. Turner was not troubled because he considered a surface sea attack on the night of August 7 to be a practical impossibility. He was, however, deeply concerned about attack on August 8—either day or night. Because of this he had expressed doubts about plans to search The Slot and had requested Admiral McCain to make sure that Flying Fortresses would patrol that sea-corridor in the morning.

Otherwise, Turner was confident. The first day of invasion had gone off beautifully. Perhaps 17,000 Marines had been landed. Fletcher's carriers were still to the south and would not depart until Sunday, August 9. On that clear calm Friday night of August

7 sailors on watch could congratulate themselves on being safe at sea and not ashore like the Marines on Tulagi, whence came the sounds of battle.

Red Mike Edson had expected the Japanese to counterattack at night, and they did.

Marines in their shallow foxholes could hear the enemy assembling. The Japanese crawled noisily out of their caves and dugouts. They shouted their war cry *"Banzai!"* in a kind of gurgling turkey-gobbler whoop. They howled threats which, they had been assured, would turn American hearts cold with fear.

"Japanese boy drink American boy's blood!"

"Blood for the Emperor!"

They attacked, coming in ragged bands or sometimes as solitary infiltrators. They fired their rifles as they charged, deliberately trying to draw giveaway fire so that they might grenade the source of muzzle flashes. Where they threw grenades they were grenaded, where they closed with knives they were met with knives. Four times they charged, striking savagely at Marine positions in the center.

Here they came against Private First Class Johnny Ahrens and his Browning Automatic Rifle, and each time Ahrens and his chattering BAR broke them up. Just before dawn the Japanese were finally repulsed.

Captain Lewis ("Silent Lew") Walt came quickly to the foxhole held by Ahrens. He found the youth dying. He was covered with blood. His eyes were closed and he was breathing slowly. There were bullet holes in his chest and thick blood rose slowly from three deep bayonet wounds. Next to Ahrens lay a dead Japanese sergeant. A dead officer was sprawled across his legs. Around his foxhole thirteen more Japanese bodies lay crumpled in grotesque, ungainly death. Johnny Ahrens lay dying, still clinging to his BAR, and Walt, a big, powerful man, bent to lift the youth in his arms.

"Captain, they tried to come through me last night," Ahrens gasped, "but I don't think they made it."

"They didn't, Johnny," Walt replied gently. "They didn't."[11]

The attack on Tanambogo had re-commenced.

At 8 A.M., August 8, the Third Battalion, Second Marines,

landed on Gavutu to help mop up. By noon Gavutu was cleared and Lieutenant Colonel Robert Hunt signaled that he was ready to attack Tanambogo. He asked for an air strike. Six Dauntlesses came swooping down—to drop their bombs on Gavutu! Three Marines were blown apart and six others badly wounded. Enraged and helpless, Colonel Hunt hurled a stream of invective at the departing "friendly" planes. Then *San Juan* stood into the harbor to shell Tanambogo briefly and withdraw. Next another group of carrier bombers arrived. They were going to knock out a Japanese position crowned by a Japanese flag. Once again, several bombs fell short—and more Marines on Gavutu were killed and wounded.

Hunt asked that he be spared further air "support."

At four o'clock he called on the destroyer *Buchanan* to attempt short-range fire. *Buchanan* ran boldly inshore and blasted Tanambogo so thoroughly that a company of Marines were able to land standing up. An hour later they tore down the flag that had so disastrously intrigued the dive-bombers, and next day mopping-up operations cleared both Tanambogo and Tulagi of the remaining Japanese.

About 750 Japanese had died defending Tulagi and Gavutu-Tanambogo, while 144 Americans were killed and 194 wounded. Capture of the harbor islands had not been costly—as "prices" are measured in the heartless business of war—and yet it seemed so when compared to the effortless conquest of Guadalcanal.

Chapter 2

VANDEGRIFT'S main body—some 10,000 Marines—hit the middle of Guadalcanal's northern coastline shortly after nine o'clock the morning of August 7.

Two battalions of Colonel Hunt's Fifth Marines came in abreast, fanning out on a front of 2000 yards to cover for Colonel Cates's First Marines landing behind them in a column of three battalions.

They were unopposed.

The Americans were stunned. Many of these youths had sincerely expected to fight for their lives from behind a barricade formed by the bodies of fallen comrades. Instead they had trotted into an exotic grove of coconut palms, and some of them celebrated this pleasant introduction to modern war by shinnying up the palms to throw down coconuts to their buddies. Bayonets honed razor-sharp were drawn to cleave, not enemy skulls, but the outer husks of coconuts, and next to puncture softer inner shells yielding a cool and tasty milk.

"Knock off openin' them coconuts!" screamed an outraged sergeant who had memorized the "Know Your Enemy" manual by heart. "They might be poisoned!"

"Damfine poison," Lew Juergens murmured, drinking happily, and Lucky shot back disdainfully, "Who'n hell's gonna poison a whole damn grove of coconuts?"[1]

A few minutes later, the Fifth Marines wheeled west to work toward the village of Kukum, and the First Marines plunged south toward Grassy Knoll, or Mount Austen, a high patch of ground which dominated the airfield from the south. Grassy Knoll was supposed to be only two miles inland across passable terrain. Actually it was four miles away and over the sort of tortuous terrain with which Martin Clemens—still crouching by his radio at Ma-tanga—had become painfully familiar.

Throughout the day men whose bodies had softened during weeks of shipboard life scrambled up the faces of muddy hills and slid down the reverse slopes. Rifles rang against canteens and falling helmets rattled on the stones. Gasping in humid heat, bathed in a stream of enervating sweat and burdened with packs and ammunition loads that were far too heavy, the First Marines moved through dripping rain forests with all the stealth of a trav-eling circus. They blundered through fields of sharp kunai grass as tall as a man and sometimes became lost in them or shot at each other there. They forded what seemed to be river after river but what was actually one or two streams doubling back on them-selves. Half of the time they had no scouts out ahead of them and most of the time they had no flankers probing the jungle to either side, and if the Japanese had chosen to sit in ambush that day there could have been a slaughter.

But the enemy was absent. Only a few—Mr. Ishimoto among them—were east of the Tenaru River. Most of them—about 1700 naval laborers, with their protectors of a Naval Landing Force—had fled to the west of that Lunga River against which the Fifth Regiment was advancing.

The Fifth was also moving slowly, but without the excuse of difficult terrain. They were attacking, as General Vandegrift an-grily told Colonel Hunt, as though they expected to encounter the entire Imperial Army. Hunt passed the general's rage along to his leading battalion commander, and the Fifth finally reached the day's objective about two miles west of the landing beach.

Both regiments dug in to pass nights made miserable by rain and mosquitoes, and fitful by the wild firing of trigger-happy sen-tries shooting at land crabs, wild pigs, shadows, and—with occa-sional tragedy—their own men. At midnight Vandegrift directed Cates to forget Grassy Knoll and to swing west toward the Lunga River in the morning, coming in on the airfield from the south.

On Saturday morning the First Marines quickly overran the air-field. Here was the prize of the campaign, and it would soon be named Henderson Field in honor of Major Loften Henderson, a Marine flying hero who was killed at Midway. Besides Henderson Field there was a complex of wharves, bridges, ice plants, radio stations and power and oxygen plants. The Japanese "termites," as the Marines were contemptuously calling the enemy laborers and their impressed Korean allies, had thrown all this up in slightly more than a month.

Meanwhile, the Fifth Regiment continued its cautious advance against Kukum. Patrols did not reach the camp until midafternoon. They found a litter of uniforms, those two-toed, rubber-soled shoes called *tabis,* shirts, helmets, caps, packs, mosquito netting, blankets, rifles, tea cups, chopsticks, and—most indicative of the panicky flight induced by *Quincy's* opening shells—rice bowls containing half-eaten breakfasts. Later, the Fifth Marines found great stores of rice, wormy, gummy rice which the Marines then spurned but which they did not, fortunately, destroy: it would one day stand between them and starvation.

In less than two days Admiral King had obtained his coveted airfield and General Vandegrift had occupied nearly all the ground he required to defend it. It would have seemed incredibly easy, if the fighting had not then been continuing across the Bay, and if Vandegrift's supplies were not mounting in target-size piles on the beach.

This, the unloading problem, had turned out to be Vandegrift's biggest headache. Because he had put five of his six infantry battalions into action and kept one in reserve, he had had only a few hundred men to spare for stevedore duty. They could not possibly cope with all the supplies dumped on shore by hundreds of landing boats and lighters plying back and forth from the transports like swarms of buzzing water bugs. Confusion had multiplied the difficulties. Untrained coxswains brought rations to beaches marked for fuel or medical supplies were mixed in with ammunition. Sailors could not help, because, as they rightfully maintained, it was their job to bring material ashore and the Marines' to get it off the beach. Many Marines not committed to action might have helped, but they merely watched their comrades of the shore parties melting under the strain. "Hell, Mac, we're combat troops," they sniffed. "You unload the goddam stuff."[2] Combat troops, they said, swimming in the Bay or cracking coconuts. Eventually the disorder became so great that perhaps a hundred boats had to wait offshore, bobbing gently in the swells, while coxswains searched vainly for an open stretch of beach to land on. Even though Vandegrift had received the message, "Unloading entirely out of hand," he dared not, on this eighth of August, risk weakening his line troops. He could only hope that the supply dumps might not seem so conspicuous from the air next time the Japanese bombers came calling.

Early on August 8 the coastwatcher Jack Read began moving to a new position atop a steep ridge on northern Bougainville. At twenty minutes of nine, as he and his carriers plodded upward through the jungle, they heard the thunder of low-flying aircraft. Directly overhead passed flights of Betty bombers escorted by Zeros layered above them and to their flanks. Read started to count, while two carriers set up his aerial. A few minutes later he had signaled Townsville, Australia:

"Forty-five bombers going southeast."

From Townsville the message was flashed to Melbourne and thence to Pearl Harbor, and at 9:10 o'clock that morning the alarm was received by the fleet in Iron Bottom Bay. Unloading ceased. Beaches were emptied of working parties. All ships got underway while *Saratoga* stacked flights of Wildcats over Savo at altitudes of ten, fifteen, and twenty-five thousand feet.

This time the Japanese avoided Savo. Fifty miles away from the island they swung to the north, turning southeast again to come in over Florida Island unharried by the American fighters. This time the Bettys carried torpedoes. This time they skimmed the treetops and went thundering among the transports.

They counted on a slaughter. They flew low, only twenty to forty feet above the water, hoping to come in under the guns' depression limit, as they had done against British warships. But the American ships were equipped with better fire-control systems and their guns were built to depress.

It was the Japanese who were slaughtered. They flew into a literal storm of steel and were torn apart. Up at Bougainville stony-eyed Jack Read smiled softly to hear an excited voice on the radio shouting: "Boy, they're shooting them down like flies, one, two, three . . . I can see eight of them coming down in the sea right now!" Everywhere the Bettys were blowing up, flaming, disintegrating. American ships were showered with pieces of wings and fuselage. On one transport sailors swept the limbs and torsos of Japanese airmen over the side. But one Betty did succeed in sending a torpedo flashing into the side of destroyer *Jarvis,* sending her staggering south to be caught by more Japanese bombers the next day and sent to the bottom with all hands. Another Betty crashed and exploded on the deck of *George F. Elliott* and set her hopelessly afire. The creaking old ship which had brought Johnny Rivers and Al Schmid and Phil Chaffee and Lucky and the rest of the Second Battalion, First Marines, from San Francisco to Guadalcanal would eventually perish.

So did all but one of the forty-five Bettys that flew to Iron Bottom Bay that day. The surviving bomber pilot landed at Rabaul and announced that he had sunk a battleship.

Pilots of all nations commonly exaggerate the results of their missions. The height and speed of aerial war only magnify the human tendency to make all destroyers battleships or to confuse a smokescreen for a funeral pyre. Some pilots exaggerate out of overenthusiasm, others out of unashamed mendacity. Japanese pilots, as Admiral Mikawa might have known, are more susceptible to the affliction, because, like Japanese admirals, they cannot lose face.

Nevertheless, Mikawa sailed down The Slot warmed by reports from Rabaul pilots to the effect that yesterday they had sunk two cruisers, a destroyer, and six transports, while heavily damaging three cruisers and two transports. Then, at noon, a search plane from *Aoba,* returned to report that the great American fleet still lay in the harbor unscathed.

Mikawa was shocked, and the news aggravated his earlier dismay at having been discovered by the enemy.

At 10:20 that morning a Lockheed Hudson bomber was sighted circling above a group of Mikawa's ships. Eighth Fleet commander had cannily divided his forces to deceive the enemy, and the Hudson sighted the larger group. The enemy plane hovered overhead for a quarter-hour before flying off toward Australia. At eleven o'clock another Hudson appeared over the smaller section, to be driven off by massed guns. Admiral Mikawa had no doubt that these planes had alerted the Americans. He was sure that the enemy carriers had been warned.

Mikawa's dismay increased at the sight of Zeros returning from Guadalcanal in straggling twos and threes. Their lack of formation meant that they must have been through heavy fighting. Mikawa discussed the situation with his staff during lunch. They had lost the hoped-for surprise and they had heard nothing of the whereabouts of the enemy carriers. What to do? As though by answer, Mikawa broke radio silence to ask Rabaul about the carriers. He got no reply.

At one o'clock Mikawa concluded that if the enemy carriers had not been sighted, that meant that they were far to the south— too far away from Guadalcanal to catch him after he began his getaway. He decided to continue the attack. He ordered speed increased to 24 knots and set course through Bougainville Strait.

At four o'clock Mikawa's ships turned left and entered The Slot.

Meiyo Maru was leaving Rabaul.

Almost all of the naval troops which Admiral Mikawa was sending to Guadalcanal were aboard this 5600-ton transport. Five smaller ships would escort *Meiyo* and carry her supplies. Meanwhile, many of the men below decks were making out their wills, as Japanese soldiers do before entering battle. They cut off locks of hair or pieces of fingernail and slipped them into the envelopes containing the wills and sealed them shut. Other men wound belts of a thousand stitches around their waist. They had received these bulletproof talismans from sisters or sweethearts who had stood patiently on Japanese street corners to beg a stitch from passing women. Not many of the soldiers believed in the magic powers of the belts, yet they put them on rather than be guilty of discourtesy to a loved one. A Japanese may be cruel, but he is never rude.

In early afternoon *Meiyo Maru* stood slowly out of Simpson Harbor bound for Guadalcanal.

Admiral Frank Jack Fletcher was leaving the Solomons.

The commander of the Expeditionary Force was not waiting until Sunday morning, as he had promised, but had turned his ships southward before dusk of Saturday night. He was taking with him three aircraft carriers, one battleship, six heavy cruisers and sixteen destroyers—by far the greater portion of the invasion fleet's fighting power.

Throughout that day of August 8, Admiral Fletcher had been fretting. He had bombarded his commanders with inquiries about enemy torpedo-bombers. He was remembering the Battles of the Coral Sea and Midway, when Japanese torpedoes had finished *Lexington* and *Yorktown*. With forebodings he learned of the torpedo-bomber attack in Iron Bottom Bay that afternoon. But

Admiral Fletcher did not consult Admiral Turner who had been in that battle, nor did he take comfort from reports of how completely the enemy had been devastated. Admiral Fletcher consulted chiefly with his fears. In late afternoon he radioed Vice-Admiral Ghormley:

"Fighter-plane strength reduced from ninety-nine to seventy-eight. In view of the large number of enemy torpedo planes and bombers in this area, I recommend the immediate withdrawal of my carriers. Request tankers be sent forward immediately as fuel running low."

Fletcher did not wait for Ghormley to approve or reject his recommendation for withdrawal. His carriers were already heading south as the message cleared, and it would be twelve hours before Fletcher finally received Ghormley's approval to retire. He had yet to be sighted by the enemy, his fighter strength was double the enemy's, and his bunkers held enough fuel to keep him in the area for at least two more days; but the commander of the Expeditionary Force was pulling out.

Admiral Fletcher had thought too much about a long black shape tipped with 1200 pounds of explosives—the dreaded Long Lance Torpedo of Japan.

Because, after World War I, Japan had been denied naval equality with the great powers, she felt that she must, of necessity, turn to other measures which would offset superior opposition. One of these was foul-weather or night torpedo attacks aimed at whittling the enemy down to size for decisive daylight battles.

Throughout the 1930s the Japanese Navy trained in the stormy North Pacific, seeking, in nocturnal maneuvers, the utmost in realism. Ships collided and sank and men were lost without qualm. Night binoculars were developed, for the Japanese knew nothing of electronic detection devices such as radar, and the fleet was combed for men with exceptional night vision. These sailors were trained in special techniques until they were able to distinguish objects four miles away on dark nights. Excellent starshells were also produced, as well as parachute flares. Night-fighting cruisers, some of which carried as many as eight torpedo tubes on their decks, were equipped with float planes whose crews were well-drilled in night scouting or in dropping flares to illuminate a surprised enemy.

It was with such crews and such weapons that Admiral Mikawa came steaming down The Slot, bound to destroy the American invasion fleet.

In the afternoon of that August 8, Commander Ohmae aboard *Chokai* finished drafting the battle plan. With a feeling of extreme confidence he sent it to be wigwagged to the Fleet.

"We will penetrate south of Savo Island and torpedo the enemy main force at Guadalcanal. Thence we will move toward the forward area at Tulagi and strike with torpedoes and gunfire, after which we will withdraw to the north of Savo Island."

As dusk approached every ship was ordered to jettison all topside flammables to clear the decks for battle. Depth charges and loose gear were stowed below. Gradually, as the sun began to sink, a feeling of exhilaration ran through the Fleet. Admiral Mikawa signaled:

"Let us attack with certain victory in the traditional night attack of the Imperial Japanese Navy. May each one calmly do his utmost."[3]

Gunichi Mikawa was himself calm. It was by then full dark and he had come down The Slot without an American airplane to detain him.

Defense of Iron Bottom Bay against surface attack depended upon extensive aerial reconnaissance.

Searching of The Slot began, on that August 8, with none of the additional reconnaissance which Admiral Turner had requested the night before.

Then the Flying Fortresses on routine search missed Mikawa's fleet by sixty miles.

Finally, of the two Royal Australian Air Force pilots who had sighted Mikawa from their Hudsons, only one bothered to make his report.

That report was filed after the pilot flew another four hours, returned to base in New Guinea and had tea. It then passed through seven separate relays before it was received by Admiral Turner eight hours and nineteen minutes after the sighting was made. The message said: "Three cruisers, three destroyers, two seaplane tenders or gunboats, course 120, speed fifteen knots." Reading it, Turner took counsel from what he thought the enemy would do, rather than what the enemy *could* do. He decided that the Japanese were going to set up a seaplane base at Gizo Bay in the central Solomons. Turner was not at that moment entirely calm, for he had just intercepted Fletcher's message to Ghormley.

Turner was trembling with rage. He, too, would have to leave quickly. Even though the ships were far from unloaded, he could not risk them to air attack without air cover of his own. But he would still like to discuss the situation with his commanders, so he sent for Vandegrift and Rear Admiral Sir Victor A. C. Crutchley.

Rear Admiral Crutchley was the last Briton to hold the rank of Flag Officer Commanding the Australian Naval Squadron. He was both a veteran of World War I, in which he had won the Victoria Cross, and of the present war, in which he had commanded battleship *Warspite* in the second battle of Narvik. Very tall, very charming, Crutchley was a great favorite with the Aussie sailors, who called him "Old Goat's Whiskers" for the magnificent red beard and mustache which he wore to hide an old wound-scar.

Turner had given Crutchley the Western Defense Force. Eastern Defense had gone to Rear Admiral Scott in *San Juan* accompanied by the Australian cruiser *Hobart* and the American destroyers *Monssen* and *Buchanan.* Turner did not expect trouble at the eastern entrance to the Bay because an attack there would have to follow a roundabout route.

But at the western entrance to either side of Savo an enemy coming down The Slot would have a clean shot at the American fleet. So Crutchley had gone there, and the British admiral had begun by dividing his forces.

He put his radar destroyers *Blue* and *Ralph Talbot* to either side of Savo on the outside and his six heavy cruisers to either side of Savo on the inside. Aboard *Australia,* his flagship, Crutchley sailed a north-south patrol followed by *Canberra* and *Chicago* in that order. Destroyers *Patterson* and *Bagley* were in front to screen. The cruisers were in column about 600 yards apart and they reversed course every hour.

The northern group was commanded by Captain Frederick Riefkohl aboard *Vincennes* followed by *Quincy* and *Astoria.* Destroyers *Helm* and *Wilson* formed the screen. Riefkohl sailed a box patrol, ten miles to a side, cruising at ten knots to turn right at 90 degrees every half hour.

Crutchley thought dividing his forces was excusable because he believed that six heavy cruisers would be an unwieldy force at night. Admiral Mikawa with seven cruisers did not share this belief. Crutchley also thought that he would have ample forewarning of enemy approach; it was not his fault that Allied reconnaissance had failed utterly. Then, Crutchley thought that Admiral Turner's message to come aboard *McCawley* meant that he should withdraw *Australia* from the battle line. This he did, leaving Captain Howard Bode in *Chicago* in charge. But Captain Bode remained at the stern of his column because he expected Admiral Crutchley to resume position in *Australia*. In fact, Admiral Crutchley had not drawn up a detailed battle plan. Meanwhile, Captain Riefkohl aboard *Vincennes* was not aware that *Australia* and Crutchley had left station. Anyway, Captain Riefkohl was tired and going to bed. So were all the other cruiser commanders.

Finally, the conference called by Turner served no purpose other than to reduce and confuse the Western Defense Force. Turner merely notified Vandegrift and Crutchley, at about eleven o'clock, that he was leaving in the morning. He showed them Fletcher's message. Vandegrift understood. It was a *fait accompli* foreshadowed by the conference in the Fijis. He could also agree with Turner's description of Fletcher's flight.

"He's left us bare ass!"[4]

Mikawa's staff was gathered in flag plot, when, at nine o'clock, the great news came in from Rabaul: Sunk, two enemy heavy cruisers, one large cruiser, two destroyers and nine transports; left burning, one heavy cruiser and two transports. Gunichi Mikawa forgot yesterday's exaggerations to believe today's.

A few hours later he launched three float planes. They were to drop course flares to guide the fleet in and they were to scout the enemy and illuminate his position upon order. They would also have very little hope of ever getting back to their ships. But Japanese fliers—there were three men in each plane—expected to die for the Emperor. The catapults flashed and the planes disappeared in the night.

Gunichi Mikawa went to *Chokai's* bridge with Commander Ohmae. They were supremely confident. They peered into the night to see every bridge streaming with the banners that marked them out in the dark. Keen-eyed lookouts could make out and identify every ship by its silhouette or the red or white rings painted around its funnels. All ships were sailing in line of battle: *Chokai, Aoba* with Admiral Goto aboard, *Kinugasa, Furutaka, Kako,* the lights *Tenryu* and *Yubari,* destroyer *Yunagi* bringing up the rear. No other navy had so prepared itself for night battle, Mikawa thought, remembering one of the Japanese Navy's favorite sayings:

"The Americans build things well, but their blue eyes are no match for our dark eyes in night actions."

One of the things Americans had built well was the sound tracking device installed aboard the submarine *S-38,* then submerged and tracking *Meiyo Maru* fourteen miles west of Cape St. George. At about midnight Commander Munson closed to one thousand yards. He fired two torpedoes. Both hit, and *Meiyo Maru* sank with fourteen officers and 328 men. Her five sister ships were recalled to Rabaul. The first attempt to reinforce Guadalcanal had failed and in the morning sharks were splashing among bloated bodies bound with belts of a thousand stitches.

Another thing well built by the Americans was the radar installed aboard destroyers *Blue* and *Ralph Talbot.* But this far-ranging electronic eye must also be understood to be effective. Neither Admiral Crutchley nor the destroyer commanders were aware that their search-legs needed to be coordinated. When these picket ships outside Savo stood at the extreme end of their search-legs they left between them a hole in the radar screen twenty-five miles wide. As August 8 neared its end *Blue* and *Ralph Talbot* sailed toward each other and then away from each other.

Aboard *Talbot* lookouts could see past Savo Island to their rear toward Tulagi, where *George F. Elliott* still burned. Her fire silhouetted some of the ships of the northern force. Over Savo there was a storm making up. Lightning flashes glimmered. The warm moist air was becoming more oppressive. Just before midnight *Talbot's* lookouts heard motors overhead.

An airplane with flashing lights flew over them.

Astonished, *Talbot's* watch gave immediate warning over the Talk Between Ships. But this and similar alarms were discounted by commanders who considered Mikawa's scouts to be "friendly." Would the Japanese dare show lights?

Blue and *Talbot* sailed on, together and apart, together and apart.

Before midnight the Japanese ships picked up the first marker lamp thirty miles off Cape Esperance. They were on course! Speed was increased to twenty-six knots. Shortly afterward a light was sighted in the direction of Tulagi. Admiral Goto reported that the sky was red over the island.

The ships steamed on . . .

On *Chokai's* bridge Gunichi Mikawa stood erect and tense. His fingers whitened as he gripped the splinter-screen and peered ahead. At 12:40 A.M., August 9, hulking Savo Island loomed out of the darkness. Three minutes later a lookout sighted a ship steaming ahead from right to left. He had seen it on a black night at a distance of five miles.

It was *Blue.*

"Left rudder," Mikawa ordered. "Slow to twenty-two knots."[5]

Every gun, every eye in the fleet was trained on *Blue.* The slightest indication that she had seen, and *Blue* would be blown to bits. Thirty seconds . . . a minute . . . and *Blue* turned about! She reversed course and sailed back to Guadalcanal.

"Ship sighted, twenty degrees to port."

Heads and guns again swiveled. It was *Ralph Talbot,* and she was sailing away.

"Right rudder," Mikawa ordered. "Course one hundred and fifty."

They went through the gap and the wolves were now in the pasture.

At 1:25 A.M. Mikawa gave the order: "Prepare to fire torpedoes."

Destroyer *Yunagi* lost speed and dropped behind to keep an eye on *Blue.*

"Cruiser, seven degrees port," a lookout cried, sighting a ship nine miles distant, illuminated in the glow of the burning *Elliott.* But it was too far north. Mikawa bored on, hunting for the southern force.

"Three cruisers, nine degrees starboard, moving to the right."

There they were, the ones he wanted, in reality *Chicago* and

Canberra with destroyer *Patterson,* and Mikawa gave the order: "Commence firing." Giant steel fish leaped from loaded torpedo tubes and went hissing through the black water. "All ships attack," Mikawa ordered, and great spiky guns fingered the sky.

At last *Patterson* had seen the enemy and was broadcasting the tocsin:

WARNING! WARNING! STRANGE SHIPS ENTERING HARBOR!

It was too late. The Long Lances were flashing on their way and parachute flares came swaying down from Mikawa's scout planes. Marines lying on their ponchos in Guadalcanal's whispering blind rain forests were made suddenly fearful to see all made grotesque and ghostly about them by this wavering pale green light.

Out on the Bay black water glittered evilly under the flares. *Chokai* in the lead, the Japanese cruisers came on with bellowing guns.

A few seconds later a pair of Mikawa's deadly steel fish finished their run and rammed with titanic thrust into the hull of *Canberra*. Twenty-four shells whistled in and broke her body. Her captain and her gunnery officer were killed. Fires started and spread. *Canberra* was done for and would have to be scuttled.

Another torpedo blew off the bow of *Chicago*. Captain Bode tumbled topside out of a sound sleep. He had a column of cruisers to shoot at, and he sailed out of the battle in the wrong direction. He also neglected to inform the northern force that he was under attack.

It took the Japanese only a few fiery minutes to blast and rout the southern force, and now Mikawa divided his column and turned left to take on the northern force.

Archer Vandegrift limped painfully below on the mine layer *Southard*. He had twisted an old football knee leaving *McCawley* for Admiral Crutchley's barge. Crutchley had offered to take him to *Southard*. As they parted, the admiral said: "Vandegrift, I don't know if I can blame Turner for what he's doing."[6] The general made no reply. Reproach, at this moment, was beyond him; even if he did think that the behinds of his Marines were somewhat barer then Turner's, who was leaving in the morning.

Vandegrift was going to Tulagi to see if Rupertus had been able to get any supplies ashore. Guadalcanal had received something less than half of its sixty-day ration, but Tulagi, busy fighting, surely had less.

In *Southard's* wardroom Vandegrift gratefully sipped hot coffee, until a sailor's voice came booming through the bridge tube: "Commodore, you better come up here. All hell's broke loose!"[7]

Racing topside unmindful of his bad knee, Vandegrift came on deck to see flares burning far off *Southard's* stern and hear the boom of naval guns. He was elated. He thought that the Americans were winning. It might not be too long before Turner would be back.

Suddenly the beams of powerful searchlights slashed the western night.

Astoria was last in column. In 1939 *Astoria* under Captain Richmond Kelly Turner had carried the ashes of Ambassador Hirosi Saito to Japan from America. Now, in the morning of August 9, *Chokai's* big guns were saying thanks. Salvo after salvo of eight-inch shells tore into *Astoria*. The big ship shuddered and bucked. Like *Canberra,* like all the other Allied ships and unlike the Japanese, *Astoria* was heavy with flammable wood, with upholstered wooden wardroom furniture, and her decks and bulkheads were thick with paint and linoleum. Within a few minutes *Astoria* was a blazing shambles and would sink at noon that day.

It was *Aoba* who had turned on her searchlights. She caught luckless *Quincy* with her guns still pointing fore and aft. *Quincy* swung her guns and fired. Her shells crashed into *Chokai's* chartroom. But now *Quincy* was caught between Mikawa's two columns. Piece by piece and man by man, *Quincy* came apart. Her captain died just after he had ordered her helmsman to try to beach the burning cruiser on Savo. She began to turn over. "Abandon ship!" Men scrambled over her side, and some were still clinging to her, like ants on a sinking can, at 2:35 A.M., when *Quincy* rolled over and dove—the first American warship to sink to the floor of Iron Bottom Bay.

In the lead, *Vincennes* was the last to be caught. Searchlights picked her out, too, but she fought back. As *Kako's* near-misses sent geysers of water pluming above her, *Vincennes* hurled shells at *Kinugasa* and hit her. But then Japanese shells exploded the airplanes on the American's fantail and *Vincennes* was doomed. One after another the Japanese cruisers swept by the staggering, burning American ship to rock her with more torpedoes and gunfire. *Vincennes* sank a few minutes after the death of *Quincy*.

In thirty-two minutes the Japanese had destroyed four Allied heavy cruisers and damaged another. As they sped toward the regrouping rendezvous northwest of Savo, their wakes washed over a thousand oil-covered American seamen clinging desperately to empty shell cases, life rafts, orange crates—to any piece of flotsam or jetsam that might keep them afloat. Marine Corporal George Chamberlin, wounded five times by shrapnel, was saved when a sailor named Carryl Clement swam to his side, removing Chamberlin's shoelaces and tying the wounded man's wrists to ammunition drums. Other wounded were not so fortunate, for Savo's shores abounded in sharks. Blood attracted them. Throughout the night men vanished with horrible swiftness. At dawn rescue operations would begin and sailors and Marines would stand on the decks of rescue craft to shoot sharks while others hauled 700 survivors aboard, blanching, sometimes, to see men with streamers of tattered flesh flopping on the decks like octopus or others so badly burned that corpsmen could find no place to insert hypodermic needles. But Gunichi Mikawa's guns had taken the lives of 1270 men and wounded 709 others.

Meanwhile, northwest of Savo, Mikawa prepared to make short and bloody work of the thin-skinned American transports. It was clear to him that he had destroyed the sheep-dogs and the sheep were now his to devour. But then, he faltered.

It was not that he feared any of the remaining warships; he would have been overjoyed to put more enemy combat vessels on the bottom. Mikawa was just not aware of either Admiral Scott's Eastern Force or Admiral Crutchley in *Australia*. Mikawa honestly believed that he had sunk five cruisers and four destroyers, almost all of the American warships that his planes had not reported "destroyed." No, it was the American dive-bombers that Gunichi Mikawa feared. He, too, had been at Midway. All the way down The Slot his chief fear had been for the American carriers. It had seemed incredible to him that he could enter the Bay unchecked. Now, he would not stretch his luck. He would not tarry to be destroyed by American air with the advent of daylight. Like Admiral Fletcher, Admiral Mikawa fled his fears.

At 2:40 A.M. he ordered his ships to make full-speed north for Rabaul.

That afternoon Admiral Turner's amphibious fleet upped anchor and made full-speed south for New Caledonia.

An hour later a battalion of the First Marines moved from Henderson Field to the beach to take up new positions. The men gaped in amazement at empty Iron Bottom Bay. Even the most obtuse private could grasp the meaning of that vacant expanse of shimmering blue water.

They were all alone.

Chapter 3

KELLY TURNER stood on *McCawley's* lower bridge yelling through a megaphone to Archer Vandegrift standing below him in a tossing small boat.

Turner did not know the details but Crutchley's covering force had been badly mauled. Turner was leaving as soon as his boats had finished fishing survivors from the water. Turner did not say when he would be back. Turner waved and Vandegrift waved, and then the general's boat beached on Guadalcanal and Vandegrift limped ashore.

He called a meeting of his staff and all regimental and battalion commanders.

They came straggling through the rain to the Division Command Post near Alligator Creek. They were colonels and lieutenant colonels and majors. New beards were sprouting raggedly on their chins. Their eyes were bloodshot and their baggy dungarees were stained with mud. They stood watching the rescue operations on the Bay or speculating on what all the shooting had been about last night. Coffee had been brewed over a smoking, sputtering fire and the hot black liquid was passed around in C-ration cans. Some of the officers cursed when the hot metal burned their lips. Others swore when concussions from the west shook the palm fronds and showered them with rainwater. The explosions were from *Canberra* being scuttled by torpedo and *Astoria* dying by compartments.

Offshore, the mists lifted to reveal the foreshortened shape of a prowless cruiser making slowly eastward between two destroyers.

"Chicago," someone said in a shocked voice.

Archer Vandegrift came out of his tent.

He spoke quickly and bluntly. The Navy was leaving and no one knew when it would be back. Only God could say when and

if they would get air cover. They were now open to every form
of attack: troops by land, bombs from the air, shells from the
sea. And they were to inform every officer and man in their command of this unlovely truth: they were all alone.

But, said Archer Vandegrift softly, his strong jaw lifting, they
would also tell their men that Guadalcanal would not be another
Bataan. Marines had been surviving such situations as this since
1775. Here also they would survive—and that was all the general
had to say.

Now Colonel Gerald Thomas, the division's operations officer,
took over. Thomas said they would now:

Organize the defense of Guadalcanal.

Get the supplies inland.

Finish the airfield.

Patrol.

They were going to hold a perimeter roughly 7500 yards wide
from west to east and penetrating inland about 3500 yards. It
would be bounded on its eastern or right flank by the Tenaru
River and on the west or left by the Kukum Hills. Its northern
or seaward front would be the most heavily fortified, because it
was here that Vandegrift expected the Japanese to counterattack.
Its landward rear would be the most lightly defended, for here
the terrain was jungle and jumbled hills and could be held by
outposts tied together by roving patrols. The First Marines were
to hold the Tenaru and the beach line west to the Lunga River.
The Fifth Marines would hold the beach from the Lunga west
to Kukum and around back to the Lunga. Colonel Pedro del
Valle, commander of the Eleventh Marines, would set up his 75-
mm and 105-mm howitzers in central positions from which to
strike any point on the line. The 90-mm antiaircraft guns of the
Third Defense Battalion were to emplace northwest of Henderson
Field, and the 75-mm half-tracks were to dig in north of the airfield to be ready for movement to prepared positions on the beach.
In the meantime, Vandegrift would hold his tank company and
one battalion from the First Marines in reserve.

This was the line which the Marines were to hold in isolation
against an enemy who now possessed the initiative and all the
ships, airplanes, guns, and men required to press it. Trained to
hit, United States Marines were now being forced to hold.

Except for the damage to *Chokai's* chartroom, Admiral Mikawa's ships had escaped the battle of Savo Island unscathed. Not a plane had pursued them as they sped up The Slot. They were jubilant. At midday of August 9, Mikawa signaled Goto to make for Kavieng with *Aoba, Furutaka, Kinugasa,* and *Kako,* while he led the remaining ships to Rabaul.

Early next morning Goto's ships proceeded confidently toward Kavieng Harbor. As they went, they passed through the eye of a periscope clutched in the hands of Lieutenant Commander J. R. ("Dinty") Moore aboard submarine *S-44.* Dinty Moore was excited. The cruisers seemed huge to him. He decided to attack the last in column, *Kako.* He waited until he was close enough to see the Japanese officers on *Kako's* bridge, a distance of about seven hundred yards, and then he fired a spread of four torpedoes and dove.

Thirty-five seconds later the first of Moore's torpedoes struck *Kako* with a thunderous explosion. One by one the others hit.

Kako's boilers blew up. Far below the stricken cruiser, American sailors looked at each other with fearful eyes, listening to the hideous water noises of a disintegrating ship. *Kako's* death rattle was worse than the enemy depth charges. It was as though giant chains were being dragged across the submarine's hull.[1] But the submarine survived, as *Kako* did not, although this solitary American underwater victory of the Guadalcanal campaign was omitted from the paeans of praise which the Japanese press had begun to pour out on the victors of Savo Island.

Eventually and in private, Admiral Isoroku Yamamoto would reprimand Gunichi Mikawa for his failure to sink the American transports. In public and immediately, however, Mikawa and his men were hailed as heroes. Victory parades were held in every city, and in Tokyo exulting crowds thronged the streets.

Headlines proclaimed "great war results . . . unrivalled in world history," Australia had "absolutely become an orphan of the southwest Pacific." Twenty-four warships and eleven transports "filled to capacity with Marines" had been sunk.[2]

The House of Peers directed that a certificate of gratitude be presented to the Minister of the Navy, and English-language broadcasts coyly announced that there was still "plenty room at bottom of Pacific for more American Fleet—ha! ha!"

In America there was silence. There were also disturbing estimates such as the one sent to General Marshall by Major General Millard F. Harmon, commander of Army forces under Admiral Ghormley. On August 11, Harmon wrote: "The thing that impresses me more than anything else in connection with the Solomons action is that we are not prepared 'to follow-up' . . . Can the Marines hold it? There is considerable room for doubt."[3]

Admiral King may also have had doubts. He betrayed the possibility of their existence by his exasperated refusal to comment on Japan's exaggerated reports of Savo. After his public information officer asked him what he should tell Washington's importunate reporters, King snapped: "Tell them nothing! When it's over, tell them who won."[4]

The Marines on Guadalcanal were the least impressed by reports of their impending doom. Hearing Tokyo Rose describe them as "summer insects which have dropped into the fire by themselves," they hooted in derision or made uncharitable estimates of the virtue of Japan's lady propagandist. The truth was that Vandegrift's Marines were actually on a kind of ignorantly blissful frolic.

They had already made light of Savo by renaming it "The Battle of the Five Sitting Ducks," and they gave proof of how little they understood the consequences of that naval disaster by talking confidently of returning to New Zealand in three weeks, or whenever it was that the Army, the lowly "dogfaces," would arrive to relieve them, the heroes of the Pacific. Then these invincible young warriors—most of whom had yet to see the silhouette of the enemy's mushroom helmet—would bask in the tender and accommodating admiration of the young ladies of Wellington while consuming acres of steak-and-eggs and quaffing cool oceans of down under beer. In the meantime, they gamboled.

They discovered and plundered a warehouse stuffed with quarts of Japanese beer and balloon-like half-gallon flasks of Japanese sake. They buried the loot in the cool sands of the sea, digging it up at night to drink and revel just like the good old moonshining days at New River; and sometimes, because they had underestimated the power of enemy wine, there were ferocious night "battles" fought between tipsy sentries.

Almost every night there was the burlesque provided by men who could not pronounce the passwords. All of the passwords—

Lollipop, Lallapaloozer, Lolligag—were loaded with L's because of the Japanese difficulty with that sound.[5] But polysyllabic passwords also sat awkwardly on the tongues of Marines such as the rifleman who awoke to relieve himself on the night the password was "Lilliputian."

"Halt!" the sentry cried.

"Fer Gawd's sake, Lucky, don't shoot. It's me, Briggs."

"Gimme the password."

"Lily-poo . . . luly . . ."

"C'mon, c'mon! The password, or I'll let you have it."

"Luly-pah . . . lily-poosh . . ." Silence, and then, in outrage: "Aw, shit—shoot!"[6]

The Guadalcanal frolic was not uninterrupted. General Vandegrift's supplies had to be moved inland and this meant working parties toiling in the alternating extremes of drenching rains or blistering sun. Men were also needed to bury ammunition on the edges of Henderson Field, and the field itself required the unrelenting labor of Marine engineers working with Japanese equipment. On August 12, Henderson was pronounced operational, or at least able to receive a Catalina flying boat piloted by an aide of Admiral McCain's. Actually, Henderson Field was only 2600 feet long, it was muddy and bumpy, it had no covering of steel matting or taxiways, and it was not drained. But the admiral's aide optimistically rated it suitable for fighter operation.

Meanwhile, to conserve food, the island had gone on a twice-daily ration composed chiefly of captured enemy rice, a wormy paste which nauseated some of the daintier spirits among the conquerors until they came to realize that they would have to swallow it—"fresh meat" and all—or starve. Occasionally the mess was spiced by a few lumps of Argentine bully beef or a dubious delicacy described as New Zealand lamb's tongue, and sometimes a marksman among the Marines would bring down a plantation cow. Phil Chaffee shot one. He had not yet caught a gold-toothed enemy head in his sights, but he shot a cow through the eye at 200 yards.

Gradually, the mood of innocent gaiety gave way to one of grim wariness, starting on August 9 when the Emperor's "glorious young eagles" came winging down from Rabaul to make Guadalcanal shiver and shake with 500-pound bombs and those grass-cutting fragmentation bombs which kill and maim; gradually the fact of isolation was grasped by even the most facetious, for the Tokyo Express had begun to run and each night Japanese destroyers or cruisers slid into the Bay to shell Americans cringing in sodden holes, and each day submarines surfaced to sink everything in sight; gradually, these lighthearted young men began to realize that they were all alone with only a few pounds of rice and the bullets in their belts to keep them alive—and then came the massacre of the Goettge patrol and they knew that they were at war.

Lieutenant Colonel Frank Goettge was Vandegrift's intelligence officer. It was Goettge who had gone to Australia to scrape together all available information on Guadalcanal, and it was Goettge who, on August 12, decided that the Japanese to the west might be willing to surrender.

On that day a Japanese seaman was captured. He was a sour little man, answering questions in a surly voice until a few ounces of medicinal brandy improved his manners and brought the admission that hundreds of his comrades were starving in the jungle and were anxious to surrender. This intelligence was coupled with a report the previous day that a Japanese "white flag" had been seen at a Japanese position west of the west-lying Matanikau River.

That night Goettge asked General Vandegrift if he might investigate. Vandegrift looked up from his meal of cold beans and shook his head. Goettge pressed him, and the general reluctantly agreed.

Twenty-five men, the cream of the Division Intelligence Section, as well as some of the best scouts in the Fifth Marines, were chosen to accompany Goettge. Shortly before midnight, under a moonless sky, leading the Japanese seaman by a rope around his neck, the Goettge patrol departed by Higgins boat for the "surrender area."

They landed opposite Matanikau Village. They moved inland to set up a perimeter opposite a group of huts. Goettge and a few others went forward to reconnoiter and were cut down by converging streams of machine-gun fire. One by one, the others received their mortal wounds. Only three men survived. They escaped by swimming. They tottered into Marine lines with blood streaming from flesh slashed and torn by coral. One of them reported that as he fled just before daybreak he turned for a last look and saw sabers flashing in the sun.

Sabers flashing in the sun.

That was the phrase and the image that carried Vandegrift's men from a merry to a murderous mood. So the enemy had chopped up wounded Marines who had come on a mission of mercy to save the wretched enemy. So be it. Now let the enemy come so that these Marines—products of a soft and effete civilization—could also kill, could also chop up wounded; and with their own sabers.

Patrols that had been cautious to the point of timidity now turned aggressive. Marines who would one day dread recurrent combat now hoped openly for battle. No longer would the cry "Condition Red!" send men flying to their dugouts and air-raid shelters to sit out, with fear and prayer, the daily wail and crash of enemy bombs; no, they remained above-ground to watch with gleeful hate while Henderson's antiaircraft gunners brought down Betty after Betty and gradually forced the enemy to escalate their bombing runs from a devastating ten thousand feet to an ineffective twenty-five thousand. Sometimes, now, Marines dueled enemy warships with their puny 75-mm howitzers or ran half-tracks down to the beach to engage the enemy's arrogant submarines, and once old Gunny Lew Diamond attempted to pursue a red-balled submarine with an 81-mm mortar mounted on a Higgins boat. Fortunately for Lew, he was restrained; but his gesture nevertheless reflected the rising ardor among his younger comrades.

These enraged young men had no way of knowing that the enemy "surrender" flag luring Goettge to disaster had actually been a Japanese flag hanging limp, thus concealing the rising sun at its center. It would never be known whether or not the captured Japanese seaman had been a deliberate plant. Nor would anyone think of criticizing Goettge for allowing curiosity or compassion to cripple his common sense. No, all that these Marines could consider was those inhuman sabers flashing and dripping and they swore that they would have their revenge.

From now on there would be no quarter.

Lieutenant General Haruyoshi Hyakutake was annoyed.

On August 13, the day on which the Goettge patrol was slaughtered, Imperial General Headquarters directed him to squelch the pests in the southern Solomons. He would, of course, continue his operation against Port Moresby. But, under a new Central Agreement signed by General Sugiyama and Admiral Nagano, his 17th Army would have to attend to Guadalcanal first.

The new orders irritated Hyakutake because he was in a hurry to get on with his beautiful new plan for conquering Moresby and because he considered the "insignificant" Guadalcanal incursion a distraction. Moreover, the general was having difficulty rounding up troops. As was common among the Japanese, the 50,000 men comprising his 17th Army had been presented to him unassembled. The famous 2nd Division—called the Sendai after the city near Tokyo in which it was recruited—was in Java and the Philippines; the 38th or Nagoya Division was in the Dutch Indies; some 17th Army antitank units were as far away as Manchuria, and other units were engaged in New Guinea; the 35th or Kawaguchi Brigade was in the Palaus; and the crack Ichiki Detachment which was to have captured Midway was still on Guam.

It seemed to Hyakutake that Colonel Ichiki's force would be enough to take care of the two thousand Americans to the south. After all, Ichiki had two thousand highly trained men, the elite of the famous 28th Infantry Regiment which had fought Russians at Nomonhan during the unproclaimed—and unpublicized—Russo-Japanese border war of 1939, and which had thereafter battled Chinese in Manchuria. Two thousand battle-hardened Japanese against two thousand soft Americans? It was like sending a man on a boy's errand.

With contempt and with confidence Lieutenant General Hyakutake ordered Colonel Kiyono Ichiki to proceed to Guadalcanal.

Martin Clemens was coming down at last.

On August 12 a scout had brought him a message directing him to enter Marine lines. Next day, bestowing a fond farewell pat on the teleradio that had been his companion for five months, presenting the village headman's aged father with a pair of gorgeous yellow corduroy shorts, Clemens departed for the Tenaru River accompanied by ten scouts.

They encountered Sergeant Major Vouza enroute. Vouza proudly told Clemens of his private war against the Japanese on eastern Guadalcanal. At Koli Point he had invited three Japanese into a hut for refreshments. After the door closed Vouza and his comrades subdued their guests, slung them on poles like dressed pigs, and carried them down to American headquarters. Grinning with happy cruelty, Vouza explained that he had decided to bind his captives because, "They walk slow too much."

Clemens and his scouts passed the night in a deserted village. On the morning of the fourteenth they struck out through kunai grass five feet high. Clemens still carried his only pair of shoes, padding along on sore and swollen feet sheathed in heavy woollen miner's socks. Coming around a bend in the coast, Clemens saw the green, scum-crested Tenaru. Across it he could see Marines in light green dungarees hauling supplies along the beach.

Clemens halted his ragged band. He adjusted the pistol on his hip and glanced at his rifle-bearer to make sure he was carrying the weapon smartly. They dressed ranks. Clemens put on his shoes. He straightened and gave the order to move out.

There was a lump in his throat and he could barely whisper his name to the guards, but Martin Clemens came marching in.

Bull Halsey was well again.

Dermatitis had kept him invalided for two months in hospitals at Pearl Harbor and in Virginia, but he had finally been certified as fit for duty and he was returning to the Pacific. Before he did, he took a short leave. Hoisting a convivial drink with friends at his family's home, he was astonished to see one of his grandsons come tearing into the room shouting:

"Look, Granddaddy! You're famous! Here you are in the funny papers!"[7]

> *Corpses drifting swollen in the sea depths,*
> *Corpses rotting in the mountain grass—*
> *We shall die, we shall die for the Emperor.*
> *We shall never look back.*

It was the ancient Japanese battle oath and the modern national anthem, and the men of the Ichiki Detachment chanted it while boarding ship at Truk. They had come there from Guam, for Colonel Ichiki had moved with customary speed. Now, August 16, he took nine hundred men aboard six fast destroyers and sailed south. Colonel Ichiki was going to land at Taivu Point, about twenty-two air miles east of the Tenaru River, at midnight of August 18. Simultaneously, about 250 men of a Naval Landing

Force would land west of the Americans as a distraction. The remainder of Colonel Ichiki's force—about 1500 troops—would follow in slower ships.

Colonel Ichiki's orders from General Hyakutake were: ". . . quickly recapture and maintain the airfields at Guadalcanal. If this is not possible, this detachment will occupy a part of Guadalcanal and await the arrival of troops in its rear." Ichiki, of course, contemplated no such waiting period. He was eager to close with the enemy and his military mustache fairly bristled with the ardor of his yearning. Though he was a trained infantry officer with a high reputation among his colleagues, Ichiki was also fond of what the Japanese call "bamboo-spear" tactics. He believed that Japanese "spiritual power" was ultimately invincible. He made sure that his men read the battle instruction, which said: "When you encounter the enemy after landing, regard yourself as an avenger come at last face to face with his father's murderer. The discomforts of the long sea voyage and the rigors of the sweltering march have been but months of watching and waiting for the moment when you slay this enemy. Here before you is the man whose death will lighten your heart of its burden of brooding anger. If you fail to destroy him utterly you can never rest at peace. And the first blow is the vital blow."[8]

Colonel Kiyono Ichiki was going to deliver that first blow.

Archer Vandegrift was both heartened and uneasy. He was encouraged because Admiral McCain had begun to send supplies in. On August 15 destroyer-transports *Little, McKean,* and *Gregory* arrived with a small Marine Air operations detachment headed by Major Charles Hayes, four hundred drums of aviation gasoline, almost three hundred bombs, belted aircraft ammunition, tools, and spare parts. All this was an earnest of Slew McCain's earlier promise:

> The best and proper solution, of course, is to get fighters and dive-bombers onto your field. *Long Island* arrives Vila the early morning of the 17th. Trained pilots will be put aboard and she will proceed to fly-away positions off south tip of San Cristobal. Planes will be flown off to reach field between 4 and 5 in the afternoon probably the 18th, and if not the 18th, the 19th, of which you will be duly advised. As I understand, she has one squadron of fighters and one squadron of dive-bombers . . .

General Vandegrift was therefore sure, on the afternoon of August 15, that he would soon have the vital air cover that he now needed more than ever, for Naval intelligence had sent word of something big brewing up north, and on that very day Japanese transports had dropped containers, meant for their countrymen west of Kukum, within Marine lines. Inside one of the cylinders was the ominous message: "Help is on the way! Banzai!"

The following day, as Vandegrift quickly learned, the destroyer *Oite* landed supplies on western Guadalcanal, plus 200 men of the Fifth Sasebo Special Naval Landing Force.

Worse, there were now reports of an enemy build-up to the east. A patrol east of the Tenaru had encountered an American missionary, a priest named Father Arthur Duhamel, who spoke of an increase in Japanese numbers. This fact had been confirmed by the young coastwatcher, Clemens, who came to Vandegrift's headquarters to put himself at the general's service. Vandegrift regarded Clemens and his native scouts as a godsend, able replacements for all of the trained Marine scouts lost on the Goettge patrol.

They were put to use after another disturbing report. Just before midnight of August 18 men along the beaches reported the wash of ships moving east at high speed; at about three o'clock they reported the wash going west again. At dawn there were rumors of an enemy landing to the east. Colonel Thomas ordered Sergeant Major Vouza to conduct a patrol around the entire perimeter from east to west. Meanwhile, a Marine patrol under Captain Charles Brush was sent probing eastward along the coast. Finally, on that same day of August 19, three companies of the Fifth Marines attacked west against the Japanese concentrated on the Matanikau River.

The western attack was a minor success.

At Matanikau Village the Japanese counterattacked in the first daylight banzai bayonet charge of the war. The Marines slaughtered them with automatic weapons. Sixty-five Japanese were killed against four Marines dead and eleven wounded.

At Kukumbona Village farther west another company attempted an amphibious assault. Enroute, their boats were shelled by a submarine and two Tokyo Express destroyers lurking in the Bay. Hugging the coast, the Marines got through to storm Kukumbona and drive the enemy into the jungle.

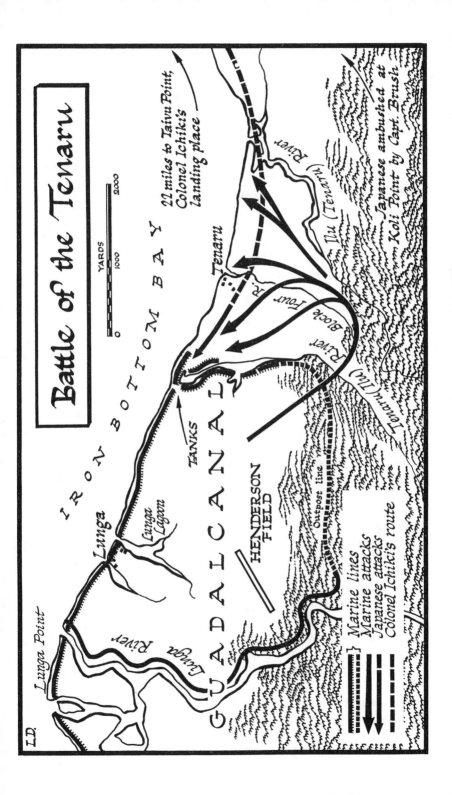

Battle of the Tenaru

L.D.

YARDS
0   1000   2000

IRON BOTTOM BAY

Lunga Point

Lunga River

Lunga

Lunga Lagoon

GUADALCANAL

TANKS

HENDERSON FIELD

Outpost line

Tenaru

Tenaru R.

Block Four

River

Ilu (Tenaru) River

Tenaru (Ilu) River

22 miles to Taivu Point,
Colonel Ichiki's
landing place

Japanese ambushed at
Koli Point by Capt. Brush

Marine lines
Marine attacks
Japanese attacks
Colonel Ichiki's route

It had been the six destroyers carrying Colonel Ichiki and his 900 men which caused the wash observed by Marine coastal sentries. The Japanese had come ashore at Taivu, twenty-two miles to the east of the Tenaru River. Colonel Ichiki decided to attack immediately, without waiting for the arrival of the rest of his troops, as General Hyakutake had suggested he might do. Ichiki shared Hyakutake's contempt for Americans. He was going to attack at night, because, as the battle studies said: "Westerners— being very superior people, very effeminate, and very cowardly— have an intense dislike of fighting in the rain or the mist, or at night. Night, in particular (though it is excellent for dancing), they cannot conceive to be a proper time for war. In this, if we seize on it, lies our great opportunity."[9]

Colonel Ichiki seized on it. He wrote in his diary: "18 Aug. The landing. 20 Aug. The march by night and the battle. 21 Aug. Enjoyment of the fruits of victory."

It was then only August 19, but Colonel Ichiki was a tidy man. He foresaw that he might die before he had a chance to make the last two entries, so he merely postdated them for posterity— and then he sent out a company to lay communication wire.

Captain Charles Brush did not convey the impression of tidiness. Shambling along in his baggy dungarees, Captain Brush was as debonair as a bear in overalls. But crusty "Charlie," as his men called him with a notable lack of filial affection, was a capable company commander—one of those reservists who could compel a regular officer's admiration.

On the morning of August 19, Brush led his patrol of eighty men eastward from the Tenaru. Shortly after noon, his advance scouts caught sight of the Ichiki wiremen moving slowly westward. Brush attacked.

He pinned the enemy down while Lieutenant Joseph Jachym led a squad off to the right and took up a position in the Japanese left rear. The Marines then struck the enemy front and rear with converging automatic fire. In a fight of about an hour's length Brush's men killed thirty-one Japanese while three others escaped into the jungle. Three Marines were killed and three wounded.

Sensing something unusual in the enemy patrol, Brush posted security and personally searched the bodies. He found, for the first time, helmets marked with the Japanese Army star rather than with the Navy's chrysanthemum. He found an unusual number of officers among the dead. Four carried swords and field glasses, wore polished boots and were clad in neatly pressed uniforms decorated by rows of campaign ribbons. Brush rifled their map cases. He was astonished. Although the maps' markings were in Japanese they were startlingly clear and they pinpointed the Tenaru line's weak points with appalling accuracy.

Brush withdrew and made his report to Colonel Cates's headquarters. General Vandegrift was notified. Some of his staff advised him to push rapidly eastward to surprise this new enemy. Vandegrift demurred. His mission was to hold the airfield. But he did order immediate strengthening of the Tenaru flank, and Colonel del Valle's artillerymen quickly "zeroed-in" on every point along the line.

The evening of that momentous August 19, unknown to Vandegrift and his Marines, President Franklin Roosevelt radioed Joseph Stalin: "We have gained, I believe, a toehold in the Southwest Pacific from which the Japanese will find it very difficult to dislodge us. We have had substantial naval losses there, but the advantage gained was worth the sacrifice and we are going to maintain hard pressure on the enemy."[10]

If Admiral Robert Ghormley back in Nouméa had seen the Chief Executive's cable he probably would have been astounded at its optimism—for Admiral Ghormley had already gotten off pessimistic dispatches to Nimitz and King—and if Admiral Yamamoto to the north in Truk had seen it, he would have dismissed it as typical of American soft-soap salesmen.

That American toe, as Yamamoto confidently expected, was about to be squashed flat by Operation Ka.

Chapter 4

KA, the first syllable of the Japanese word for Guadalcanal, was the code name for the joint Army-Navy plan to recapture that island. Colonel Ichiki's force—the 900 already on Guadalcanal and the remaining 1500 still steaming down The Slot—represented the Army's contribution. It was to be supported by much the greater part of Yamamoto's Combined Fleet.

Since August 7, the admiral had been gathering ships from all over Greater East Asia. Within about a dozen days—or at least by the time Captain Brush's Marines had met and destroyed the Ichiki patrol—there were three aircraft carriers gathered around Truk,* supported by three battleships, five cruisers, eight destroyers, one seaplane carrier, and numerous auxiliary ships. To this could be added Admiral Tsukahara's Rabaul force composed of one hundred planes of the Eleventh Air Fleet and four cruisers and five destroyers of Admiral Mikawa's Eighth Fleet.

Combined Fleet's carrier aircraft were to clear Solomons waters of all American surface ships.

Eleventh Air Fleet's planes were to hammer Marine positions on Guadalcanal by day.

Mikawa's ships—the Tokyo Express—were to batter the Marines by night.

All of this was in support of 2400 troops: it was a whale backing up a weasel. But it was typically Japanese, and it reflected, once again, the Army's unshakable conviction that there could not be more than a few thousand Americans on Guadalcanal, and the Navy's fixed determination to lure out and destroy the American fleet.

Moreover, General Hyakutake had given Colonel Ichiki orders

* Truk was Japan's naval bastion of the Pacific. It lay about seven hundred miles north of Rabaul.

which permitted him to attack immediately, without waiting for *anyone* to move, if he saw fit. And Ichiki, on August 19, had already decided to attack. The weasel would strike without waiting for the whale.

To the south of Guadalcanal a flying whale was fighting a flying elephant.

A huge four-engined Kawanishi flying boat homeward bound for the Shortlands after scouting American waters had blundered into a Flying Fortress returning to Espiritu Santo after scouting Japanese waters.

Captain Walter Lucas brought his more-maneuverable Fort up under the Kawanishi's belly. The American's guns began stuttering. The Japanese began to weave from side to side to bring the American within range of his 20-mm tail cannon. Captain Lucas whipped his big plane broadside to the lumbering Kawanishi's tail. Sergeant Vernon Nelson in the Fort's waist triggered a killing stream of bullets into the enemy tail gun.

Lucas cut in sharper. The big Kawanishi weaved away. Now on this side, now on that side, these great groaning mastodons of the sky fought each other. They turned and twisted for twenty-five minutes, until, at last, the Kawanishi broke off to flee and the Fort bored in to kill.

Nelson and Sergeant Chester Malizeski shot out three of the Kawanishi's engines, and the whale went down for a water landing near an island. Lucas pursued. He brought his winged elephant in low over the taxiing whale, and Sergeant Edward Spetch, another gunner who had so far failed to fire a shot, caught the enemy full in his sights, pressed the trigger and watched him blow up and burn.

It was August 20, a date to remember for men accustomed to the dull routine of aerial reconnaissance.

American reconnaissance—plus reports from Australian coastwatchers—had warned Admiral Ghormley of the impending Ka Operation. Ghormley ordered Vice-Admiral Frank Jack Fletcher to protect the Solomon sea lanes with the three-carrier force he had withdrawn from Guadalcanal. A fourth carrier, *Hornet*, with her supporting cruisers and destroyers, left Hawaii to join them. Meanwhile, new battleships *Washington* and *South Dakota*, together with the antiaircraft cruiser *Juneau* and escorting destroyers, were ordered from the East Coast through the Panama Canal.

Admiral King was preparing for a showdown battle at Guadalcanal. He was deliberately pushing in the blue chips. Like all of the other high commanders, King was aware that in mid-August of 1942 the entire war had come to crisis. Everywhere—in Russia, in North Africa, in the North Atlantic, in the Pacific—the enemy was on the verge of triumphant breakthrough. Stalin was clamoring for more supplies, so was Britain's General Montgomery in Eygpt, the BOLERO build-up was still going forward, and Churchill and Roosevelt had agreed to massive Allied landings in North Africa. What claim could Guadalcanal advance among such lofty preferences and priorities? Alone among the high commanders, Admiral Ernest King considered Guadalcanal paramount and urgent.

On Guadalcanal the Marines holding the Tenaru line had also sensed that a critical time had come. From the first light of August 20, the Second Battalion, First, under Lieutenant Colonel Al Pollock had been busy fortifying the west bank of the river.

Actually, the Tenaru* was not a river but a backwater. It flowed sluggishly north to the sea, but was barred from entering it by a broad sandspit. The sandspit was like a bridge across the river and was thus the focal weak point. Here Pollock concentrated most of his machine guns and rifles and a 37-mm antitank gun dug in behind a single strand of barbed wire strung across the sandspit. Pollock also had 81-mm mortars, of course, and the guns of the Eleventh Marines behind them.

Next, Pollock decided to extend his right flank. He ordered a group of riflemen to take up positions south along the river, and he pulled machine guns off the beach to support them.

Among the riflemen was Phil Chaffee and among the gunners were Lucky and Lew Juergens and their comrades Bud Conley and Bill Smith. Grumbling, they broke down their guns. Juergens spread-eagled that heavy iron instrument of torture known as the tripod across his back and Lucky hefted the gun on his shoulder. The others grasped the water cans and ammunition boxes and moved out.

---

* Months later it was found that the "Tenaru" was actually the Ilu.

Vouza was not dead. He awoke in darkness. His chest was sticky with blood. He could feel the cut beside his tongue where the enemy steel had entered. Yet, he was alive. He must warn the Americans. He began biting the ropes that bound him. He felt himself weakening from pain and loss of blood. He chewed on. Finally, the ropes parted. Vouza slumped to the ground and began crawling west.

It was dark along the Tenaru. Only the faint light of stars glinted on the river's black surface.

In the center of the line Al Schmid lay on his blanket with mosquitoes droning in his ears and his leg throbbing with pain. He wondered if he would have to leave his buddies. One of them had promised to "cook it" out of him, saying: "When we get up I'll get some salt water and heat it up in the pot, and you put your foot in there when it's boiling hot. That'll draw the goddam lump down."[3] Now, Schmid felt waves of heat pass through his body. Then he felt cold and began to shiver. Did he have malaria, too?

Farther to the right Lucky and Juergens sat on sentry duty outside the unfinished gunpit—a gaping black square in the dark night—peering at the river between them and the coconut grove. From far to their left came the gentle murmur of the sea. Suddenly a strange rippling V appeared to their right moving downstream. Two greenish orbs were at its center. It was a crocodile, and a Marine on their right whooped and fired at it. It dove and disappeared.

"Goddam, Lew," Lucky whispered, glancing uneasily at the coconuts, "I could stand a cigarette."

"They'd spot it, Lucky. Anyway, those Jap butts taste like they're half tobacco and half horseshit."

"You ask me, Lew, they're a hundred per cent horseshit."[4]

Suddenly there were lights swinging and bumping across the river. The two Marines were astounded.

"Who goes there?" Juergens bellowed.

The lights bumped on.

"Who goes there? Answer, or I'll let you have it!"[5]

The lights went out.

Now all of the men on the right flank were excited and awake. They crowded about the gunpit, speculating, searching the darkness with straining eyes.

Sometimes Vouza was able to walk and make better time. He lurched along the trail, yet sure of every step; for Vouza had been born on Guadalcanal and knew the trails as they can only be known by a man who has spent his boyhood on them. At other times, though, Vouza was so weak he had to crawl. When this happened he wanted to weep. He was sure that he was dying and he wanted to live only long enough to warn the Americans of the impending attack.

Just before midnight, perhaps a half mile from the Tenaru, Vouza blundered into Marine outposts.

"Me Vouza," he called. "Me Sergeant Major Vouza."

Warily, they let him approach. He began to blurt out his tale, and they carried him to Colonel Pollock's command post.

By the time Vouza reached Pollock, the battalion's outposts had detected enemy to their front. They exchanged rifle fire. Pollock gave them permission to withdraw and turned to deal with the bleeding, gasping native who had come to warn him.

"How many Japs?" Pollock asked sharply.

"Maybe two hundred-fifty, maybe five hundred," Vouza gasped.[6]

Round numbers were enough for Pollock, and he wheeled to call Regiment to send down Martin Clemens, for whom the dying man kept calling, and at that moment a flare rose from the river bank and the Ichiki charge began.

Colonel Ichiki had gathered his nine hundred men in the woods east of the sandspit. He was going to hurl about five hundred of them across the sandspit. After they had broken through, he would pour more of his men through the gap. At some time around half-past one in the morning of August 21,[7] the Ichiki shock troops began gathering in the shallows. Their mortars fell on Marine lines. Nambu light machine guns spoke with a snapping sound. Heavier automatics chugged. And then, silhouetted against the sea by the eerie swaying light of a flare, the Ichikis charged.

They came sprinting and howling and firing their rifles, and the Marines were ready for them. Like a train of powder, the American lines flashed alight. Machine guns spat long lines of curving tracers. Grenades exploded in orange balls. Rifles cracked and their muzzles winked white like fireflies. Mortar shells plopped smoothly from their tubes, rising silent and unseen until they had climbed the night sky and fallen among the enemy with flashing yellow crashes that shook the earth. Everywhere were tongues and streaks and sparks, orange and white, red and yellow, and the night was herself a slashed and crisscrossed thing. Everywhere also was the counterpointing of the guns, the wail of battle, the mad orchestration of death—and running through it all like a dreadful fugue came the regular *wham!* of the antitank gun spewing out its mouthfuls of death.

In the center Al Schmid had rolled out of his sleep and come crawling into the gunpit. Johnny Rivers was already at the trigger, his helmet on. Corporal Lee Diamond burst inside. He began pushing sandbags away from the gun so that they could fire it into the water if the enemy tried to swim. Rivers saw a dark, bobbing mass on the opposite shore. It looked like cows coming down to the river to drink. "Fire!" Diamond yelled, and Rivers' gun began to stutter and shake. With screams and movement, the crowd broke up.

To the right Lucky and Juergens had seized their unemplaced gun and were triggering short bursts at the sound of movement in the coconuts. They moved the gun up and down the river bank to give the impression of massed weapons, to confuse the enemy whose tracers came gliding out of the black toward them.

Down at the sandspit the barrel of the antitank gun glowed red in the dark. It cut swathes in the ranks of the enemy still pouring to the attack; squad after squad, platoon after platoon, running low with outthrust bayonets, gurgling *"Banzai! Banzai!"* But the short squat shapes were falling. Singly, in pairs, sometimes in whole squad groups, the antitank's canister sickled them to the sand. Banzais changed to shrill screams of pain or the hoarser trailing cries of death. Now a grenade sailed into the antitank position. It exploded in a flashing roar. The gun fell silent. But a squad of riflemen leaped into the pit and the gun glowed red again.

Now the Ichiki charge was mounting in its fury. It flowed up against the barbed wire and seemed to be dammed up there. Baffled, jabbering, the Japanese milled around—and Marine fire struck them down and stacked their bodies high. But some of the Japanese got through. They closed with Marines in their pits. Three of them made for the hole held by Corporal Dean Wilson. Wilson brought his BAR around. It jammed. "Marine you die!" a Japanese soldier screamed, hurtling toward Wilson with lunging bayonet. Wilson seized his machete and swung it. The Japanese sank to the ground with his intestines squirting through his fingers. Wilson swung his thick-bladed knife twice more, and disemboweled two more enemy.

A Japanese jumped into Corporal Johnny Shea's hole. He drove his bayonet twice into Shea's leg. He lifted it to slash upward through the groin, and Shea kicked and jammed the Japanese against the foxhole, struggling to free his jammed tommy gun. The bolt sprang home and Shea shot the man to death.

The bolt on Johnny Rivers' machine gun raced madly back and forth. Johnny had unclamped the gun and was firing freely. But the enemy was fighting back. They had spotted the American position. They poured bullets into it. Sand and log chips flew about the pit. Rivers hunched forward, searching for the enemy gun. There was a little grin on his face, the same expression Schmid had seen there when Johnny got hit in the ring.

A burst of bullets tore into Johnny Rivers' face. Blood spurted from the holes and he fell backward dead.

Al Schmid jumped into his place. He fought on, dueling the Japanese gun located in an abandoned Marine amtrack a hundred yards upriver. Corporal Diamond was shot in the arm, but he stayed alongside Schmid. Eventually, they silenced the enemy. And then a grenade sailed sputtering into the pit to fill it with roaring light. Al Schmid was thrown flat on his back. He could not see. He put his hand to his face and felt blood and pulp. He was blind. He felt for his pistol and waited for the enemy rush. If he could not see, he could still smell. At the first whiff, he would . . .

But the Ichiki charge had been annihilated. Only a few dazed bands of the five hundred men who began it had survived; they dragged themselves east across the torn and lifeless bodies of their comrades, crawling over sand that was thick and clotted with blood.

At about five o'clock in the morning, Colonel Ichiki struck again.

This time he tried to get around the sandspit. His mortars and some light cannon pounded Marine positions while a reinforced company waded out beyond the breakers. Then they moved west, wheeled to face the beach, and came charging through the surf with bared bayonets. And the second carnage was more bloody than the first.

Running erect and with no attempt to get below the American fire, the Japanese soldiers were cut down by Marine machine guns firing from the west. Artillery strikes came whistling and crashing down upon them. Balked by the wire, struck from the side by bullets and from the sky by shells, the Japanese perished almost to a man—falling one upon another until they lay three deep in death for the tide to bury them in the morning.

With daylight, a crackling rifle fire began along the line. The Marines lay on their bellies to pick off the remaining Ichikis flitting among the coconuts. Colonel Pollock came down to the river to stride among his marksmen, shouting: "Line 'em up and squeeze 'em off!" Seeing a man being treated for a wound in the groin, Pollock grinned and called: "I hope the family jewels are safe."[8]

All along the line automatic rifles and machine guns were pouring bullets into the grove where Colonel Ichiki and his wretched remnant lay. Sometimes enemy soldiers jumped into the water to swim away, as though they preferred death by drowning to being stung by the swarms of invisible bees buzzing among the coconuts. Their heads bobbed on the surface like corks, and the Marines shot them through the head.

Far to the right four terrified Japanese came sprinting along the Tenaru's east bank, and Lucky jumped on the unemplaced machine gun to cut down three of them with a swift, swinging burst. Then the machine gun broke down, plowing up earth with bullets. Lucky seized a rifle to shoot the fourth.

"Cease fire!" came a command from farther right. "First Battalion coming through."

Gradually the line fell silent while Marines of Vandegrift's reserve battalion crossed the river and fanned out through the coconuts. Vandegrift had released them to Colonel Cates after

Cates and Thomas agreed that the time had come to swing his right at Ichiki and drive the enemy into the sea. Slowly, like an inexorable broad blade, the right flank swung to the north.

General Vandegrift came to Cates's command post. He listened to reports of the fighting. He swore softly after he heard of how wounded Japanese would lie still until American medical corpsmen came up to examine them, and then blow themselves and their benefactors to bits with hand grenades. The only answer to that, Vandegrift told himself, was war without quarter[9]; and he gave Cates a platoon of light tanks to finish off the treacherous foe.

The tanks completed the slaughter. They clanked across the sandspit after the American battalion had driven Ichiki's remnant into a pocket where Marine artillery and the newly arrived Marine aircraft could shell and strafe them. Like the scything chariots of the Persians, the tanks ground remorsely over dead and wounded alike. They chased Japanese while belching canister and spraying machine-gun bullets. They ran up to enemy positions to take them under muzzle-blasting fire or butted coconut trees to shake down Japanese for riflemen to shoot. Those Japanese whom they could not shoot or flail with canister they ran over, until, with all the literal and gory reality of that battle for Guadalcanal which was now irrevocably without quarter, their rear ends resembled meat grinders.

The first organized Japanese counterthrust at Guadalcanal had ended in disaster. Some 800 of Colonel Ichiki's men lay dead, and there were very few of the survivors who were not wounded; some of whom would also die. Marine casualties were less than a hundred, of whom forty-three were dead. Most important of all, the legend of the Japanese superfighter had been shot into a sieve and would no longer hold water. Emperor Hirohito's "devil-subduing bayonets" had been broken by a foe superior in Japan's own vaunted "spiritual power" as well as in firepower. The soft, effete Americans had shown how savage they could be.

That afternoon, even as Sergeant Major Vouza began his amazing recovery, even as Al Schmid—who would regain part of his sight years later—was taken out to a destroyer, the last of the Japanese were finished off. Souvenir-hunters began swarming among the dead. Phil Chaffee was one of them. He had begun prospecting. Moving warily, he kicked dead mouths open; he flashed his light inside them, his eyes darting about until they came upon what he sought—and then he put in his pliers and yanked. Thus, one of the victors taking one of the grislier trophies.

Far to the east Colonel Kiyono Ichiki tasted his own "fruits of victory." He burned his colors and shot himself through the head.

Chapter 5

WHEN COLONEL ICHIKI and his men sped south in six fast destroyers on August 16 they set in motion Admiral Yamamoto's Operation Ka.

Although Ichiki had failed in his rash decision to destroy the Americans "at one stroke," Ka was continuing as planned. Two slow transports carrying the remaining 1500 Ichikis continued south from Truk, followed by the faster and bigger transport *Kinryu Maru* loaded with a thousand men of the Yokosuka Fifth Naval Landing Force. All were bound for Guadalcanal under command of Rear Admiral Raizo Tanaka.

Tanaka, the veteran destroyer leader who had commanded the Landing Force at Midway, had been placed in command of the Guadalcanal Reinforcement Force and assigned to Eighth Fleet at Rabaul. And "Tanaka the Tenacious," as he would one day be called by his admiring enemies to the south, had not liked his new assignment any more than he had favored the ill-fated expedition against Midway. He considered that landing troops in the face of an armed enemy was the most difficult of military undertakings and he was dumfounded that Imperial General Headquarters was attempting such operations without prior rehearsals or even preliminary study.[1] But his opinion had not been asked, nor would it ever be—a fact which also irked him—and so Tanaka the Tenacious took over as ordered, convinced that Guadalcanal reinforcement would be a failure and certain that Eighth Fleet did not know what it was doing.[2]

At first, he was surprised and gratified to hear that Captain Yasuo Sato's six destroyers had successfully put the Ichiki spearhead ashore at Taivu. Next, he was aggrieved and dismayed to hear of Colonel Ichiki's destruction. Then, he was shaken to learn that American aircraft had landed at Henderson Field, thus making his attempt to put troops ashore more difficult than ever.

Nevertheless, Tanaka the Tenacious plowed on. At least he would have the support of Combined Fleet, which had sortied from Truk shortly after his own departure.

Isoroku Yamamoto had assembled his customary massive armada. He was going to direct it by radio from aboard *Yamato,* cruising in the vicinity of Truk.

There was the Advance Fleet force of battleships led by Vice-Admiral Nobutake Kondo and the Striking Force of three carriers commanded by Chuichi Nagumo. Yamamoto was going to bait the American carriers with light carrier *Ryujo.* While their aircraft were away attacking her, planes from *Shokaku* and *Zuikaku* would make surprise strikes on them. After they were destroyed, Kondo's fleet would batter Guadalcanal. And Kondo had the battering power. Yamamoto, an old battleship man much as he might emphasize air power, had seen to that. Big *Mutsu* and the bombardment sluggers *Hiei* and *Kirishima,* backed up by six heavy cruisers, would wreck Henderson Field and mangle the Marines so that the troops aboard Mikawa's transports would only have to mop up.

Moreover, there was added insurance: about a dozen submarines had been sown in waters southeast of Guadalcanal. They lay athwart the American supply line. One day, American sailors would give those waters the descriptive name of Torpedo Junction.

By August 20, Yamamoto knew that Admiral Fletcher's carriers were at sea. Two days later he had placed Combined Fleet in position to attack about two hundred miles north of the southern Solomons. Fletcher's three carriers—*Saratoga, Wasp,* and *Enterprise*—were about three hundred miles to their southeast. The Americans were operating as independent groups for fear of Torpedo Junction's numerous torpedoes.

By the same date Fletcher also knew that the enemy was at sea. One of Slew McCain's long-ranging Catalinas had detected Tanaka's transports. Tanaka had himself realized that he had been observed. From flagship *Jintsu,* a light cruiser, he reported to Rabaul. Admiral Mikawa at once ordered him to turn about and make north. Tanaka obeyed. And then he received a message from Admiral Tsukahara commanding Southeast Area Force, and therefore superior to Mikawa, instructing him to proceed as ordered.

Furious, Tanaka was now positive that Rabaul did not know what it was doing. But he did not turn about as Tsukahara had ordered, for it would be impossible to reach Guadalcanal the morning of August 24 as scheduled. And that was indeed fortunate for Tanaka.

By August 22 General Vandegrift was also aware of Tanaka's approach. He felt chilled at the prospect of large-scale enemy reinforcement. As yet, he had no way of knowing that the First Marines had all but destroyed the enemy to the east. Vandegrift debated risking his new Cactus Air Force, so-called after the code name for Guadalcanal. He decided that he must, and sent Mangrum's bombers and Smith's fighters roaring aloft. He watched them go from the top of the Japanese pagoda-like structure which had become Cactus Air Force's headquarters.

The Marine planes ran into a solid front of weather. Driving rain misted their windshields. Visibility fell close to zero, and they had to turn back. Vandegrift watched them come in. He was pacing the Pagoda's muddy floor when Mangrum entered to make his negative report. Vandegrift thanked his pilots courteously, but Mangrum thought that the general was deeply distressed.[3]

Next day, in clearing weather, the Marine fliers again went on the hunt; but Tanaka had turned north as ordered and they missed him.

Vandegrift's distress deepened.

Martin Clemens was very much distressed. He was worried about Mr. Ishimoto. His capture and torture of Vouza made it clear that as long as Ishimoto was alive, Clemens's scouts were in mortal danger. They could not feign neutrality and mingle with the enemy with Ishimoto about.

After the battle of the Tenaru, Clemens had had his men comb the battlefield for Ishimoto's body. They did not find it.

Then Gumu, a scout who had become separated from the Brush patrol, came into the perimeter reporting he had been caught by Ishimoto. Gumu had been sitting beside a track with ten stones to count the Ichikis as they passed. He made a movement and was discovered by Ishimoto and four soldiers. They had Father Oude-Engberink, Father Duhamel and Sister Sylvia and old Sister Edmée of France and Sister Odilia of Italy with them. The missionaries were under guard, having been brought from their mission at Ruavutu.

Gumu said Ishimoto had tried to make the fathers go back to the Americans and tell them that the Japanese were too powerful and that they should surrender. They refused, and they and the sisters were taken east.

Ishimoto also tried to make Gumu carry his pack. When Gumu said he was sick and could not lift it, Ishimoto hit him across the mouth. Gumu continued to feign illness and was at last released. Coming west, he met another native who told him he was the lone survivor of five natives who had carried a wounded Marine back to American lines. Ishimoto and his soldiers had bayoneted the other four to death.

According to Gumu there were quite a few parties of Japanese wandering about in the east. But no new force had landed. For this news, at least, Clemens was thankful; and he passed it along to Marine intelligence.

Haruyoshi Hyakutake was puzzled, as well as distressed.

General Hyakutake had heard from signal men whom Colonel Ichiki had left behind at Taivu and their report was astounding. Annihilation? It had never happened before. Moreover, in a military given to writing reports wearing rose-colored glasses, there was absolutely not a single euphemism available to describe it. Hyakutake at last notified Imperial General Headquarters: "The attack of the Ichiki Detachment was not entirely successful." Then he ordered Major General Kiyotake Kawaguchi and his brigade of five thousand Borneo veterans to stand by for movement to Guadalcanal.

Admiral Raizo Tanaka had resumed course for Guadalcanal. Shortly after noon of August 24 his lookouts sighted heavy cruiser *Tone* speeding southward on the eastern horizon, followed by *Ryujo* flanked by destroyers *Amatsukaze* and *Tokitsukaze*. Tanaka was encouraged. These ships were his indirect escort to Guadalcanal. Even though *Ryujo* was to decoy the Americans, she could still fly off aircraft to bomb Guadalcanal.

Commander Tameichi Hara stood on the bridge of *Amatsukaze* steaming at twenty-six knots off *Ryujo's* starboard beam. He looked at the 10,000-ton decoy and wondered how her green pilots—replacements for the veterans lost at Midway and latterly over Guadalcanal—would stand up to *Ryujo's* first battle test.

Grimly recalling how his and Admiral Tanaka's fears had been realized at Midway, Hara kept glancing apprehensively upward. He looked at *Ryujo* steaming serenely along and wondered if her skipper was not taking her decoy role too fatalistically. She had no aircraft ready to fight. True, *Ryujo* had flown off fifteen fighters and six bombers to attack Guadalcanal. Nevertheless, Hara knew that she still had nine more fighters below decks and he wondered why some of them were not at least armed and ready.

Even after American scouts sighted them, *Ryujo* acted like a mesmerized ship, sending two fighters up only after *Amatsukaze* and the others had begun blasting with antiaircraft guns. Hara lost his temper. He dashed off a message for an Eta Jima classmate aboard *Ryujo*.

"Fully realizing my impertinence, am forced to advise you of my impression. Your flight operations are far short of expectations. What is the matter?"[4]

It was a rude message—incredible for a Japanese—and the *Ryujo* force was dumfounded by it.

Yet, Hara's classmate sent the reply: "Deeply appreciate your admonition. We shall do better and count on your co-operation."[5]

Seven more Zeroes quickly appeared on *Ryujo's* decks. Their propellers were just beginning to spin when *Amatsukaze's* lookouts shouted: "Many enemy planes approaching."

They were from *Saratoga*. Thirty Dauntlesses and eight Avengers under Commander Harry Felt. The dive-bombers flew at fourteen thousand feet above broken and fleecy cloud cover, but the torpedo planes circled at a lower level waiting to strike when all enemy guns were turned toward the Dauntlesses.

Now the dive-bombers came sliding down a staircase of clouds.

They came out of a bright sun that blinded enemy gunners and polished the white caps ruffling a dark blue sea; thirty pilots diving one after another through tracers reaching up like yellow straws, thirty pairs of hands and feet working sticks and rudder-bars to steady aircraft bucking beneath the onslaught of heavier flak; and thirty rear-gunners sitting tensely to watch the narrow tan deck of *Ryujo* growing larger and larger. Five thousand feet, and the pilots bent to their bombsight tubes to center that deck in the crosshairs. Two thousand feet and they seized release handles. Thirty thousand-pounders falling on wildly weaving *Ryujo*, thirty great eggs describing their yawning parabola in full view of morbidly fascinated Japanese seamen; and then the pilots were drawing back hard on sticks, pulling out fast and flat and away while tracers seemed to wrap them in confetti and their own gunners cursed with fierce joy and raked the enemy decks with bullets.

Then the Avengers came skimming in off *Ryujo's* bows, launching an anvil attack from either side so that no matter which way the enemy carrier turned to evade she would still be exposed to warheads.

Ryujo never had a chance.

Scarlet flames shot up from her. Explosions staggered and punctured her. Smoke billowed upward in huge balls that thinned as they rose into the air like pillars. As many as ten bombs had pierced her decks and at least one torpedo flashed into her side. She was an iron red sieve and Commander Hara watched in agony as she rolled over to expose her red-leaded belly. There was a hole in that, too. Then Hara's ship and the others were rushing to her side to take off survivors. Three of her Zeros appeared, returning from the Guadalcanal strike. They circled wistfully overhead before ditching alongside the destroyers. The pilots were rescued. *Ryujo* would sink shortly after dusk with a hundred Japanese still aboard her.

To the west, Rear Admiral Mikawa saw the smoke columns rising from the dying carrier, and he turned to look fearfully in the direction of Henderson Field.

Ryujo's fighters and bombers had joined with about a half-dozen Betty bombers from Rabaul to raid Henderson earlier that afternoon. All of Captain Smith's available Wildcats had been waiting for them. They shot down sixteen enemy planes. Captain Marion Carl flamed two bombers and a Zero, and Lieutenants Zennith Pond and Kenneth Frazier and Marine Gunner Henry Hamilton shot down a pair apiece. Four Wildcats were lost, but only three pilots.

It was far from being the most famous aerial battle in Solomons history, but it marked the beginning of the end for Japanese air power.

When Admiral Nagumo heard of the attack on *Ryujo* he thought that the time to avenge Midway was at hand. He still believed that Fletcher had three big carriers in the vicinity, unaware that *Wasp* had been sent south to refuel. The flattops which a float plane had reported sighting after two o'clock were *Enterprise* and *Saratoga*.

Certain that Fletcher had flown off all his planes against sacrificial *Ryujo*, Nagumo ordered *Zuikaku* and *Shokaku* to send every eagle they could fly screaming against the Americans.

They missed *Saratoga* entirely, but they caught *Enterprise* at about half-past four—and they also caught a tiger by the tail.

Fletcher had not forgotten *Lexington* or *Yorktown*, and he had not flown off all of his planes. He had fifty-three Wildcats stacked in the skies, waiting. They tangled with the Japanese planes— dive-bombing Vals and single-engine torpedo-launching Kates heavily protected by layers of Zeros—and a wild scrimmage raged overhead. Even returning American dive-bombers and torpedoplanes roared into the battle.

But most of this action raged at the edge of a perimeter far outside the range of *Enterprise's* guns; far, far beyond the sight of lookouts squinting into the bright tropic afternoon. The *Big E*, yet to be scratched in the Pacific War, still sailed along at twenty-seven knots with all her planes up and all her Marines and sailors at battle stations. A few minutes after five o'clock a 20-mm gunpointer caught the flash of sun-on-a-wing. It was a Val turning over, the first of thirty.

Enterprise's guns opened up. Behind her, mighty *North Carolina* belched out an umbrella of steel and smoke over the imperiled flattop. But the Vals kept coming down. Every seven seconds one of them peeled off and dove. They attacked with all the skill that Felt's dive-bombers had shown over *Ryujo*. Even though square-winged Wildcats slashed and growled at them coming down, risking friendly aircraft fire, the Japanese pilots never faltered.

Soon *Big E's* gunners could see the landing-gear "pants" of the leading Val, could make out the horrible dark blob of an egg nestling between them, and could see, with indrawn breath, that blob detach, yawn, and fall.

There was a monstrous shuddering slap against *Enterprise's* side. The first bomb had near-missed.

Big E twisted and turned. Her own gunners and *North Carolina's* spat networks of steel across the sky, but at 5:14 the big carrier took her first bomb-hit of the war. A thousand-pounder crashed through the after elevator. It penetrated to the third deck before its delayed-action fuse exploded it with a whip-sawing roar that flung every man aboard up-down-and-sideways. Thirty-five sailors were killed. Huge holes were torn in the deck and side-plates were ruptured. Thirty seconds later, the second bomb hit —only fifteen feet from the first.

Again a violent whipping motion, again death—thirty-nine sailors—but this time smoke and fire. Stores of five-inch powder bags had been hit.

Listing and pouring out smoke, the *Big E* still raced along at twenty-seven knots—and then she took a third bomb.

Fortunately, it was only a 500-pounder, and its fuse was defective. Damage was comparatively slight. *Enterprise* was still moving ahead, and all that Captain Arthur Davis and his men need do now was to save their burning ship.

From Lieutenant Commander Herschel Smith in Central Station came the orders. Surrounded by deck plans and diagrams of every system—fresh and salt water, oil and gasoline, ventilation, steam, electricity—and flanked by a battery of telephone-talkers, Smith relayed his instructions to teams of fire-fighters, repairmen, and rescuers.

Men with hoses played streams of water on burning bedding or clothing, men with foam generators smothered burning oil, men with CO_2 extinguishers put out electrical fires; and men in asbestos suits and breathing-masks shambled into burning compartments to rescue wounded or burned sailors, bringing them to other men in gauze masks and white coats who sewed flesh or straightened bones or sprayed charred skin with unguents. Other men with axes trimmed shattered timbers around deck holes, hammering square sheets of boiler plate over them. Debris parties cleared the decks of bomb fragments or replaced torn planking. Weakened and dangerous areas were marked off. Gradually, *Big E* was prepared to receive planes topside. Below decks, officers and bluejackets strove to get her on an even keel again. Three portside ballast tanks were flooded while those to starboard were pumped out. Flooded storerooms had to be pumped dry. Carpenters began repairing two big holes in *Enterprise's* side, above and below the water line. Working up to their armpits in water, using emergency lighting, they built a cofferdam of two-by-six planking placed vertically a foot from the side of the ship. They covered the holes from the inside with heavy wire meshing. Between the meshing and the cofferdam they packed mattresses and pillows. Then they wedged the cofferdam tight against the packing and began pumping.

An hour after the last bomb struck, *Enterprise* turned into the wind at 24 knots to receive aircraft.

Less than an hour later, the helmsman reported, "Lost steering control, sir," and a few minutes later the rudder had jammed and *Enterprise* was turning, turning helplessly to starboard.

Captain Davis slowed to ten knots. He broke out the "Breakdown" flag. He ordered the rudder fixed. And *Enterprise* circled like a defenseless whale while *North Carolina* and cruiser *Portland* stood close by and the group's destroyers raced around and round them, sniffing for submarines. Below, Chief Machinist Mate William Smith buckled on a rescue-breather-vest and put on his breathing-mask. He filled his pockets with the tools that he thought he would need and stepped into the rubble-strewn oven that was the elevator machinery room. At the other end, behind a dogged-down hatch, was the steering engine room . . .

Above, *Enterprise's* big air-search antenna swung—and stopped. "Large bogey. Two seven zero, fifty miles." It was Nagumo's second strike. Thirty Vals from *Zui* and *Sho*. And *Enterprise* still turned . . .

Below, the heat had sent Smith sagging to the deck. He was dragged back. He recovered and returned, accompanied by Machinist Cecil Robinson. They stumbled through the debris to the hatch. They got their hands on the dogs, and passed out . . .

Above decks the seas and the skies were darkening. Anxious gunners tilted their chins into the gathering gloom. The big bedspring antenna swept the skies . . .

Smith and Robinson had been rescued. They had revived and had stumbled to the hatch again. They swung it open. Smith darted inside. He saw that the mechanism had not completed its shift to port. He completed it. The rudder moved again.

Above, the helmsman reported: "Steering control regained, sir." *Enterprise* straightened and sailed south.

Nagumo's eagles had missed her. They had flown past fifty miles away, going southeast. *Enterprise* recovered the last of her planes. One flight of eleven Dauntlesses led by Lieutenant Turner Caldwell was too far away to return. They flew on to Guadalcanal, landing after dark by light of crude flares. They were warmly welcomed, and they would prolong their "visit" for almost a month.

And now all of Fletcher's ships were retiring. Admiral Kondo's battleships and cruisers came tearing after them. In a night action, they could blow the lightly armed flattops to bits, they could overwhelm *North Carolina* and her cruisers.

But Fletcher's caution this time had thwarted the enemy. Kondo could not catch up. The Battle of the Eastern Solomons had ended indecisively. Nevertheless, *Ryujo* was forever lost and *Enterprise,* though knocked out of action for two months, would come back to fight for Guadalcanal again, and again.

Admiral Tanaka's convoy of troops had withdrawn to the northeast again while Admiral Nagumo's pilots struck at *Enterprise.* Then, hearing reports that two enemy carriers had been left burning and probably sinking, Admiral Mikawa in Rabaul ordered Tanaka to turn south again.

With a sinking heart, Tanaka obeyed.

Night of the twenty-fourth came and his ships plowed on.

Below him, off Guadalcanal, five destroyers of his command bombarded the Americans. Then they sped north to join Tanaka. They were aged *Mutsuki* and *Yayoi,* and the newer *Kagero, Kawakaze,* and *Isokaze.* They joined up early in the morning of August 25 at a point 150 miles north of Henderson Field. Tanaka was delighted to have them. He drew up his signal order for their movements and formations, and just as it was being wigwagged the enemy Dauntlesses broke through the clouds.

The dive-bombers were Mangrum's Marines and Caldwell's "visitors" from *Enterprise.* They had caught the Japanese unawares, not even able to ready their guns to return fire.

Lieutenant Larry Baldinus planted his bomb forward of Tanaka's flagship *Jintsu*. Near-misses staggered the big cruiser and showered her with tons of geysering water. Another bomb struck the forecastle. Men fell and steel fragments flew. Tanaka was knocked out. He recovered consciousness in clouds of choking smoke. As the smoke cleared, he saw a Dauntless flown by Ensign Christian Fink swoop down and set *Kinryu Maru* afire with a well-placed thousand-pounder. Admiral Tanaka ordered *Jintsu* to limp back to Truk for repairs, and began transferring to *Kagero*. He instructed *Mutsuki* and *Yayoi* to take off *Kinryu Maru's* troops. Then he took *Kagero* and the other destroyers speeding north out of airplane range.

But the Dauntlesses had radioed Tanaka's location and their message brought eight Flying Fortresses over *Kinryu* and her ministering destroyers. In a shower of deadly eggs *Kinryu* was finished off and *Mutsuki,* lying motionless in the water, was sunk almost instantaneously.

Commander Kiyono Hatano of *Mutsuki* was one of the survivors fished from the water by men of *Yayoi*. To him had fallen the ignominious honor of skippering the first Japanese ship to be sunk by horizontal bombers, and he took it with resignation, saying: "Even the B-17s can make a hit once in a while."[6]

Then *Yayoi* put about and sailed north.

More ships and more soldiers had been lost to the Emperor. Of the troops who were finally put ashore in the Shortlands, many were wounded or burned and none had their weapons.

Ka had failed and American toes still clung to Solomons soil.

Chapter 6

TRUK was quiet.

Major General Kiyotake Kawaguchi and most of his brigade had sailed south in the big transports *Sado-maru* and *Asakayama-maru,* and the Nagumo and Kondo fleets had refueled and set out for waters northeast of Bougainville, where they would cruise on call while the carrier aircraft joined the onslaught on Henderson Field.

Weary sailors of the few warships still anchored inside Truk Lagoon took advantage of the respite. They swam or merely loafed aboard ship, watching the blue ocean boil white over the fringing reef. Others fished. The lagoon abounded in fish of all varieties and the men had their fill of *sashimi,* thin strips of raw fish which Japanese consider a delicacy.

Aboard destroyer *Amatsukaze* one day the men caught a falcon which had fluttered down and perched on the mast. They put it in a crude cage. Then someone caught a rat. The rat was placed inside the cage with the falcon and *Amatsukaze's* crew gathered around to watch. Hearing their voices, Commander Tameichi Hara came out on deck to investigate.

The falcon sat calmly on its perch. Its eyes were closed. The rat raced around in terror. Suddenly, the falcon blinked and swooped on the rat. It put out one of the rat's eyes, and the sailors cheered. Now the rat scurried around the cage with the falcon whirring after it. One turn, and the falcon put out the rat's other eye. The men roared their approval, and Commander Hara returned to his cabin with tightened lips.

Hara was not dismayed by the cruelty of his men. It just seemed to him that the falcon was an American dive-bomber and the rat was a Japanese destroyer.[1] And "Rat," as Commander Hara knew, was the code word for the new plan of reinforcing Guadalcanal.

Admiral Tsukahara commanding Southeast Area Force had decided that Japanese strength was to be built up steadily on Guadalcanal by stealthy night landings from destroyers. He directed Admiral Tanaka, still steaming up The Slot, to carry out the first Rat Operation the night of August 27.

Tanaka quickly instructed his Shortland headquarters to place about 400 men and supplies for three times that many aboard three destroyers. They were to leave the Shortlands, which was still out of range of Henderson Field, at five in the morning and arrive at Taivu on Guadalcanal at nine that night. Two hours after they had departed, Tanaka, then safely home, received an Eighth Fleet order postponing the landing until the next night. Tanaka quickly replied that the ships had already left, but Eighth Fleet countered: "Recall destroyers at once."

Tanaka obeyed. But his patience was wearing thin. For the third time since he had assumed command of Guadalcanal Reinforcement Force he had received conflicting orders from Tsukahara and Mikawa. Again Tanaka rued the haphazard character of the Guadalcanal operation. If such confusion continues, he thought, how can we possibly win a battle?[2] Probably, Tanaka would have been horrified if he had known the extent of that confusion.

At Rabaul, Tsukahara and Mikawa operated from separate and apparently rival headquarters. Each interpreted intelligence reports as he saw fit and each drew up his own plans.[3] The result was confusion for Tanaka the Tenacious, who had to struggle to keep his bow into those contrary winds.

So the three destroyers were recalled, refueled and set to marking time in the harbor pending departure at the same time next morning.

That night, cruisers *Aoba* and *Furutaka* slid into Shortland Harbor with Tanaka's old friend Aritomo Goto. Both admirals expressed their fears over Rabaul's slipshod management. Then Tanaka learned that four other destroyers being assigned to him were headed for Guadalcanal from Borneo loaded with an advance echelon of the Kawaguchi Brigade. They also were to land at Taivu on the night of August 28.

So Tanaka ordered Captain Yonosuki Murakami to take his three refueled destroyers, plus one more, and join up with the Kawaguchi group then at sea. But the Kawaguchi destroyers radioed that a fuel shortage prevented their stopping in the Shortlands; they would go on to Guadalcanal.

They did go on, sailing on a Rabaul schedule that put them within daylight range of Henderson Field. Colonel Mangrum's Dauntlesses went boiling aloft and caught them squarely in The Slot. *Asagiri* with Captain Yuzo Arita aboard took one 500-pounder in her innards and blew up. *Shirakumo* was left dead in the water and *Yugiri* was staggered and sent limping home.

Tanaka was consumed with rage upon hearing the report. Once again ships and men had been lost because Rabaul would not or could not understand that landings in the face of enemy air power were suicidal. A midnight conference was called to discuss the disaster, and then, Captain Murakami radioed that he was turning back to the Shortlands. Tanaka was speechless. Much as he wanted to, he could not order Murakami to take his troop-laden destroyers to Guadalcanal as ordered, because now they could not make it before dawn and would be easy prey to American planes.

Admiral Tanaka contented himself with tongue-lashing Captain Murakami in the morning. Then Tanaka, in turn, took a blistering reprimand from Tsukahara and Mikawa. He passed it along with interest to Murakami and sent him hotly south.

After breakfast that morning *Sado-maru* and *Asakayama-maru* sailed into Shortland Harbor with Major General Kawaguchi and his main body. Kawaguchi, a fine figure of a man with his guardsman's mustache and his neatly-pressed khakis, came aboard Tanaka's new flagship, the heavy cruiser *Kinugasa*. Kawaguchi said he was anxious to get the bulk of his brigade to Guadalcanal as quickly as possible. Tanaka said he would have his wish. When properly planned, Rat runs were swift and safe. American air might be a daylight danger but at night Guadalcanal and The Slot were Japanese. Moreover, air cover could now be supplied. The new airfield at Buka on northern Bougainville was operational and had received 29 Zeros on August 28.

General Kawaguchi demurred. With consummate courtesy he explained that he detested destroyer transportation. He preferred barges. He had landed successfully in Borneo after a 500-mile voyage by barge. Destroyers had little space, and it was because of this limitation that Colonel Ichiki had been forced to land with reduced rations and insufficient equipment. Big barges could carry all of Kawaguchi's men and equipment. That equipment, as Kawaguchi did not inform Tanaka, included the general's dress white uniform. He intended to wear it during flag-raising ceremonies at Henderson Field. And that, said General Kawaguchi, was that: barges it would be, just as General Hyakutake had agreed.

No, said Admiral Tanaka, it would be destroyers; just as Admiral Mikawa had ordered. Barges were far too slow and much too risky. With the conference now at stalemate, Tanaka informed Kawaguchi that he was radioing Mikawa for instructions and suggested that Kawaguchi do the same with Hyakutake.

From Rabaul, Tanaka learned nothing except that an American force of two transports, one cruiser and two destroyers, had been reported at Lunga Point. Admiral Mikawa had personally directed Captain Murakami to attack this force after he had unloaded his troops.

Next morning Captain Murakami returned to Shortland to announce that he had unloaded troops safely at Taivu. However, he had *not* attacked the American ships.

"There were moonlight conditions," Murakami explained falteringly. "American planes were up."[4]

Tanaka relieved Murakami on the spot.

That morning *Amagiri* and *Kagero* entered the harbor with the remnant of the Kawaguchi advance echelon which had been bombed August 28. They had *Shirakumo* in tow. Admiral Tanaka quickly put more Kawaguchis aboard undamaged *Kagero* and *Amagiri* and filled up *Yudachi* with another batch. General Kawaguchi protested. Tanaka was compelled to unload *Yudachi* and send her south to Guadalcanal with naval troops. That night he asked Rabaul for instructions and was criticized for not having sent *Amagiri* and *Kagero* down The Slot.

Admiral Tanaka and General Kawaguchi met again on that day, August 30. Kawaguchi still refused destroyer transportation. His staff agreed, especially Colonel Akinosuka Oka. Exasperated, Tanaka readied eight destroyers for departure next morning. Either Kawaguchi would go south on these, or he would stay north. Kawaguchi refused. That night, a message arrived from Eighth Fleet: "Under our agreement with Seventeenth Army, the bulk of the Kawaguchi Detachment will be transported to Guadalcanal by destroyers, the remainder by large landing barges."[5]

It was a typical Japanese denouement, a face-saving agreement that if the time is not six o'clock or seven o'clock, let it be agreed that it is half-past six. In the morning of August 31, General Kawaguchi sped south on one of Tanaka's eight destroyers. They landed safely at Taivu at midnight.

A few days later a thousand men under Colonel Oka proceeded south by barge. Hiding out by day and creeping down The Slot by night, they approached their destination undetected until the last night. Then, delayed by heavy seas, they were caught offshore by Henderson Field's dawn reconnaissance. American aircraft came roaring down on them, spraying bullets into the ranks of soldiers crowded helplessly aboard tossing boats. Four hundred men were lost. The remainder, under the drenched but undismayed Colonel Oka, eventually made the western coast of Guadalcanal.

The direful predictions of Tanaka the Tenacious had been turned into tragic reality. But he was no longer around to foretell fresh disaster. On August 31 he received the reward so often reserved for an accurate prophet of doom: he was relieved of his command.

On that same day Imperial General Headquarters issued an official directive making Port Moresby secondary to the Guadalcanal campaign. General Hyakutake was notified that he must go on the defensive in New Guinea until the Solomons were reconquered. He must utilize all available units of his 17th Army to oust the Americans. Admiral Tsukahara would cooperate with all the airplanes of his Southeast Area Force and all the ships of Admiral Mikawa's Eighth Fleet. The Nagumo and Kondo fleets would continue to cruise northeast of Bougainville and Combined Fleet itself, with Yamamoto aboard *Yamato,* would stand by in a supporting position a bit farther north. More submarines were to be fed into Torpedo Junction.

All of the uncommitted power of Imperial Japan was now pointed like a pistol at Henderson Field.

Chapter 7

IN MARCH of 1942 the Army Air Force's 67th Fighter Squadron arrived at Nouméa, New Caledonia, by ship. They had their planes with them in crates. They took them ashore and uncrated them. To their astonishment they found an unfamiliar plane.

It was the P-400, an export version of the early models of the P-39, and originally built for Britain. None of the mechanics had ever worked on a P-400 before, and there were no instructions for assembly included in the crates. Nevertheless, the mechanics got the ships together and the 67th's pilots learned to fly them.

On August 22 five P-400s led by Captain Dale Brannon and guided by a Flying Fortress flew across 640 miles of open water from Espiritu Santo to Henderson Field. Five days later nine more of them arrived. Cactus Air Force, already composed of the Marines of Smith's and Mangrum's squadrons and Turner's Naval visitors from *Enterprise,* became a joint command.

Unfortunately, the Army fliers had come to the right place with the wrong plane. The P-400 lacked proper supercharger equipment and its oxygen system was of the high-pressure type. Since there were no bottles of high-pressure oxygen available on Guadalcanal, Cactus's new pilots could fly only at low levels, usually ten to twelve thousand feet, well beneath high-flying Japanese bombers and Zeros. Moreover, even if they could have flown high enough, the plane was even less of a match for the Zero than the P-39 Airacobra which pilots such as Saburo Sakai and the others of Lieutenant Sasai's squadron had slaughtered over New Guinea.

Nevertheless, Washington would continue to insist that the Airacobra was just the airplane for the Pacific. General Harmon on Nouméa might write letter after letter to General Arnold in Washington pleading for the new, fast, and long-ranged P-38 or Lightning fighter, but General Arnold would not be moved.

In the meantime, the Airacobra's lame sister—the P-400—was quickly shot from Solomons skies. Within six days only three of the original fourteen were operational. General Vandegrift withdrew them from aerial combat and assigned their pilots to bombing and strafing Japanese outside the Marine perimeter. Here, with its nose cannon and its light and heavy machine guns, with its ability to carry a 500-pound bomb, the P-400 proved itself a scourge of enemy ground forces. So would the Airacobra, and both planes were to become devastating after depth charges were slung under their bellies and dropped into enemy-held ravines. The concussions were dreadful; they literally blew the Japanese out of their shoes. Nevertheless, neither P-400 nor Airacobra was of much use against the aerial onslaught roaring daily south from Buka and Rabaul, and defense of that Henderson Field for which the Japanese were also now pushing in the blue chips became the sole concern of Captain Smith's dwindling band of Marine pilots.

In one week these Marines blasted the legend of the invincible Zero into flaming wreckage. Within a week they were shooting down both bombers and fighters at a rate of six to eight for every one of their own lost. Saburo Sakai's comrades, fighter pilots who had vaunted themselves as all-conquering in the skies, were sent crashing into jungle or plummeting into the sea. Lieutenant Junichi Sasai was the first to die, shot down in a fighter sweep on August 26: the second of the roaring-tiger belt-buckles had come to rest on the floor of Iron Bottom Sound. It was the turn of Ota next, and after him Sakai's wingmen, Yonekawa and Hatori. Of eighty fighter pilots who had followed Commander Nakajima to Rabaul, only Nakajima himself, plus the peerless Nishizawa—who would live to surpass Sakai, but also to die in the Philippines—and six others would survive the deadly firepower of these stubby American fighters. Not all of these Japanese aces fell to the flaming wing guns of Captain Smith's men alone, for more Marine fighter squadrons were to enter the battle; nevertheless, they did perish as a result of battle tactics devised by Henderson's early defenders.

Very early these men realized that the Zero was still able to outclimb, outspeed, and outmaneuver the Wildcat. Just because of this superiority the Japanese pilot was still fond of individual combat; he had no appreciation of team tactics. The Americans, flying a sturdier plane mounting more firepower—a Zero could not take two seconds fire from a Grumman, but the Grummans could take as much as fifteen minutes from a Zero—began flying in pairs. Alone they could not stand up to the Zero, but flying wing-to-wing two Wildcats could take on four or five enemy fighters. It was thus that they fought: warned by the coastwatchers, and later by radar, they climbed high into the sun awaiting the enemy bombers —still their prime target—to come flashing down in a direct overhead or high-side pass calculated to avoid the Bettys' tail stingers, and then, after a quick flaming burst at an intercepting Zero, they dove for home.

Home was a cot and a tent pitched in the mud under shrapnel-scarred coconuts surrounding Henderson Field. It was a mash of dehydrated potatoes and rice and hunks of sodden Vienna sausage spooned from mess gear borrowed from the foot Marines. Home was the center of the Japanese bombers' bull's-eye, the heart of the target for the nightly shells of the Tokyo Express. It was a black and airless dugout in which men who had fought at high altitudes all day crouched to hear the whispering whistle of the bombs dropped by Washing Machine Charley, those nocturnal prowlers so named for the sound of their offbeat motors, or, worse, to listen to the droning approach of Louie the Louse—a cruiser scout-plane—and to see the greenish light of flares filtering through the dugout's burlap door and to realize that the long dark shapes out on the Bay now had their targets spotted and in a moment there would be a giant roaring and thundering all around them and that for some inexplicable reason it would be difficult to keep the mouth open to reduce concussion and to pray to God at the same time. That was home, and in the dirty gray morning they were up, aching from fatigue induced by vitaminless diets or from sucking on oxygen all day; up to down the blessed cups of scalding black coffee and to walk to the runways where sometimes tractors had to tow their Wildcats from concealing coconut groves; up to squeeze into cockpits and to see the first light glinting weakly off spinning propellers, to inhale lungfuls of blue smoke swirling from coughing motors and to feel it souring the stomach where clots of undigested sausage lay like bits of rubber; and then they were feeding power to the motors, racing down the runway to go climbing, up, up, and up, showing the sea the sky-gray of their bottoms and the sky the sea-blue of their tops, climbing from extreme heat into those high cold altitudes where guns can freeze, climbing from solid earth into a floating world where the neck must swivel like a feeding bird's, where the only sounds are the thunder of motors or hammering of the guns, where there is cloud mist on the windscreen in one instant and the sparkle of a drying sun in the next, and where, from time to time, a pilot's eyes dart toward his wingman's tail to see if there are mud-brown wings and a round red ball and smoking cannon there.

That was the pilots' life at Henderson Field, a sun-blistered desert of black dust that fouled motors, or a rain-drenched slop of sticky black mud from which aircraft took off with all the easy grace of a fly rising from molasses.[1] Dust or mud, Dauntless dive-bombers equipped with hard rubber wheels for carrier landings churned up this strip like plowshares when they landed. Here was an airfield at its most primitive: when the Dauntlesses took off, their 500-pound bombs had to be lugged and loaded by hand, for there were no hoists; and just to refuel aircraft was an operation of several hours undertaken with 55-gallon drums and a handpump and a chamois strainer, or else by wheeling planes beneath drums slung in the rafters of the rickety hangars built by the Japanese.

And yet, six days after that August 24 on which they began Henderson's defense by shooting down sixteen of Rabaul's and *Ryujo's* airplanes, most of these men were aces with five kills to their credit. Captain Smith was by then one plane shy of being twice an ace, for on that August 30 he destroyed four Zeros.

Sixteen Bettys heavily protected by Zeros had come winging over Iron Bottom Bay in a vee-of-vees, promptly sinking *Colhoun,* one of the two transports which the moonstruck Captain Murakami had ignored the night before. Turning to flee, they were attacked by Smith's Marines. Smith shot down his first Zero easily, coming up on the enemy's rear with such terrible speed that the pilot never knew what killed him. Smith picked the second Zero off his wingman's tail, banking sharply to catch him full in his gunsight. The third nearly shot down Smith. Hanging on its nose, the Zero struck straight up under Smith's belly. His bullets were stitching the Wildcat's fuselage. Smith nosed over and came at the Zero nose-to-nose. An enemy bullet hit Smith's windshield but missed Smith. Chunks of steel were flying from the Zero as both planes roared toward each other. They tore past each other fifteen feet apart, and Smith looked over his shoulder to see the Zero start spinning earthward out of control. Heading home with low tanks and only a few remaining bullets, Smith was skimming over the coconuts when he caught a Zero hedge-hopping along the coast. Smith came up behind him, pushed the gun-button, and sent the enemy crashing into the Bay.

Then he landed to receive the congratulations of Cactus Air Force's new commander, Colonel William Wallace. Wallace led in nineteen more Wildcats under Major Robert Galer and twelve Dauntlesses under Major Leo Smith. They had had a typical arrival, coming in at the height of the battle, and, in the case of the Wildcats, joining it.

Lieutenant Richard Amerine was among the new arrivals. But he did not reach Henderson. His oxygen apparatus went out and he was forced to parachute from his Wildcat over the Guadalcanal jungle. He landed safely at Cape Esperance, and started walking east through enemy lines.

General Vandegrift now had a total of eighty-six pilots and sixty-four planes—three of them Army, ten Navy, the rest Marine —in his Cactus Air Force. This was approximately double the size of the force that had, since August 21, destroyed twenty-one enemy bombers and thirty-nine Zeros while blocking Admiral Tanaka's reinforcement attempt.

Nevertheless, as Vandegrift knew, the Japanese were now reinforcing more heavily than the Americans. Cactus got thirty-one new planes on August 30, but two days later Rabaul got fifty-eight. The Japanese were also building up ground forces to east and west of Vandegrift's perimeter. They were fresh troops, whereas the Americans were already emaciated by their twice-daily ration of rice and the exhausting routine of working or patrolling by day and fighting by night; they were racked with dysentery, eaten by the rot, and now, as August ended, the rate of malarial victims was rising with a disquieting steadiness.

Obviously the enemy build-up would continue and grow greater. There seemed to be no way of stopping the Tokyo Express. American warships either could not or would not contest them. Obviously it was up to the planes to hit the Tokyo Express ships before it got dark. But the Dauntlesses and Wildcats were short-range planes. What was needed was long-rangers such as the new Lightning.

Such, basically, was Vandegrift's thinking, and it was approved and seconded by Slew McCain after the wiry little admiral paid his first visit to Guadalcanal on August 31. Vandegrift broke out his only bottle of bourbon in his honor. There was just enough for about one drink apiece for the two men and their staffs, and then the Japanese siren announced the advent of Japanese bombers. That night a Tokyo Express cruiser bombarded the airfield. In the morning, more bombers arrived. Sitting in Vandegrift's dugout while the bombs came whistling down, McCain blinked his intense small eyes and said: "By God, Vandegrift, this is your war and you sure are welcome to it. But when I go back tomorrow I am going to try to get you what you need for your air force here."[2]

McCain did. He sent a dispatch to Ghormley, MacArthur, Nimitz, and King, declaring:

"Two full squadrons of Lightnings or Wildcats in addition to present strength should be put into Guadalcanal at once with replacements in training to the south . . . The situation admits of no delay whatever . . . With substantially the reinforcements requested Guadalcanal can be a sinkhole for enemy air power and can be consolidated, expanded, and exploited to enemy's mortal hurt. The reverse is true if we lose Guadalcanal. If the reinforcement requested is not made available Guadalcanal cannot be supplied and hence cannot be held."

Visiting with Ghormley in Nouméa, Undersecretary of the Navy James V. Forrestal became concerned by McCain's reports. He grasped the importance of holding Guadalcanal, and he would, upon his return to Washington, inform the Joint Chiefs of its aircraft needs. But that was yet to be. At the moment, Ghormley asked MacArthur if he could send Guadalcanal some Lightning fighters. MacArthur replied, with truth and reason, that he needed his handful of Lightnings for defense of New Guinea and Australia. Could Ghormley possibly lend him one or two of his four carriers? No, said Ghormley, he needed them to keep the sealanes to Guadalcanal open.

Besides, there were now only three.

Stately old *"Sara Maru,"* as her crew called *Saratoga,* was steaming on defensive patrol about 260 miles southeast of Guadalcanal. There had been a submarine scare, but now, at about seven in the morning, the sea sparkled serenely in the sun and a bugle called all hands to breakfast.

Chow lines formed while *Sara Maru's* screen moved dutifully around the big ship. Outside the screen, off *Sara's* bow, all this was observed with rising excitement by a Japanese officer watching through submarine *I-26's* periscope. At about a quarter of eight, six Long Lance torpedoes went hissing from the submarine's tubes.

A minute later destroyer *MacDonough* sighted the periscope about thirty feet off her bow. She hoisted the torpedo warning, and moved in. She dropped two depth charges which had no depth setting, and were therefore useless, and then, simultaneously, her hull scraped against the diving submarine's side and a torpedo porpoised astern.

On *Saratoga* Captain DeWitt Ramsey swung his rudder hard right and rang up full speed. Slowly, ponderously, old *Sara Maru* turned toward the torpedo wakes. But not enough . . . Two minutes later a torpedo smashed her starboard side abreast of the island superstructure.

It did not seem too bad. No one was killed and only twelve men, including Admiral Fletcher, had been slightly wounded. But after *Saratoga* finally made it with a tow back to Tongatabu, it was discovered that it would require three months to repair her.

Saratoga was out of the fight for Guadalcanal.

Next day, Vandegrift learned of her loss with a sinking heart, for he had also heard of General Kawaguchi's landing to the east the night before. Crisis was recurring, and he ordered the Raiders and Paratroopers to move from Tulagi to Guadalcanal.

Part 3

AT BAY

Chapter 1

AN HOUR after dark on the night of September 3 a message arrived at Cactus "Operations." A transport was arriving and the airfield would have to be illuminated.

Seven jeeps bounced to the south end of the strip and switched on their lights. There was a thundering overhead and some of the drivers instinctively ducked. The transport's wheels cleared them by a few feet and the big plane bumped to a halt. The door swung open and a cold white grizzly bear in khaki stepped down.

Brigadier General Roy Geiger had flown up from the New Hebrides, where he was supposed to be commanding the First Marine Air Wing, to take charge of Cactus Air Force. With him were his chief of staff, Colonel Louis Woods, and his Intelligence officer, Lieutenant Colonel John Munn.

They were three of the most experienced air officers in the Marine Corps, led by a general who won his wings in 1916 and had flown every type of aircraft from the open-cockpit crates of World War I to the newest-model Grumman fighters then parked in Henderson's coconuts. Roy Geiger was also a Parris Island classmate of Archer Vandegrift, and he had helped him fight Cacos in Haiti by ordering his pilots to load a small bomb aboard a Jenny and drop it on an enemy stronghold simultaneously with a ground attack launched by Vandegrift. The day after Geiger arrived, pitching his tent not far from the Pagoda, he called on his old friend. He brought him a package from Admiral Nimitz marked "fan mail." Vandegrift opened it. It was a case of Scotch. But Geiger was aware that Vandegrift, a Virginian, subscribed to the Virginian's belief that a man who drank Scotch rather than bourbon was either a tourist or a show-off, and so, he said:

"Archer, I have a case of bourbon, and I'll trade you level—even though mine are quarts."[1]

Vandegrift was delighted and the two generals placed the Scotch—as rare as bathing beauties on Guadalcanal—into a jeep and drove off to Geiger's tent. Geiger looked for his bourbon, and found that it was gone. Some pink-cheeked fly-boy with more red balls on his fuselage than hairs on his chin had made off with his general's refreshments, and the general's face beneath his thatch of snow-white hair was also round and red and his bleak blue eyes were icy with rage. Archer Vandegrift, Virginian though he was, decided that he was not now in Virginia: he would keep the Scotch. He gave his old friend two bottles, and departed; and Geiger took command of Cactus Air Force in a humor so foul that even Colonel Woods, accustomed to his chief's harsh cold furies, was impressed.[2] In such mood, Geiger drove his fliers from a splendid August into a superb September.

Henderson's old-timers and the new arrivals of Colonel Wallace had already learned to fight together, having knocked down seven of forty enemy attackers on September 2, two of them falling to Major Galer's guns; and the following day Leo Smith's dive-bombers joined Mangrum's to fall upon Colonel Oka and his thousand Kawaguchis barging down The Slot. On Geiger's first day of command, Wildcats were sent to help the Dauntlesses make Oka's passage even more harrowing than Admiral Tanaka had predicted, and on the ensuing two days scout-bombers went ranging 200 miles to the northwest to strike at Gizo Bay, the heretofore too-distant daylight hideout of the Tokyo Express. Gradually, Geiger's inordinately bad temper subsided into his normal curtness. He became fond of his young fliers, jaunty in their dark-blue baseball caps and shoulder holsters. In turn, they ceased to think of him as ruthless but as single-mindedly aggressive and they called him the Old Man. A magnificent band of fighters had found the right leader, and it was well, for the Tokyo Express was recruiting cruisers and destroyers by the dozen and Rabaul and Buka were reinforced with aircraft to the extent that Geiger would be outnumbered 180 planes to seventy by mid-September. Nevertheless, the men of Cactus Air Force continued to whittle the enemy, growing in offensive spirit and gathering almost nightly at the Hotel de Gink, Henderson's hostelry for visiting pilots, to toast each other in medicinal alcohol—or perhaps "borrowed" one-star bourbon—while bellowing out a popular parody of "On the Road to Mandalay":

> *In Cactus "Operations"*
> *Where the needle passes free*
> *There's a hot assignment cookin'*
> *For Marine Group Twenty-three.*
> *As the shells burst in the palm trees*
> *You hear "Operations" say*
> *"Fill the belly tanks with juice, boys,*
>
> *Take the Scouts to Gizo Bay*
> *Take the Scouts to Gizo Bay."*
> *Oh, pack a load to Gizo Bay*
> *Where the Jap fleet spends the day.*
>
> *You can hear their Bettys chunkin'*
> *From Rabaul to Lunga Quay.*
> *Hit the road to Gizo Bay*
> *Where the float plane Zeros play*
> *And the bombs roar down like thunder*
> *On the natives, 'cross the way.*

Meanwhile, as the Solomons aerial war grew fiercer, the Seabees began working on Henderson Field.

The Sixth Naval Construction Battalion arrived at Guadalcanal on September 1. Like all other Seabees—a nickname based on the initials CB—these men were experienced craftsmen. They were tractor drivers, carpenters, masons, dynamiters, electricians, ship-fitters, machinists, and so on, who had volunteered to put their skills at their country's disposal. Most of them were well past the draft age; some of them were veterans of World War I. Their average age of thirty-five was nearly double the age of many of Vandegrift's Marines who watched the Seabees coming ashore and thought that they were being reinforced by their fathers.

"What the hell, pop! They running outta men at home?"

"Hey, pop—you get your wars mixed up or somethin'?"

"Hang onto yer false teeth, grandad—the Jap's're dropping sandwiches."

The Seabees grinned weakly, until one of the Marines inevitably went too far, chortling: "Seabees, huh? Stands for Confused Bastards, you ask me. What'n hell you old geezers gonna do here?"

"I'll tell you what, you mother's mistakes," a Seabee roared back. "We're gonna protect the Marines!"[3]

It was not exactly true, but it had the effect of provoking sweet shouts of anguish from the indignant Marines. Thereafter —and throughout the Pacific war—both Seabees and Marines were drawn together in a rough but affectionate camaraderie based upon mutual respect.

Having been rushed to Guadalcanal, the Sixth Battalion's men had very little equipment: two bulldozers, six dump trucks and a big, waddling carryall capable of scooping up twelve cubic yards of earth. But they also had Japanese trucks and tractors, graders and rollers, Japanese cement, and Japanese poles, lumber and soil pipe. With this, and with gradually increasing supplies of their own, they took over the job of completing and enlarging Henderson Field, while also repairing the strip after enemy air raids.

Repair was vital, and it had to be done quickly. The moment the Japanese approach was signaled, all of Henderson's Wildcats roared aloft to intercept, while the Dauntlesses and P-400s— "Klunkers" as they were now called—took off either to fly out of range or to bomb and strafe the Japanese at either end of the island. But every plane which survived the raid would be coming back, returning to a field pocked with craters. One afternoon in early September, the Seabees watched in agony while seven fighters came in one after another, and cracked up.

So the Seabees discovered that the enemy's 500-pound bomb usually tore up 1600 square feet of Marston steel matting, and packages of that much matting were placed alongside the strip. Trucks loaded with exactly the amount of sand and gravel required to fill such a crater were parked out of sight at strategic points. Compressors and pneumatic hammers to pack the fill were placed in readiness. Assembly lines for passing and laying matting were organized. At the moment of the enemy's approach, all of the Seabees—cooks included—raced to their stations. The moment the bombers departed, sometimes while Zeros shrieked down to strafe, they made for the airstrip. Twisted matting was torn from the craters even as the loaded trucks roared up from the coconut groves. Fill was poured into the holes while men with hammers and compressors leaped in to pack it. New matting was passed, laid, and linked to undamaged strips. Inside forty minutes, the hole would be completely filled and covered.

Repairing shell-holes, of course, took longer. The Seabees had to wait before going to work; for as everyone on Guadalcanal knew, if the bombers left as quickly as they came, it seemed that the Tokyo Express would never leave.

It was next to impossible for Cactus Air Force to derail the Tokyo Express at night. The Japanese ships were only visible during periods of bright moonlight, and these, of course, were the nights when they usually stayed home. Moreover, weather conditions worsened during September and the moon was on the wane, and the wily Tanaka had instructed his skippers never to reveal position by firing on American aircraft at night. They only fired when they were ready to depart, sailing westward through the Bay, blasting Henderson and the Marine positions as they went, and hitting top speed as they cleared Savo and turned northwestward for home.

Nevertheless, Henderson's pilots always took to the skies whenever the Tokyo Express was reported landing troops or supplies. They tried to illuminate the Bay with flares and sometimes they went down as low as five hundred feet looking for long dark shapes. But they seldom did more than keep the Japanese on the alert.

Warships equipped with radar might sink the enemy ships, but the American Navy had not been back in force since Savo. Nor were American sailors the equal of Japanese seamen in nightfighting. They were still cautious, fearful of firing on friendly ships; and they were not trained to recognize the enemy by silhouette as the Japanese were. *Blue,* the destroyer that had been blind to Admiral Mikawa's approach at Savo, gave tragic demonstration of these failings the night after the Battle of the Tenaru. With another destroyer, *Henley,* she tried to intercept a Japanese landing. Four minutes after her sonar and radar had made a contact on a strange ship, and just as she was bringing her guns and torpedo tubes to bear, she was racked by a Long Lance from the enemy destroyer *Kawakaze,* which had just put troops ashore. *Blue* lost several feet of her stern and had to be scuttled.

After this, although perhaps not on account of this, there were fewer and fewer American warships entering Iron Bottom Bay at night.

Little and *Gregory* were two of a rare kind at Guadalcanal: ships that stayed. Sisters of sunken *Colhoun,* they were old four-stack destroyers converted into fast transports. They had brought Red Mike Edson and the Raiders and Parachutists from Tulagi to Guadalcanal, and on September 4 they took aboard a party of Raiders under Colonel Griffith to patrol Savo Island.

Aboard *Little* a lookout cried "Periscope!" and the ship prepared to close with depth charges before the "periscope" was sheepishly recognized as the mast of a sunken American ship. Ashore on Savo, the Raiders found no Japanese but only charred and oily debris and the mounds of shallow graves, still more grim testimonials to the efficiency of Admiral Mikawa's ships. A native named Allen-luva told the patrol that the Japanese had not been on Savo since July.

"Take bananas, chicken, pumpkin, everything," Allen-luva said angrily.

"Him talk pidgin?" someone asked.

"Like drunk man," Allen-luva snorted. "Him talk 'aeroprane' and 'Guadarcanar.' "[4]

The Marines laughed and went back aboard *Gregory* and *Little*. They returned to Guadalcanal at dusk. Because it was an extremely dark night, *Little* and *Gregory* did not go back to Tulagi Harbor as was customary. Commander Hugh Hadley in *Little* decided to patrol off Lunga Point.

At one o'clock next morning the Americans observed gunfire flashes in the east near Taivu.

Destroyers *Yudachi, Hatsuyuki,* and *Murakumo* were to provide diversionary bombardment while transports put the last of General Kawaguchi's men ashore at Taivu. At about one o'clock in the morning, they began. And then the startled gunners looked to the west where two small American destroyer-transports were beautifully outlined in the light of five beautiful American flares.

Little and *Gregory* both thought the gunflashes were from a Japanese submarine. They sped eastward, and then, a Catalina on patrol a half mile ahead also saw the flashes and also thought that they came from a submarine, and helpfully dropped a string of flares to mark the target.

In that light the three enemy destroyers, each nearly as big as a light cruiser, began battering Americans mounting only one four-incher, some 20-mm guns and a few light and heavy machine guns. *Little* and *Gregory* fought bravely, but within a few salvos of feelers the Japanese had the range. Commander Hadley was killed on *Little's* bridge. *Gregory* was shredded by salvos of five-inch shells and set blazing from stem to stern. Both ships were blazing wrecks, but the Japanese made certain of their destruction. They sailed between them, hurling shells to both sides. Many Americans in the water were killed by those shells. Some of them dove deep to get beneath burning oil, to avoid flaming embers cascading down from their ships. They tried to swim out of seas of fire, and sometimes, if they were lucky, water which had risen into the sky in long geysering plumes came raining down to put out the fires around them. Others, such as Lieutenant Commander Harry Bauer, skipper of *Gregory,* were not so fortunate. Badly wounded, Bauer struggled to escape both burning oil and the suction of his sinking ship. Two men—Clarence Justice and Chester Ellis—swam to his side to pull him free. Bauer heard a sailor cry out that he was drowning. He directed his rescuers to the man's aid, and he was never seen again.

Once more tragedy had overtaken American ships and men on the dark brooding surface of Iron Bottom Bay, and far to the west Lieutenant Richard Amerine heard the thundering and saw the flashing and he wondered what was happening now on this satanic paradise.

The Japanese had not seen Amerine parachute into the jungle around Cape Esperance. No one had come for him. But Amerine was growing weak. He had been subsisting for five days on snails and insects. He knew which ones were edible because he was an entomologist. In fact, he had seen such an astounding variety of insects that he had been brokenhearted not to have a butterfly net with him.

That day, though, he would have traded it for a rifle.

He had nearly blundered into a party of Japanese. Luckily, he had found one enemy soldier sleeping beside a track and he had seized a boulder and smashed the man's head like a china doll's. Then he took the dead soldier's pistol with which he killed two more of them, shooting one and battering the other with the pistol butt.

Now, in the early darkness of September 5, he lay in the whispering, dripping jungle and wondered if there were more Japanese between him and the Marine lines.

With daylight, he arose and began walking east again.

There was "pogey-bait" on Guadalcanal.

It would seem absurd that during a time of critical shortages in fuel and goods and ammunition anyone should bother to bring in candy, and yet, on September 5, a Skytrain flown by Lieutenant Colonel Wyman Marshall came in under fire loaded with pogey-bait and cigarettes. Then Colonel Marshall flew out with a load of wounded.

Next day more Skytrains arrived, carrying drums of fuel, ammunition, machine guns, and mortar shells—departing, again, with wounded. Thus was begun the famous shuttle operation called SCAT after South Pacific Combat Air Transportation Command.

Meanwhile, the Marines were issued pogey-bait at the rate of one bar of candy to a squad. Rather than divide it and provide too little for all, the men drew lots. The blushing winners took their prizes and went slinking into the bush to devour it beyond the reproachful eyes of the losers.

Combined Fleet had returned to Truk.

After ten days of useless cruising north of Guadalcanal, fifty-odd ships led by great *Yamato* sailed into the lagoon to refuel.

Admiral Yamamoto called a conference aboard his battleship. He was taciturn as he spoke to his commanders. For the first time he cautioned against underestimating American fighting strength, and he issued two simple orders:

1 – Keep the location and movements of Japanese carriers unknown to the enemy.

2 – Make initial air assaults against the enemy as strong as possible.

These instructions were to cover Combined Fleet's support of Major General Kawaguchi's attempt to capture Henderson Field. The all-out aerial assault was to be launched September 12 in concert with Kawaguchi's attack.

Commander Tameichi Hara came back from the conference to

his destroyer *Amatsukaze*. Lieutenant Kazue Shimizu, his gunnery officer, met him with a doleful face.

"What's the matter with you?" Hara snapped.

"We failed to catch a single fish today," Shimizu said. "This super fleet of ours has exterminated every fish in the atoll in just three days."[5]

On September 9 the super fleet shoved off again, bound for the Solomons.

Lieutenant Amerine had come back from the dead. On September 6, gaunt and staggering, he wandered into Marine lines at Kukum. He was brought to Vandegrift's headquarters to inform Intelligence of what he had seen. But Amerine had little to tell. The Japanese he had killed had been stragglers and he had not come upon any large bodies of enemy troops.

Colonel Thomas still believed that the large enemy formations were to the east. Clemens's scouts continued to report a Japanese build-up at the village of Tasimboko, about a mile west of Taivu. In fact, Thomas and Colonel Twining had already begun to plan a raid on Tasimboko, and Colonel Edson came to headquarters to propose just such an operation. The night of September 6, Thomas informed Edson that he could go ahead with it.

"We must not overrate the importance of our successes in the Solomons," the President was saying warningly in his annual Labor Day speech to the nation, "though we may be proud of the skill with which these local operations have been conducted."

Franklin Roosevelt was preparing America for bad news. Even as Vandegrift's men marched toward their ships to attack Kawaguchi's men at Tasimboko, the President in the White House was minimizing the campaign with the deprecating phrase "local operation." Then, the announcement of Japanese victory on Guadalcanal would not come like the crack of doom.[6]

Chapter 2

KIYOTAKE KAWAGUCHI was as confident of victory as Colonel
Ichiki had been. He had 6200 men ashore whom he would hurl
at Henderson Field in a three-pronged attack.

1 – The major blow would be led by himself. He would take a
battalion of the 124th Infantry and the two remaining Ichiki
battalions to the south of the airfield, wheel and attack north.

2 – Another battalion of the 124th would strike west across
the Tenaru.

3 – From the vicinity of the Matanikau River two reinforced
battalions under Colonel Oka would cross the Lunga River and
hit the airfield from the northwest.

Meanwhile, the main blow was to be supported by naval gunfire and air strikes.

It was a tidy plan, worthy of any textbook or any army that
marches on maps. General Kawaguchi had devised it in the Shortlands in between arguments with Admiral Tanaka. It did not occur
to him then, as it did not now occur to him, that he might scout
the battlefield and the enemy before drawing up a battle plan.

Like Colonel Ichiki, he was making free and fiery interpreta-
tion of General Hyakutake's measured instructions to "view the
enemy strength, position and terrain" to see if it was "possible
or not to achieve quick success" with his present strength. An
impatient man, Kawaguchi had no intention of wasting time
studying the enemy. To him there was no question of quick success. The Americans were few in number and inferior in quality.
Japanese "spiritual power" would triumph. Moreover, by stealing
stealthily south, by "tunneling through the jungle" as he called it,
he would come up on the American rear and surprise them. The
map had shown him a hogbacked ridge which ran down into the
airfield. It seemed to be undefended.

In such confidence, General Kawaguchi went sloshing southwest. The Ishitari Battalion moved off directly westward. Colonel Oka's force, gathering at the Matanikau, marked time for the appointed hour on the night of September 12.

Left behind at Tasimboko were three hundred men guarding General Kawaguchi's food, part of his artillery, and a trunk containing his dress whites.

After dark on September 7 the Raiders under Colonel Edson boarded two destroyer-transports and a pair of converted California tuna launches now dignified with the initials YP, meaning patrol boat and translated "Yippy." The Marines sailed east to Tasimboko, their approach announced by showers of bright red sparks pouring from the Yippies' funnels.

In a misty dawn, the Raiders clambered into their Higgins boats. The Japanese, aware of their presence, prepared to receive them with a pair of 47-mm antitank guns capable of blowing the American boats out of the water.

But then the shredding mists revealed the large transports *Fuller* and *Bellatrix* escorted by a cruiser and four destroyers. They were enroute to Lunga Point, but Kawaguchi's rear guard thought they were coming to Tasimboko. The Japanese broke and ran, abandoning the antitank guns, their own weapons and their breakfasts.

Landing unopposed, the Raiders quickly removed the antitank guns' breech blocks and hurled them into the sea. Then they struck inland half a mile and wheeled west through a coconut plantation.

In the meantime, General Kawaguchi's panicky soldiers had informed the brigade commander that a major enemy landing was being made in his rear, and he, in turn, had notified Rabaul.

General Hyakutake was at last distressed. He ordered the 41st Infantry Regiment to mark time at Kokoda in New Guinea for possible transfer to Guadalcanal, and then he radioed Tokyo that Kawaguchi was "sandwiched." Tokyo quickly notified two battalions in the East Indies to stand by, even as Admiral Mikawa planned a night bombardment with a cruiser and eight destroyers and the Tokyo Express shipped two battalions of the Aoba Detachment aboard.

It was a first-class flap which continued to flutter until word came from Kawaguchi suggesting that his earlier report had been exaggerated.

Nevertheless, General Kawaguchi could not turn to strike the Raiders. He was bogged down. Among other things he had underestimated the jungle. His engineers had not been able to hack out the clear straight "tunnel" that had been promised, and three thousand men of the Kawaguchi Brigade were strung out in a snaking column three miles long. They clawed up slime-slick slopes or stumbled through swamps sometimes armpit-deep, or were tripped at every turn by tangles of root and creeper and fern, ravaged, as they went, by clouds of stinging wings and all those jungle creatures that fall, fasten, and suck.

No, Kawaguchi could not turn; he could only send his rear guard the peremptory order:

"Confront the enemy."

Plucking up their courage, they did. Two mountain guns and a pair of howitzers and numerous Nambu machine guns began firing from the coconut groves and Edson's men were pinned down.

Edson immediately called for aerial support and sent a company led by Clemens's scouts along a jungle trail to turn the enemy's right flank. Then Captain Dale Brannon's shark-nosed Klunkers arrived to strafe and bomb the Japanese. At noon, the encircling company had deployed in the Japanese rear. Caught in a crossfire, the enemy fled again. Twenty-seven dead bodies were found draped over six heavy machine guns. Most of Kawaguchi's food supply was also discovered, and fifty men were detailed to jab their bayonets into cans of sliced beef and crabmeat while others dragged thousands of bags of rice into the surf. All Japanese weapons were destroyed and the field pieces towed into the Bay. Enemy maps, charts, and notebooks were gathered up and a powerful radio set was wrecked.

Then, with great hoarse shouts of joy, the Marines blundered into a thatched warehouse loaded with beer and sake. When they returned to their waiting ships late that afternoon they were loaded down with bottles and with cans of beef and crab, which, as they sheepishly explained to the gently inquiring Colonel Edson, they had somehow forgotten to destroy.

It is delicious to drink the enemy's wine and to eat his sweetmeats, and it is glorious to make him grind his teeth, as the Raiders did, sailing west to Kukum with Kiyotake Kawaguchi's fancy white duds nailed to the masthead.

Mr. Ishimoto had been in the vicinity of Tasimboko and he reacted swiftly to the American raid.

He rounded up the missionaries and demanded again that they advise the Americans to surrender. Father Oude-Engberink replied that he could not. As he had said to Martin Clemens, he was neutral. But it would be difficult for Ishimoto to consider white skin and large noses neutral, and he shouted:

"It is useless to resist the Japanese. They are too strong for you. You cannot win and you must leave Guadalcanal."[1]

Again, the priests refused. Political affairs were not their concern. Ishimoto ordered them tied and thrown into a native hut where they were tortured and bayoneted to death. Old Sister Edmée, her body swollen and deformed by elephantiasis, was sent blundering off into the bush. But Sisters Sylvia and Odilia, both young, were also murdered.

After they were raped.[2]

The night of his return Red Mike Edson had gone to Colonel Thomas at Vandegrift's headquarters. "This is no motley of Japs," he said in his throaty whisper.[3] Next morning, smiling his cold white smile, Edson was back. Thomas looked up from patrol reports and Intelligence interpretations of the captured Tasimboko documents. "They're coming," Thomas said.

Edson nodded. But from where? He pointed to a ridge on an aerial photograph and whispered: "This looks like a good approach."[4]

Thomas was startled. Edson had fingered the very ridge to which General Vandegrift, tired of jumping in and out of airfield dugouts, was planning to move his command post. Edson was unperturbed. The ridge was a perfect approach to the airfield. It was a broken hogback running parallel to the Lunga River south of the airfield. South, east, and west—that is, front and both sides—it was surrounded by jungle; but to the north or rear it ran gently down into Henderson Field. What better approach, Edson argued, and Thomas, agreeing, took him to see the general.

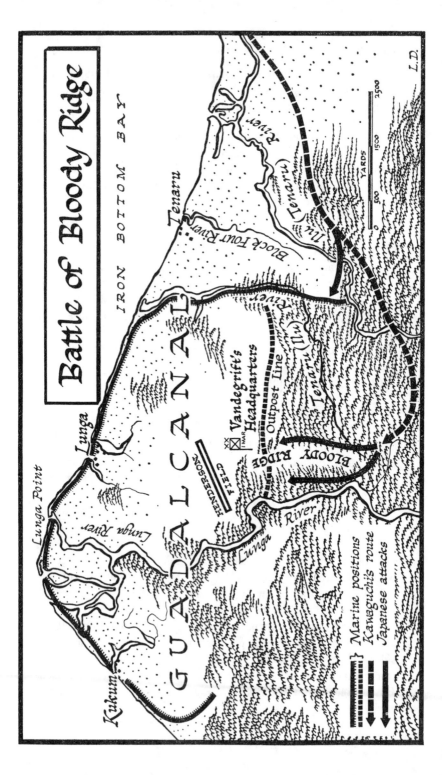

Battle of Bloody Ridge

IRON BOTTOM BAY

Lunga Point

Kukum

Lunga River

Lunga

Lunga River

GUADALCANAL

HENDERSON FIELD

Vandegrift's Headquarters
XX
1 MAR

Outpost Line

BLOODY RIDGE

Lunga River

Tenaru (Ilu) River

Block Four River

Tenaru

Ilu (Tenaru) River

Ilu River

Marine positions
Kawaguchi's route
Japanese attacks

YARDS
0   500   1500   2500

L.D.

Vandegrift was pleased to see the two men unfold their map and confidently pinpoint the avenue of enemy approach.

"Where is that?" he asked.

Respectful but reproachful, Edson said: "The ridge you insist on putting your new CP behind."[5]

Vandegrift smiled softly. He had already rejected some rather profane objections from his staff regarding his new command post, and he was not now going to change his mind. Engineers were already at work building a pavilion 35×18 feet which would house the living and working quarters of Vandegrift and his chief of staff, Colonel Capers James. It was to have Japanese wicker furniture and a Japanese icebox run by kerosene and it would be surrounded by woods filled with the colorful parrots and macaws which Vandegrift found so delightful. No, he would not change his mind, even if he could immediately grasp the danger of leaving that ridge undefended. So the general courteously ignored the colonel's respectful rebuke and ordered him to take his composite battalion of 700 Raiders and parachutists and block that open ridge.

Then the general returned to such urgent matters as his repeated request for reinforcements. He wanted at least one regiment, preferably, if he could get it, his old Seventh Marines.

The Seventh Marines had been in Samoa since the middle of May. Trained as an assault elite, they were withering as garrison troops. There was enchanted moonlight filtering through the branches of banyan trees and the soft plinking of native guitars. There was also a ration of two cans of beer daily and hot food from the galleys. And there was the tsetse fly that brings "mumu," as the Samoans call elephantiasis.

None of these things are typical of a Corps dedicated to the principle that hunger and hardship are the school of the good soldier. "Nothing is too good for you," the Marine Corps tells its men, adding: "But we'll let you have it anyway."

But on Samoa the Seventh was "living it up" in comparison to its brother regiments on Guadalcanal and the spectacle of Colonel James Webb—"Gentleman Jim" in his natty whipcord breeches and his gleaming low-quarter shoes—leading hikes in a station wagon was also not calculated to inflame its men with ardor.

It was up to the battalion commanders to try to keep their men battle-fit. One of these leaders was Lieutenant Colonel Herman Henry Hanneken, the veteran of the Banana Wars who had killed the Caco chieftain, "King" Charlemagne, in personal combat. Another was Major Chesty Puller.

At forty-four, Puller was already a Marine legend. He had won two Navy Crosses in Haiti and Nicaragua. He was that very rare bird of war: a man who actually loves combat and who is beloved by his men. Puller's Marines delighted in repeating those numerous Pullerisms, true or false, such as his remark when he saw his first flame-thrower: "Where do you fit the bayonet on it?" They boasted of his bullhorn voice and they claimed that his huge chest bulging from an otherwise spindly frame hardly five feet six inches high was capable of repelling enemy bullets. Puller's military credo contained two articles: conditioning and attack.

On Samoa he repeatedly ordered his men out on long hikes beneath a brazen sun, instructing his officers: "Gentlemen, remember to have every man carry a one-inch square of beef suet in his pack. If they'll grease their feet daily, and avoid so much washing, they'll have no blisters. An old trick from the Haitian soldiers, and it never fails. You can't march men without feet, gentlemen."[6]

But Puller, like the other professional officers, soon began to mourn the Samoan confinement: "Here I am, stuck out here to rot on this damned island while other people fight the war. They've marooned us."[7] Hearing of the Battle of the Tenaru, he cried: "They mowed 'em down! One of these days we'll be giving 'em hell like that. *Better* than that."[8]

A few weeks later the Seventh Marines were ordered to Espiritu Santo. It was rumored that they were not going to Guadalcanal, but to New Guinea to fight for General MacArthur.

Admiral Ghormley pondered a most disturbing message. Admiral Nimitz was ordering Ghormley to turn over to General MacArthur one reinforced regiment of "experienced amphibious troops," together with the ships required to mount them. Ghormley was puzzled. The Joint Chiefs of Staff, who had originated this order, surely must know that the only "experienced" amphibious troops in the Pacific were fighting for their lives on Guadalcanal. Could he mean the Seventh Marine Regiment, even then sailing toward Ghormley's area? Ghormley asked the advice of Richmond Kelly Turner. He got a very straight answer:

"The only experienced amphibious troops in the South Pacific are those in Guadalcanal and it is impracticable to withdraw them." Turner then laid it on the line:

"I respectfully invite attention to the present insecure position of Guadalcanal. . . . Adequate air and naval strength have not been made available. Vandegrift has consistently urged to be reinforced at once by at least one regiment . . . I concur."

What might have been a very soft filching of Guadalcanal's dwindling strength was thus prevented.

And Vandegrift's strength was dwindling. Malaria was now ravaging his ranks as the enemy had not been able to do. Every day new shortages appeared—in bombs, bullets, starter cartridges, oxygen, tires, and lubricating oil—thus complicating old and constant shortages in food and fuel.

General Geiger's strength was being whittled by shortages rather than by Zeros. Eight airplanes cracked up on take-off on September 8. Two of them were restored to readiness but the others were hauled off to the "boneyard" where sharp-eyed mechanics cannibalized them for spare parts.

On September 10 there were only eleven Wildcats available, and the enemy aerial onslaught was mounting. Combined Fleet's sortie from Truk and the steady reinforcement of northern airfields were ominous signs. Admiral Nimitz did not fail to observe them. On that same September 10 he ordered all carrier aircraft "that could be spared" to be flown to Guadalcanal, thus contradicting the Navy's doctrine that carrier aircraft should fly from carriers, as well as countermanding Ghormley's promise to Fletcher that his fighters would not be committed to Guadalcanal. Pledges made in all sincerity in response to reasonable requests, the niceties of command prerogatives, military dogma, all had to go by the boards, now, for the enemy was obviously mounting a major bid to recover Guadalcanal.

Crisis had come.

General Vandegrift knew it as he moved into his new command post behind the ridge that would be called Bloody, and Red Mike Edson knew it going down to Kukum to tell his men that they were moving to a "rest area."

"Too much bombing and shelling here close to the beach," Edson said. "We're moving to a quiet spot."[9] He smiled, enjoying the joke. The men moved out. Twice they were forced to take cover from air raids, but by two o'clock in the afternoon they were fortifying Bloody Ridge.

Edson put the parachutists under Harry Torgerson—the singed dynamiter of Gavutu—on his left or eastern flank. The Raiders took over the center and right with the right flank company strung out thinly toward the Lunga. Edson's own command post was in a gully about a hundred yards south of Vandegrift's new headquarters. Here he put his reserve, a depleted company of Raiders.

None of the men really believed that they had come to a "rest area," and some of them were already cursing Edson as a glory-hound who hung around headquarters sniffing out bloody assignments for his men. None of them, however, actually suspected that they, and they alone, stood between an approaching enemy and that Henderson Field which was now the prize of the Pacific war. So some of these men did not dig so deeply as they might have, for to dig into coral with truncated entrenching tools which are little better than trowels can be so painful and exhausting that only the fear of death can impel some men to attempt it.

That fear came upon these Marines next morning. Stringing barbed wire and hacking out fields of fire in the undergrowth, they heard the cry "Condition Red!" Twenty-six Bettys with twenty escorting Zeros were on their way. The man kept on working. The target would be, as always, the airfield behind them.

But the target was Bloody Ridge.

That tan, hump-backed mound rearing out of the dark green jungle sea like the spine of a whale leaped and shuddered as though harpooned.

Those who had dug pits hurled themselves into them, those who had not stood erect or tried to run and were killed or maimed.

And then the raid was over. It was quiet on the Ridge, beneath the growl and whine of aerial combat in which Marine fliers destroyed seven enemy planes and in which Major Robert Galer, shot down in the Bay, survived to swim ashore. But the men on Bloody Ridge did not know this. They knew only that the enemy was after their Ridge and they brushed dirt from their dungarees and began to dig with desperate fury.

"Some goddam rest area," a corporal snarled. "Some goddam rest area!"[10]

Out in the jungle, General Kawaguchi's toiling column of three thousand men took comfort in the sound of Japanese bombs falling on American Marines. But it was small comfort. Their march to the battle area had become an excruciating torment. It was a blind blundering stagger through a malevolent green labyrinth. Kawaguchi had no guides. The policies of Mr. Ishimoto had seen to that. Nor did the general have accurate maps or aerial mosaics.

Nevertheless, he pressed on. General Hyakutake had insisted that September 12 was to be the night of the attack and Kawaguchi could not miss that rigid deadline. He closed his eyes to the sight of limping soldiers and took an iron grip on his confidence. He would still prevail. Two of the Ichiki battalions would make the breakthrough and then the powerful unit led by Lieutenant Colonel Kusukichi Watanabe would dash to the airfield. Kawaguchi's forces to east and west would close in simultaneously.

And then the surrender ceremony that day . . .

Remembering his lost white uniform General Kawaguchi's face darkened and his hand fell to his saber hilt.

Vice-Admiral Richmond Kelly Turner also heard those Japanese bombs. He flew in just before "Condition Red!" was sounded and the Japanese bombers who raked the Raiders' ridge also introduced Kelly Turner to the grim realities of life on Guadalcanal.

He sat out the raid in Vandegrift's dugout just a hundred yards north of the quaking Ridge. He was discomfited, but after the bombers left, Vandegrift noticed that he still looked tense. He was. He pulled a folded sheet of paper from his pocket and silently handed it to Vandegrift. Color drained from the general's face. He winced. He was reading Admiral Ghormley's estimate of the situation on Guadalcanal. Commander, South Pacific, summarized the enemy build-up: naval forces were gathering at Rabaul and Truk, aerial reinforcements were arriving daily, dozens of transports were in Simpson Harbor waiting to put troops aboard; an overwhelming push against Guadalcanal was likely. Then Ghormley scrutinized his own situation. He listed shortages in cruisers, carriers, destroyer-transports, and cargo vessels.

Admiral Ghormley concluded that he could no longer support the Marines on Guadalcanal.

Without a word Vandegrift handed the message to Colonel Thomas. The colonel read and looked up dumfounded.

"Put that message in your pocket," Vandegrift told him. "I'll talk to you about it later, but I don't want anyone to know about it."[11]

Thomas nodded, watching Admiral Turner pulling a bottle out of his bag. He poured three drinks, and said: "Vandegrift, I'm not inclined to take so pessimistic a view of the situation as Ghormley does. He doesn't believe I can get the Seventh Marine Regiment in here, but I think I have a scheme that will fool the Japs."[12]

Turner's plan was simply to bring the Seventh over a course well to the east of the normal approach, while carriers *Wasp* and *Hornet* and their screen sailed out of sight of the transports as though on normal patrol.

Vandegrift was encouraged at the thought of receiving 4000 fresh troops, but in Turner's next breath he was dismayed. The admiral was playing general again. Because he was still Amphibious Force Commander, and because Guadalcanal had not yet taught the Americans that Landing Force Commanders such as Vandegrift must be at least the equal of the Amphibious Force Commanders when on the ground, Kelly Turner was still Archer Vandegrift's superior. In that capacity he wanted to use the Seventh Marines to carve out little American enclaves on Guadalcanal. He was hopeful of establishing another airfield at Aola Bay, the point far to the east where Martin Clemens had had his district office. Vandegrift protested. Henderson Field was the prize. It was protected by a perimeter. All troops should be used to hold that perimeter until it was time to go on the offensive to drive Japan from the island.

The two men could not agree, and their discussion of how to use the Seventh Marines ended in stalemate.

That afternoon reinforcements of a different order arrived: twenty-four Wildcats from crippled *Saratoga* flew into Henderson Field led by Commander Le Roy Simpler.

That night the Tokyo Express was on schedule. For almost two hours Japanese naval shells combed Bloody Ridge. Once again the coral shivered and shook and Edson's men dug their noses into damp coral and prayed. Once again Kelly Turner took shelter in Vandegrift's dugout. He heard the shells whispering hoarsely overhead, heard them crash and felt their shock waves rattle the dugout. He had time to reflect on his earlier criticism of Vandegrift as being "unduly concerned" for the safety of his perimeter.[13]

In the morning Vandegrift showed him the carnage, especially the field hospital struck by a big shell. Before Turner departed he told Vandegrift: "When I bring the Seventh in I will land them where you want."[14]

Aboard *Saratoga* in Pearl Harbor that afternoon, Admiral Chester Nimitz was about to present decorations. All hands were lined up on the flight deck. Nimitz stepped to the microphone and said, "Boys, I've got a surprise for you. Bill Halsey's back!"

A storm of applause greeted Admiral Halsey as he stepped on deck, and the light blue eyes beneath the bristling gray eyebrows filled with tears. Halsey was ready for his new assignment, command of a carrier task force built around *Enterprise;* but his ships were not ready, yet. In the meantime, he would tour the South Pacific on an itinerary that would take him, he hoped, to Guadalcanal.

General Vandegrift had seen Admiral Turner safely off. Now he was walking back to his command post with Colonel Thomas. Vandegrift was preoccupied, thinking of Ghormley's gloomy estimate. Then his jaw lifted and he said:

"You know, Jerry, when we landed in Tientsin in 1927, old Colonel E. B. Miller ordered me to draw up three plans. Two concerned the accomplishment of our mission, the third a withdrawal from Tientsin in case we got pushed out." Vandegrift's words came soft and slow. "Jerry, we're going to defend this airfield until we no longer can. If that happens, we'll take what's left to the hills and fight guerrilla warfare. I want you to go see Bill Twining, swear him to secrecy and have him draw up a plan."[15]

Thomas went to see Twining. "We can't let this be another Bataan, Bill. We'll go to the headquarters of the Lunga. We'll take our food and bullets."[16] Twining agreed. He went to his tent and wrote out, by hand, an operation order which had neither date nor serial number. He put it in his safe.

Over at the Pagoda, Archer Vandegrift spoke to Roy Geiger. He told him that the Marines were staying on Guadalcanal, Navy or no Navy. "But if the time comes when we no longer can hold the perimeter I expect you to fly out your planes."

Geiger said, "If we can't use the planes back in the hills, we'll fly them out. But whatever happens, I'm staying with you."[17]

Vandegrift nodded appreciatively, and then, the siren wailed and the cry arose:

"Condition Red!"

Forty-two enemy airplanes were winging down from the north. To meet them Cactus Air Force sent eleven Marine and twenty-one Navy fighters thundering skyward. Sixteen enemy planes were knocked down at a loss of one American ensign killed in a dead-stick landing. But some of the bombers got through. Once more Marines on the Ridge dove without hesitation into their holes, again sticks of 500-pound bombs and strings of daisy-cutter fragmentation bombs walked the Ridge—killing, maiming, stunning.

Now the men of Red Mike Edson drove themselves to complete their fortifications. Spools of wire stripped from less-threatened positions were brought up and hastily strung. Extra grenades and belted machine-gun ammunition were put into the pits. To the rear, batteries of 105-mm howitzers had been moved to new positions to give Edson close support. Artillery fire plans had been drawn and maps gridded. An artillery observer was stationed in Edson's command post on the southern snout. Communication wire ran backward to a fire direction center and Vandegrift's headquarters.

The general's slender reserve, the Second Battalion, Fifth Marines, moved into supporting positions. Its officers scouted approach routes which they might have to follow in darkness.

Every gun, every Marine on Guadalcanal was now committed. It was now up to the Raiders on the Ridge. The enemy was coming that night, Vandegrift was certain. Clemens's scouts had come in with reports of three thousand men moving toward assembly points on the Lunga's east bank.

Darkness came quickly as it does in the tropics. In swiftly dying sunlight homing birds lost the brilliance of their plumage. Above the Ridge the skies were clouding over. Soon that long knobby peninsula was blending into the black of the jungle flowing around it. It was silent. The last spade had clinked on coral, the last command had been shouted. Marines in their holes closed and re-opened their eyes to accustom them to darkness. They listened for the regular sounds of men among the irregular sounds of nature. Sometimes their mouths twitched to hear an iguana bark or the *crrrack* of the bird whose cry was like the clapping of wooden blocks.

It began to rain.

General Kawaguchi's iron confidence was rusting in the rain forest. The jungle had scattered his detachments. He was not ready to attack, and yet he must. Rabaul was counting on it. He would like another day to prepare, but he could not ask for it, even if he had dared, because the Americans had destroyed his radio at Tasimboko. Helpless, he put his available forces along the Lunga opposite the Marine right flank and awaited the naval bombardment that was to precede his attack.

Louie the Louse droned overhead.

Around nine o'clock he dropped a flare.

A half hour later a cruiser and three destroyers shelled the Ridge. Some of their projectiles crashed around the Marine positions, some fell short, but most of them exploded harmlessly in jungle west of the Lunga.

Edson's men tightened their grip on their weapons.

The shelling ceased twenty minutes after it began, a rocket rose from the jungle, machine-gun and rifle fire broke out like a sputtering string of firecrackers, and the Kawaguchis came pouring out of the black.

"*Banzai!*" they screamed. "*Bonnn—zaaa—eee!*"

"Marine you die!" they shrieked. "Marine you da—eee!"

They drove the Raiders back. They sliced off a platoon on the far right flank, cut communications wire and went slipping farther down the Lunga to attempt an encirclement.

On the left the Japanese struck the parachutists half a dozen times, punched holes in their front and broke them up. And then they milled wildly about, unable to capitalize on the impetus of their blows, and before dawn Edson was able to pull back his left flank and re-form it.

But General Kawaguchi had no such control. His troops battled beyond his reach. Their attacks became purposeless and fragmented. On the right where they had gained the greatest success, they lost their way once they had departed the straight going of the river bank. They thrashed and fell in the underbrush. Their jabbing bayonets met empty air or dug up earth. Meanwhile, Marine mortars flashed among them and Marine artillery whistled down into pre-plotted areas and found Japanese flesh there as anticipated.

Gradually, the American platoon that had been cut off fought its way back to the right slope of the Ridge.

At dawn the Japanese melted back into the jungle.

The Marines rose up and counterattacked to regain lost ground. Bloody Ridge had held.

That morning, Red Mike Edson called a conference of staff officers and company commanders. They sat around him in a semicircle, drinking coffee and smoking. Red Mike sat on a log, his legs crossed, spooning cold hash from an open can. He chewed slowly as he talked.

"They were testing," he said. "Just testing. They'll be back. But maybe not as many of them." He smiled. "Or maybe more." He paused, his jaws chewing. "I want all positions improved, all wire lines paralleled, a hot meal for the men. Today: dig, wire up tight, get some sleep. We'll all need it." His officers rose. "The Nip will be back," Red Mike said. "I want to surprise him."[18]

Major Kenneth Bailey was among the officers who set to work preparing Edson's surprise: a pullback from the previous night's positions. Bailey had been wounded at Tulagi and sent to a hospital in New Caledonia. Leaving without permission and before his wound was fully healed, he had hitchhiked an airplane ride back to Guadalcanal in time for the battle.

Edson's pullback served to tighten and contract his lines. It improved the field of fire for automatic weapons, and it confronted the Japanese with a hundred yards of open ground over which they must move to close with the Marines.

Many of those Marines had the look of sleepwalkers by afternoon of this September 13. They stumbled along the Ridge, lifting their feet high like men in chains. Seventy-two near-sleepless hours —hours of shock and sweat and pain beneath the enemy's bombs and shells, in the face of his bullets—had numbed them. They had expected to be relieved by Vandegrift's reserve, but intermittent aerial attacks had kept that battalion under cover.

Three separate air raids struck at Henderson Field that day. But there were now ample fighters on hand to meet them. Wildcats had come in from carriers *Hornet* and *Wasp* and Guadalcanal received its first torpedo-bombers with the arrival of six Avengers. Although Admiral Ghormley was as pessimistic about Guadalcanal as he had been at the start, he was nevertheless giving the beleaguered Marines all the air he had: in toto, sixty planes.

But Rabaul got more.

On September 12 the 26th Air Flotilla which was to have relieved the riddled 25th came into the Guadalcanal battle as reinforcement instead, and 140 aircraft were added to those already based at Rabaul and Bougainville.

Next day many of them were on the runways, propellers turning, while pilots sat in ready huts awaiting word to fly south. Loaded troop transports stood by with idling engines. All was in readiness for the surrender ceremonies.

But there was no word from General Kawaguchi.

Neither General Hyakutake nor Admiral Tsukahara had been able to communicate with Kawaguchi since the enemy landing at Tasimboko. He had, of course, sent them his message of September 11 in which he notified them of his intention to take possession of the airfield the night of September 12–13. Since then, nothing . . .

Tsukahara sent four scout planes south. They came back with bullet holes suggesting that the Americans were still in possession of Henderson. Rabaul's top commanders postponed the fly-down for the surrender ceremony one day. The customary attacks were renewed on Henderson, but it was considered unsafe to attack the Ridge. Instead, it was decided to strike the enemy force which had landed at Tasimboko to "sandwich" Kawaguchi.

Twenty-six Bettys and a dozen escorting Zeros thundered south. They came in low over Florida Island and pounced on Kawaguchi's rear echelon. In one moment these Japanese were dancing for joy to see the sun flashing off the red balls on their comrades' wings, in the next they were being blown flat or apart or were dragging themselves to the beaches to stop the slaughter by spreading their own red-balled flags out on the sand. The Zeros only strafed them where they lay, and one day Martin Clemens's scouts would bring these bullet-pierced and blood-caked flags into the perimeter as souvenirs.

Out at sea Combined Fleet's scout planes had also reported the

Americans in possession of the airfield, thereby contradicting Rabaul's message claiming that it had been captured.

Admiral Yamamoto was as annoyed as the commanders in Rabaul. Where was Kawaguchi?

He was grinding his teeth in the jungle and preparing a fresh attack.

At one time during last night's abortive assault General Kawaguchi found himself alone but for his adjutant, his orderly and a few soldiers. The assault had been that haphazard.

Moreover neither Colonel Oka in the west nor the Ishitari Battalion in the east had attacked as scheduled.

But tonight, Kawaguchi thought grimly, they would. He had seen to that, contacting both commanders. Moreover, he had been able to get some kind of order into his own force, still well over 2500 men. Once again he would strike with two reinforced battalions until a hole had been ripped open for Colonel Watanabe's elite. It was unfortunate that his artillery had been lost at Tasimboko and that the Americans had captured the Ishitari guns supposed to batter the Ridge; nevertheless, Japanese spiritual power should still suffice to overwhelm these contemptible Americans.

Of whom, unknown to General Kawaguchi, there were only 400.

"Gas attack!"

A cloud of vapor drifted over the Marine right, and the too-precise voice came again:

"Gas attack!"

But there was no gas, only smoke, an attempt to mask that 100-yard approach, and a trick to shake American nerves.

But the Marines held to their holes, watching the jungle while flares made a ghoulish day of the night. And then the jungle spewed out short, squat shapes.

Two thousand men, launching two major attacks, they came sprinting toward the Marines in waves. They came on to a rising, shrieking chant:

"U. S. Marines be dead tomorrow."
"U. S. Marines be dead tomorrow."

"You'll eat shit first, you bastards!" a BAR-man screamed, and the Ridge erupted with the mad wail of battle.[19]

Japanese fell, but still they came on. Platoon after platoon, company after company, flowed from the jungle and went bowlegging it through the flickering green light. They bent back the Marine lines like a horseshoe. But they could not break them. Marines fought back individually. Pfc. Jimmy Corzine saw four Japanese setting up a machine gun on a knob. He rushed them. He bayoneted the gunner, and swung the gun around to spray the enemy with his own death. Then Corzine was killed.

On the right the Japanese were once again chopping up the Americans into small groups. Captain John Sweeney's company was cut up into small pockets of resistance. His own right flank was gone and he was down to sixty men, and on the left a mortar barrage and another Japanese charge was splintering Torgerson's parachutists.

Torgerson rallied his faltering men. He went among them and taunted them. He held roll call on the Ridge and challenged each man to go forward by name. They went. They fought back with machine guns. But the Japanese singled out the automatic weapons and lobbed grenades down on them. Sergeant Keith Perkins crept over the Ridge searching for ammunition for his two machine guns. One by one, his gunners were struck down. Perkins jumped on his last gun and was also killed.

Now there was another iron tongue baying over Guadalcanal.

Even as the Raiders were resisting that first fierce charge, Louie the Louse flew over Henderson Field. He cut his motors, coasted, dropped his flare, and seven destroyers in Iron Bottom Bay began shelling the field. They fired for an hour, their voices thrumming like a bass viol beneath the clatter and screaming of the Ridge, the jabbering of the Japanese and the coarse cursing of the Marines.

Then the Japanese ships fell silent. They had heard firing south of the airfield. They waited for the flare from General Kawaguchi signaling its capture. Then they heard firing from the east.

The Ishitari Battalion was attacking the Third Battalion, First Marines. They had crossed the Tenaru River upstream and emerged into a broad field of kunai grass. They formed and charged. Halfway across they ran into barbed wire and the massed fire of Marine guns. American 75-mm howitzers rained shells among them. They broke and fled. They re-formed east of the field for a stronger attack, and came again.

Once more they hit the wire and were torn apart. But some of them got through. Captain Robert Putnam rang up Lieutenant Colonel William McKelvy, to report:

"Some Japs just got inside my barbed wire." There was a pause, and then Putnam concluded: "There were twenty-seven of them."[20]

Squat dark shapes were running low toward the Ridge when Red Mike Edson's telephone jangled. A voice said cautiously:

"What name do you identify with Silent?"

"Lew," Edson whispered.

"That is correct," Captain Lew Walt said, and began his report. Another voice broke in:

"Our situation here, Colonel Edson, is excellent. Thank you, sir."[21]

Edson swore softly. It was the enemy. They had cut the wire and Captain Sweeney on the right was still cut off. How to reach him? Red Mike seized an iron-lunged corporal and sent him forward. The man cupped his hands to his lips and bellowed:

"Red Mike says it's okay to pull back!"[22]

Out in the wild spitting blackness of the right flank Sweeney's isolated remnant fought back to the contracted Marine line.

For Red Mike Edson was shortening his position. The battle had come to crux and he was taunting his men to win it. He lay within ten yards of his foremost machine gun. He lay with his arm curled about his telephone and shielding his face against fragments whizzing from the blasts that lifted him up and slammed him to the ground. He saw men drifting toward the rear and he ran at them. He seized them and spun them around and pointed his finger at the enemy and snarled: "The only thing they have that you don't is guts!"[23]

Major Bailey also darted at retreating Marines. He had been running back and forth from the Ridge to the rear for grenades and ammunition. He crawled over the bullet-swept Ridge to bring them to Marine foxholes. He caught at the arms of dazed men and slapped them, screaming: "You! Do *you* want to live forever?"[24]

It was the cry of old Dan Daly echoing across the decades from Belleau Wood, and it made another generation of young Americans ashamed of what they were about to do. They turned and went back.

They fought on while Colonel Edson lay on his belly bringing his own artillery in closer and closer to the charging enemy. A corporal named Watson who would be Lieutenant Watson in the morning spotted the enemy for him. He marked the Japanese rocket signals and directed redoubled fire to break up the enemy's massing points.

"Closer," Edson whispered. "Closer."[25]

The Ridge shook and flashed. A terrible steel rain fell among Marines and Japanese alike. Terrified enemy soldiers dove into Marine foxholes to escape death above ground. Marines knifed them and pitched them out again. The night was hideous with the screams of the stricken, for artillery does not kill cleanly: it tears men's organs with jagged chunks of steel, it blows off their limbs and burns their faces black.

But now the Kawaguchis were falling back again. Now the short squat shapes were springing to their feet and sprinting back into an opaque wall of darkness, jabbering once they had gained cover—for it was the chief failing of these jungle-fighters that they could not keep silent in the jungle. At two o'clock they came again behind another mortar barrage which cut wires to Vandegrift's headquarters and the artillery.

"Marine you die!" the Japanese shrieked again, but with a notable lack of their former fervor, and the Marines, already exultant with the scent of victory, replied with strings of obscene oaths and streams of bullets, and they cut the enemy down.

At half-past two in the morning of September 14 Red Mike Edson called headquarters and said:

"We can hold."[26]

Chapter 3

BATTLES do not end suddenly, they die down.

Throughout that long dawn of September 14 the Battle of Bloody Ridge sputtered on like an expiring fuse. Before daylight General Kawaguchi launched two more attacks which came after units of Vandegrift's reserve had groped their way into Edson's support. But they were faltering thrusts which hardly began before Marine artillery broke them up.

At six o'clock the Army P-400s roared over the Ridge at twenty feet, spewing cannon into Kawaguchi's assembly points with devastating effect.

Two thousand yards to the east on the Ishitari Battalion front, five Marine tanks clanked rashly past their own wire in an attempt to repeat the Tenaru slaughter. Three of them sank in the mud and were knocked out by antitank fire. Nevertheless, the Ishitaris retreated rapidly east.

On the Ridge the random pinging of sniper's bullets still kept Marine heads low. Souvenir-hunters such as Phil Chaffee would pause yet a bit before venturing among more than five hundred Japanese bodies strewn about these muddy slopes. Marines were still dying. At eight o'clock a jeep loaded with wounded was riddled by machine-gun fire that killed Major Robert Brown, Edson's operations officer, and almost all the other occupants. One of the wounded drove the shattered vehicle out of range on its starter: it hopped out of sight like a monster toad.

Some of the Japanese had infiltrated. Three of them slipped into General Vandegrift's command post.

"Banzai! Banzai!"

Vandegrift looked up from messages he was reading outside his pavilion. He saw two onrushing enemy soldiers and an officer swinging a saber. The officer hurled the saber like a spear at a nearby sergeant, transfixing him. Inside a tent Sergeant Major Shepherd Banta heard the enemy scream: he turned from casti- gating a clerk to rush outside with drawn pistol and shoot the enemy officer dead. A Marine corporal tried to shoot one of the soldiers, but his pistol jammed. He dove at the intruder; just as he hit him shots rang out all over the command post and both Japanese soldiers fell dead.

Vandegrift continued reading his messages. They indicated to him that Edson had won the most critical battle of the campaign. But they also made it plain that he could not go over to the offensive to destroy his shattered enemy. Colonel Thomas had al- ready fed the Second Battalion, Fifth, into the battle and left Vandegrift without any reserve. Even though Edson had won a great victory at a loss of only fifty-nine Marines dead or missing and 204 wounded, his composite force was reeling. The para- chutists were in tatters, down to 165 officers and men of an original 377, and he would have to get them off the island. The Raiders were down to 526 effectives out of an original 750. Van- degrift dared not weaken any point in his line by pulling out troops: there had been the attack to the east and there were re- ports of enemy forces massed at the Matanikau. No, Archer Van- degrift could only be thankful for Red Mike Edson and his men and let the enemy withdraw.

General Kawaguchi was withdrawing. He was departing in tears.

Throughout the morning he had heard the roll call of disaster: 708 of his men dead, 505 of them wounded. American firepower had been ferocious. Even now the American aircraft with shark- teeth painted on their sharp snouts were pumping cannon into his survivors. And shame had dishonored his defeat: Colonel Watanabe had failed to join the action. The powerful battalion which was to dash to the airfield had spent the night marking time. When Kawaguchi heard of this he wept openly. His guards- man's mustache quivered, and he sent for Colonel Watanabe.

"Coward," he cried as the colonel approached, "commit hara- kiri!"[1]

Colonel Watanabe hobbled closer and Kawaguchi relented. The man could barely stand, and Watanabe explained that the jungle march had ruined his feet and he had been unable to lead his troops. He did not say why he had not turned his command over to his executive officer, and Kawaguchi was too distressed to press him on it.

The general had to choose between returning to Taivu in the east or marching west to join Colonel Oka at the Matanikau. Still unclear on the nature of the American force that had landed in his rear at Tasimboko, wishing to gather his forces, he decided to go west. In mid-morning he gave the order to break through the jungle toward the headwaters of the Matanikau. Some 400 badly wounded men were placed on improvised litters, four and sometimes six soldiers to a litter, and Kawaguchi's ragged, beaten, bleeding column began snaking south.

In mid-afternoon they heard firing to the west. Colonel Oka was at last launching his attack from the Matanikau. The firing died down almost as soon as it began, indicating that Oka was not only tardy but also timid.

Overhead, above the matted jungle roof that gave them cover, Kawaguchi's men could hear the familiar growling of dogfighting airplanes.

Rabaul had still not heard from General Kawaguchi, although it was plain that Henderson Field was still in American hands. Therefore the customary bombing formations were sent south, and they were met by the customary flights of Marine Wildcats.

There was now a rivalry among these fliers, and Captain John Smith and Captain Marion Carl were tied for the lead with twelve kills apiece. That day neither of them shot down another enemy plane, but Carl's fighter was so badly riddled that he was forced to bail out over Koli Point to the east.

His parachute blossomed above him and he drifted down into the Bay. He freed himself from his harness and swam ashore. Waiting for him on the beach was a powerful, smiling Fijian named Eroni. He was one of Martin Clemens's most valued men, a "medical practitioner" who was highly respected by the natives. Eroni promised to take the tall American back to Henderson Field.

Kelly Turner was keeping his promise to Archer Vandegrift. On that morning of September 14 he sailed in *McCawley* at the head of a force bringing the Seventh Marines from Espiritu Santo to Guadalcanal. Admiral Ghormley, who had not favored

Turner's plan, had nevertheless given his beetle-browed amphibious commander all that he could, once he saw that Turner could not be dissuaded. A strong carrier group built around *Wasp* and *Hornet* and commanded by Rear Admiral Leigh Noyes was to protect Turner's convoy of six transports.

Throughout the day these transports went zigzagging toward Torpedo Junction. Reports of enemy activity multiplied: carriers and battleships to the north, Tokyo Express warships to the northwest.

At noon a big Kawanishi lumbered overhead and Turner knew he had been spotted. He decided that he must withdraw: he could not dare to risk these four thousand Marines who might be the saving of Guadalcanal. But he would continue on until nightfall to delude the enemy into thinking he had held course. After dark, he would retire to await a more favorable opportunity.

Wasp and *Hornet* with mighty *North Carolina* and their screens held toward Torpedo Junction.

September 15 dawned cloudless and blue. Six miles of white-plumed waves separated *Wasp* and *Hornet*. The morning passed with no reports of the enemy, either above or below the sea. Some time after noon combat air patrol shot down a two-engined flying boat beyond the range of the carriers. At 2:20 o'clock *Wasp* turned into the wind to launch and receive planes.

Commander Takaichi Kinashi, skipper of submarine *I-19*, watched this maneuver through his periscope. His joy was unbounded. *Wasp* was in an awkward position and none of her six circling destroyers seemed to have sighted his submarine yet.

Captain Forrest Sherman aboard *Wasp* sounded the routine whistle for a turn, and bent on 16 knots to return to his base course, and Commander Kinashi sent a spread of four torpedoes hissing toward the swinging ship.

"Torpedoes!" starboard lookouts yelled.

Captain Sherman ordered rudder full right. But the Long Lances were running fast and true. Two of them struck forward to starboard and a third broached and dove to strike the hull fifty feet forward of the bridge.

Wasp was whipsawed. She leaped and twisted like a stricken monster. Planes were lifted and slammed to the deck. Men were hurled against steel bulkheads, generators were torn from their foundations, and the great ship took a dangerous list. Fires broke out, and *Wasp* was a floating torch whose smoke and flames were ominously visible to *Hornet* a half dozen miles away.

Now *Hornet* had to meet her own ordeal, for submarine *I-15* had joined the attack. Her skipper loosed his own spread of steel fish. They sped unseen toward *Hornet,* until destroyer *Mustin* on *Hornet's* port bow sighted a wake ahead and to port. *Mustin* swung hard left to avoid it, hoisted the torpedo warning and gave the alarm by voice radio.

Hornet got out of the way.

But one of *I-15's* torpedoes passed under *Mustin's* keel and ran 500 yards into the side of *North Carolina.* A great roar, a pillar of water and oil shooting into the sky, five men killed—and a gash 32 feet long and 18 feet high was torn twenty feet below *North Carolina's* water line. But battleships are built to take it. Forward magazines were flooded as a fire-prevention measure and within five minutes the great vessel had lost her list and was steaming majestically along at twenty-five knots.

Destroyers are not so husky, and another of *I-15's* torpedoes tore into *O'Brien* to deliver what was to be her death wound: she would break up and sink while attempting to return to West Coast ports.

And now *Wasp* was a holocaust. Flames raged out of control. At three o'clock a shattering explosion shook her, killing men on the port side of the bridge and hurling Admiral Noyes to the deck, his clothes burning. Captain Sherman evacuated the bridge. He conferred with his officers on the flight deck and concluded that the ship was lost.

"Abandon ship!"

Wounded were gently lowered over the side onto life rafts and floating mattresses and then *Wasp's* men jumped and dove for their lives. Destroyers picked them up. Of 2247 men aboard, 193 were lost and 366 wounded. All but one of *Wasp's* airborne planes landed safely on *Hornet,* and Rear Admiral Norman Scott in cruiser *San Francisco,* now in command of the group, ordered destroyer *Lansdowne* to sink the ship that had fought German U-boats in the Atlantic and saved Malta.

Lansdowne fired five torpedoes. All hit, three exploded, and at nine o'clock that night *Wasp* went to her death in the Pacific.

Hornet was now the only American carrier operational in the

Pacific. *O'Brien's* special antiaircraft firepower was lost to her, *North Carolina* was also out of the fight for Guadalcanal, and *Washington* was the only new battleship still available.

And four thousand Marines had lost half the protection required to get them safely through the waters of Torpedo Junction.

News of *Wasp's* sinking sweetened the bitter taste in Admiral Yamamoto's mouth. Commander, Combined Fleet, had been chagrined to receive reports of the American carrier force at the very moment when his ships were low on fuel. He had had to spend three days refueling at sea at a point two hundred miles north of Guadalcanal, and had missed the chance to strike.

Then, on September 15, he had heard reports of the Kawaguchi disaster, and had been filled with bitter anger.[2] Rather than waste more valuable fuel sailing aimlessly around, he had ordered his ships back to Truk. Enroute, he received Commander Kinashi's joyful report of having destroyed *Wasp*.

At Truk a conference was held between Yamamoto's staff and General Hyakutake's staff. It was decided that more troops would be needed in addition to the Sendai Division already assembling at Rabaul. Tokyo was notified and two days later Imperial General Headquarters assigned the veteran 38th or Nagoya Division to Hyakutake.

Japan's high command also instructed Hyakutake to suspend the Port Moresby operation indefinitely. On September 14 his troops had looked down on the lights of the Allied port, but now they were to retire to Buna to await the successful conclusion of Operation Ka.

In the meantime three new carriers then training in home waters would join Yamamoto at Truk. They would not arrive, however, until the second week in October, much to the consternation of some officers who believed that to delay a full-scale counteroffensive for almost a month was to grant the enemy a respite which might prove suicidal for Japan. They wanted to strike immediately, break in on the Americans while they still had their backs to the wall.

But Isoroku Yamamoto was adamant. He wanted those three carriers. Besides, it would take nearly a month to get the Sendai Division into Guadalcanal.

The loss of *Wasp* was to deepen Admiral Ernest King's conviction that the desperate situation at Guadalcanal could not be retrieved without more airplanes for Henderson Field. King made this conclusion clear at a meeting of the Joint Chiefs of Staff on September 16.

General Arnold replied that the need was landing fields, not planes. If Guadalcanal had more than eighty or a hundred planes the craft would sit idle on the fields and their pilots would get stale. In England planes and pilots could be used against Germany every day.

"There should be a reconsideration of allocation every time there is a new critical situation," King said. "The Navy is in a bad way at this particular moment."[3]

It was an astounding admission from King the confident, and the Navy's commander-in-chief followed it up by asking for Lightning fighters for Guadalcanal. Arnold reluctantly agreed to divert fifteen of them from the North African invasion scheduled for November. That was all he could spare, and he could not say when he could spare them. King insisted that the South Pacific had to be saturated with such planes, and Arnold exploded:

"What is the saturation point? Certainly, not several hundred planes sitting on airdromes so far in the rear that they cannot be used. They will not do us any good, and may do us some harm."[4]

King left the meeting in exasperation. Next day, his pen impelled by reports of the *Wasp* disaster, he prepared a memorandum for General Marshall. Of sixty-two Wildcats delivered to Guadalcanal since August 20 only thirty were operational. The Navy, he wrote, could not "meet this rate of attrition and still operate carriers." It was therefore "imperative that the future continuous flow of Army fighters be planned, starting at once, irrespective of, and in higher priority than, the commitments to any theater."

King had ceased to make requests. Now he was demanding.

Although shaken by the loss of *Wasp,* Admiral Turner was also aware that Guadalcanal probably could not be held without the Seventh Marines, as well as a valuable load of aviation gasoline which he was bringing with him. On September 16—which would be September 17 back in Washington—he decided to push on to Guadalcanal.

He was favored by overcast skies. General MacArthur came to

his assistance with a series of bombing raids on Rabaul, and so did Admiral Yamamoto by sailing back to Truk.

Turner slipped through Torpedo Junction to stand off Lunga Roads at dawn of September 18. Four thousand fresh Marines with all their equipment came flowing ashore, while destroyers *Monssen* and *MacDonough* paraded the Bay hurling five-inch shells at enemy-held sections of Guadalcanal.

That night Kawaguchi's men prepared to rest in a ravine south of Mount Austen. Soldiers hacked a clearing in the jungle. The wounded were laid on the ground to the rear so that their cries and the horrible smell of their gangrenous wounds would not keep the others awake. Then the able tottered to their feet to search for food.

The men had become ravenous since the rice gave out. They tore bark from trees or grubbed in the earth for tree roots. They drank from puddles and in a few more days they would gnaw their leather rifle slings. Some of them had already buried their mortars and heavy machine guns, but they had been too weak to bury hundreds of comrades dying along the way. The dead were left beside the trail to become moving white mounds of dissolution, true "corpses rotting in the mountain grass."

That night as these barefoot and ragged scarecrows sucked on their agony in insect-whirring blackness, someone switched on a short-wave radio to a patriotic mass meeting held in Hinomiya Stadium in Tokyo. Captain Hiraide of the Naval Staff announced the recapture of the airfield on Guadalcanal and a great gust of cheering drowned out the moans of the Kawaguchi wounded. Hiraide said:

"The Marines left in the lurch have been faring miserably since they were the victims of Roosevelt's gesture." There was more applause, and again Hiraide's voice: ". . . the stranded ten thousand have been practically wiped out."[5]

It was well that it was dark, so that no one need look the other in the eye.

In the morning, while the Kawaguchis swung west to cross the upper reaches of the Lunga River, abandoning helmets, packs, light machine guns—all but their rifles—a decrepit old launch wheezed up to the beachmaster's jetty at Kukum.

Corporal Eroni held the tiller while Captain Carl brought the balky old engine to a coughing silence. Both men calmly stepped out to introduce themselves to a band of startled Marines. Then they borrowed a jeep and drove to General Geiger's headquarters. Carl strode into the Pagoda. Geiger looked up in glad surprise. Carl had been given up for dead. Then Geiger grinned slyly.

"Marion," he said, "I have bad news. Smitty has fourteen planes, now. You still have only twelve. What about that?"

Carl stroked his lantern jaw, hesitating. Then he burst out:

"Goddamit, General, ground him for five days!"[6]

Corporal Eroni had gone from the Pagoda to see his old friend, Sergeant Major Vouza, and his chief, Martin Clemens.

Vouza had completely recovered from his wounds. In fact, shortly after his throat had been sewn up, he had asked for something to eat. Now, as September turned toward October, Vouza was back at work scouring the trails for Japanese prisoners. He could deliver them on schedule and to order, always trussed and slung, perhaps a bit more painfully tight than heretofore, because Vouza had scars on chest and neck to remind him of Mr. Ishimoto.

Vouza was highly popular among the Marines. He wore their dungaree uniform when inside the base, the medal they had given him pinned proudly on the jacket.

Martin Clemens was also a favorite, something like a celebrity whom Intelligence kept trotting out for the entertainment of visiting personages. The day Eroni arrived a colonel was brought to see Clemens. The colonel seemed very interested in the natives. He asked if they had known how to write before the advent of the white man.

"Not very well," Clemens replied. "You see, they had no paper."[7]

Even Eroni joined the shout of laughter, and then he left, accompanied by a Marine radio operator, bound for Marau on the eastern tip of Guadalcanal. The Marine's mission was to set up a coastwatching station for submarines.

After the ships of the Tokyo Express streaked up The Slot, they were replaced by Japanese submarines which entered the Bay from the other end. They lay there to fire their torpedoes at transports anchored off Lunga Roads. Sometimes they surfaced to attack smaller vessels with their deck guns. At other times they duelled Marine 75-mm howitzers on Tulagi. The Marines had smaller cannon but they usually could drive the submarines down by shelling their gun crews.

All of these actions were clearly visible to men on the beach defenses, or to other Marines who had come down to the shore to take a swim—in the way that Pfc. Richard McAllister went swimming near Lunga in late September while a small cargo vessel was being unloaded. McAllister saw an enemy periscope break the water. He saw a torpedo go flashing toward the cargo ship. Then he saw it come curving just off the ship's stern and come running straight at him.

McAllister turned and swam. His arms flailed the water like a racing windmill. He swam wondering if there was enough metal in his dog tags to draw the torpedo toward him. He looked back wildly and saw the torpedo coming closer. He looked ahead and saw a beach working party scattering and taking for the coconuts.

He looked again backward and saw the torpedo's steel snout only a few feet behind him. He swerved and dug his face into the water and flailed. His feet felt the sand beneath him just as the torpedo skimmed past him and drove up on the beach not three feet to his side.

But McAllister did not pause to measure the miss. Nor did he tarry for his clothes. His legs were now free and pumping and he entered the coconut grove going very, very fast. Later, this precious Long Lance would be disarmed and shipped home to instruct American manufacturers in the things that they did not know about torpedoes.

The military correspondent told General Vandegrift that the American people did not know what was going on at Guadalcanal. He said that they had been led to believe that the Marines were firmly entrenched and occupied almost the entire island. Today, September 19, the correspondent said, he had discovered that this was far from true. It was obvious that American troops were besieged within a small perimeter at the end of a riddled supply line.

Moreover, he said, in Washington the high command seemed

about ready to give up on Guadalcanal, and in Nouméa a spirit of defeatism had seized Admiral Ghormley's headquarters. There were at that moment upwards of sixty ships lying unloaded in Nouméa because of the confusion at Ghormley's headquarters and because the ships' officers and crews, already drawing exorbitant "combat-zone" pay, wanted to be paid overtime rates to unload them. The correspondent had seen all this and he wanted to know what the general thought about it.

Vandegrift said that he did not like it at all. He would like the American public to know what had been done, that Japan had been stopped for the first time. He discussed the situation pro and con and concluded firmly that the enemy had actually been hurt more. He said he would like the public to know how his men had stood up to ordeal, and especially with what magnificent high spirit they continued to hang on. The correspondent was surprised. He examined the general shrewdly.

"Are you going to hold this beachhead?" he asked. "Are you going to stay here?"

"Hell, yes!" Archer Vandegrift snorted. "Why not?"[8]

Chapter 4

GENERAL VANDEGRIFT'S confidence rested upon the fact that he now had more than 19,000 men and could go over to a cordon defense.

Hitherto his line had been continuous only on the northern beaches and the Tenaru barrier to the east. On the west and south he had held strong points tied together by patrols with the gaps covered by artillery. Now he could draw a ring around Henderson Field. He could advance south to a deeper ridge line and do the same to the west, and there would be no gaps anywhere. It meant spreading a lot of men thin, defending at every point weakly rather than at vital points in depth, and it also meant that wherever the enemy chose to attack he could concentrate his most against Vandegrift's least. But Vandegrift did have superb artillery, he would have more with the arrival of five-inch naval rifles and eventually 155-mm "Long Toms," and he thought he could build a line strong enough to withstand any attack until he could counter with his now-ample reserves.

Build was the word. With bulldozers, barbed wire, axes, shovels, sandbags, and machetes made of cut-down cavalry sabers, Vandegrift's men built a bristling defensive ring in an energetic style which would one day prompt a Japanese officer to snort that the U. S. Marines were actually not genuine jungle-fighters because "they always cut the jungle down." He was not wrong. In the jungle ravines between the ridges sweating Marines hacked out fields of fire of up to a hundred yards. In the fields they burned the kunai grass to clear even longer lanes between their guns and the enemy's cover. In the coconut groves axes rang and great trees came crashing down to cries of "Charge it to Lever Brothers!" and then the trunks were chopped into sections and the logs dragged across holes that were now deeper and more thickly cushioned

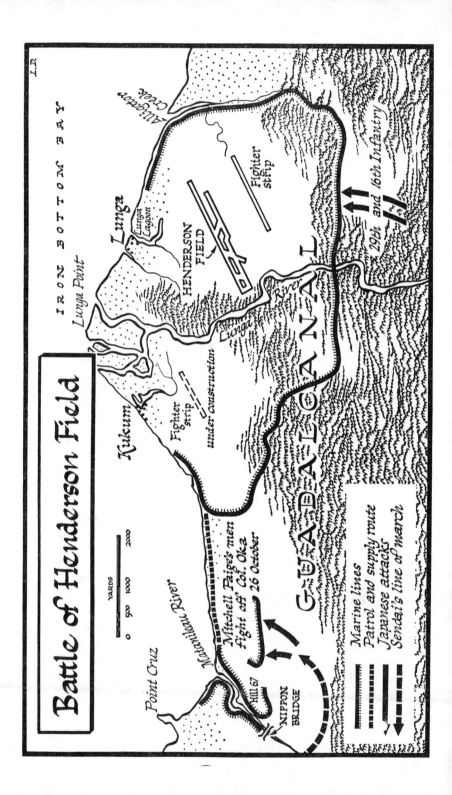

Battle of Henderson Field

IRON BOTTOM BAY

GUADALCANAL

Alligator Creek

Lunga Point

Lunga

Lunga Lagoon

Lunga River

HENDERSON FIELD

Fighter strip

29th and 16th Infantry

Kukum

Fighter strip under construction

Point Cruz

Matanikau River

Mitchell Paige's men fight off Col. Oka 26 October

Hill 67

NIPPON BRIDGE

YARDS
0   500 1000   2000

Marine lines
Patrol and supply route
Japanese attacks
Sendai's line of march

L.D.

with sandbags. Clumps of grass were planted atop the logs and in a few days tropic moisture had fastened them there so that the gunpits gave the appearance of low hummocks. Barbed wire was now plentiful and the Marines strung apron after apron of it until the outer rim of Vandegrift's ring was formed of concentric collars of cruel black lace. Outside this rim mortarmen and artillerists marked all the likely assembly points and trails. All approaches were mined or booby-trapped. Hand-grenade pins were partially withdrawn and fastened to wires intended to trip unwary feet. Inside the rim riflemen dug Japanese spider-holes, deep vertical pits in which, if they were not filled with rain, a man could stand and shoot. Machine gunners, meanwhile, interlocked their guns or registered them for night firing. They placed cans of gasoline in trees and pressed cartridges into sandbags under their gunbutts to mark the exact spot to fire at night and set the cans afire.

On and on they worked, cursing, cursing, cursing as they did, for these filthy, ragged, gaunt, undaunted men could no more work without the name of God on their lips than a preacher can preach without it. They cursed everything and everyone about them, calling down the Divine wrath upon friend and foe alike, upon the barbed wire that ripped their flesh and the flies that fed on the blood, or on the female anopholes mosquito who carried malaria and bit with her tail straight up; they cursed the rain that drenched them or the sun that scorched them, the sweat that made their tools slippery or the dysentery growling in their bowels; they spoke unspeakables about Washing Machine Charley and the Tokyo Express, and when they were at the chow line in the galley they were not delicate in describing the mess plopping wetly on their outstretched messgear or in delineating the lineage of the cooks who could not make it palatable—and yet they had not exhausted themselves, having saved the most anguished and insulting oaths for that moment, when, approaching the end of the line cursing the tasteless black liquid sloshing around in canteen cups now so hot that they burned their fingers, they were told to halt and open their mouths while corpsmen threw into them those bitter yellow atabrine pills which were supposed to suppress malaria, but which would also, as these infuriated men would believe until the war was over, make them impotent. "You shanker-mechanic!" they howled. "You think I want a broken arrow?" And so they virtually swore Vandegrift's new line into existence, only shutting their mouths when it was their turn to go on patrol.

The patrols went out daily. They were Vandegrift's eyes and ears. They usually went out in squads—ten or a dozen men—occasionally in company strength up to two hundred. They were lightly armed. The men carried only one canteen of water and enough bullets to beat back an ambush. They smeared their faces with mud and adorned their bodies with branches. They moved silently along the trails, spaced out at intervals of a dozen feet to left and right of the track. Progress was agonizingly slow, often at a rate of no more than a mile in a day. They moved and halted, moved and halted, investigating every turn, searching every defile that might lead to ambush.

There were frequent ambushes during late September. On one of them a company scouting the Lunga south of the perimeter was struck by machine guns and pinned to the ground. Unseen Japanese sat behind their weapons calling, "Come here, please. Come here, please." The Marines began a fighting withdrawal, pulling back gradually, but leaving behind men who had fallen in the jungle. One of them was Private Jack Morrison. He had been shot in the chest and toppled into the underbrush with his feet sprawled across the trail. Another Marine lay moaning behind a log, and a Japanese soldier hurdled the log to jab downward twice with his bayonet. There were no more moans. Morrison clenched his teeth against his own outcries.

Pfc. Harry Dunn also lay in the underbrush. But he was not hurt. He was playing dead. Throughout that waning afternoon the enemy tramped through the ambush area, stripping the dead, laughing and calling to each other. But they did not notice Morrison's outflung feet. Morrison passed from consciousness to unconsciousness. His mind was like a boat drifting from mist to sun, from mist to sun. He felt the blood oozing from his wounds, felt himself growing weaker. The last time he awoke it was dark. A hand was over his mouth. He stiffened in horror, but then a voice spoke gently in his ear: "It's all right. It's me—Harry Dunn."

Dunn pulled Morrison back from the trail into a thicket. He tried to bind his wounds with Morrison's shirt. But the garment became soaked with blood and Dunn threw it away. Then Dunn crept among the bodies of his comrades looking for water. The Japanese had taken all the canteens. Next he crawled to the river bank. He could see the Lunga gleaming darkly. He could hear murmuring wavelets. But he dared not cross a clearing in full view of the Japanese.

All that night and the next day Dunn and Morrison lay in their thicket, among the flies and ants and slithering things, their tongues beginning to swell with thirst, their noses filled with the sweet stench of flesh already decadent, and with Dunn's hand firmly clamped over Morrison's mouth.

Night fell again and Dunn decided that the Japanese had withdrawn upriver. He dragged Morrison to the Lunga. He pulled him gently down into the water. They drank for the first time in two days. Then Dunn sank into the river and pulled Morrison onto his back. He began crawling down the river bank. He watched the river fearfully for widening V-shaped wakes, for he knew that the Lunga was infested with crocodiles. Sometimes Morrison cried out, and Dunn had no way to silence him. Sometimes Dunn passed out from exhaustion, but he always regained consciousness and crawled on.

At daybreak Dunn reached the perimeter. Morrison was carefully lifted from his back and carried, still bleeding, to a jeep that rushed him to the airfield. There a plane flew him out to a base hospital and eventual recovery. Dunn who had at last passed out from exhaustion, was taken to the Guadalcanal hospital.

The Japanese who had ambushed Harry Dunn's company were from Colonel Oka's command. They were on patrol from the Matanikau River line which it was Oka's responsibility to hold, and it was to this haven that Major General Kawaguchi was bringing his beaten troops.

But it was not a haven. There could be no rest beneath the constant strafing and bombing of American aircraft and there could be no rehabilitation without rice. Oka's men were also hungry. They had brought only enough rations to tide them over until General Kawaguchi captured the airfield. After that they would live off American food. But the Americans had not surrendered and Oka had requested emergency rations from Rabaul. Unfortunately, the provisions that were put ashore at Kamimbo Bay to the west had to be brought east over fifty miles of jungle trail and through the clutching hands and hungry mouths of the two thousand men of the 8th Base Force who had fled the airfield the day that the Americans landed. Another seven hundred men from a Naval Landing Force also stood between Oka's thousand souls and their food. Thus, when the first of the Kawaguchis stumbled into camp on September 22, they found themselves among friends nearly as miserable as themselves.

Colonel Oka blanched at the sight of them. He had never seen such human wrecks. They did nothing but beg rice from his own hungry troops or wander among them with lit fire cords in their mouths pleading for a few crumbs of tobacco. Fighting Americans had not been like fighting the Chinese,[1] he was informed. Some of these survivors who had been with Colonel Ichiki at the Tenaru had horrible tales to tell of the Marines. They said they were foul-mouthed beasts, the refuse of jails and asylums. They cut off Japanese soldiers' arms and legs and ran over their bodies with steamrollers.

Neither Colonel Oka nor General Kawaguchi considered such stories fit for the ears of the defenders of the Matanikau, still less for the men of the 4th Infantry Regiment which had arrived at Cape Esperance in mid-September. Led by Colonel Nomasu Nakaguma these fresh and well-equipped troops, part of the crack Sendai Division, had marched east to reinforce the Matanikau. It would be unwise to allow them to mingle with the Kawaguchi scarecrows and catch that most deadly of military diseases: defeatism. So the survivors of Bloody Ridge were sent farther west again, to the food stores and doctors and quinine at Kamimbo Bay and Cape Esperance, and, for the more fortunate among them, for shipment to Rabaul and hospital treatment via destroyers.

For the Tokyo Express was running at full throttle again.

In late August, just before he had left for the South Pacific, Brigadier General Roy Geiger had encountered Lieutenant Colonel Albert Cooley in San Diego.

"Al," Geiger grunted, "got your Group ready for war?"

Cooley gulped. His dive-bomber squadron had just been split four ways to form new squadrons and his fighters were new and untrained. But he smiled weakly and said: "Not ready, sir—but willing."

"Well, you're going next Saturday," Geiger grunted.[2] And they did.

In the last week of September, Cooley and five Dauntless pilots were flown into Guadalcanal by SCAT. Geiger immediately put Colonel Wallace in charge of all fighters and Cooley in charge of the bombers, with orders to stop the Tokyo Express.

On September 21 Cooley led the Dauntlesses against destroyer *Kagero* unloading troops at Kamimbo, but failed to sink her.

Next day they attacked the enemy assembly point at Visale, a few miles north of Kamimbo. Roy Geiger flew one of the bombers. Disgusted to hear pilots complaining that the bomb-pocked airstrip was risky, fifty-seven-year-old Geiger had lumbered from the Pagoda to squeeze into a Dauntless cockpit. Then he thundered aloft to drop a thousand-pounder on the Japanese. That night more bombers struck at a group of destroyer-transports.

On September 24 Cooley's planes bombed and strafed destroyers *Umikaze* and *Kawakaze*—the killer of *Blue*—in Kamimbo Bay.

Nevertheless, the Tokyo Express still ran as scheduled. The troops were getting through, and Vandegrift, alarmed by patrol reports of strong defenses on the Matanikau, decided that he had better attack.

It was from Chesty Puller that Vandegrift heard of the enemy strength.

Puller was a lieutenant colonel now, and on September 21 he was just where he wanted to be: at the head of a body of Marines hunting the enemy. His Crusader's Cross around his neck, his jungle-stained copy of Caesar's *Gallic Wars* in his pocket, his stump of a cold pipe in his mouth, Puller was leading his men toward the headwaters of the Matanikau.

And the Japanese were waiting for him. They struck repeatedly at his column, and these unseasoned men of the First Battalion, Seventh Marines, proved themselves not as jungle-wise as they might be. On the night of the first day they were all but exhausted from the ordeal of moving through the sort of terrain which had ruined General Kawaguchi's brigade. Colonel Puller was also out of breath, from swearing at them.

In the morning they were hit again. One of the casualties was Captain Jack Stafford. He was torn about the face and neck by the explosion of his own rifle grenade. Puller came to his side just as a corpsman gave him morphine. He saw that Stafford was

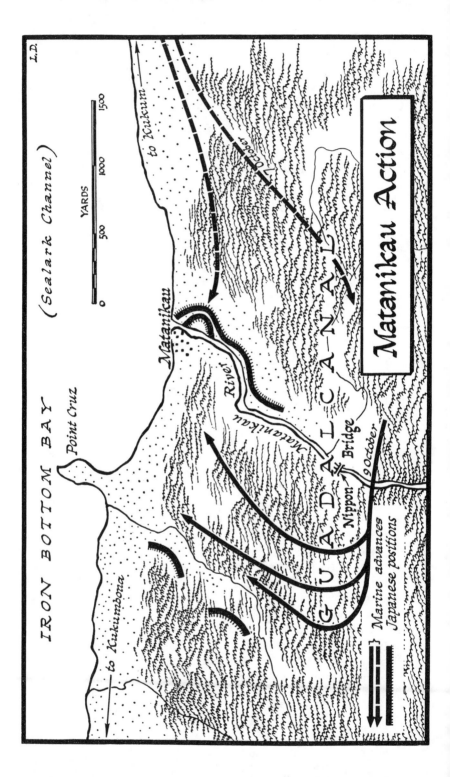

IRON BOTTOM BAY

(Sealark Channel)

Point Cruz

Matanikau

to Kukumbona

YARDS

0   500   1000   1500

to Kukum

Matanikau River

GUADALCANAL

Nippon Bridge

9 October

Matanikau Action

Marine advances
Japanese positions

L.D.

strangling in his own blood. He unsnapped a big safety pin from his bandoleer. He reached into Stafford's mouth, seized his tongue, and pinned it neatly to the man's dungaree collar. Puller's action saved Stafford's life, and it convinced his men that perhaps this little leader with the big chest and the big voice was even bigger than his legend.

They were an improved force, when, on September 23, they struck out again for the upper Matanikau. This time, though they lost seven dead and twenty-five wounded in fights with Oka's outposts, they gave much worse than they got. But there was still no crossing the Matanikau. Oka had blocked all the fords. On the morning of September 26, Puller called for air and artillery support. But the enemy was dug in and could not be dislodged. So Puller swung north and moved down the east bank of the Matanikau toward the coastal road. Japanese mortars and automatic weapons emplaced on the Matanikau's west bank struck them as they moved. Weary, they reached the coast at sundown.

From reports of Puller's foray it was clear to Vandegrift that the enemy held the Matanikau west bank in strength. He decided on a three-pronged operation to dislodge him.

The First Raiders, now under Lieutenant Colonel Sam Griffith, were to march inland along the Matanikau's east bank. They would cross the river at a log crossing called Nippon Bridge, and then wheel right to attack downstream to the sea.

As the Raiders attacked, the Second Battalion, Fifth Marines, would strike across a sandbar at the mouth of the Matanikau.

Simultaneously Puller's battalion would sail west to Point Cruz, land to the west of this promontory, turn left and attack to the east along the coastal track.

The operations were to be under Red Mike Edson, now in command of the Fifth Marines. They began on the morning of September 27, and they began with immediate trouble.

As Griffith and his Raiders approached Nippon Bridge they were struck by a storm of fire. The gallant Major Bailey was killed. Colonel Griffith attempted to swing around the blocking force and come down on its rear. But this slow and painful maneuver was eventually spotted by the Japanese and they opened fire. Griffith was wounded and his Raiders were stalled.

But garbled messages led Vandegrift and Edson to believe that the Raiders were safely across the river. Edson ordered the

Marines at the river-mouth to attack across the sandbar. They did, and were beaten back.

At this moment, Puller's battalion, under Major Otho Rogers in the absence of Puller, who was with Edson, sailed west to Point Cruz. They came quickly ashore and prepared to swing to their left. But the Japanese had seen them coming and had wisely pulled back and allowed them to penetrate about 400 yards inland. Then they struck at the Americans from three sides. They poured mortars and bullets into them and within a few minutes Major Rogers was killed—blown apart by a mortar landing almost under his feet—as were half a dozen others. Captain Charles Kelly took command. The toll of dead and wounded rose, especially in the company commanded by Captain Regan Fuller. The only way out for these Marines was the way they had come, now completely covered by enemy fire. And then the Japanese moved to surround them.

Colonel Edson had called for aerial support of the Marines trapped down at Point Cruz, but his message was never received. One of the heaviest air raids of the month came roaring down from Rabaul to knock out all of Henderson Field's communications.

While the raid was at its height, Chesty Puller hurried down to Kukum to hail the old four-stack destroyer, *Ballard,* which had escorted his men up to Point Cruz. He came aboard and *Ballard* began sailing west to the rescue.

Marines on Point Cruz were fighting desperately. Mortarmen fired at almost point-blank range. They held the mortars in place by lying on their backs to support the tubes with their feet. Captain Kelly tried to contact Captain Fuller's outfit. But Sergeant Robert Raysbrook, the communications man, reported that he had forgotten to bring his radio.

HELP

Lieutenant Dale Leslie saw it underneath him, tiny but distinct, in white letters that might be T-shirts. Leslie was flying his Dauntless along the coast in search of targets. He came down closer, saw the trapped Marines, and radioed Edson. Then he began patrolling the area, waiting to help. Beneath him on the Bay he saw an American destroyer approaching.

Sergeant Raysbrook was redeeming himself. He saw *Ballard's* approach, saw the black smoke boiling from her four stacks, and saw her guns begin to raise into position. He seized the T-shirts and jumped erect to wigwag the ship while reading her responses.

Chesty Puller was on *Ballard's* deck. He could see Raysbrook through his field glasses.

"Return to beach immediately," he had *Ballard* signal.

"Engaged," Raysbrook wagged. "Cannot return."

"Fight your way. Only hope."

There was no reply, and Puller had another message sent:

"Give me your boundaries right and left. Will use ship's fire."[3]

Raysbrook obliged, and *Ballard's* five-inchers began hurling shells into the jungle between the Marines and the sea. They cut huge swathes in it. To the east, a battalion of Marine artillery began battering the tip of Point Cruz to prevent the Japanese from occupying it and cutting off the retreat.

And Puller's men were coming down. They came plunging down the slopes with wild yells, firing as they came. They were halfway to the beach before the enemy tried to halt them. Platoon Sergeant Anthony Malanowski told Captain Fuller, "I'll handle the rear. I'll be with you in a few minutes." Malanowski took a BAR from a wounded man and laid it across a log. He knelt down. He was never seen again, although the men he was covering heard the bursts from his automatic rifle.

The Marines crowded down to the beach, and the enemy came after them slipping from tree to tree and nearly indistinguishable in their green uniforms. A Japanese officer sprang from the bush. He swung his saber with both hands and beheaded a Marine. The officer jumped back into cover just as a grenade thrown by Fuller flushed a tottering and dying enemy soldier from a thicket.

Landing boats from *Ballard* were roaring inshore, led by a Coast Guard coxswain named Donald Munro. Munro held his tiller with one hand and raked the enemy with machine-gun fire with the other. He was killed. Some of the boats faltered. The Dauntless flown by Dale Leslie came roaring in behind them, shepherding them toward the beach. Leslie's gunner sprayed bullets into the onrushing Japanese. But the enemy came closer. Some of the coxswains were unwilling to wait for the last stragglers. Captain Fuller persuaded them with his pistol, and before the sun was low in the western sky all of the trapped battalion had been drawn off, including twenty-three wounded and most of the bodies of twenty-four dead.

It might have been a slaughter if the battalion had broken. But the Marines kept their nerve and their ranks and the rescue took some of the sting out of the Matanikau defeat.

Defeat it was, and General Vandegrift was quick to admit it. His operation had been based on faulty intelligence which underestimated both the terrain and the enemy—hitherto an exclusively Japanese characteristic—and he had drifted into it. Having lost sixty dead and one hundred wounded, Vandegrift withdrew his forces to await a more favorable opportunity.

On September 28, one day after the Matanikau defeat, General Vandegrift received the following letter from Admiral Turner:

> . . . now would seem to be the time to push as hard as possible on the following items: (a) continue clearing out all the nests of enemy troops on the north side of Guadalcanal, initial operations continuing to the westward. I believe you are in a position to take some chances and go after them hard. I am glad to see Rupertus is cleaning up Florida Island; and believe he should establish detachments on Sandfly Passage, the north coast, Matumba Bay at the eastern end of Florida, as soon as justified. Here we are working up a scheme to start out within a few days with the two destroyer-transports available and two companies of the Second Raiders, to attack the Jap outposts entrenched at Cape Astrolabe, Malaita; at Marau Bay on Guadalcanal, and at Cape Hunter. We want to co-ordinate these operations with you, and get your approval of our plan; therefore the Commanding Officer of the Second Raider Battalion, after conference with me, will shortly fly up and see you and go over our plans with you. One question to decide is whether or not to leave small detachments of the Second Raiders at these places; at a later time, we would relieve them with other line troops.[4]

Vandegrift was infuriated. Here he was crossing swords with Kelly Turner again over the same old issue: the admiral's fondness for the general's troops. It had begun in New Zealand and had continued into Guadalcanal when, after the Savo disaster, Turner had sailed away with 1400 men of the Second Marines. He had then attempted to form them into a "2nd Provisional Raider Battalion," and had written to Admiral Ghormley recommending the overhaul of all Marine regiments so that each one would carry a raider battalion for special missions. Turner wrote that he did not believe Marine regiments would be needed in the Pacific, adding: "The employment of a division seems less likely." All of these moves and recommendations had been made without consulting Vandegrift, and it had required the intervention of Admiral Nimitz to scuttle Turner's plans for the Marines. Now, with the arrival in the New Hebrides of the "authentic" Second Raiders—the outfit that had raided Makin under Lieutenant Colonel Evans Carlson—Turner was once again putting down the sextant and reaching for the baton. To Vandegrift, who admired and respected Turner when he was at sea, the proposal was nonsense.[5] He answered it bluntly:

> From reconnaissance it is estimated the Japanese are now holding this river [Matanikau] line in force of about fifteen hundred men as outpost line of resistance. Information received from a captured prisoner, a copy of his testimony which is enclosed with this letter, would tend to show that we may expect an attack in force from additional troops to be landed some time around the first of October when the moon is favorable to such landing and operations. If the testimony of this prisoner is true, and an additional division is landed to the west of us and puts down a major push in depth through our west or southwest lines, they are now so thinly held and our reserves so few that it could well be dangerous to our position.
>
> I regret that Major Bailey of the Raiders was killed and that Lieutenant Colonel Griffith, the present Commander of the Raiders, was wounded in the shoulder. I have talked the question over with Edson, its previous Commander, and I believe that with the losses sustained in both officers and men of this battalion, and the strenuous work that they have done, that they should be returned to Noumea or some other place for rebuilding. If this is done, I urgently recommend that the Second Raider Battalion be sent in to replace them as we will need all the strength we can get for this next push which I feel sure will be a major one.[6]

Vandegrift dictated his reply confident that he had at least one ally in Nouméa. That was Major General Millard F. Harmon, who had spent a night on Guadalcanal a few days before, and who had agreed with Vandegrift's estimate of the situation. Moreover, Harmon had told Vandegrift that he would never place an Army division on Guadalcanal under Turner's command.[7] So Vandegrift stuck to his guns, and two days after he did he had gained another ally.

It was the last day of September and a furious thick rain was heralding the onslaught of the monsoon. Above Guadalcanal a Flying Fortress had lost its way, and then, coming very low, the pilot had seen the island and Henderson Field. He landed with twin V's of dirty water curving away from his big rubber wheels and then he taxied slowly through the mud toward a group of officers standing beneath a cluster of palm trees.

A ramp was run up to the Fort and a slender, white-haired man in khaki with four stars pinned to his collar stepped out.

General Vandegrift stepped forward and saluted smartly.

Admiral Chester Nimitz, Commander-in-Chief, Pacific Ocean Area, had come to Guadalcanal.

Vandegrift was not sorry that Nimitz had made an arrival typical of Guadalcanal. He wanted him to see what he and his men were up against, and he took him to see his perimeter. That night Vandegrift had no trouble impressing Nimitz with the necessity of concentrating forces to defend the airfield. Later, as the two men relaxed over a drink, Nimitz said:

"You know, Vandegrift, when this war is over we are going to write a new set of Navy Regulations. So just keep it in the back of your mind because I will want to know some of the things you think ought to be changed."

"I know one right now," Vandegrift replied grimly. "Leave out all reference that he who runs his ship aground will face a fate worse than death. Out here too many commanders have been far too leery about risking their ships."[8]

Nimitz smiled and said nothing.

In the morning it began to rain hard again. Vandegrift and Geiger hurried their guest to the airfield, both of them buoyed by Nimitz's promise of "support to the maximum of our resources."[9] At the field Nimitz decided that he would like to fly in the Flying Fort's nose. He crawled forward over the protests of his staff, and the big plane's motors coughed. It began thundering down the runway. Roy Geiger blanched. The Fort had not enough take-off speed. Suddenly the pilot shut off power and slammed the brakes, and the plane began to slide.

It slid almost the length of the strip and came to a halt with its distinguished nose hanging over the edge of the field not far short of the trees.

Admiral Nimitz went meekly to the back of the plane and the Fort finally took off safely.

It was not too soon. For the rain had stopped and clearing weather suggested that the noon raid in the enemy's mounting aerial onslaught would be down on schedule.

It was on September 25 that Rabaul received the reinforcements required to crush the enemy to the south: one hundred Zeros and eighty bombers were brought to Vunakanau and Lakunai fields. Two days later the attack began.

Thirty-one bombers struck at Henderson in the raid that knocked out communications between Vandegrift and his Matanikau forces, but the Navy and Marine fighters who intercepted them shot down six Bettys and five Zeros at no loss to themselves.

Next day close to sixty of the Emperor's eagles came winging down and the Americans shot down twenty-three bombers and one Zero. Jubilant, Vandegrift radioed Nouméa: "Our losses: no pilots, no planes, no damage. How's that for a record?"

When September came to an end, three of Henderson's Marines were the top aces of America: Major John Smith had nineteen kills, Captain Carl had sixteen and Major Galer had eleven. Since aerial battle began, the Americans had shot down well over two hundred enemy aircraft against thirty-two of their own lost. And the Americans had lost fewer pilots. Japanese fliers, fighting over enemy territory, scorning parachutes as beneath the dignity of the samurai who cannot surrender, usually went down with their aircraft.

Nevertheless such staggering losses were suicidal for the Japanese, and they began October determined to wipe out American fighter strength. A few bombers were used as bait for swarms of Zeros. On October 2 the trick worked: four Americans were shot down, against only five enemy planes, and among them were Major Smith and Major Galer.

Galer had shot down a Betty when a Zero came up on his tail and riddled his Wildcat. Galer knew he would be forced to land, but he wanted to retaliate first. He dove into a cloud as though he was trying to get away. Instead of coming out below, he came out on top—and caught the Japanese waiting beneath him. He pressed his gun button, and both aircraft went down in flames.

It was the second time Galer had been shot down, but he landed safely in a field and walked home.

Major John Smith crashed in the jungle. He jumped from his Wildcat and began running west. His breath came as quickly as his perspiration but he kept running through the silent, eerie jungle, hastening to get out of it before dark.

It was dusk when Smith reached the Ilu. He forded the river and ran through a wood into a field of kunai grass. Across the field he saw two men in a vehicle. He thought they were Japanese. Then he heard them yelling in English and ran up to them.

It was Colonel Cates and his jeep driver. Cates had heard that Smith had been shot down. He had studied his map to calculate the route he would take if he were in Smith's place, and he had driven to the field and waited there.

Smith poured out his thanks in an Oklahoma drawl, rueful, meanwhile, at the loss of his lucky baseball cap and his failure to destroy his plane. But even this was vouchsafed him by the solicitous Cates. A patrol from his First Marines found and burned Smith's plane and brought back his baseball cap.

Next day, quickly recovering from the enemy's stratagem, the Wildcats resumed their old team tactics, as well as their slaughter of enemy aircraft; while Dauntlesses and Avengers, joined by Flying Fortresses from New Hebrides, went ranging up The Slot to strike at the Tokyo Express again.

Even the pessimistic Admiral Ghormley sent *Hornet* and a screen against the enemy massing in the Shortlands, although the carrier strike was thwarted by the bad weather upon which Hyakutake and Mikawa had been counting.

Alone in August, the Marines had held; at bay in September they had fought the enemy off; but now the month of crisis was at hand: October was beginning with those monsoon rains and moonless nights which lay like a concealing cloak over troops of the Sendai Division then sailing steadily south.

Part 4

CRISIS

Chapter 1

IN ALL the Imperial Japanese Army there was no unit more illustrious than the 2nd or Sendai Division. It had been founded in 1870 when the Emperor Meiji, making a modern Japan, organized a modern army. Into its ranks came sturdy peasant youths recruited from the Sendai region north of Tokyo, and although they were not samurai, they demonstrated, during the savage Satsuma Rebellion of 1877, that they could fight the warrior-caste on even terms or better.

The Sendai considered themselves the Emperor's own, and their motto was a couplet taken from Meiji's rescript to soldiers and sailors:

> *Remember that Death is lighter than a feather,*
> *But that Duty is heavier than a mountain.*

The Sendai fought in the Sino-Japanese War of 1894–95, and in the Russo-Japanese War of 1904–05 the division distinguished itself by capturing Crescent Hill at Port Arthur in a bloody night attack. The Sendai were also distinguished for their ferocity during the Rape of Nanking in the Chinese War, they had fought the Russians at Nomonhan, and had had an easy time of their invasion of Java.

For two years between action in Manchuria and Java, the Sendai was at home replenishing its depleted ranks with young recruits. Many of its soldiers sailing south to Guadalcanal in this October of 1942 could remember, with swelling hearts and misting eyes, the day on which they went off to war. In each town the entire community assembled to honor the departing conscripts. The mayor read to them portions of the Imperial Rescript:

"I am your Commander-in-Chief, you are my strong arms. Whether I shall adequately fulfill my duty to the Ancestors depends upon your fidelity . . . If you unite with me, our courage and power shall illuminate the whole earth."

Regimental commanders such as Colonel Masajiro Furumiya of the peerless 29th Infantry succeeded the mayors, bowing to the audience to say, in a typical speech delivered in ringing tones:

"As the dying leopard leaves its coat to man, so a warrior's reputation serves his sons after his death. You will see that these sons of yours will be nurtured by the Army. They will be given the courage that will impel them to leap like lions on the foe. In the moment of national crisis our lives are no more significant than feathers, and immense treasures are as valueless as the dust in your streets. Each subject, *as each least handful of earth,* is in the service and possession of the Emperor.

"Tomorrow," he told the recruits, "you will report to your regiment, but today, before you leave, you will observe the ancient ritual of your fathers. You will say farewell at the cemetery before the tombs of your ancestors, and receive from them all the inherited loyalty for the Emperor that your family's generations have cherished."[1]

Later the Sendai's recruits were lined up on the parade ground to receive their rifles from the hands of an officer, who told them: "Conscripts, your rifle enables you to serve the Emperor just as the sword of the samurai made him strong and terrible in the Imperial service. You will keep its bore as bright and shining as the samurai kept his blade. On the outside it may, like yourselves, become stained with mud and blood, but within, like your own warrior's soul, it will remain untarnished, bright, and shining."[2]

And so, like knights receiving their spurs, the Sendai accepted their rifles, making a profound obeisance before them, and in the morning they were introduced to the harsh brutal life of the Japanese soldier, one so pitilessly purposeful that it would provoke the westerner to mutiny, but one which these youths, trained almost from the cradle in disciplined adversity, regarded as the penultimate step toward a glorious destiny: fighting and dying for the Emperor.

All day long they heard drill sergeants bellowing, *"Wan-hashi, wan-hashi"—wan* for the teacup which all Japanese hold in their left hands, *hashi* for the chopsticks grasped with the right. *"Wan-hashi, wan-hashi.* Teacup-chopsticks, teacup-chopsticks."

It was a tantalizing chant for men accustomed to a crude and tasteless diet of soybean curd for breakfast; rice, pickled fish and sliced radishes for lunch; and raw fish, rice or beets and a cup of sake for dinner. But the Sendai's menu was not devised to please but rather to inure men to privation. In the field it was worse: rice balls and soybean curd. On this, the men of the Sendai had been trained to endure as had no other troops in the world. Before they left Japan, the men of Colonel Furumiya's 29th Regiment had marched 122 miles in seventy-two hours, carrying their weapons, 150 rounds of ammunition and a forty-pound pack, sleeping only four hours, and then, with the roofs of their barracks in sight, they had double-timed the last few miles.

This was the division and these were the men with whom Lieutenant General Haruyoshi Hyakutake would at last crush the Americans. Although Hyakutake was no longer contemptuous of his enemy, he was still confident of defeating him; and he still underestimated his forces at about ten thousand after making allowances for the eight or nine thousand "killed" by Colonel Ichiki and General Kawaguchi. Nevertheless, he was not going to allow his forces to drift into battle piecemeal as formerly. He was going to concentrate them, and he had already ordered the 38th Division to move from Borneo to the Shortlands for shipment to Guadalcanal. Finally, he would no longer trust impetuous subordinates: General Hyakutake was going down to Guadalcanal to take personal command. He expected to arrive the night of October 9 with his 17th Army Headquarters.

In the meantime, he got the Sendai on their way. Admiral Mikawa's ships had already landed one unit—the 4th Infantry Regiment—on western Guadalcanal in mid-September. The remainder under the Sendai's commander, Lieutenant General Masao Maruyama, would make three separate runs led by a cruiser also named *Sendai*.

The first, with Maruyama aboard, was to leave October 3.

Admiral Nimitz arrived in Nouméa on the third of October. He conferred with Vice-Admiral Ghormley and was disturbed by what he learned. Nimitz was not so much impressed by the confused supply situation—which could not be blamed on a man who had been given an entire area tied in a shoestring—but by Ghormley's deep pessimism about Guadalcanal. When the possibility of reinforcing the island was discussed, Ghormley protested. He said it would be unsafe to strip rear-area islands of their garrisons. The Japanese "might break through and attack our lines of communication."

Nimitz did not challenge Ghormley's convictions. After all, he was the man in charge. But Nimitz returned to Pearl Harbor wondering if perhaps there should not be someone else in command, someone more aggressive, someone who shared his own optimism about Guadalcanal.

It was very difficult for Chester Nimitz not to think of Bull Halsey.

That same October afternoon Martin Clemens was thinking that the time had come to rescue Snowy Rhoades and Bishop Aubin's missionary party at Tangarare.

For the past few weeks Rhoades had been reporting a steadily deteriorating situation at the mission station on the southwest coast. Both he and Schroeder, the frail old Savo storekeeper turned coastwatcher, were down with malaria. Dysentery had all but done for Bishop Aubin, and the entire party was without food. The Japanese, unimpressed by the bishop's policy of neutrality, had taken it all.

Clemens asked Vandegrift if it would be possible to divert a Catalina flying boat to the rescue. The general, preparing a third offensive west of the Matanikau, was annoyed at being distracted by what he called "a bunch o' nuns."[3] But then Rhoades signaled, "Bishop requests also evacuation of native nuns as if left behind they will be raped,"[4] and Vandegrift consented to Clemens's request.

On the afternoon of October 3, however, the *Ramada* sailed over from Malaita and Clemens dropped his plans for the Catalina. *Ramada* was the old Guadalcanal District vessel, a wooden schooner forty feet long and powered by a diesel engine at a speed of six knots. Her hull was black and her awnings gray and she was marked by two white crosses.

Ramada had come to Guadalcanal with three Japanese airmen who had been captured after their bomber crashed, and Clemens asked her skipper, Peter Sasambule, if he would make the rescue trip to Tangarare. Sasambule demurred. Even though he was among the best of the native captains, a sailor who could creep like a cat among the uncharted Solomons waters, he did not like the prospect of sailing his flimsy craft past enemy-occupied territory by day and by night through the southern terminus of the Tokyo Express. But Clemens persuaded him. Early that afternoon, escorted by a fighter-plane, *Ramada* swung wide off the Guadalcanal coast and went chugging northwest.

Two hours later a coastwatcher radioed that six Japanese destroyers led by *Sendai* were 140 miles distant from Cape Esperance. They would arrive there about four o'clock the next morning.

Marine and Navy dive-bombers immediately prepared to strike. They took off before dusk. In the half-light of a dying day they found the Japanese convoy and came screaming down to plant a direct hit on *Sendai* and another on a destroyer.

Nevertheless, the ships carrying General Maruyama and his troops pressed on. At four o'clock in the morning they set Maruyama and another Sendai regiment safely ashore on Guadalcanal.

Ramada, which had turned Cape Esperance around midnight, also made a safe passage to Tangarare. On October 4 she sailed back under the friendly square wings of a Wildcat fighter. She arrived off Lunga after supply ships *Fomalhaut* and *Betelgeuse* and their destroyer escorts had entered Iron Bottom Bay from the other direction on a daring run of the Torpedo-Junction gantlet. Landing boats and lighters were swarming on the Bay and destroyers were prowling up and down the coast when *Ramada* made her entry, steaming sedately along loaded to the gunwales with Rhoades, and Schroeder; Bishop Aubin, frail and weak in his white soutane, a pectoral cross on his breast and his umbrella grasped in his hands; six priests, six European nuns and double that many native sisters, all of them dressed in white habits. The sailors gaped as *Ramada* dropped anchor and the Wildcat overhead dipped its wings in salute and flew away.

Martin Clemens came aboard and quickly put the six priests on one of the supply ships. They scrambled up the bosun's ladder. The European sisters, however, offered a different problem. A mail boat was lowered, the nuns stepped into it, and then the little craft was drawn neatly aboard to the cheers of all within view. Bishop Aubin came ashore to spend the night with General Vandegrift, who received him graciously. In the morning, he returned to

Ramada. Together with the native nuns, and a party from the Church of England mission on Tulagi, he sailed for Buma Mission on Malaita.

In a war without quarter, neutrality had not been possible.

On the day that the missionaries left Tangarare, a group of far-from-neutral natives set out from the abandoned mission station. Led by Constable Saku, one of Clemens's best scouts, they were out to kill Japanese.

Two days later—October 5—they came upon ten Japanese soldiers gathering wild nuts by a river. The soldiers had piled their rifles on a rock. Saku and his comrades crept up to the rock, took the rifles and hid. Saku warned his men not to shoot and thus draw help to the enemy. The Japanese returned, and the natives leaped from the bush swinging axes and spears. Terrified, the Japanese bent to seize stones—and they were slaughtered to a man.

Saku's merciless band repeated the same tactics against nine more Japanese soldiers, and they fought a pitched rifle battle with another dozen. Eventually they killed thirty-two of the last of the Kawaguchi stragglers still making their pitiful way west, and they buried a hundred of their rifles. Along the route of the Kawaguchi retreat they found heaps of whitening bones and in the jungle they discovered wrecked and rusting red-balled aircraft with charred skeletons in flight suits still erect in their seats.

The jungle wept at the enemy's misery, but Saku's band continued to hunt him without pity.

Pity was also not a quality describing Lieutenant General Masao Maruyama. Haughty was a better word; haughty, irritable, and unbending—and the commander of the Sendai Division had found the situation on Guadalcanal one calculated to make these characteristics quickly known to Colonel Oka and General Kawaguchi.

First, Maruyama was displeased that these two officers had allowed the Americans to get away from the Point Cruz trap so easily. But he was above all infuriated to find that they had allowed the wretched veterans of this miserable campaign to mingle with men of his fresh 4th Infantry Regiment and to spread their tales of horror among them. On October 5—the day that Saku began slaughtering Japanese—Colonel Nomasu Nakaguma had brought Maruyama a letter written by one of the 4th's soldiers. It said:

> The news I hear worries me. It seems as if we have suffered considerable damage and casualties. They might be exaggerated, but it is pitiful. Far away from our home country a fearful battle is raging. What these soldiers say is something of the supernatural and cannot be believed as human stories.[5]

Lieutenant General Maruyama promptly issued a general order to all troops:

> From now on, the occupying of Guadalcanal Island is under the observation of the whole world. Do not expect to return, not even one man, if the occupation is not successful. Everyone must remember the honor of the Emperor, fear no enemy, yield to no material matters, show the strong points as of steel or of rocks, and advance valiantly and ferociously. Hit the enemy opponents so hard they will not be able to get up again.[6]

Then General Maruyama began planning an advance to the east bank of the Matanikau River. He, too, had recognized the advantages to be had from that position. He could put artillery there and shell Henderson Field and he could use the east bank as a jumping-off point for the grand attack scheduled for October 17.

Maruyama ordered Colonel Nakaguma to take the 4th Infantry across the Matanikau early in the morning of October 7.

Then he sat down at his field desk, mopped his streaming face with a towel, and resumed the study of his maps. The mouth of the Matanikau, it seemed to him, would be the most suitable place for the American commander to surrender his sword.

General Vandegrift also studied the mouth of the Matanikau on his maps that October 5. It occurred to him that the river and the terrain offered the same possibilities which Robert E. Lee had exploited at the Chickahominy. He would make a demonstration at the river mouth while other forces crossed the Matanikau upriver to swing right and close the trap at the rear.

This time he would use five full battalions.

Two battalions from the Fifth Marines would mass at the river mouth under Edson.

Two battalions of the Seventh—Puller's and Herman Henry Hanneken's—and a battalion from the Second Marines reinforced by Colonel William Whaling's scout-snipers would make the march inland. Whaling would be in command. He would be the first to cross Nippon Bridge, wheel north and march toward the sea. Hanneken would cross the river next, and move farther west before turning to the sea himself. Then Puller would cross and make the deepest western penetration, swinging round to march toward Point Cruz. Once Puller held that point, the Fifth would charge west across the river mouth.

The attack was to commence October 7, the same day that Maruyama had chosen for Nakaguma's attack.

On that morning the two forces collided.

Edson's men met Nakaguma's men at the river mouth and Whaling encountered Japanese while still east of the river and marching toward Nippon Bridge. Edson called for help and Vandegrift sent him the remnant of the First Raiders. Under Silent Lew Walt, now, these exhausted Marines entered their last battle. They helped the Fifth push the enemy into a pocket, and when the desperate Japanese attempted to break out that night in a banzai charge they killed sixty of them.

October 8 it rained. It came down in monsoon sheets and both forces lay mired in the muck and murk of a Solomons downpour. Then Vandegrift learned, as had happened so often before when he attempted to break up enemy concentrations, that an enemy task force was bearing down on Guadalcanal. He would have to trim his ambitions.

Next day the three battalions crossed the Matanikau upriver as planned, but with instructions to swing east once they had reached the sea. Then they would pass through the Fifth Marines at the river mouth and enter the perimeter.

They did, but before they did Chesty Puller flushed an entire battalion of the enemy.

Marching north toward Point Cruz his scouts caught sight of large numbers of enemy soldiers at the bottom of a ravine. It looked like a bivouac area. Puller called for artillery fire and set his battalion on high ground to watch.

The Japanese were trapped.

Shells from the Marine 105-mm howitzers shrieked and crashed among them. They came without warning, and because they did they devastated the enemy and made terrified, milling cattle of them. They sprinted in terror for the sanctuary of a ridge behind them, but as they broke from cover the Marines drove them back into the ravine with mortars and machine-gun fire. Back they tumbled, back into thickets of flashing death. Up toward Puller's position they flowed, and once again the mortars and the machine guns swept death among them.

And so it went, back to be blasted or torn apart, up to be riddled to pieces—and very few of them survived.

No less than seven hundred men fell in that slaughter-pen of a ravine, and General Maruyama's first meeting with the Marines ended in sharp defeat. His 4th Infantry Regiment was shattered, for another two hundred men had been killed by the other American forces.

And so the Third Matanikau came to an end on a familiar critical note. With 65 dead and 105 wounded, Vandegrift's battalions came back along the coastal road to resume positions along that Henderson Field perimeter that was now threatened as never before. As they did they heard airplane motors thundering overhead. Looking up they saw twenty Wildcats. Major Leonard (Duke) Davis was bringing his squadron into Guadalcanal. General Geiger would now have forty-six fighters to hurl into an aerial battle even then blazing up with unprecedented fury.

Chapter 2

We asked for the Doggies to come to Tulagi
But General MacArthur said, "No."
He gave as his reason:
"It isn't the season.
Besides, you have no U.S.O."

THUS did the Marines on Guadalcanal bawl out their derision of the Army, singing, to the tune of "Bless 'Em All," an uncomplimentary and inaccurate estimate of why it was that they were still alone after two months of uninterrupted ordeal. For General MacArthur had nothing to do with Guadalcanal, except to mount formations of Flying Fortresses against the Japanese bastion at Rabaul, and Army troops had not been included in the operation in the beginning.

Yet, even as the Marines on Guadalcanal continued to sing so caustically, there *were* Doggies coming to Tulagi.

They were coming because their commander in the Pacific, Major General Millard Harmon, did not share Admiral Ghormley's reservations about reinforcing Vandegrift. Moreover, Harmon thought that Kelly Turner's continued insistence upon carrying out the occupation of Ndeni in the Santa Cruz Islands—over Vandegrift's protests—would prove inimical to the entire campaign. On October 6, Harmon sat down and addressed an unsolicited recommendation to his chief, Admiral Ghormley. He said:

"The occupation of Ndeni at this time represents a diversion from the main effort and dispersion of force . . .

"If we do not succeed in holding Guadalcanal our effort in the Santa Cruz will be a total waste—and loss. The Solomons has to be our main effort. The loss of Guadalcanal would be a four-way victory for the Jap—provide a vanguard for his strong Rabaul position, deny us a jumping-off place against that position, give him a jumping-off place against the New Hebrides, effectively cover his operations against New Guinea.

"It is my personal conviction that the Jap is capable of retaking Guadalcanal, and that he will do so in the near future unless it is materially strengthened. I further believe that appropriate increase in strength of garrison, rapid improvement of conditions for air operations and increased surface action, if accomplished in time, will make the operation so costly that he will not attempt it."[1]

Harmon's letter had the effect of tearing off Ghormley's smoked glasses and letting him see the situation a little less darkly. Perhaps the admiral was stung by the general's reference to "increased surface action," or perhaps, as had happened in September when Kelly Turner argued strongly for dispatching the Seventh Marines to Guadalcanal, Admiral Ghormley's hesitant nature, like a rundown battery, needed periodic recharging from the more volatile spirits around him. Whatever the reason, Admiral Ghormley became all energy and determination.

He postponed the Ndeni operation and alerted the 164th Infantry Regiment of the Americal Division for movement to Guadalcanal. On October 8 at Nouméa—the day on which the monsoon mired Vandegrift's and Maruyama's men in the jungle—the 164th's soldiers began filing aboard *McCawley* and *Zeilin*. Next day—the one on which the Marines withdrew triumphantly and the Wildcat reinforcements arrived—Admiral Turner led these transports north. Escorting him were three destroyers and three mine layers.

Ranging ahead of him went a Covering Force of two heavy and two light cruisers and five destroyers under Rear Admiral Norman Scott. Two Striking Forces, one built around carrier *Hornet* and the other around battleship *Washington*, also sortied north.

Vice-Admiral Robert Ghormley was giving Guadalcanal everything he had. The island was going to be reinforced at all costs, and the United States Navy was at last sailing toward The Slot with open guns.

It was pitch black at Aola, but Martin Clemens knew the coastline as well as he had known his "digs" in Cambridge. Besides, three scouts and three Americans were stationed along the shore. All seven men held hooded flashlights. Hearing the murmur of motors offshore, they began to signal with them.

The murmur rose, then lessened. Clemens heard the lapping of wavelets against a hull, and then, the scraping of a keel on sand. One of the Marines called "Halt!," and an American voice answered with the password. Lieutenant Colonel Robert Hill of the Second Marines came out of the darkness. With him was his staff. He told Clemens that his two companies of Marines were enroute to Aola in Higgins boats towed by a pair of Yippies. Unfortunately, one of the Yippies had towed one boat under at a loss of fifteen men drowned. But there would still be about 500 rifles available for the attack on Gurabusu and Koilotumaria, the villages to the west of Aola in which the Japanese radios were located.

Clemens assured Hill that the enemy was unaware of their presence. Two nights ago he had come to Aola with three scouts and three Americans. They had spent the intervening days mapping the target area and alerting village headmen to provide scouts and carriers.

Clemens thought there would be no difficulty surprising the Japanese and destroying the radios as General Vandegrift had ordered. He also thought, although he did not say it aloud, that he would find Ishimoto among the enemy.

Far to the west on the darkness of that same night—October 9—a destroyer put Lieutenant General Haruyoshi Hyakutake ashore on Guadalcanal. With him were his senior staff officer, Colonel Haruo Konuma; Major General Tadashi Sumuyoshi, commander of 17th Army Artillery; and Major General Kiyotake Kawaguchi, who had been to Rabaul to brief staff officers on the difficulties presented by both the Americans on Guadalcanal and the island's terrain. Like Maruyama before them, the staff officers could not believe that any terrain or any enemy could deter Japanese soldiers. And yet, the moment Kawaguchi set foot again on the island which had taught him otherwise, he heard himself vindicated: an officer from Maruyama's staff stepped forward to tell Hyakutake that the American artillery had "massacred" the 4th Infantry that very day.

His face bleak, Hyakutake followed Kawaguchi to his 17th Army command post, which had been established "in the valley of a nameless river about three kilometres west of Kokumbona."[2] There, he immediately called for a daybreak meeting with Maruyama.

The conference convened and Hyakutake heard additional recitals of defeat. The Sendai Division had been forced to retreat for the first time in history, the east bank of the Matanikau had been lost as a platform from which to bombard the airfield and to launch an offensive, and both the Ichiki and Kawaguchi remnants were of more use to the enemy than the Emperor. Moreover, food and medicines were scarce, the roads and trails were hardly passable, and there was a shortage of artillery shells.

Hyakutake sat listening, his small face and large round glasses giving him the look of a preoccupied lemur. Then he announced that the attack was to proceed as planned, and turned to issuing orders and making his own report.

He notified the 38th Division in the Shortlands to send down the 228th Infantry Regiment and the 19th Independent Engineer Regiment. He told Imperial General Headquarters in Tokyo: "The situation on Guadalcanal is far more aggravated than had been estimated."[3] He called for reinforcements.

And so, Admiral Gunichi Mikawa in Rabaul began collecting ships again, and Pistol Pete was readied for a voyage south.

Pistol Pete was the name which the Marines were to confer on all of Hyakutake's artillery. Actually, the guns were six-inch howitzers. Eight of them, plus a few guns of smaller bore, with their ammunition and tractors, medical supplies, sixteen tanks, miscellaneous equipment and a battalion of troops, were loaded aboard seaplane carriers *Chitose* and *Nisshin*. Another thousand men were placed on six destroyer-transports. Three heavy cruisers and two destroyers were formed as a covering force.

This was to be the largest Sendai movement so far, and Admiral Mikawa demanded ample aerial protection for it.

The Tokyo Express, now run by Rear Admiral Shintaro Hashimoto, had not lost any troops so far this month; but its ships had been battered. Since the night of October 3, when *Ramada* and the cruiser *Sendai* crossed contradictory courses, American bombers from Henderson Field had been appearing over The Slot in growing numbers. On October 5 they severely damaged destroyers *Minegumo* and *Murasame,* on October 8 they had so blasted northern terminals in the Shortlands that traffic down The Slot was snarled for twenty-four hours, and on the night of October 9 they struck at *Tatsuta* and other destroyers carrying Hyakutake south.

Admiral Mikawa asked Admiral Tsukahara to do something about it. Tsukahara promised that he would neutralize Henderson Field on October 11, and Mikawa gave the order for the Tokyo Express to move on that date.

It did. The first to leave was the Covering or Bombardment Force composed of big destroyers *Hatsuyuki* and *Fubuki* and heavy cruisers *Aoba, Kinugasa,* and *Furutaka,* veterans of the Battle of Savo Island. Commanding was another veteran of that great victory: Rear Admiral Aritomo Goto, the first admiral from either side to sail into Iron Bottom Bay.

Rear Admiral Norman Scott had been in the Bay on that momentous night of August 8–9, but he had been in command of the Eastern Defense Force and had been unable to sail to the aid of Admiral Crutchley in the west. Nevertheless, Scott, an aggressive and thorough sailor, thirsted for revenge.

For three weeks prior to departing Nouméa, Scott had been training his men in night fighting. He drove them without stint, and he insisted that his commanders teach themselves the proper use of radar. When Ghormley chose him to lead the force covering the 164th Infantry Regiment which Turner was bringing to Guadalcanal, Scott regarded the mission as an opportunity to avenge Savo.

Twice, on October 9 and 10, Scott led his ships toward Cape Esperance. But General Geiger's bomber pilots had cleared The Slot. Aerial reconnaissance reported no suitable targets.

On October 11 a Flying Fortress from the New Hebrides reported Goto's force sailing south. Two more aerial sightings were made, and at six o'clock that night Goto was reported a hundred miles north of Cape Esperance.

Scott eagerly signaled his approach order to his ships. He calculated that the enemy force should appear west of Savo just before midnight.

But Norman Scott would be there first.

There was a sudden rain shower at dawn of October 11. Martin Clemens, lying on a slope outside the Japanese encampment at Gurabusu, felt the water being dammed against his body. He hunched up slightly to release it—and then the Marines around Gurabusu attacked.

The Japanese fought back. They opened fire and Captain Richard Stafford raised his head above his coconut log to see what was happening. He fell back with a bullet between the eyes.

Clemens jumped up and joined the attack. A Japanese officer swung a saber at him. The Japanese missed and a Marine shot him dead. The other enemy soldiers turned to flee and charged straight into the bullets of American machine guns. Suddenly, it was quiet. The skirmish was over. Thirty-two enemy had been killed with only Captain Stafford lost.

Clemens went through the Japanese encampment. He found a gold chalice belonging to the missionaries. It was being used as an ash tray. One of the dead enemy soldiers lay wrapped in the altar cloth he had been using for a blanket. Then Clemens found vestments and the unmarked graves of the priests and nuns whom Ishimoto had murdered. Clemens watched his scouts. They prowled among the bodies, turning them over and shaking their heads in a disappointed negative.

Colonel Hill came back from Koilotumaria. The action there had not been successful. The enemy had run off into a swamp. Only three of them were killed, and two Marines were lost.

But one of the dead Japanese, according to a native scout, was Mr. Ishimoto.

Clemens could never be sure. The wounds inflicted by modern arms tend to make identification difficult. Nevertheless, the former carpenter from Tulagi was never heard from again.

The skies were still overcast when the men aboard Admiral Goto's ships heard the thundering of aircraft motors above them. They were momentarily fearful, but then, realizing that they were still about two hundred miles north of Guadalcanal, they decided that the unseen planes were their own.

They were. Thirty-five Bettys escorted by thirty Zeros were flying at 25,000 feet. They came over Henderson Field shortly before four o'clock and found, to their dismay, that a shift of clouds had covered the target. More, scores of enemy Wildcats were growling and slashing among them. The bombers fled east, dropping their explosives in the sea.

And some of the bombs fell right in front of the landing boats bringing the Marines from Gurabusu to Aola.

It was as though a Martian cornucopia had been overturned, showering these returning victors with geysering bombs, spurting bullets and cartridge cases that fell on water like pebbles or rang sharply on steel decks.

Suddenly there was a terrible rising scream and a Wildcat came plummeting straight down. The pilot cleared his plane at about a hundred feet above the water and he struck it with such force that his clothing was torn off. He was rescued, but he died ten minutes later. Another Marine pilot crashed into the Bay. He was hauled into Clemens's boat with an eye hanging out. He was taken to Aola where the efficient Eroni put the eye back in and bandaged it, and the pilot was back in action within a month.

And so Admiral Tsukahara's stroke to neutralize Henderson Field was a failure. At the cost of these two Wildcats shot down, the Marines had destroyed seven bombers and four Zeros. Henderson had not been harmed. Yet, General Geiger's fliers had been kept so active that Admiral Goto was able to steal safely down The Slot.

That was why, that midnight at Aola, the Marines and Martin Clemens saw a flashing and heard a rumbling that was neither thunder nor lightning.

There had been glimmerings of true lightning over the dark horizon that night as Admiral Scott's ships formed into battle column and sailed for Savo.

Three destroyers—*Farenholt, Duncan,* and *Laffey*—held the lead, followed by four cruisers, Scott's flagship *San Francisco, Salt Lake City,* and *Helena,* with the tail of the column formed by two more destroyers, *Buchanan* and *McCalla.* They swung wide around Guadalcanal's west coast, moving at top speed. Conical Savo loomed grimly ahead and speed was dropped to twenty-five knots, then to twenty. Scott prepared to launch planes. As Mikawa had done two months ago, so would Scott do on this dark breezy Sunday night.

Catapults flashed aboard *San Francisco* and *Boise* and two Kingfishers swooshed off into the black. *Helena,* which had not been notified, dumped hers overboard as inflammable material. *Salt Lake City* attempted to launch hers, but the plane was set afire by her own flares and was also jettisoned.

The burning aircraft's flames could be seen fifty miles to the north by men aboard Admiral Goto's ships. Goto thought it was Hyakutake signaling from his beachhead or else the seaplane carriers carrying Pistol Pete. He ordered replies blinkered. When no answer was forthcoming, some of Goto's officers aboard flagship *Aoba* were suspicious. But Goto continued to flash his signal lights, hoping to lure any American ships in the vicinity away from the landing area. Goto did not really expect to find any, The Slot and Iron Bottom Bay having been such incontestable Japanese preserves during the past few months.

His column sailed on—cruisers *Aoba, Furutaka,* and *Kinugasa,* with destroyers *Fubuki* and *Hatsuyuki* off *Aoba's* beam—a giant T speeding south to shell Henderson Field.

Below, Scott got his first scout-plane report: "One large, two small vessels, one six miles from Savo off northern beach, Guadalcanal." Could this be the big force reported earlier that day? It did not seem so. Nor was it. It was part of the Supply Force. Scott continued to sail to the west of Savo on a northerly course. At half-past eleven he ordered a countermarch to the south.

Goto still rushed toward him.

Inadvertently, Norman Scott had "crossed the T." His ships were sailing broadside to the approaching enemy column: all his guns could be brought to bear to rake Goto stem-to-stern.

Helena got a radar contact!

Fifteen minutes before midnight Captain Gilbert Hoover broadcast a two-word signal: "Interrogatory Roger," which meant, "Request permission to open fire." Admiral Scott thought he meant "Roger" as employed to acknowledge receipt of a previous message. He replied, "Roger," which also meant "Commence firing!" But Scott did not want to commence firing. Hoover was uncertain. With unsuspecting *Aoba* closing the range to a mere 5000 yards, with *Helena's* gunners fingering their mechanisms in agony, Hoover repeated his former inquiry and Scott repeated his former, "Roger."

Helena opened fire.

Six- and five-inch shells howled toward *Aoba.* They missed, but the second salvo caught the enemy cruiser full amidships. Now

Salt Lake City and *Boise* were thundering at Goto's stricken flagship. Not white flashes but orange flames gushed from the muzzles of heavier eight-inch guns. *Aoba* bucked and shuddered. Her bridge buckled. Admiral Goto was mortally wounded. He lay dying on his twisted bridge, gasping:

"*Bakayaro! Bakayaro!* Stupid bastard! Stupid bastard!"[4]

Goto thought friendly ships were firing on him. He thought vessels of the Supply Force had blundered, and as his own guns began to speak, he gave the order to cease fire.

Norman Scott also thought his ships were firing on each other —which was true in the case of *Duncan* and *Farenholt*—and he also gave the order to cease fire.

Then the dying Goto gave the command to turn right.

The movement enabled the Japanese ships to aim all their guns, but it also gave the Americans the opportunity to mass their fire at each ship as it approached the frothing white water that marked the turning point. They did, for Scott's gunners were slow to respond to his orders to cease firing. Some of them never did, and *Aoba* and *Furutaka* were battered repeatedly and set ablaze.

Nine minutes before midnight Scott ordered: "Resume firing!"

Once again shock waves went rolling over black water and Marines crouching in Guadalcanal's sodden holes heard again those familiar iron tongues of midnight.

Captain Charles ("Soc") McMorris of *San Francisco* heard the order just as his lookouts sighted a strange warship on a parallel course three quarters of a mile to the west. *Frisco's* searchlights leaped alight to illuminate a destroyer with a white band around her second stack. American gunners, now trained, knew her as *Fubuki*.

They opened up from all sides. They poured a horrible punishing fire into the enemy ship, and she blew up and sank at seven minutes before midnight.

Now all the American ships were pursuing fleeing *Aoba* and *Furutaka*. They pummeled them by turns. But now *Kinugasa* was fighting back.

With destroyer *Hatsuyuki*, the big Japanese cruiser had misread Goto's orders and had turned left rather than right. The mistake saved them. It took them out of the fight, and it gave *Kinugasa* the chance to open up on *Boise* at eight thousand yards.

Eight-inch shells straddled the American and a spread of torpedoes came running toward her. Captain Mike Moran ordered hard right rudder and *Boise* swung around to comb the wakes.

Then *Boise* spotted *Aoba* and put her searchlights on her. *Aoba* fired back, and *Kinugasa* made a bull's eye of the American's light. For three minutes *Boise* took a fearful pounding, until heroic *Salt Lake City* interposed her own bulk between her and the enemy, while silencing *Aoba* and driving *Kinugasa* off.

And now it was the twelfth of October. *Furutaka* was dragging herself toward her watery grave twenty-two miles northwest of Savo, *Fubuki* was gone, *Aoba* was so badly damaged she would have to limp all the way home to Japan for repairs, while slightly damaged *Kinugasa* and unscathed *Hatsuyuki* were streaking north for sanctuary.

Behind them destroyer *Duncan*, fired on by both sides, was also in her death throes: she would take the plunge at two o'clock in the morning.

And *Boise* was ablaze. Her gallant crew was struggling to quench the flames that streamed off her tail as she joined up with the victorious American column and sailed south for Nouméa. Aided by sea water which flowed through her pierced sides to flood the magazines, *Boise* made it.

The Battle of Cape Esperance was over. It was an American victory, and though it was not as decisive as Savo, it was at least some measure of vengeance for that defeat. Moreover, it made it clear to the enemy that The Slot was no longer a Japanese channel, and it heartened the Marines on Guadalcanal to know that the Navy was coming out fighting again.

But the Battle of Cape Esperance did not prevent Pistol Pete from coming ashore. The enemy supply ships went boldly about unloading Hyakutake's big guns, his tanks, his shells and his medical supplies. They paid dearly for their insouciance: that same October 12 Dauntless dive-bombers from Henderson Field caught destroyers *Murakumo* and *Natsugumo* in The Slot and sent them to the bottom loaded with survivors from Goto's stricken ships.

In all, Japan had lost one heavy cruiser and three destroyers against one American destroyer sunk. And Henderson Field had been spared bombardment.

But not for long.

Chapter 3

THE JAPANESE did not consider the Battle of Cape Esperance to be an unmitigated defeat. Rather, they regarded the outcome as salutary: Admiral Scott had sailed his ships south and the way was now clear for heavier bombardment of Henderson Field.

Much, much heavier—for Combined Fleet was now ready.

On October 9 the big converted carriers *Hiyo* and *Junyo* with smaller *Zuiho* sailed into Truk lagoon, and Vice-Admiral Kakuji Kakuta—a Japanese giant standing six feet tall and weighing two hundred pounds—left his flagship, *Hiyo,* to report to Admiral Yamamoto aboard *Yamato.*

With Kakuta's arrival, Yamamoto now had five carriers, five battleships, fourteen cruisers and fourty-four destroyers—backed up by about 220 land-based airplanes to deploy against the enemy. On October 10 most of these ships sortied from Truk as part of the Guadalcanal Supporting Forces commanded by Vice-Admiral Nobutake Kondo. Yamamoto, remaining behind, watched them go.

As always, it was a stirring sight. Out of the reef passages they sailed, battleships leading—standing to sea in a stately column of ships. Then they were in open water and the escort ships broke column, heeling over with strings of signal flags tautening in the wind, while the queens of the fleet—the carriers—steamed majestically into position surrounded by protecting rings of cruisers and battleships.

They sailed south to take up supporting positions north of the Solomons, and to carry out Yamamoto's instructions: ". . . apprehend and annihilate any powerful forces in the Solomons area, as well as any reinforcements."

A few days after they departed Truk, their own reinforcements began going aboard six fast transports in the Shortlands. These were the last of the Sendai and some of the soldiers of the 38th Division: about ten thousand men in all. They were to arrive at Guadalcanal the night of October 14–15, joining General Hyakutake's 17th Army in time for the big push now scheduled for October 20. Before they sailed, Henderson Field would be knocked out to guarantee them safe passage.

That was why, a few days after the grand sortie from Truk, battleships *Kongo* and *Haruna* under Vice-Admiral Takeo Kurita peeled off from Kondo's forces and made for Guadalcanal. Each carried five hundred horrible fourteen-inch bombardment shells, plus ammunition of smaller sizes. Both were escorted by seven destroyers and flag cruiser *Isuzu* carrying Tanaka the Tenacious back to The Slot. These ships were also loaded to bombard, as were four heavy cruisers scheduled to deliver later attacks.

But The Night of the Battleships would be first: on October 13.

Kelly Turner's luck had held.

While Norman Scott had been sailing south in triumph, Turner had pushed on to the north with 3000 soldiers of the 164th Infantry Regiment. The huge Japanese armada which Yamamoto had ordered to destroy American reinforcements had left Truk too late to intercept him. Fourteen Japanese submarines screening Torpedo Junction had somehow let his two transports filter through.

As dusk of October 12 approached, Kelly Turner sighed with relief. He had made it. At dawn next morning he would be off Lunga with the first American soldiers to join the first American offensive.

> *Oh, some PT's do forty-five*
> *And some do thirty-nine;*
> *When we get ours to run at all*
> *We think we're doing fine.*

Lieutenant Alan Montgomery's four torpedo boats were truly not running at all when they arrived at Guadalcanal that afternoon of October 12. They had been towed from the New Hebrides by destroyers *Southard* and *Hovey,* entering the great battle of the Pacific and Iron Bottom Bay in a pedestrian style that delighted the hearts of the uninhibited deep-water sailors who greeted them.

"Rub-a-dub-dub, five gobs in a tub!"

"Tootsie-toys, yet! The Japs got the Tokyo Express and we got the Toonerville Trolley."

Under tow the torpedo boats were indeed unlovely and unformidable sights, but once they had been freed and fallen astern and had drowned the taunts of their detractors in the great throaty roar of their powerful motors, they went thundering across the Bay with lifted prows, planing gracefully along and throwing out huge bow waves that showered torpedo tubes and machine-gun mounts with spume and trailed a thick wide wake of frothing white behind them.

With their arrival the battle for Guadalcanal became complete.

Marines and sailors, soldiers and fliers, Seabees, native scouts and Japanese laborers, every type of warrior or martial worker imaginable had fought above, around, and upon this island; they had struck and hacked and shot at each other on foot or from every type of ship or aircraft or vehicle, wielding every kind of gun or knife, fighting with spears and axes, with fists and with stones—and now the bold little cockleshells were here to round out the roster and complete the arsenal of modern arms. As they came into the fight, taxiing up to Government Wharf in Tulagi Harbor, the Skytrains of SCAT were overhead flying south with the last of that valiant band of Marine fliers who were the first to fight for Cactus Air Force.

Major Richard Mangrum was himself the only pilot of his bombing squadron able to walk away from the field. Seven other fliers were dead, four had been wounded, and the remainder flown out with malaria or other illnesses. Four of Mangrum's rear-gunners had also been killed, and another wounded.

Major John Smith was going home as America's leading ace: nineteen enemy warplanes shot down in less than two months. But six of Smith's fighter pilots had been killed and six others wounded. Captain Carl was still alive, victor in sixteen aerial battles, and he, too, went home that afternoon of October 12—after the Skytrains had unloaded their cargoes of precious gasoline.

Fuel supplies were again critically short at Henderson Field. Although a Skytrain could fly in enough 55-gallon drums to keep twelve Wildcats aloft for one hour, what they brought in on October 12 would certainly be gone by October 13. Once again General Roy Geiger appealed to Nouméa, and an emergency barge-towing convoy was made up.

Cargo ships *Alchiba* and *Bellatrix,* PT-tender *Jamestown,* fleet tug *Vireo* and destroyers *Meredith* and *Nicholas* each towed a barge loaded with two thousand drums of gasoline and five hundred quarter-ton bombs.

They set out from Espiritu Santo late in the afternoon of October 12, a few hours after Japanese engineers began surveying a road to the south of Henderson Field.

Lieutenant General Masao Maruyama had graciously consented to Captain Oda's request that the trail to the assembly areas be called "The Maruyama Road." That had been on October 10. The next day Captain Oda and his engineers sat down with Colonel Matsumoto, the Sendai Division's intelligence officer, to study aerial photographs of the route. They saw the roof of a solid jungle. It seemed straight going. Oda was sure he could blaze the trail to the upper Lunga without difficulty. Meanwhile, Colonel Matsumoto would continue to torture captured Americans to extract information from them. None of them had talked so far, much to the surprise of Matsumoto and the concealed admiration of Colonel Masajiro Furumiya of the 29th Infantry,[1] and they had had to be beheaded in the honorable way. But more prisoners would be taken, and perhaps more forthright measures would produce better results.

Leaving Matsumoto, Captain Oda and his engineers cheerfully set out to cut The Maruyama Road.

"Hey, Lucky—the doggies are here!"

"Yeah, I know, Lew," Lucky grunted. "They came in on the New York bus."

"It's the straight dope. They're out in the Bay. You want to take a look?"

"We can't. We've got to stand by to move out. We're moving to new positions today or tomorrow."[2]

It was true, both that the 164th Infantry Regiment had arrived safely off Lunga Point, and that this latest reinforcement had induced General Vandegrift to shift his troops again. He expected the gathering enemy to strike hard from west of the Matanikau and he was moving his strength in that direction. The Tenaru line to the east would be held by the newly arrived 164th under Colonel Bryant Moore. To the south of Henderson Field, farther inland and a little to the east of Bloody Ridge, Vandegrift stationed Chesty Puller's battalion.

Almost exactly at the point where The Maruyama Road was to terminate.

"Condition Red!"

The cry was almost meaningless to these American soldiers hearing it for the first time on that afternoon of October 13, and it was raised too late.

Up north Japanese patrols had at last flushed the coastwatchers from their hideouts. Paul Mason and Jack Read were on the run, unable to warn Guadalcanal, and Henderson Field's new radar had also been remiss. And so, twenty-four Bettys with escorting Zeros came thundering over the big runway and Fighter One while forty-two Wildcats and thirteen P-400s and Airacobras hung roaring on their noses in a desperate attempt to gain altitude. Eventually, one bomber and one fighter would fall to their guns, but not before huge gashes were torn in both runways, parked aircraft were blasted apart, five thousand gallons of gasoline were set afire, and the men of the 164th Regiment had felt the first scorching licks of a baptism of fire that none of Vandegrift's Marines had ever experienced.

Some of the bombs fell on Colonel Moore's men only a few minutes after they set foot on Guadalcanal. Corporal Kenneth Foubert was killed—the first American soldier to die on the island—and two other men were wounded. Casualties mounted during another savage raid—again without warning.

All of the planes of the second raid got safely away, except for the Zero which fell to the flaming wing guns of a square-jawed, cigar-smoking Marine captain named Joseph Jacob Foss. Then Foss took a bullet in his oil pump and came rocketing down from 22,000 feet to a dead-stick landing while a trio of Zeros took turns trying to shoot off his tail. It was Captain Foss's first victory, and it was a hair-raising flying feat which was to be typical of Henderson's newest and greatest fighter pilot.

Individual victories, however, were of small solace to Archer Vandegrift on that black-bordered day of October 13. Henderson Field was now out of action for the first time. Geiger had almost no gasoline. The fury of the enemy onslaught suggested that a period of comparative lull had ended and that the Japanese were now opening their third and heaviest bid for victory. Far away in Australia General Douglas MacArthur was planning an all-out defense of the island continent in the event that the Solomons were lost, a huge Japanese bombardment force had been reported on its way south, forcing Admiral Turner to flee for the New Hebrides again, and as dusk introduced The Night of the Battleships, Archer Vandegrift heard a new voice speaking over Henderson Field.

Sergeant Butch Morgan was preparing the general's dinner when Pistol Pete spoke.

His first shell screamed over Vandegrift's pavilion and struck the big runway with a crash. Sergeant Morgan seized his World War I helmet and raced for the dugout. Another shell screeched overhead. Morgan slammed on his helmet and dove for cover.

Crrrrash!

General Vandegrift looked up in thoughtful surprise.

"That wasn't a bomb," he said. "That's artillery."[3]

Sergeant Butch Morgan came out of the dugout, his face a crimson match for his red walrus mustache. He looked around him furtively to see if any boots had witnessed the discomfiture of the Old Salt who had fought in France and knew all about artillery barrages.

"Aw, hell," Morgan muttered, taking off his helmet and going back to his makeshift stove. "I mean, only artillery . . ."

If it was "only" artillery, it was still authoritative enough to reach the airfield and to introduce a new element of danger into the harried lives of the Seabees there. Formerly, after attack from bombers or warships, repairmen might rush to the torn-up runway to fill the craters without fear of lightning striking twice in the same place. But now, Pistol Pete could fire one shell, wait until the Seabees were at work, and then drop another in the very same place.

Moreover, Vandegrift's heretofore matchless artillery was now outranged. Even his biggest guns, five-inch rifles, were of lesser bore than these six-inch howitzers of Hyakutake's; and his field pieces, 105- and 75-mm howitzers, that is, roughly four- and three-inch cannon, were far outweighed by them. Nevertheless, the Marine artillerymen were unafraid to duel the Japanese in counterbattery firing; if only they could locate them. The Marines had no sound-and-flash ranging equipment on Guadalcanal, and General Geiger could not consume precious gasoline keeping observation planes aloft.

Pistol Pete would speak for many, many days, unsilenced even by the five-inch rifles of visiting destroyers; speak as he was speaking now in the fading light of October 13, churning up the runways and forcing Marine ground crews to dare his flying fragments while moving parked aircraft to the comparative safety of Fighter One, ranging in on Kukum to chew up naval stores, hurling desultory shells into the Marine perimeter and moving from there, accidentally, into the heart of the 164th Infantry's bivouac area, raining shells upon these soldiers with such ferocity that one of them—a sergeant—crawled about begging his men to shoot him.

Then it was dark.

Pistol Pete thundered on, red flares shot up from the jungle, enemy bombers roared overhead—flashing in and out of Marine antiaircraft fire and thick pencils of searchlight crisscrossing the sky—and everywhere there was a thumping and lashing of tortured earth and a whistling of invisible steel, while dazed and sleepless men stumbled in and out of their pits and foxholes, bracing for the enemy to appear once the uproar ceased.

At half-past eleven Louie the Louse planted a green flare directly over Henderson Field and The Night of the Battleships began.

Screened fore and aft, and flanked to each side by *Isuzu* and Admiral Tanaka's seven destroyers, battleships *Haruna* and *Kongo* raced down The Slot at twenty-five knots.

Just before midnight, west of Savo, speed was dropped to eighteen knots. Gunnery officers could see the first of many flares burning brightly over Henderson Field. They began calculating the mathematical problems. At half-past one, at a range of about ten miles, sixteen great fourteen-inch guns swiveled toward Henderson, gouts of flame gushed from their muzzles, and huge red blobs went arching through the blackness with the effect of strings of lighted boxcars rushing over a darkened hill.

Henderson Field became a sea of flame.

Fires and explosions were visible from the darkened bridges of the Japanese ships. Sailors cried out in glee and excitement. To

Admiral Tanaka the battleships' pyrotechnic display seemed to make the famous Ryogoku fireworks show a pale candle by comparison.[4]

Ashore the Americans were passing through an agony not to be repeated in World War II. It was a terror of the soul. It was as though the roar of colliding planets was exploding in their ears. Self-control was shattered, strong faces went flabby with fear, men sobbed aloud or whimpered, others put their pistols to their heads. It was not possible to pray.

It was possible only to crouch in gunpits to watch, through the rectangles of the gun embrasures, a horizon quivering with gun flashes, and to hear the soft, hollow thumping of the enemy's salvos—

Pah-boom, pah-boom. Pah-boom, pah-boom, pah . . .

—to feel the dry constriction of the throat and to hear the great projectiles wailing hoarsely overhead,

Hwooo, hwoo-ee,

and then to be thrown violently to earth and feel the stomach being kneaded as though by giant fingers of steel, while the eardrums rang and the head ached and the teeth were rattled by the perfection of sound, a monster clanging as though the vault of heaven were a huge casque of steel and giants were beating on it with sledgehammers, beating one-two, one-two-three, as the salvos came crashing in from two-gun turrets, three-gun turrets, and the flogged earth leaped and bucked and writhed.

It went on for an hour and a half, while Henderson Field's airplanes were blown to bits or set afire or crushed by collapsing revetments, while Tanaka's destroyers thickened the battleships' fire with their own five-inch shells, while Marine shore-batteries on Guadalcanal and Tulagi bravely but vainly attempted to drive off an enemy far out of range, and while Lieutenant Montgomery's bold little PT boats came racing out of Tulagi Harbor to challenge the intruders. Even the Japanese were astonished at these impetuous waterbugs charging at a pair of whales, although they recovered from their surprise in time to swing ponderously about and comb the American torpedo wakes. Then the destroyers turned on their searchlights and drove them off.

Kongo and *Haruna* bellowed on. Until, at three in the morning, a sudden quiet came over Guadalcanal.

At dawn the Americans came sleepwalking from their holes to

gaze in awe upon huge baseplates and shell fragments and to congratulate the Japanese gunner who had zeroed-in on a ration dump, making mince of cases of Spam to feed it, bit by detestable bit, to Guadalcanal's populous colony of rats. Otherwise, there was nothing to laugh about.

Forty-one men—many of them pilots—had been killed, and a score more were wounded. Many men were buried alive and had to be dug out, among them Michael, Martin Clemens's cook, who was pulled out of a collapsed dugout with his face streaming blood.

Henderson Field was a ruin. Smoke still curled skyward from burning fuel dumps, jagged sections of steel runway matting lay hundreds of yards away from cratered airstrips, part of the hospital was wrecked, tents flapped in the wind like canvas sieves, and there were great swathes cut in the coconut groves where the trees stood in serried rows of serrated stumps.

Neither of the runways was usable. General Geiger had had thirty-nine Dauntlesses operational when he went to bed the night before, but when he tumbled groggily to his feet on this morning of horror, he had only five. Sixteen of his Wildcats were twisted ruins, and every one of the twenty-four remaining required repairs. Most of the Avenger torpedo-bombers recently arrived were useless, and the Army aviators, whose P-400s and Airacobras were still usable, received this chilling briefing from a Marine colonel:

"We don't know whether we'll be able to hold the field or not. There's a Japanese task force of destroyers, cruisers, and troop transports headed our way. We have enough gasoline left for one mission against them. Load your planes with bombs and go out with the dive-bombers and hit them. After the gas is gone, we'll have to let the ground troops take over. Then your officers and men will attach yourselves to some infantry outfit.

"Good luck and good-by."[5]

Up went the Army craft beside four Dauntlesses. They found the enemy convoy and they attacked. But they failed to sink them and the Japanese ships pressed on.

Back at Henderson Field, Seabees and Marine engineers drove themselves to repair the airfields. Squadron commanders conferred anxiously with their repair officers.

"What's left, Lieutenant?"

"You'd need a magnifying glass to find it, Colonel."

"Well, start using one then. How about Number 117?"

"*Her?* Oh, she's great—wasn't even scratched. Except that she needs an engine change. Other than that, all she needs is both elevators, both stabilizers, the right auxiliary gas tank, right and center section flaps, right aileron, windshield, rudder, both wheels and the brake assembly. But she's still in one piece, sir, and I guess we can get her up in six days."

"Six days!"

"Dammit, Colonel, back in the States it'd take six months to do it!"

"All right, all right—but let's keep those junk-pickers of yours busy."[6]

Henderson's mechanics patched up ten more bombers that day. They did it even as bombs fell upon them from twenty-five unchallenged Betty bombers which came winging in at noon; an hour later, when fifteen more bombers and ten Zeros arrived overhead, they had twenty-four fighters aloft and waiting. Nine bombers and three Zeros were shot down, at a cost of two Marine pilots and one Army flier.

And then it became clear that Cactus Air Force was out of gas.

Admiral Ghormley's headquarters was aware of the critical situation at Henderson Field. General Vandegrift's urgent message requesting twenty bombers "immediately" had been received by Vice-Admiral Aubrey Fitch—who had replaced Admiral McCain as commander of South Pacific Air—but the best Fitch could do was send six more Dauntlesses to Guadalcanal.

In Espiritu Santo, Admiral Turner readied another emergency shipment of gasoline. Destroyer *McFarland,* now converted to a seaplane tender, was loaded with 40,000 gallons of gasoline, in tanks below and in drums topside, together with a dozen torpedoes, airplane flares and supplies of 37-mm shells.

McFarland would get to Guadalcanal about the same time as the slower barge-towing convoy which had set out from Espiritu two days before.

Admiral Yamamoto was elated by Admiral Kurita's reports of the destruction of Henderson Field. His carriers could now venture close to Guadalcanal without fear of land-based air, and he notified Admiral Kondo to move toward the island at top speed.

Kondo's mission was to destroy the American naval forces which Yamamoto mistakenly believed to be in the vicinity, and to support General Hyakutake's attack on the American airfield.

In the meantime, Admiral Mikawa would pick up where Kurita had left off.

Again Louie the Louse, again the flares, again the long sleek shapes gliding down The Slot—and once more Guadalcanal's earth quivered while cursing Americans blundered blindly through the darkness toward their holes.

This time it was Gunichi Mikawa with flagship *Chokai* and big *Kinugasa,* the lucky battler of Cape Esperance. They began shelling even as six transports from the Shortlands began unloading troops and supplies off Tassafaronga, only fifteen miles west of the Marine perimeter.

Chokai and *Kinugasa* hurled 750 eight-inch shells into the American beachhead. Racing north unmolested, Mikawa jubilantly radioed Yamamoto that the enemy airfield was *zemmetsu:* wiped out.

With dawn of October 15, Marines on the southern ridges could look west past Kukum and see, with chilled hearts, the Japanese ships calmly unloading, while destroyers screened them to seaward and enemy planes patrolled the skies above them.

Behind these dispirited but not yet despairing Marines there was a ruined airfield, only three Dauntlesses that could fly, and not a drop of gasoline.

"No gasoline?" Roy Geiger thundered. "Then, by God, find some!"[7]

Then Geiger radioed Espiritu Santo to fly in nothing but fuel that day, while his startled supply officers hurried from the Pagoda to start hunting gasoline. First, they drained the tanks of two wrecked Flying Fortresses, getting four hundred gallons out of one of them, and next someone remembered four hundred drums of Japanese aviation gasoline that had been cached outside the airfield's outer rim during the early days.

It was enough to contradict Admiral Mikawa's estimate of Henderson Field's fighting capacity.

"Always pray," Lieutenant Anthony Turtora had written to his parents, "not that I shall come back, but that I shall have the courage to do my duty."[8]

Shortly after daybreak on October 15, Lieutenant Turtora climbed into one of Henderson's three flyable Dauntlesses. His motor roared and the stubby powerful ship went zigzagging down the bomb-pocked runway, struggling aloft while ground crews watched with caught breath. Then Turtora flew down to Tassafaronga to do his duty. He did not return, but after him came scores of pilots who also had the courage to do their duty.

They should not have been airborne, by every law of logic Admiral Mikawa should have been right; and yet, all day long the ragtag Cactus Air Force struck at the enemy transports. Flying on gasoline supplies which were always on the verge of giving out, until another Army or Marine transport roared in from Espiritu, the Wildcats and P-400s and Airacobras tangled with Japanese Zeros or swept in low to strafe enemy troops. Seated in the cockpits of Dauntlesses and Avengers which Henderson's magnificent mechanics had patched together in fulfillment of their vow to salvage everything but the bullet holes, the bombers showered the enemy ships with 1000- and 500-pound eggs, or dove down through streamers of antiaircraft fire to strafe and to blast supply dumps.

Late in the day Flying Fortresses came up from Espiritu to join the Tassafaronga assault, their majestic formation provoking cries of delight from Marines atop the ridges who had been cheering on the airmen throughout the day. And then a great shout broke from their lips. They had seen a clumsy Catalina lumbering west with two torpedoes tucked under its belly.

It was the *Blue Goose,* General Geiger's personal plane, and Mad Jack Cram was at the controls.

Major Cram had flown into Guadalcanal to deliver torpedoes. He had begged the use of one of them, and an ensign who had already been down to Tassafaronga told him he could have both. Then Cram gathered his crew and climbed back into *Blue Goose.*

He nursed the awkward Cat into the sky. He made for a rendezvous with eight fighters and a dozen Dauntlesses a few miles east of Henderson. Beneath him, Major Duke Davis and his Wildcats were cakewalking down the runway between the bursts laid down by Pistol Pete.

Blue Goose was roaring along with the Dauntlesses and Wildcats toward the transports and thirty Zeros flying cover above them. Then the dive-bombers were going over, flashing down through the flak, and big bulky *Blue Goose* was going over with them.

She was built to make 160 miles an hour, this Catalina, but she was diving at 270. Her great ungainly wings shook and shrieked in an agony of stress. She would surely fall apart.

Cram pulled the stick back. He leveled off at one thousand feet. Then he went over again. *Blue Goose* came thundering over two transports at seventy-five feet. She shuddered and bucked in their flak blasts. Cram sighted off his bow at a third transport. He yanked the toggle release. His first torpedo hit the water and began running straight and true. He yanked again, and the second fell. It porpoised, righted—and followed the first into the transport's side.

Blue Goose had broken the transport's back. She was done. Her skipper drove her up on the beach. Soon two more transports were beached, and the other three had turned and raced back toward the Shortlands.

Now *Blue Goose* was fighting for her life. Five Zeros went after her. Cram stood his big plane on one wing and raced for Henderson Field. The Zeros took turns raking his tail. Cram began rollercoastering, rising and diving, rising and diving. He came over the main strip with his ship wailing through a hundred holes. But he was going too fast to land. He made for Fighter One. He began letting down, while Marine antiaircraft gunners shot two Zeros off his tail.

Then a third came after him, just as Lieutenant Roger Haberman brought his smoking Wildcat down with lowered wheels.

Haberman shot the Zero off Cram's tail and *Blue Goose* went plowing up the strip in a pancake landing. Cram and his crewmen emerged unscathed, only to hear Geiger bellow:

"Goddamit, Cram! I ought to court-martial you for deliberate destruction of government property!" Then Geiger strode into the Pagoda to write out a recommendation for a Navy Cross.

And so the "safest" run of the Tokyo Express was all but wrecked. The three beached ships would eventually be turned into charred and rusting skeletons; many of General Hyakutake's reinforcements were lost and the remainder would have to complete the southern movement by barge, ravaged by American torpedo boats at night, scourged by their aircraft by day. In all, about 4500 men would reach Hyakutake in time for the big push. But he would not get all his supplies. Many of them were already burning and American destroyers would set other depots afire. As the day came to an end, three Japanese transports had been lost, in effect, and five Zeros and three Bettys shot down; against the loss of seven of Geiger's aircraft.

It had been a memorable fifteenth of October, and tomorrow *McFarland* and the barge-towing convoy would arrive.

Early in the morning of October 15 the Japanese fleet reached a station two hundred miles north of Guadalcanal. Admiral Kondo took personal command of heavy cruisers *Myoko* and *Maya* and led them toward The Slot. Meanwhile, Nagumo's carriers flew off scout planes to search for the American fleet. They found no carriers, but at ten o'clock in the morning they reported sighting a force of one cruiser, two destroyers, and two transports at a point a hundred miles south of Guadalcanal.

Nagumo decided to attack, even though the target was three hundred miles distant. Twenty-seven Vals and Kates roared aloft from *Zuikaku,* speeding toward what was in actuality the barge-towing convoy from Espiritu.

But they would find only two targets.

Nagumo's scout plane had already made transports *Alchiba* and *Bellatrix,* destroyer *Nicholas* and PT-tender *Jamestown* conclude that it would be wise to withdraw. Fleet-tug *Vireo* and destroyer *Meredith* plowed on. Shortly before eleven they beat off a two-plane attack. Then they received word that enemy ships were close by, and they, also, decided to reverse course.

But *Vireo* moved too slowly, and so, *Meredith* ordered her abandoned and prepared to sink her with torpedoes—just as Nagumo's warbirds came tumbling out of the sky.

They fell on *Meredith.*

Bombed, torpedoed, and machine-gunned, the destroyer sank almost instantly. Her men took to the life rafts. One raftful succeeded in boarding drifting *Vireo.* But the others could not and these rafts became floating horrors. Wounded and dreadfully burned sailors lay in the boiling sun across the gratings while salt water washed across their open cuts and burned bodies. Other men clung to the lifelines, waiting for someone aboard to die so that they could take his place.

The sharks found them. They dragged the men on the lifelines under. One great scaly beast flipped onto a raft and tore a chunk of flesh from a dying man's thigh before his horrified comrades could seize the flopping creature by the tail and heave it back into the sea again.

After three days and three nights of agony unrivaled, eighty-eight survivors of *Vireo* and *Meredith* were eventually rescued by destroyers. But 236 were not.

Thus did the Navy suffer to keep the Marines and soldiers on Guadalcanal alive and fighting.

They were out in the Bay again.

Heavies *Myoko* and *Maya* were there, with Admiral Kondo in command, and ordeal was renewed and red again.

Parading within less than five miles of the island, Kondo's cruisers fired a crushing 1500 rounds of eight-inch shell into the American perimeter.

In the morning, General Geiger counted fifteen ruined Wildcats. His Cactus Air Force numbered only twenty-seven planes, and it was again out of gasoline.

Henderson Field's only hope now rested in Lieutenant Colonel Harold ("Indian Joe") Bauer's fighter squadron at Espiritu Santo, alerted for movement north, and in *McFarland*, still bending it on for Iron Bottom Bay.

"I am your Commander-in-Chief, you are my strong right arms. Whether I shall adequately fulfill my duty to the Ancestors depends upon your fidelity . . . If you unite with me, our courage and power shall illuminate the whole earth."

Tears streaming down their cheeks, the men of the Sendai Division stood outside the encampment at Kukumbona, their faces toward the Emperor and their ears filled with the familiar words of the Imperial Rescript.

They were marching against the Americans.

On this morning of October 16, while Roy Geiger contemplated the ruins of his air force, seven thousand of them prepared to march through the jungle to an assembly area south of Henderson Field.

As always, General Maruyama was supremely confident. Captain Oda and his engineers had sent back encouraging reports on the progress of the Maruyama Road. The Sendai should easily be in place by "X Day," now tentatively set for October 22. So the general ordered his men to take only five days' rations.

Then, stroking his thin line of supercilious mustache, he suggested to General Hyakutake that the appropriate place to receive the surrender of the American commander was at the mouth of the Matanikau River.

After which, at noon of October 16, he set out along the Maruyama Road.

A few hours later his rear guard heard the welcome sound of Japanese aerial bombs falling on American ships in Iron Bottom Bay.

McFarland got to Guadalcanal ahead of Joe Bauer's fliers.

A floating gasoline dump and ammunition depot, the brave little ship entered the Bay on the morning of October 16. Her crew and her skipper, Lieutenant Commander John Alderman, were understandably eager to unload, and they quickly began lowering drums over the side into waiting lighters while dropping a fuel line to a barge which had come alongside.

Commander Alderman and his crew were not quite so eager to take aboard their return cargo: 160 hospital patients, half of whom were those exhausted and battle-fatigued men who were still, in those days, ungraciously described as "war neurotics."

At five o'clock Alderman sighted a periscope and decided to get under way. He did, with the gasoline barge still alongside taking on fuel.

Some time later Colonel Bauer's squadron of nineteen Wildcats, plus seven Dauntlesses, came winging overhead. They came in with fuel tanks almost empty, and they began lowering quickly down for a landing. Bauer would come in last.

And then nine Japanese dive-bombers fell without warning on *McFarland.*

Alderman rang up full speed and ordered the barge cast off. She was, in time to be holed and sunk.

Then an enemy bomb burst among the depth charges on *McFarland's* fantail. Huge explosions racked the ship. The neurotics panicked. They stampeded through the passageways and tried to tear weapons and life jackets away from sailors struggling desperately to save their ship.

Above, Joe Bauer saw *McFarland* plodding along at barely five knots. She was a helpless target for about five Vals which had still to make their dive. With his gas tanks nearly empty, Bauer went wolfing swiftly among the enemy.

He shot down four of them before he came down with bone-dry tanks.

McFarland was saved, as well as her precious cargo of ammunition.

Rugged Joe Bauer, Indian Joe Bauer, one of the most inspirational of flying leaders, and also the pilot whom all Marines regarded as "the greatest," had brought off the most astonishing single feat of aerial arms in the annals of Guadalcanal. In the words of his adoring wingman:

"The Chief stitched four of the bastards end to end."[9]

Chapter 4

"IT NOW appears that we are unable to control the sea in the Guadalcanal area," the admiral reported. "Thus our supply of the positions will only be done at great expense to us. The situation is not hopeless, but it is certainly critical."

It was not Ghormley the pessimist who wrote those words on October 15, 1942, but rather Nimitz the optimist.

And his grim estimate of the situation came at a time when it was next to impossible for Admiral King in Washington to divert any additional ships or supplies or men to the South Pacific. Operation TORCH, the invasion of North Africa, was gathering. President Roosevelt had insisted that American troops be committed against Germany at some time in 1942. His Joint Chiefs of Staff had argued for a cross-Channel invasion of France but their British counterparts had objected; backed by Prime Minister Churchill they held out for the North African venture, and Roosevelt had agreed with them.

A vast concourse of ships, a logistics problem as yet unrivaled, was involved in transporting some 90,000 men to North Africa from bases as far away as England and the United States.

Moreover, Admiral King's hands were also very full contending with German U-boats, which sank eighty-eight ships and 585,510 tons of cargo in the Atlantic during October, and with supplying British forces in Egypt via the long route around the Cape of Good Hope. General Marshall was solidly for TORCH, now that Roosevelt had given it the green light, and General Arnold, although not equally enthusiastic, still cherished his never-to-be-realized dream of bringing Germany to her knees by strategic bombing, which meant concentrating aircraft in Europe.

Admiral King and General MacArthur might argue that disaster must not be courted in the Solomons and New Guinea just to get into action against the Germans, thus boosting morale on the home front as well as perhaps providing for the eventual invasion of Europe, but the Commander-in-Chief of American armed forces, Franklin Delano Roosevelt, was not to be moved. TORCH still burned with the green light.

And so Nimitz knew that the Guadalcanal situation was critical simply because the Japanese Navy was concentrating all its forces there and he had not equal forces to oppose them.

Then, on October 16, the day the Sendai marched south on Guadalcanal, Nimitz received a shattering message from Admiral Ghormley.

"This appears to be all-out enemy effort against Guadalcanal. My forces totally inadequate to meet situation. Urgently request all aviation reinforcements possible."

The following day Ghormley came through with an estimate of what he needed to save the day: all the submarines in MacArthur's area, all the cruisers and destroyers in Alaska, all the PT boats in the Pacific except those at Midway, a review of the entire destroyer assignment schedule in the Atlantic and the Pacific, and from the Army Air Force ninety heavy bombers, eighty medium bombers, sixty dive-bombers, and two groups of fighters, including those Lightnings which General Arnold was reluctant to release.

Nimitz, a calm and orderly man, was staggered. Obviously such recommendations did not spring from a hopeful mind. Such forces, even if they could be made available, could not be furnished instantly. And the time was one for instantaneous action with the forces that were available. Chester Nimitz sighed and came reluctantly to a decision.

Back in Washington on that same day—October 16 in Washington, the seventeenth in the South Pacific—Secretary of the Navy Frank Knox was meeting the press. Came the question: Can Guadalcanal be held?

"I certainly hope so," the Secretary said. "I expect so. I don't want to make any predictions, but every man out there, ashore or afloat, will give a good account of himself."

That night on Guadalcanal the Marines heard of the Secretary's shy little pep talk with hoots of derision.

"Didja hear about Knox? It was on the 'Frisco radio. He says he don't know, but we're sure gonna give a good account of ourselves."

"Yeah, I heard—ain't he a tiger?"[1]

The following day a four-engined Coronado flying boat circled above Admiral Ghormley's flagship, *Argonne,* in the harbor at Nouméa.

The pilot eased back on the throttle and brought the plane down gently on the water's surface. An admiral with a craggy face and tufted gray eyebrows clambered out just as a motor whaleboat drew alongside. The admiral jumped into the tossing whaleboat.

A young junior grade lieutenant stepped up to him, saluted, and handed him a sealed envelope marked "Secret."

The admiral tore it open and read. He read it again, blinking, and then he handed it to his Marine adviser and friend, Colonel Julian Brown. It said:

YOU WILL TAKE COMMAND OF THE SOUTH PACIFIC AREA AND SOUTH PACIFIC FORCES IMMEDIATELY.

"Jesus Christ and General Jackson!" Bull Halsey swore. "This is the hottest potato they ever handed me."[2]

On Guadalcanal, men who had never once lost hope of victory, who were entering their eleventh week of battle still confident of it, heard the news with shouts of jubilation.

A real tiger was taking over.

Chapter 5

THE ARRIVAL of the 164th Infantry Regiment's three thousand soldiers had given Archer Vandegrift 23,000 men on Guadalcanal, with another four thousand under General Rupertus on Tulagi. Guadalcanal, however, was the prize; and Vandegrift again reorganized his defenses there.

Sector One comprised seven thousand yards of beach front held by a composite force of Marines from the Third Defense Battalion, Special Weapons, Amtracks, Engineers, and Pioneers. On its right or eastern flank it joined the 164th holding Sector Two, a 6500-yard line south along the Tenaru which curved back west short of Bloody Ridge. Here it tied in with Sector Three held by the Seventh Marines, less one battalion, for another 2500 yards west to the Lunga, Sector Four, defended by the First Marines, less one battalion, stretched an additional 3500 yards west until it merged with Sector Five, which, held by the Fifth Marines, curved back north to the sea.

Essentially, this was the same perimeter which the Marines had been holding since August 7, except for one new feature: a battle position on the east bank of the Matanikau.

Here two independent battalions of Marines, backed up by artillery and 75-mm half-tracks, held a line from the river mouth left to Hill 67 about a thousand yards inland. Although this position was about three thousand yards to the west of the perimeter, it could be supplied along the coastal road. It could also depend upon Marine artillery registered to fire anywhere along the entire defense.

In reserve, Vandegrift held one infantry battalion and most of the tank battalion. Regimental commanders all held a third of their strength in reserve, as did lesser commanders down through companies.

It was a neat and efficient cordon depending upon the mobility offered by interior lines, and it had, of course, that single exception on the Matanikau. But it was here, from the Japanese assembly area at Kukumbona, that Archer Vandegrift expected the main thrust.

And he was wrong.

Lieutenant General Haruyoshi Hyakutake still depended upon the Sendai Division then marching south to deliver the main blow in his three-pronged assault involving 22,000 men.

General Maruyama was to attack at a point a bit east of the area in which General Kawaguchi had met defeat. His seven thousand men were to seize the airfield, the very nerve center of the American defense.

To assist him, Hyakutake had arranged for a reinforced battalion of the 38th Division to land to the east of Koli Point. This "Koli Detachment" would be boated and ready to land on order.

On the west, Hyakutake planned a heavier distraction. Here he would use a tank-infantry-artillery unit under Major General Tadashi Sumoyoshi, commander of 17th Army artillery. Sumoyoshi's guns had already been at work battering the enemy airfield and perimeter. Now they would support the remnants of Colonel Nakaguma's Fourth Infantry Regiment as they charged across the Matanikau River mouth behind sixteen tanks. Farther inland, Colonel Oka's composite force would cross the river to flank the Americans on Hill 67. Then, while Nakaguma was striking the enemy at the river mouth, Oka would turn north to come in behind the American battle position and isolate it.

In the meantime, Rabaul would mount sustained aerial attacks, covered by Zeros based on Buka and the new field at Buin on southern Bougainville. Combined Fleet's battleships and heavy cruisers would crush the Americans with sustained bombardment. Once the airfield was captured, Yamamoto's eagles would fly in to operate from it. His gunfire ships would cut off the American retreat.

All depended on the capture of the airfield, all depended on the peerless Sendai striking from their secret position to the south.

They would not, they could not fail. Guadalcanal airfield should again be Japanese by the morning of October 22.

October 22?

Isoroku Yamamoto was annoyed. What was wrong with the Army? First, the deadline had been moved back from October 17 to October 20. And now there was another postponement of two days. The huge Guadalcanal Supporting Forces had been at sea since October 11, at sea doing nothing; doing nothing and consuming fuel. Was the Army not aware that a fleet feeds on oil? All the Army had to do in Operation Ka was supply a few divisions of men; they had not contributed so much as a single airplane—and here they were dragging their feet again.

While they did, the Americans would surely reinforce. Isoroku Yamamoto did not subscribe to any of those wildly optimistic evaluations of the American change of command, especially not the one predicting "withdrawal of all American naval forces from the South Pacific."[1] Yamamoto could only admire the daring skill which had brought off the Doolittle raid on Tokyo. He did not think that a rude, aggressive man like Halsey—with his insulting boast that he would ride the Emperor's white horse down Pennsylvania Avenue—could have the slightest intention of withdrawing. Halsey would attack, he would reinforce; and the Army was playing into his hands.

And there, Yamamoto was exactly right.

The *Big E* was coming back to battle. The mighty proud flattop that had been in almost every action since the Pacific War began was whole again, the damage she had suffered August 24 during the Battle of the Eastern Solomons had been repaired. On October 16 she cast off her last lines and stood out to sea from Pearl Harbor.

On her flag bridge was Rear Admiral Thomas C. Kinkaid, bareheaded and shirt-sleeved as always among his helmeted and jacketed sailors, pacing the deck with binoculars around his neck. Kinkaid was to take tactical command of South Pacific Force after his own carrier and screen had made rendezvous with *Hornet* and her screen. Then, for the first time since *Wasp* went down on September 15, the Americans would have two carriers to oppose the Japanese.

Enroute to the rendezvous area, Kinkaid received a message

from his new chief, Halsey, urging him to proceed at all possible speed. Kinkaid obeyed. But he could never join *Hornet* before daybreak of October 24.

And that, according to Hyakutake's timetable, was just two days too late.

Masao Maruyama was almost in tears. Kawaguchi had been right. The terrain was incredible. And that unspeakable Captain Oda, could he not have realized that if his lightly equipped trailblazers could very easily crawl up and down these terrible cliffs, heavily laden combat troops could not?

Every one of Maruyama's men carried sixty pounds of personal equipment, besides machine guns or grenade launchers. Each man carried an artillery shell. They had no mules to pull the guns, 37-mm antitank pieces, 70- and 75-mm howitzers. All the division's horses had been left in Rabaul. The only way to get the artillery up and down the cliffs was by hand and by ropes. It was impossible to do this in daylight because of the American aircraft. It had to be done at night; as a result, the artillery was dropping far behind.

Thirty-five miles, that was all that they had to go, and yet, after five days marching, the advance guard had gone only twenty-nine. Six miles of foul, impenetrable jungle still lay between them and the assembly area. And these were the Sendai! These were the men of Colonel Furumiya's matchless 29th Infantry who had marched 122 miles in seventy-two hours.

But the men had been splendid. They had gone on half-rations without a murmur, and they plodded on inspired by the sight of officers who also were hungry, who also carried guns or artillery shells. Nor had the Sendai forgotten its heritage. Each morning the march was renewed with the memorable words:

"I am your Commander-in-Chief, you are my strong arms . . ."

Each time the men seemed to be on the verge of collapse their officers rallied them by turning them to face toward the Emperor, to sing:

> *"Corpses drifting swollen in the sea depths,*
> *Corpses rotting in the mountain grass . . ."*

They sang with tears streaking their mud-caked cheeks, uncaring if American patrols were in the vicinity. But for all their endurance, for all their sacrifice, General Maruyama knew by October 21 that he could not possibly make the deadline. He radioed General Hyakutake back in Kukumbona that he would have to postpone the attack until October 23.

It was October 22 and it was obvious that Admiral Kakuta's flag carrier *Hiyo* was not going to be of use. *Hiyo* had developed engine trouble. Her power-plant, originally designed for a merchant ship, could not provide the speed required by a carrier. Kakuta sent *Hiyo* back to Truk at her top speed of six knots and took his flag, together with the Emperor's picture, aboard his last flattop, *Junyo*.

On October 23, General Maruyama had reached the end of his march. He set up his headquarters on a rise called Centipede-Shaped Ridge and made his final dispositions.

The point he chose to attack was slightly to the east of the ridge at which General Kawaguchi had met defeat. Unknown to Maruyama, it was defended by the Marine battalions commanded by Chesty Puller and Herman Henry Hanneken.

Facing north toward the sea, the Japanese right consisted of the 29th Infantry, with antitank guns, mortars, mountain artillery, and engineers. It was commanded by General Kawaguchi. The left wing, composed of similar arms and similar strength, was led by Major General Yumio Nasu. In reserve was the 16th Infantry, which Maruyama intended to use once Kawaguchi and Nasu had broken through.

The attack would begin just after sunset, following the scheduled aerial bombardment of the Americans.

October 23 seemed like a dull day to the fighter pilots on Henderson Field. The big enemy push was expected hourly, and yet the skies were free of red-balled aircraft. In the morning, Captain Joe Foss and a few other Wildcat pilots escorted a Catalina south toward Nouméa. Lieutenant General Thomas Holcomb, Commandant of the Marine Corps, was aboard. Holcomb had come to visit Vandegrift, and now, he and some other generals were flying down to confer with Admiral Halsey.

Foss and his comrades dipped their wings in farewell, and flew back to Henderson.

At noon they were hanging on their noses clawing for altitude. Sixteen Japanese bombers were coming in, escorted by a few Zeros. The Wildcats closed. In the rear of the formation, Joe Foss took a last look around. High above, like a flight of silvery flying fish, he spotted about eighteen Zeros. They were coming down in a screaming dive. They flashed beneath him.

Foss dove to overtake them. A Wildcat crossed his course firing into a Zero trying desperately to escape. Another Zero was on the Wildcat's tail. Foss swung in behind him. Only a few feet away, he pressed the button.

Ba—loom!

The enemy plane was gone. It had blown up with the vehemence characteristic of the Zero. Foss saw the pilot pop from his cockpit like a pea pressed from a pod. The motor went spinning into space, and Foss tore through an aerial dustbin of bits and pieces of aircraft. Below him, the plane's wing section was sailing downward like a leaf.

Foss banked hard. He went after a Zero which went into a dive, pulling out and looping. Foss cut close inside, and the Zero went over on its back. Foss was upside-down, too, when he triggered a leading shot at the red-balled fighter and caught him in a terrible, converging burst.

His second kill had blown up.

Foss ducked again to avoid debris, and suddenly a Zero came from nowhere, slow-rolling as though in a victory celebration, and Foss's plane again shook from the recoil of its wing guns. There was a disintegrating flash, and the pilot popped from his cockpit and nearly hit Foss's plane.

Now there were two Zeros coming at Foss, one head-on, the other from an angle. Foss rushed at the first one. The planes drove toward each other with smoking guns. The Japanese swerved right, and Foss aimed a burst behind his motor. Streaming flames, the Zero came on—exploding off Foss's right wing and rocking the Wildcat with the force of the blast.

Now Foss's plane was smoking. The enemy had scored hits. Foss went over in a dive for home. A Zero came after him, overran, and Foss fired his last rounds at him in a useless burst. Another Zero raked him on a side pass. Foss radioed for help, and two Marine fliers came roaring over to shoot down both Zeros.

Foss reached the field safely, bringing in his fourth damaged plane since he had begun fighting from Henderson on October 10. One more shot-up Wildcat, he thought, and I'll be a Japanese ace.[2] But he was already twice an American ace, with eleven aircraft downed in fourteen days.

Other newly made aces were rolling exultantly over the field, among them Lieutenant Jack Conger, a wiry gamecock who had chased a Zero all the way up to Savo before sending him down in flames. Of the twenty Zeros that came down to Guadalcanal that October 23, every one was destroyed. So was one bomber, while four others staggered home trailing smoke and flames.

Once again the Cactus Air Force had fought to save the ground troops, for Maruyama's anticipated bombardment never came off.

Nor would his attack.

General Maruyama was beside himself. Shortly after the raid from Rabaul was repulsed, he was notified that General Kawaguchi had not yet reached his assembly area. He could not possibly attack at sunset. Maruyama had no alternative but to postpone his assault another day. He did, and then, in an icy rage, he telephoned Kawaguchi and relieved him of his command. Colonel Toshinaro Shoji took his place.

Next, Maruyama attempted to reach General Sumoyoshi to tell him to postpone the Matanikau thrust until sunset of October 24. He could not reach him. As happened so frequently to both sides in that moist, dissolving jungle, communications had broken down.

But Maruyama did reach Hyakutake, who quickly informed Yamamoto, who angrily sent his fleet tankers south and ordered Kondo's force to withdraw for refueling.

Yamamoto was incensed. One carrier had already been lost because of delays, and here he was forced to withdraw his entire fleet from the target area. More, he was made uneasy by reports of growing American naval strength along the supply line to Guadalcanal. A patrol plane from the Gilbert Islands had sighted *Enterprise* steaming north, and a few days before that *Hornet* had been detected. Then, suddenly, like ghosts, the American carriers had vanished. What did it mean? Neither Yamamoto nor Chuichi Nagumo, both of whom carried the memory of Midway burned in their brains, could supply the answer. One thing Yamamoto knew, though: he would brook no more delays, and he informed Hyakutake of his displeasure.

Hyakutake contacted Maruyama again. There was no doubt: the attack would go forward at sunset of October 24. By early morning of October 25 Hyakutake should receive the message signaling capture of the airfield. It was one word: *"Banzai!"* Upon receipt of it, the Koli Detachment would be ordered to land to the east.

Meanwhile, Maruyama inquired, had he remembered to specify that when the American commander came to the mouth of the Matanikau to surrender, he must come unarmed and accompanied only by an interpreter?

The American commander was not on Guadalcanal.

The Catalina which Foss and his comrades had escorted south that morning of October 23 also carried Alexander Archer Vandegrift. Admiral Halsey had had the grace and the common sense to summon the ground commander to an important conference at Nouméa. Kelly Turner was there, too, along with Lieutenant General Holcomb, Major General Harmon, Major General Alexander Patch, commander of the U. S. Army's Americal Infantry Division from which the 164th was drawn, and which was now scheduled to relieve the First Marine Division—when and if it was possible.

Halsey sat smoking while the others settled around a table. Then he asked Vandegrift to outline the situation. Vandegrift did. His soft, courteous voice was charged with urgency. The question was one of reinforcement of every kind. He needed more airplanes and the rest of the Americal Division and a regiment from the Second Marine Division, then enroute to the Pacific. His men were worn out. There were now seven hundred new cases of malaria a week.

Holcomb and Harmon spoke. They agreed, vigorously. Kelly Turner spoke. He was stung by the implied rebuke to his efforts. He rehearsed all of his attempts to supply the island, he said there were getting to be fewer transports and fewer warships to protect them. There were no sheltering bases at Guadalcanal. They still needed the seaplane base at Ndeni to provide aerial cover of the supply line. Solomons' waters were too narrow for maneuver. Torpedo Junction swarmed with submarines.

Halsey heard him out, his knuckly fingers drumming the desk, his eyes thoughtful under the shaggy gray brows. Then he turned to Vandegrift.

"Are we going to evacuate or hold?"

"I can hold," Archer Vandegrift said softly. "But I've got to have more active support than I've been getting."

"All right," Halsey said. "Go on back. I'll promise you everything I've got."[3]

Archer Vandegrift did go back, to find Guadalcanal ablaze with battle again.

In the United States Marine Corps there is a legend concerning the battle between *Serapis* and *Bonhomme Richard*. After the British commander summoned John Paul Jones to surrender, and after that doughty sailor had flung back his immortal, "I have just begun to fight," it is said that one of the Marines* who had been fighting very briskly in the rigging looked down upon John Paul in disgust, and snorted: "There's always some poor slob who doesn't get the word."

On the night of October 23 the unfortunate Major General Tadashi Sumoyoshi was one of those who did not get the word. Maruyama had not reached him to postpone his attack on the Matanikau, Hyakutake had not done so either, and Sumoyoshi was himself lying in his dugout in a malarial coma.

His attack went forward at six o'clock that night.

Once again Colonel Nakaguma's Fourth Infantry was torn apart. Ten battalions of Marine artillery had registered their guns on the Matanikau mouth and the coastal track behind it, and they blew the massing Japanese apart with a howling hurricane of steel.

Then Sumoyoshi's tanks burst from the cover of the jungle and went racing with spinning inner wheels toward the sandspit. One came, two came, three, four, five, six, seven, eight, nine—and then the Marine gunners in dug-in half-tracks on the west bank decided that there were enough targets.

Wham! Brrranng! Ba—loom!

---

* They were French Marines.

Seventy-five millimeter rifles smoked and recoiled, howitzers to the rear bucked and bellowed, 37-mm antitank guns spat out flat trajectories, everyone opened up—riflemen, machine-gunners, BAR-men, mortarmen—and in a single disintegrating outburst lasting at the most three minutes, they halted or blew apart all but one tank and sent bullets or shells into the backs of the crewmen who leaped from them to flee.

The surviving tank was the first one, carrying Captain Maeda, the tank commander. It came whizzing over the sandbar. It rolled over strands of barbed wire and crushed a pillbox and wheeled to its right to come clanking down on a foxhole occupied by Private Joe Champagne.

Champagne ducked. The tank rolled over his hole and paused, as though Captain Maeda was taking his bearings. Champagne pulled a grenade from his belt, stuck it in the tank tread, and pulled the pin while the tank resumed speed and clattered away.

Barrrooom!

Maeda's tank sloughed around out of control. A Marine half-track drove down to the sandbar. Its seventy-five flashed and Maeda's tank shivered. It fired again. Flames gushed from the tank. Its ammunition locker had been hit, and it was blown twenty yards into the sea where it was finally finished off.

And now those massed battalions of American artillery were walking their fire back along the coastal road, raking the assembly area, knocking out three more tanks, and putting the dreadful seal of annihilation upon the Fourth Infantry Regiment of the Sendai Division.

Another 650 men had been killed, and in the dawn of October 24 Marines along the Matanikau heights could look down upon a silent sandbar clogged with broken, burned-out tanks and the bodies of the enemy. Nothing moved but the crocodiles swimming hungrily downstream.

Chapter 6

Enterprise had arrived in time to fight.

Guadalcanal's tortuous terrain, General Maruyama's overconfidence, his own and General Hyakutake's failure to appreciate that plans possessing precision and power on paper often wobble and weaken in time and space—all these factors had conspired to grant the Americans the time they needed to double their carrier strength in the Pacific.

All these factors, and Vandegrift's dauntless Marines; for even as *Enterprise* and her screen reached the rendezvous area 850 miles southeast of Guadalcanal at daybreak of that October 24, Admiral Kinkaid knew that the enemy's latest attempt to seize Henderson Field had been repulsed. He knew also that the Marines were bracing for a far more furious attempt that night.

If they could hold again, could fight for just one more day's grace, then perhaps Kinkaid's ships would have the time to strike the enemy fleet.

And so, *Enterprise* and her escorts met the tanker *Sabine,* slipping two at a time to either side of the big fleet cow to fill their tanks with thick black oil. Later in the day, lookouts sighted the silhouettes of *Hornet* and her screen standing over the rim of the horizon with slow majesty. When they joined, Halsey had at sea two carriers, two battleships, nine cruisers, and twenty-four destroyers to oppose Admiral Yamamoto's four flattops, five battleships, fourteen cruisers, and forty-four destroyers.

By three o'clock in the afternoon the American battleship group, *Washington,* three crusiers and seven destroyers commanded by Rear Admiral Willis Augustus Lee, had turned northwest to come up under Guadalcanal's southern coast and patrol it, and the two carriers went racing northeast to intercept or trap the enemy.

Kinkaid's orders were to take his ships north of the Santa Cruz

Islands, which are almost due east of Guadalcanal, and then to turn them southwest to cut off the enemy fleet. With any luck, they might even get behind the suspecting Japanese to batter them beneath the waves as they had done at Midway.

Chuichi Nagumo sat in his cabin aboard flag carrier *Shokaku*. The marks of Midway seemed to have been etched deeper into his face. His skin was sallow and wrinkled and his hair was gray. Beside him on a table were the immaculate white gloves he always wore on deck. In his hands was a sheet of tabulated reports of enemy ship sightings.

"The enemy carriers have been missing for a week," Nagumo muttered. "What does this mean?"[1]

He called for his chief of staff, Rear Admiral Jinichi Kusaka. "Any reports on enemy carriers?" he asked.

Kusaka shook his head, and Nagumo began musing aloud: "At Midway, the enemy struck us at a time of his choosing. Now, too, there is no doubt that the enemy pinpoints our position as if on a chessboard, but we are running blind . . ."[2]

There was a tense silence, broken by a staff officer suggesting that Nagumo wire Yamamoto for instructions. Nagumo remained silent, but Kusaka closed his eyes and dictated a message: "May I suggest halting our southward advance until we receive definite word that the Army has captured Guadalcanal airfields? There seems to be a possibility of our being trapped if we continue going like this."[3]

After a long delay Nagumo received Yamamoto's reply: "Your Striking Force will proceed quickly to the enemy direction. The operation orders stand, without change."[4]

Nagumo snorted while Kusaka bit his lip. "All right," Chuichi Nagumo said with a shrug, "start fueling the carriers."[5]

One of the results of the Japanese debacle on the Matanikau the night of October 23 was that it confirmed the Marines' belief that the major assault was to come from the west.

Roy Geiger, now a major general and in command during Vandegrift's absence, moved to reinforce there. He pulled Colonel Hanneken's battalion out of the line south of the airfield and sent it marching toward the Matanikau.

Now Chesty Puller's battalion had an entire front of 2500 yards to defend.

Masao Maruyama spent the morning conferring with his officers at his headquarters at Centipede-Shaped Ridge. At noon, he issued the following order:

The Division has succeeded in reaching the rear flank of the enemy in absolute secrecy.

In accordance with plans of my own, I intend to exterminate the enemy around the airfield in one blow.

Both left and right will begin the charge at five o'clock and penetrate the enemy lines.

I will stay at present location until three o'clock and will then head for the airfield behind the left unit.[6]

It was Kiyono Ichiki and Kiyotake Kawaguchi all over again, except that neither of these supremely self-confident men had ever dashed off such a masterpiece of vague bravado as "In accordance with plans of my own, I intend to exterminate the enemy . . . in one blow." His private plans locked in his breast, Masao Maruyama followed his left wing toward the jump-off point.

And the monsoon came down in a torrent.

Rain fell with the rattle of rifle-fire. In a single sodden minute the jungle was a streaming, swishing, gurgling swamp and the Sendai Division was segmented. Companies were lost, platoons were lost, squads were lost. Communications went out. And as the rain came steadily down, it became apparent that there would be no five o'clock attack.

Colonel Oka was still not in position.

The commander who had attacked very timidly and very tardily at the Matanikau a month ago under General Kawaguchi, was again dragging his feet under General Hyakutake. He did not cross the Matanikau upriver to come down behind the American battle position. He explained his failure with the message: "The Regiment endeavored to accomplish this objective of diverting the enemy, but they seemed to be planning a firm defense of this region."

It was not true. The Marine position in the west ended on Hill 67, where its left flank was refused, that is bent back and left dangling in the jungle. General Hyakutake knew this and could not accept Oka's alibi. He came up to the front personally and ordered Oka to get moving.

He did, and he moved too far.

Marines on top of Hill 67 spotted Japanese soldiers moving across a lower ridge to their left. They reported it to headquarters.

Geiger quickly diverted Hanneken's men then marching west toward the Matanikau, sending them south instead to organize undefended high ground about a thousand yards east of the refused left flank.

Before they swung left, these Marines passed through the headquarters area. With cots and tents and clean clothing, it seemed to them a lotus-eater's land, a place where troops dined on Spam and powdered eggs and canned fruit and other dishes that were veritable delicacies compared to front-line fare. So they helped themselves to what they saw, having no faith in a chain-of-supply which begins with the cow at headquarters and ends with the tail at the front.

In the platoon of machine guns led by hard-jawed Sergeant Mitchell Paige a small can of Spam and a large can of peaches were thus "procured."

Paige's men trudged on, confident of "living it up" tonight, because for some of them, as they suspected, there would be no tomorrow.

Chesty Puller was spreading himself thin, trying to cover the entire 2500-yard sector which fell to him after the withdrawal of Hanneken's battalion. Every man in Puller's battalion except the mortarmen was put into line.

They seized strands of wire marking a jeep-road to their rear and strung it by winding it around trees, adorning it with cans filled with stones and grenades with half-pulled pins.

Throughout the morning and afternoon Puller roved his lines, chomping on his cold stump of pipe, removing it to bellow orders ("We don't need no communications system," his men boasted, "we got Chesty!"), or speaking through teeth clamped firmly around the stem. Puller's manner was urgent because a young Marine who had fallen behind a patrol that morning had seen Japanese officers studying his position through field glasses. Puller urged his men to dig deeper, but when he came to one position he pulled his pipe from his mouth, pointed at the hole with it, and grunted:

"Son, if you dig that hole any deeper Ah'll have to charge you with desertion."[7]

The Marine grinned, and Puller strode on, pleased to see that Manila John Basilone had fortified his pair of machine guns almost in the exact center of the line.

Colonel Puller returned to his "command post"—a field telephone hardly ten yards behind his lines—to repeat his request for permission to withdraw his outpost platoon. He was convinced that the enemy was coming, and he feared that the forty men on outpost would be needlessly sacrificed. But his arguments—generally couched in ungentle roars—were unavailing. The men stayed outside the line.

Finally, Puller had all of the field phones opened so that every company and platoon could hear every message.

And then the rains came down.

At seven o'clock that night the rains slackened. Sergeant Mitchell Paige crawled forward on the nose of the ridge which his section was to defend. It was dark. Paige felt about with his hands, hunting for a good position.

"Here," he called softly. "Put the guns here."

They moved with silent swiftness. Gunners with their 53-pound tripods, assistants with their 33-pound guns, ammunition carriers with 19-pound boxed belts in each hand, all burdened with their own weapons and equipment, they slipped forward without as much as the chink of gun pintle entering tripod socket.

"Chow time," Paige whispered. "Where's the chow?"[8]

The can of Spam was present but the can of peaches was absent without leave. Its bearer mumbled incoherently about its having slipped from his grasp to roll down the ridge. Paige hissed sharp guttural uncomplimentaries in the delinquent's direction, and then he opened the Spam with his bayonet, tearing the thick soft meat into hunks and pressing it into outstretched hands.

They ate.

They sat hunched by their guns. It began to rain again. At midnight, the men on watch heard the sound of firing far to their left.

It was only about seven o'clock before General Maruyama's commanders were able to bring any semblance of order out of the confusion caused by the rain. Over on the right wing, where Kawaguchi's failure to cope with the terrain had cost him his command, Colonel Shoji, his successor, was also behind schedule. Shoji had also not reached his jump-off point.

Impatient, Maruyama ordered the left wing to attack.

Colonel Masajiro Furumiya took the 29th Infantry forward, and a few minutes later they were flowing around Colonel Puller's outpost.

Sergeant Ralph Briggs and his men on outpost hugged the ground, while Briggs rang up Colonel Puller's command post.

"Colonel," he said softly, "there's about three thousand Japs between you and me."

"Are you sure?"

"Positive. They've been all around us, singing and smoking cigarettes, heading your way."

"All right, Briggs, but make damned sure. Take your men to the left—understand me? Go down and pass through the lines near the sea. I'll call 'em to let you in. Don't fail, and don't go in any other direction. I'll hold my fire as long as I can."

"Yes, sir," Briggs said, and hung up.[9]

Then the sergeant and his men began crawling slowly on their bellies to the left. All but four of them, whom the Japanese caught and killed.

At eleven o'clock it began to rain heavily again, and the Japanese came hurtling against Puller's Marines.

Once again they were screaming:

"Blood for the Emperor!"

"Marine, you die!"

Once again the foul-mouthed raggedy-tailed defenders of democracy were bellowing:

"To hell with your goddamed Emperor! Blood for Franklin and Eleanor!"[10]

The Japanese were charging by the thousands, so many of them that the sodden ground shook beneath their feet. They hit the barbed wire even as Marine guns erupted in a bedlam of firing.

Japanese fell on the wire, others hurled themselves upon it while their comrades used their bodies as bridges.

Colonel Furumiya was at the head of his troops, shouting and waving his saber. He led the color company—the 7th—through a break in the American wire and went racing with them toward the enemy's guns.

Inspired by the breakthrough, willing to follow their colors into hell, the Japanese soldiers flowed toward the gap.

But the Marines closed it. Colonel Furumiya and the color company were cut off from the rest of the regiment.

Now the attack was veering toward dead center. The Japanese hordes were rushing at Manila John Basilone's machine guns. They came tumbling down an incline, and Basilone's gunners raked them at full-trigger. They were pouring out five hundred rounds a minute, the gun barrels were red and sizzling inside their water jackets—and the precious water was evaporating swiftly.

"Piss in 'em, piss in 'em!" Basilone yelled, and some of the men jumped up to refill the jackets with a different liquid.

The guns stuttered on, tumbling the onrushing Japanese down the incline, piling them up so high that by the time the first enemy flood had begun to ebb and flow back into the jungle, they had blocked Basilone's field of fire. In the lull Manila John ordered his men out to push the bodies away and clear the fire lanes.

Then he ducked out of the pit to run for more ammunition. He ran barefooted, the mud squishing between his toes. He ran into Puller's CP and ran back again burdened with spare barrels and half a dozen fourteen-pound belts slung over his shoulders.

As he did, Furumiya's men drifted west. They overran the guns to Basilone's right. They stabbed two Marines to death and wounded three others. They tried to swing the big Brownings on the Americans, but they only jammed them. They left the pit and drove farther to the rear.

Basilone returned to his pit just as a runner dashed up gasping:

"They've got the guys on the right."

Basilone raced to his right. He ran past a barefoot private named Evans and called "Chicken" for his tender eighteen years. "C'mon, you yellow bastards!" Chicken screamed, firing and bolting his rifle, firing and reloading. Basilone ran on to the empty pit, jumped in, found the guns jammed, and sprinted back to his own pit.

Seizing a mounted machine gun, Basilone spread-eagled it across his back, shouted at half of his men to follow him—and was gone. A squad of men took off in pursuit. They caught

Basilone at a bend in the trail, and blundered into a half-dozen Japanese soldiers. They killed them and ran on.

Then they were inside the silent pit, firing the gun which Basilone had brought, while Manila John lay on his back in the mud working frantically to free the jammed guns.

Beyond the wire in the covering jungle, the Sendai were massing for another charge.

Submarine *Amberjack* had nearly reached Guadalcanal.

Inside her sausage-shaped belly were nine thousand gallons of aviation gasoline destined for Henderson Field tanks that were again nearly bone-dry. She also carried two hundred 100-pound bombs. She had departed Espiritu Santo more than two days ago, and now, sliding along at her top submerged speed, she expected to make Lunga Point by daybreak.

But then her orders were changed. From Guadalcanal came instructions to put in at Tulagi with her cargo. Henderson Field was under major attack, the issue was in doubt, and it would be foolish to make the enemy a gift of the gasoline.

Chesty Puller called Colonel del Valle to request all the artillery support possible.

"I'll give you all you call for, Puller," del Valle grunted. "But God knows what'll happen when the ammo we have is gone."

"If we don't need it now, we'll never need it. If they get through here tonight there won't be a tomorrow."

"She's yours as long as she lasts."[11]

Both men hung up and the Marine artillery began glowing red again.

"Colonel," Captain Regan Fuller said over the telephone to Puller, "I'm just about running out of ammo. I've used almost three and a half units of fire."

"You got bayonets, haven't you?" Colonel Puller asked.

"Sure. Yes, sir."

"All right, then. Hang on."[12]

It was half-past one in the morning and the Sendai were coming again, there was a white breath around the muzzles of the Marine 105s, and Manila John Basilone had his guns fixed.

Basilone rolled from gun to gun, firing, exhausting first one belt and then another, while his men worked wildly to scrape the mud from cartridges that had been dragged along soggy trails. And the Sendai rolled forward in even greater strength, with both wings charging, now, punching holes in the Marine lines, forcing General Geiger in the rear to counter with his reserve, and leading General Maruyama to radio the one signal that all Japan was waiting for:

"*Banzai!*"

General Hyakutake heard it with elation back in Kukumbona and he relayed it north to Admiral Gunichi Mikawa in Rabaul. Mikawa immediately ordered three large destroyers carrying the Koli Detachment to land these troops on eastern Guadalcanal as scheduled.

And Combined Fleet's carriers turned south again.

Some time after two o'clock in the morning of Sunday, October 25, Sergeant Mitchell Paige and his men heard firing to their right.

A band of Colonel Oka's soldiers had slipped through the draw between Paige and Hill 67 and had overwhelmed an outpost.

Paige slipped forward on his ridge. He heard mumbling below him. He pulled the pin of a hand grenade and heaved the bomb into the jungle. His men pulled their pins and handed Paige their grenades, and he threw these bombs, too.

There were flashes and screams.

But no one came.

At half-past three General Maruyama hurled his third charge at the Americans—and this time his men heard for the first time the eight-round semiautomatic firing of Garand rifles in the hands of American soldiers.

The 164th Infantry was in action.

General Geiger had fed its Third Battalion under Lieutenant Colonel Robert Hall into the battle. Hall's soldiers marched from their bivouac behind the Tenaru to the front, sloshing through the streaming darkness guided by a Navy chaplain, Father Keough, the only man at headquarters who knew the way. Puller went to meet them.

"Here they are, Colonel," Keough called, and Puller shook his hand, grunting: "Father, we can use 'em." Then he turned to Hall: "Colonel, I'm glad to see you. I don't know who's senior to who right now, and I don't give a damn. I'll be in command until daylight, at least, because I know what's going on here, and you don't."

"That's fine with me," Hall said, and Puller continued:

"I'm going to drop 'em off along this road, and send in a few to each platoon position. I want you to make it clear to your people that my men, even if they're only sergeants, will command in those holes when your officers and men arrive."

"I understand you," Hall said. "Let's go."[13]

They went. The soldiers went into the fight, sometimes having to be guided in by hand, in that slippery darkness, and they too, held, when the Sendai came flowing toward its third futile attempt to annihilate the Americans.

By seven o'clock in the morning, the Sendai had stopped coming.

Nearly a thousand of them had stopped living. They lay in sodden heaps outside and partly within the American wire. One column of Japanese dead lay opposite Captain Fuller's antitank guns. They were in perfect formation, each man laying halfway atop the man in front of him—felled in a single scything sweep like a row of wooden soldiers.

Within the jungle, General Maruyama beheld his survivors: bands of dazed and hollow-eyed men stumbling woodenly back to their assembly areas. Nowhere could Maruyama find Colonel Furumiya. Obviously, the airfield was still American.

Masao Maruyama got off a message to General Hyakutake indicating that he was "having difficulty" capturing the field.

And then Dugout Sunday began.

Chapter 7

OCTOBER 25 was to be known as Dugout Sunday because most Americans on Guadalcanal sat out that reverberating sabbath below ground.

It was set in motion by Masao Maruyama's premature paean of victory. By the time he had retracted it and admitted that Henderson Field was still in enemy hands, Admiral Mikawa had sent the Koli Detachment destroyers speeding down The Slot, while cruiser *Yura* and five destroyers went sweeping to the north to come around Florida Island and bombard Koli Point.

Flights of Bettys were bombed-up and fueled at Rabaul and escorting Zeros at Buka and Buin stood at the ready with idly spinning propellers.

Admiral Yamamoto had also been electrified by Maruyama's *"Banzai!"* He had ordered carrier *Junyo* under Admiral Kakuta to fly off planes to land on the airfield, notified Nagumo's carriers to move south, and alerted Kondo's battleships to steam south to destroy Admiral Lee's battleship force and chew up the American supply line.

Then came the message suggesting that the airfield was not quite captured—to be followed in the afternoon by an outright admission of defeat—and the angrily perplexed Yamamoto ordered Kakuta to fly off bombing strikes instead, canceled the battleship attack, and left Nagumo more bewildered than ever.

And so, the Koli Detachment ships opened Dugout Sunday services, to the dismay of a very attentive audience in submarine *Amberjack*.

Amberjack entered Iron Bottom Bay at about daybreak. Her periscope lookouts could see the old four-stack destroyers *Trever* and *Zane* steaming out of Tulagi Harbor, to which they, too, had brought gasoline. Fleet-tug *Seminole* was moving slowly toward

Lunga Point, carrying, of course, a load of gasoline for Henderson Field.

Amberjack's skipper, Lieutenant Commander J. A. Bole, decided that Iron Bottom Bay was getting congested. He reversed course.

Thirty minutes later his periscope displayed three big Japanese destroyers racing into the Bay, hull-down, shelling Marine positions as they came. They were *Akatsuki, Ikazuchi,* and *Shiratsuyo,* and they carried the men of the Koli Detachment.

Amberjack could not risk her cargo by entering battle. She could do only one thing: she went down.

As she did, the Japanese destroyers spotted little *Trever* and *Zane.* They broke out battle signals, rang up flank speed, and swung around to a collision course with all guns firing. *Trever* and *Zane* fled, firing back with their little three-inchers. A Japanese shell exploded on *Trever's* after gun, demolishing it and its crew. *Trever* swerved hard left and then right again, and ran into the shoals of a channel between Savo and Florida. *Zane* followed. Both these ancients were now rattling along at twenty-nine knots. *Trever's* No. 2 boiler casing burned through. The Japanese closed.

And then three Wildcats came screaming down from the skies. They had somehow managed to take off from sodden, soupy Fighter One—their wheels throwing out arcs of spray as they thundered along, spinning as they rose—and then they were airborne and saw the enemy below about to finish off *Trever* and *Zane.* They had no bombs, only bullets, but they turned the Japanese destroyers around and sent them fleeing west.

Right into *Seminole* and *Yippie 284* making with agonizing slowness for the sanctuary of Tulagi Harbor.

Akatsuki, Ikazuchi, and *Shiratsuyo* nearly rammed the little Americans, they were so close—and at point-blank range they needed only two minutes to put the *Yippie* under and turn *Seminole* into a floating holocaust.

Then the Japanese were in trouble. Marines with five-inch naval rifles opened up from Guadalcanal. They scored hits. Smoke poured skyward from the destroyers. Putting out smoke of their own to screen themselves, the Koli Detachment destroyers fled up The Slot.

Meanwhile, *Yura* and her five destroyers still swept around

Florida. They intended to come around the island's eastern tip, and swing south toward Koli Point. But an unarmed search plane spotted them as they approached Florida. At the Pagoda on Henderson Field, *Yura* and her steel brood were marked for action —once the field had dried.

Dugout Sunday was turning hot and clear.

Far to the north, Chuichi Nagumo's ships were still taking on oil.

Nagumo was dozing in his cabin, when an orderly dashed in with a message from a patrol plane:

"I have shot down an enemy plane, apparently a scout."[1]

Nagumo leaped erect, shouting:

"Cut refueling! Turn the carriers around and head north!"[2]

Both the Nagumo trio of carriers and Admiral Kakuta in *Junyo* turned about and headed north at twenty knots.

Chuichi Nagumo had failed to turn his carriers away at Midway; but he was not going to make the same mistake at Guadalcanal.

The sun which warmed sailors of both fleets quickly dried the moldy uniforms of Chesty Puller's soldiers and Marines at work refortifying their positions for the anticipated renewal of battle that night. By mid-morning, the sun was blistering hot. Its scorching rays shone with dissolving intensity upon the corpses lying outside the lines beneath buzzing, conical swarms of black flies. Already, these bodies were beginning to turn lemon yellow, to swell and burst like overripe melons; already the sticky-sweet smell of corrupting flesh rose sickening and overpowering in the nostrils of these sweating Americans.

At Henderson Field, ready pilots kept glancing nervously between the quickly drying airfield and the blue skies overhead, where carrier Zeros circled unmolested, radioing the good news to Rabaul that the deadly Wildcats were up to their hubcaps in mud and would not be airborne that day.

But the Japanese, also contending with bad weather, were not able to respond quickly. By the time sixteen Bettys and escorting Zeros came roaring in, Henderson Field had dried sufficiently to allow the Wildcats to scramble aloft. Captain Joe Foss and Lieutenant Jack Conger were among those who struck at the enemy formation. Foss shot down two of three Zeros destroyed in a flight of six. But then, his fifth plane riddled beneath him, he was forced to go down for another one. Going up again, he tore into the Zeros escorting a fresh contingent of enemy bombers. He shot down two more—and he dove for home with fifteen kills to his credit during the sixteen days he had been on Guadalcanal.

Jack Conger also shot down a Zero in the second attack. Banking, he went thundering after another. He pressed the gun button. No response. He was out of ammunition. Undaunted, Conger still flew at the Zero. He hung on his nose and brought his propeller under the enemy's tail. The Zero swerved, and broke in two.

Now Conger's plane was going over in a vertical dive. He fought wildly to bring it out. It still fell. Conger strained at his escape hatch. He could see Iron Bottom Bay rising up toward him, growing larger. It was as though a great steel-gray griddle had been catapulted upward, flying up, up, and up, expanding until it was a monstrous obliterating roundness. Conger struggled with the hatch. He thought he would never get out, that the huge griddle would shatter him, and then, at 150 feet, he was out in the air, his parachute was blooming overhead, and he was into the griddle, his body jarred as though he had been slammed on the soles of his feet with an iron bar.

Just before he went under, Conger saw his Wildcat crash in the coconuts. Then he was going down deep, only to have his swift descent arrested by his rigging. He surfaced, treading water, slashing with a knife at the smothering shroud of the parachute. Twenty feet away another pilot floated gently down into the water.

He was Japanese.

A rescue boat sped toward Conger. It reached him and reduced speed. Conger was hauled aboard. Then the boat came about and headed for the Japanese pilot. Conger called to him to surrender. The Japanese pilot held his breath and sank out of sight. He came up beside the boat, kicked at it, and tried to shove himself away. Conger grabbed a boathook and snared the man by his jacket. The man struggled, snarling with hate. Conger leaned forward to boat him. The Japanese dug his hand under his armpit and whipped out a huge Mauser pistol. His malevolent eyes only inches from Conger's startled ones, he pressed the pistol to his benefactor's temple and pulled the trigger.

Click!

Conger tumbled backward, thinking: *I'm dead!* He was not, nor was his enemy who, failing to return death for life, attempted to take his own by placing the pistol to his own head, producing only a second exasperating *click*. Conger seized a water can and slammed it down on the man's head. Unconscious, he was dragged into the boat and taken to Guadalcanal.

Where the two enemies became good friends.

Mitchell Paige's men had found their peaches. Dugout Sunday's sun had picked it out in the jungle beside the ridge. The moment the men had seen it glinting there, like a lost jewel, they whooped and went scrambling down to retrieve it. Men with American names—Leiphart, Stat, Pettyjohn, Gaston, Lock, McNabb, Swanek, Reilly, Totman, Kelly, Jonjeck, Grant, Payne, Hinson—they squatted on their haunches in the drying mud and ate with great relish the only food they would get that day.

Then they dove for their foxholes, for Admiral Kakuta's *Junyo* had turned south again and her dive-bombers and Zeros were overhead.

To the east, almost exactly between Chesty Puller's position on the left and Paige's ridge on the right, Lucky and Juergens squatted on a ridgetop talking. They, too, heard the sound of motors—and almost too late.

A Zero came skimming down their ridge like a skier. They sprawled flat, bullets spurting dust around them. The Zero thundered over them and banked. Juergens dove into his dugout and dragged out his machine gun. He began setting it up, cursing. Lucky ran toward him. But the enemy fighter-plane was coming in to strafe again, and Juergens went sprawling again while Lucky whirled and ran for the edge of the ridge. The Zero pursued, roaring, spitting bullets, shedding tinkling cartridge cases. Lucky jumped and fell six feet, rolling down the hillside while the Zero went roaring out over the jungle roof. Then he scrambled back up the ridge and ran to squat beside Juergens.

Again, the Zero turned again and made for the ridge.

"C'mon, you son of a bitch," Juergens swore. "You won't find it so easy this time."[3]

In came the enemy plane, again spitting bullets, and the Marine gun was hammering its reply—and then a pair of Airacobras rose like genies from Henderson Field to the rear, catching the unsuspecting Zero full in their cannon sights and blasting him into a shower of debris.

One more of a total of twenty-six Japanese planes had fallen to Henderson's fliers—while out beyond Florida Island Henderson's bombers had caught *Yura* and were pounding her beneath the waves.

Before sunset the Japanese cruiser was a wreck. Naval and Marine dive-bombers had flown four attacks against her, Flying Fortresses had come up from Espiritu to multiply her wounds —and she was finally abandoned and sunk by her own destroyer, *Yudachi*. Destroyer *Akizuke* was also racked, and had to be beached on Santa Isabel Island. Her four sisters fled.

Dugout Sunday had seen the complete rout of the attempt to put the Koli Detachment ashore on eastern Guadalcanal.

It was not Sunday but Saturday in the United States. On the East Coast it was a sunny autumn afternoon. Football crowds flocked to the stadiums along sidewalks bordered by yellowing maples. In Washington the Joint Chiefs of Staff were in session. One of the first matters to be discussed was a message from the Commander-in-Chief. It said:

"My anxiety about the Southwest Pacific is to make sure that every possible weapon gets into that area to hold Guadalcanal, and that having held it in this crisis that munitions and planes and crews are on the way to take advantage of our success."[4]

President Roosevelt had taken a direct hand. But he had taken it on the very day on which a vast concourse of ships and men had departed East Coast ports bound for North Africa.

Even though Roosevelt requested the Joint Chiefs to canvass the entire armaments situation over the weekend, even though Admiral King might be pleased that the White House was now so concerned over Guadalcanal, all of the Joint Chiefs realized that there was at that moment very little to be spared for the South Pacific.

And by nightfall there would be one valuable ship less.

President Coolidge was sliding into Segond Channel at Espiritu Santo. The big Army transport carried the 172nd Infantry Regiment of the 43rd Division. Her civilian skipper kept her straight on course toward a minefield. Patrol craft signaled desperately, shore blinkers winked wildly—but *Coolidge* sailed on.

Then she blundered into two mines and began to sink. She went down slowly; all but two men were rescued. But the 172nd's guns and gear were gone, together with the ship that was to have taken them to Guadalcanal.

Admiral Nagumo's turnaround and run north had widened the gap between his fleet and Admiral Kinkaid's carriers. By midday of Dugout Sunday *Hornet* and *Enterprise* were west of the Santa Cruz Islands and about 360 miles southeast of Nagumo.

Kinkaid was uncertain of the enemy's position. A Catalina had detected Nagumo's ships at noon, moving southeast again, but had lost them in a squall. Rather than await the enemy's pleasure, Kinkaid decided to launch both searching and striking flights from *Enterprise*.

They found nothing. When planes of the strike returned after dark, the first one crashed on the flight deck and six others were lost in the water.

It was a bad beginning.

Masao Maruyama did not think that a poor start necessarily presaged a bad finish.

At Centipede-Shaped Ridge that afternoon he called for a "final death-defying night attack." He was committing the 16th Infantry, led by Colonel Hitoshi Hiroyasu, to replace the slaughtered 29th. Both his wings were in place. Colonel Shoji on the right was at last in position. On the left, Major General Nasu was prepared to lead the charge, just as Colonel Furumiya had done the night before.

General Maruyama was sorrowful over the loss of Furumiya. It had been because of him that he had ordered his second and third attacks. Commander of the proud Sendai, Maruyama could not turn his back on an officer who had carried a Rising Sun banner into enemy lines.[5] Even today he had sent out search parties for the colonel. They had not found him, and Maruyama reluctantly concluded that Furumiya was dead.

He was not.

Colonel Furumiya, Captain Suzuki, and seven others had survived the Americans' systematic slaughter of the Seventh Company. Throughout Dugout Sunday they lay in the undergrowth within enemy lines, their bodies draped with leaves and vines. American patrols passed them but did not see them.

Like Colonel Ichiki before him, Colonel Furumiya thought of burning his colors and committing ceremonial suicide before the smoke. But the smoke might attract attention and bring the Americans to capture the colors before they were completely destroyed. To lose the regimental flag was unthinkable. Although the 29th Infantry may have been *zemmetsu* so far as its officers and men were concerned, it lived while its flag remained unviolated. To lose that flag was to lose the 29th's honor. Annihilation in battle was a thousand times more preferable to such disgrace. This was why, according to many historians, the great General Maresuke Nogi committed suicide after the Emperor Meiji had died: he was expressing his apology for having lost his battalion colors during the Satsuma Rebellion. No, the flag, the very *esprit de corps* of the Japanese Army, could not be risked.

So Colonel Furumiya thought of escape instead. He sent Lieutenant Ono and two soldiers to look for a way out. They did not return, and Warrant Officer Kobayashi went to look for them. He, too, vanished.

Peering from his thorny hideout, Furumiya watched the Americans digging in. He made notes on their defenses, observing that their machine-gun positions were about fifty yards apart and that no one seemed to be manning them. From this he concluded that the guns were fired by remote control.

Colonel Furumiya also observed that the enemy seemed to be cheerful. Some of them even sang as they worked.

> *We have a weapon that nobody loves,*
> *They say that our gun's a disgrace,*
> *You crank up 200, and 200 more—*
> *And it lands in the very same place.*
> *Oh, there's many a gunner who's blowing his top,*
> *Observers are all going mad.*
> *But our love it has lasted*
> *This pig-iron bastard*
> *Is the best gun this world ever had.*

It was thus that Marine mortarmen sang of their stovepipes, those harmless-looking tubes that shoot straight up and down and kill men, and it was thus that Chesty Puller's mortarmen were singing while they stacked up piles of shamrock-shaped triple shell casings.

Mortar shells were the only supplies which Puller had been able to get to his lines on Dugout Sunday. All of the aerial fighting, naval shelling, and the constant pounding of Pistol Pete had made movement difficult. Nevertheless, Puller was better prepared than on the previous night, having been able to shorten his front while the 3rd Battalion, 164th Infantry, took over the leftward sector he had held. On the soldiers' left were their comrades of the 2nd Battalion, 164th.

Puller was confident, and he and his headquarters troops could hoot and jeer in derision at the English voice over Radio Tokyo which was announcing their defeat and impending demise. The fact that it was now the football season in America was not lost on the commentator, who simulated a sportscaster's staccato, and said:

"The score stands—U. S. Navy, 0; Japan, 21—with the Japanese deep in American territory, ten yards to go. Coach Roosevelt passes up and down chain-smoking cigarettes. A pass is knocked down. America calls time out and Ghormley is pulled from the game. The Rising Sun cheers loudly for Coach Tojo. Roosevelt sends in Halsey to call signals. Another pass is called, but the ball is fumbled on the one-yard line, and the heavy favorites, the U.S., are in a bad way as the gun signals the end of the first half."[6]

And then it was dark: Colonel Furumiya lay in the bushes waiting for the attack that would rescue them, the American soldiers and Marines braced behind their guns, and the Sendai came flowing out of the jungle in the heaviest of all Guadalcanal's charges.

"U. S. Marine you going die tonight," they chanted, "U. S. Marine you going die tonight."

They were greeted by the customary volleys of obscenity, particularly from American soldiers, against whom the charge was breaking with equal fury, and who were enraged that the enemy should, just like the Stateside newspapers, give all the credit to the Marines.

So the Sendai charged, and American mortars fell among them, artillery shells flashed in the assembly areas, bullets riddled them —and they were cut in two before they reached the wire. It was not a charge, this frenzied rush to destruction, it was a mere death-swarming. They flowed into American steel like moths into flame.

Without artillery preparation of their own and without adequate maps or knowledge of the enemy's position, with arrogant confidence in the superiority of "spiritual power" over firepower and a vaingloriously suicidal determination to look upon death before defeat, Maruyama and his officers sent the Emperor's best division into a holocaust.

General Nasu was killed, Colonel Hiroyasu was killed, four battalion commanders fell, half of the Sendai's officers perished, and another thousand men were destroyed.

And still the Sendai Division charged.

Colonel Oka was at last attacking.

His men struck hard at the ridge held by Sergeant Paige's section.

The Japanese came screeching up the hillside full into Paige's guns spitting orange flame a foot beyond their flash-hiders. Short shapes fell, but more came swarming in. It was hand-to-hand. Paige saw little Leiphart down on one knee fighting off three attackers. Paige shot two of them. The third killed Leiphart with a bayonet, but Paige killed the killer. Pettyjohn's gun was knocked out. Gaston fought a Japanese officer, parrying saber swings with his rifle, until the rifle was hacked to pieces. Then Gaston kicked at the blade. Unaware that part of his leg was cut away, he kicked high—and caught the officer under the chin and broke his neck.

All over the ridge the short shapes and the tall shapes flowed, merged, struggled, parted, sank to the ground or rolled down the slopes. Everywhere were the American voices crying, *"Killl! Killl!"* the gurgling whoops of the Japanese shouting, *"Bonnn—az—ee!"* or screaming "Marine you die!"

Then the short shapes flowed back down the ridge, and Mitchell Paige ran to fix Pettyjohn's disabled gun. He pried out a ruptured cartridge and slipped in a fresh belt of ammunition, just as a burst from a Japanese machine gun seared his hand.

Yelling again, the short shapes came bowling up the hill once more. They could not force the left, where Grant, Payne, and Hinson still held out, though all were wounded. In Paige's center they hit Lock, Swanek, and McNabb. They moved through the gap. Paige dashed to his right to find a gun to stop them. He found Kelly and Totman beside their gun, protected by a squad of riflemen. He ordered the riflemen to fix bayonets, and led them on a charge that drove the Japanese back. Then he set up the gun in the center and fired it until dawn.

As daylight came creeping over the jungle roof to his left, he saw one of his platoon's machine guns standing unattended on the forward nose of the ridge. Three men in mushroom helmets were crawling toward it. Paige rose and ran forward . . .

It had been a warm night at sea.

Aboard flag carrier *Shokaku* all seemed calm, until the silence was shattered by the ringing of alarms and voices crying "Air raid! Air raid!"

One of Admiral Nagumo's staff officers dashed for the bridge. He saw two Catalinas come gliding down toward *Zuikaku* about three miles astern. Four plumes of water rose into the air to starboard of *Zuikaku*. The officer held his breath. Then the plumes flowed back into the sea and *Zuikaku* sailed on unruffled.

The officer tumbled down the ladder and raced into Admiral Nagumo's cabin to report. Admiral Kusaka was there. Both admirals looked at each other, to say with one voice: "Let's turn around."[7]

On the bridge of his destroyer *Amatsukaze*—the ship whose men made such cruel sport with rats and falcons—Commander Tameichi Hara saw *Shokaku* blink the signal: "All ships turn 180 degrees to starboard!"

Nagumo's carriers were swinging north again, fearing a concentrated air raid which never came. But this second turnaround would work to their advantage. With dawn of October 26 they would not be where Admiral Kinkaid expected them to be.

With that dawn of October 26, while Sergeant Mitchell Paige raced the enemy for a machine gun, an enemy force in company strength captured a vital ridge between Paige and Puller. They set up machine guns on it and began raking the Marine flank.

Major Odell (Tex) Conoley could see vapor rising from the enemy guns as the jungle water on the barrels was condensed by hot steel. Conoley saw that the enemy's penetration could be expanded to a breakthrough. He rounded up a party of bandsmen who were serving as litter-bearers, a trio of wiremen, two runners, and three or four cooks, and charged.

There were seventeen of them in all, but they went up hurling grenades and they drove the Japanese off the ridge. Then Conoley called for mortars to lay a curtain of steel between him and the enemy while he consolidated his position, and awaited reinforcements.

They arrived to be greeted by a strutting cook who boasted of having brained an enemy officer.

"What'dja do?" a rifleman jeered. "Hit him with one of yer own pancakes?"

. . . Mitchell Paige reached the gun first.

He dove for it, squeezed the trigger, and killed the crawling Japanese.

A storm of bullets fell on Paige, kicking up spurts of dust. Paige fired back. Stat, Reilly, and Jonjeck ran to him with belts of ammunition. Stat fell with a bullet in his belly. Reilly went down kicking, almost knocking Paige off his gun, and Jonjeck came in with a belt and a bullet in his shoulder. Jonjeck bent to feed the belt into the gun, and Paige saw a piece of flesh go flying off his neck.

"Get the hell back!" Paige yelled.

Jonjeck shook his head. Paige hit him in the jaw, and Jonjeck left.

Paige moved the gun back and forth to avoid enemy grenades. He saw about thirty men rise in the tall grass below him. One of them put binoculars to his eyes and waved his hand for a charge.

Paige fired a long burst.

The enemy vanished.

Paige called to his riflemen. He slung two belts of ammunition across his shoulders, unclamped his gun, cradled the searing-hot water jacket in his arm, and went down the ridge yelling, "Let's go!"

"*Ya-hoo!*" the Marines yelled. "*Yaaaa-ho!*"

And they went racing down the hill after the dispersing enemy. The officer with the glasses popped up out of the grass and Paige disemboweled him with a burst, and then he and his Marines had burst into the jungle.

It was silent and empty.

The enemy was gone. The battle of Henderson Field was over. General Maruyama had already ordered a full retreat. Colonel Shoji was taking the remnant of the Sendai right wing to the east,

Maruyama was leading the reeling left wing to the west. Marine bulldozers were already clanking toward the front to gouge out mass graves in which to inter the reeking carcasses of 2500 dead, Colonel Furumiya and his companions lay despairing in the bush, and Mitchell Paige and his men were trudging slowly back to the ridge.

They sat down wearily. Paige felt the sweat drying coldly on his body. He watched vapor rising from his machine-gun jacket. He felt a burning sensation in his left arm. He looked down. From fingertips to forearm a long white blister was forming, swelling as thick as a rope to mark the place where flesh had held hot steel.

Out in the Bay behind him, submarine *Amberjack* had at last surfaced, had finally delivered her cargo of fuel, and was now sailing eagerly away to Australia.

Chapter 8

BATTLES on land, sometimes entire campaigns, often have depended upon the outcome of a naval battle; but seldom has a great fight been fought at sea because of what happened ashore.

Yet, the battle of Henderson Field was directly responsible for the savage carrier conflict called The Battle of the Santa Cruz Islands.

Successive postponements of the 17th Army's major assault on Guadalcanal had not only cost the Japanese the services of carrier *Hiyo* but had given the Americans time to double their carrier forces; and carrier power varies as the square: two carriers are four times as powerful as one. General Maruyama's premature message of victory had also left Admiral Yamamoto teetering on a tightrope of indecision and had very nearly sent his carriers tearing into the trap which Admiral Halsey had planned for them.

But Admiral Nagumo's two turnarounds had kept him well north of *Hornet* and *Enterprise* as they slanted northwestward from their run around the Santa Cruz Islands. Throughout the night of October 25–26, while the Sendai Division made rendezvous with ruin, the two American flattops raced along an aggressive northwestward course toward the enemy. *Hornet* had a deckload of aircraft ready for a moonlight strike, all of the ships were alerted for immediate action—but the Japanese carriers were never found.

Nagumo had been frightened into his second and most fortuitous turnaround by the fruitless attack on *Zuikaku*. After he had reversed course, the Vanguard Group of battleships and cruisers had also turned north.

Shortly before three o'clock in the morning of October 26, thirteen scouts went zooming aloft from the Japanese carrier decks. A few minutes later the entire fleet—Vanguard gunfire ships,

Nagumo's three carriers, and Admiral Kakuta in *Junyo* about 130 miles to the north—turned south again.

About five o'clock on the bridge of *Amatsukaze* Commander Hara heard his radio-room voice tube come to life with the message: "*Shokaku* scout plane reports a large enemy force at KH17. Force consists of one *Saratoga*-class carrier and fifteen other ships heading northwestward."[1] Commander Hara gasped. KH17 was an area 210 miles away on a bearing slightly to the left. The Americans were not directly ahead, or even to the right between the Japanese and the Solomons, as Nagumo's officers expected. They were to the *left*. Without those two turnarounds and runs north, the Japanese would have been far to the south and the Americans would have been in behind them.

On *Shokaku's* flag bridge, the white-gloved Nagumo grinned broadly. He ordered immediate strikes. Planes began roaring down the decks. To the rear, Admiral Kakuta grimaced angrily to discover the enemy was 330 miles away. He rang up top speed and big *Junyo's* boilers built her speed to twenty-six knots in a record ten minutes. *Junyo* even sprang ahead of her destroyers, much to their astonishment, while Kakuta ordered a strike readied. Although he was far away from the enemy, his pilots could return to the closer *Zuikaku* or *Shokaku*. And by the time he was prepared to launch a second strike, he would be much closer.

Ahead of him, forty dive-bombers and torpedo-bombers escorted by twenty-seven Zeros were airborne and burning up the miles between Nagumo's three carriers and the Americans to the south.

ATTACK. REPEAT, ATTACK.

It was only three words, but it was in the style characteristic of Bull Halsey, and it had the effect of opening the sleep-gummed eyes of sailors gulping pre-dawn breakfast on the American ships, of electrifying pilots being briefed on carrier decks, and of making everyone in Kinkaid's force aware that today there would be a battle.

Kinkaid had already ordered a search of what were to be the battle waters, a thousand square miles of South Pacific to the north of the Santa Cruz. It was a wise decision considering his lack of information on the enemy; but unfortunate in the fact that a few minutes after sixteen Dauntlesses took off, he received a Catalina report, delayed two hours, placing the enemy about two hundred miles to the northwest.

By then the Dauntlesses, each armed with a 500-pound bomb, "just in case," had paired up and fanned out over the battle water by twos.

Some of the pairs found the Vanguard Group commanded by Rear Admiral Hiroaki Abe, and a few of them made unsuccessful attacks on cruiser *Tone*.

But it was not until a few minutes before seven that Nagumo's carriers were located. They promptly put up smoke and altered course. The Dauntlesses began fighting off the Zeros buzzing in on their tails. But their report also drew Lieutenant Stockton Strong and Ensign Charles Irvine to the area. They saw the smaller carrier *Zuiho* below them. They nosed over, a pair of small bombs between them, and went screaming down.

Commander Hara gaped. The American scout planes had come down from the overcast undetected and were already pulling up over *Zuiho*. Hara could see the silver streaks of their bombs flashing toward the unsuspecting ship. Then Hara groaned. A pair of explosions shook *Zuiho* and black clouds rolled skyward.

Just two bombs, and both had hit in almost the same place, tearing open a fifty-foot hole in *Zuiho's* flight decks, knocking out gun batteries and starting fires. *Zuiho* signaled that she could launch planes but could not receive them. Nagumo ordered her to fly off all of her fighters and withdraw.

Of five flattops which had sailed from Truk, only three were left.

Moreover the Lord, thy God, will send the Hornet among them until they that are left, and hide themselves from thee, be destroyed.

To *Hornet's* fighting sailors, many of whom carried this capital-H quotation from Deuteronomy inside their wallets, no comment on the battle could be more appropriate. And at half-past seven that morning *Hornet* was first to strike at "they that are left and hide themselves." Lieutenant Commander William ("Gus") Widhelm led fifteen Dauntlesses, six Avengers and eight Wildcats aloft, to be followed by forty-four additional aircraft from both carriers.

Behind these seventy-three aircraft winging northwestward, the American ships prepared to receive Nagumo's sixty-seven warbirds roaring southeast.

Aboard the carriers flammables were heaved over the side, deck hoses were shut off and men stood by with buckets of foamite to fight flames. Liquefied carbon dioxide was fed into gasoline lines to freeze and crystallize as protection against fire. Damage-control units fanned out through the ships while men who worked the huge sprinkler systems stood by in control rooms ready to flood any section of the ship upon order.

Sailors and Marines everywhere put on their helmets and flash clothes, their life jackets as well, if they did not interfere with movement, and the brigs were thrown open and prisoners temporarily freed to take up their battle stations: in the sick bays, in the engine rooms, in the galleys, or on the guns.

Inside soundless turrets made of thick steel, gunners and ammunition passers checked the chains which brought up shells and powder bags from magazines below, while less protected gun crews on weather deck mounts stood by their sights or wiped the oil from gun barrels. Aboard *Enterprise,* men trained to fire the new 40-mm antiaircraft guns spoke confidently to each other of what these sleek new beauties would do to "bastards," as American seamen, with characteristic delicacy of phrasing, called enemy aircraft.

Big new battleship *South Dakota* also mounted the new gun, an American version of the famous Swedish Bofors, and she had them because of an accident.

Rushed to the South Pacific through the Panama Canal, *South Dakota* had torn her belly open on a coral pinnacle near Tongatabu, and had had to limp into Pearl Harbor for repairs. While there, she was fitted with dozens of the new forties. And her skipper, Captain Thomas Gatch, had made sure his men could shoot them, for Gatch may not have had much passion for clean fingernails or white-glove inspections, but he did like a bull's eye. All the way from Pearl Harbor, Gatch had kept his men busy at target practice. Squeegees and buckets lay neglected in *South Dakota's* lockers and the big ship became a slattern. At Santa Cruz she was probably the dirtiest ship in the United States Navy, but also one of the deadliest.

And so the ships made ready, and on *Hornet,* thoughtful cooks baked thousands of mince pies and doughnuts. They hoped, if there was a lull in the battle, to take them throughout the ship, along with buckets of hot coffee, to feed *Hornet's* hungry fighters.

Colonel Masajiro Furumiya was in a torment of hunger and thirst. The preceding night, he and the five other survivors of the Seventh Company, had attempted to break out of the American lines and rejoin their comrades. They had gotten to within a hundred yards of the American wire and had been pinned to the ground by the terrible hail of fire which riddled General Maruyama's second nocturnal assault.

They had crept back to a clump of underbrush, and now, as they lay there on the morning of October 26, tortured by hunger cramps, their lips cracked and their mouths swelling—tantalized by the smell of cooking issuing from the nearby encampment of Marine mortars—Furumiya again toyed with the idea of suicide. But then, he decided to make one more attempt to escape and save the colors.

At nightfall, calling upon all the strength remaining to them, they would break up into two-man groups and try to crawl to freedom.

There would be no lulls for hungry sailors.

Shortly after nine o'clock that morning, while *Enterprise* slipped into the sanctuary of a rain squall, the Japanese fliers found *Hornet.*

There were twenty-seven of them—fifteen Val dive-bombers, twelve torpedo-carrying Kates—and they pressed their attack with great courage, straight into a storm of five-inch and lesser fire from *Hornet* and her screen. Such attacks seldom fail, and mighty *Hornet* began to rock and shudder from enemy hits.

The first struck the starboard side of the flight deck aft, and then two near-misses hammered her hull. Next, the Japanese squadron commander came thundering down on a suicide dive. He carried three missiles—one 500-pound bomb and two 100-pounders—and one of the smaller bombs exploded as he smashed into *Hornet's* stack. His own momentum and the thrust of the explosion drove him on down through the flight deck, where the second 100-pounder exploded and tore into a ready room below. The big bomb was a dud, but it remained wedged below decks to menace the men of the *Hornet* as they turned to face the far greater ordeal of the torpedo-bombers.

Though some of the Kates blew up and others plummeted into the sea, the others bored in low astern. Two torpedoes struck to starboard in swift staggering succession, tearing away the ship's armor and ramming into the engine rooms.

Belching smoke, ablaze from gasoline fires set by the suicider, *Hornet* lurched to starboard, slowed to a stop, and began taking in water.

Two more 500-pounders struck aft and a third landed slightly forward.

And then a blazing Kate made a suicide run from dead ahead, crashing into the forward gun gallery and blowing up near the forward elevator shaft.

In five minutes *Hornet* had been left a helpless, drifting, blazing hulk. Her fire mains were broken and her power lines were cut, communications were out, and six fires were burning fiercely, threatening at any moment to engulf the ship, or worse, detonate the deadly 500-pound egg lodged in her vitals.

She seemed surely lost, and there was one despairing moment when Captain Charles Mason issued the order, "Prepare to abandon ship!" But minutes later the bullhorns blared: "Belay that . . . Belay that . . . Fires under control!"

Hornet was being avenged.

Her Dauntlesses had found *Shokaku,* accompanied by still-smoking *Zuiho.* Just as the Japanese had struck at their own ship, the Americans went plummeting down through layers of flak with enemy fighters clawing at their tails, and they put three to six 1000-pound bombs into *Shokaku's* vitals.

Pouring out columns of smoke, her flight deck shredded and her hangars in ruins, all of her guns useless, *Shokaku* turned away.

Commander Hara aboard *Amatsukaze* watched her departure in agony, but then he hastened to obey the retiring Admiral Nagumo's orders to join the screen protecting *Zuikaku.*

Fortunately for Japan, the American Avengers never found *Shokaku,* and were unable to finish her off with torpedoes. They struck, instead, along with riddled flights from *Enterprise,* at Admiral Abe's Vanguard Group, damaging cruiser *Chikuma* and forcing her to withdraw. But they had missed the prize: the carriers.

Even so, big *Shokaku* was out of the war for nine months.

Hornet looked like a good risk.

Damage-control teams led by Commander Henry Moran, and greatly assisted by destroyers *Morris* and *Russell* lying alongside to hose the burning ship with sea water, had brought all fires under control by ten o'clock in the morning. Commander Pat Creehan's black gang had provided steam by hooking up three undamaged boilers to unruptured pipes ingeniously connected to the after engine room. *Hornet* was fit to be towed, and cruiser *Northampton* came cautiously forward to secure a· line to her.

But then a lone Val swooped down to drop a bomb that missed, but which also canceled towing operations and sent the apprehensive screening ships racing wildly around the crippled giant.

They need not have bothered, for the enemy aircraft were at that moment concentrating on *Enterprise*.

"I think," Commander John Crommelin said thoughtfully, studying one of the diving Vals with professional detachment, "I think that son of a bitch is going to get us."[2]

He was right.

Plunging at an angle, the 500-pounder slammed through the forward overhang of *Enterprise's* flight deck, came clear for fifteen feet, ripped through the fo'c'sle deck, and tore out of the ship's port side to explode under the port bow, ripping jagged holes in the ship's side and blowing a Dauntless into the sea.

Thus, at 11:17 A.M., the onslaught on the only undamaged American carrier in the entire Pacific was begun.

Only an hour before, *Enterprise* had already lost destroyer *Porter* out of her screen. Japanese submarine *I-21* had launched a spread of Long Lances at *Big E,* but *Porter* had taken them in her fire rooms and had had to be sunk by gunfire from destroyer *Shaw.*

And so Captain Osborne Hardison, *Enterprise's* new skipper, had also to think of subsurface attack when the enemy divebombers came hurtling down from the blue. Fortunately, he did not also have to deal with simultaneous aerial torpedo attack. The Japanese had planned it that way, but of the forty-four planes that were to make co-ordinated torpedo and bombing assaults, the twenty-four dive-bombers arrived a half-hour earlier and went immediately into action.

Steel and flame spouted up to meet them. Aboard mighty *South Dakota* a hundred muzzles flamed and fell, flamed and fell, like lethal pistons, and a cloud of dark-brown powder smoke drifted off her stern. *South Dakota* would claim thirty-two enemy aircraft shot down that day, she would be officially credited with twenty-six, but she, and all the other gunfire ships, all of *Enterprise's* guns taking full aim at the relentless Vals coming straight down on their twisting, maneuvering ship, could not deny the enemy.

Moments after the first bomb struck, another crashed abaft the forward elevator, breaking in two on the hangar deck where one half exploded and the other half drove down to the third deck before exploding and killing forty men. Fires broke out; light, power, and communications lines were cut; and then a third bomb hit aft of the island superstructure to starboard.

Enterprise was whiplashed. She shook along every inch of her 800-foot length. Nearly every man on his feet was slammed to the deck, her entire foremast turned a half inch in its socket— knocking the antennas on it out of alignment—and a fuel tank was torn open to trail a wake of oil behind as Hardison swung his stricken ship hard to port.

Then the bombers departed and the torpedo-bombers arrived.

There were eleven dark-green Kates in the first wave, but after Lieutenant Stanley ("Swede") Vejtasa got through with them there were only five. In one of the great flying feats of the war, Swede Vejtasa, who had already shot down two Vals over *Hornet,* sent six torpedo-planes into the sea before he ran out of ammunition. Three or four more Kates were shot down by other Navy pilots, but still, fifteen broke through the fighter screen. They came flat over the water toward *Enterprise,* boring in off both bows.

Captain Hardison stood on the *Big E's* bridge, his helmet in his left hand, watching the enemy aircraft, staying on course, with *South Dakota* following a thousand yards distant like a wingman, watching while American firepower whittled the enemy. Five miles out a Kate burst into flames and dove into the ocean with a brief plume of spray. Three miles out another skidded into the water.

Two more came apart. But then, five Kates on the right bow made their drops.

Hardison looked quickly to the left. Four more Kates were coming in but had not yet launched. He looked again to his right.

Like a dreadful V, three torpedoes sped straight and true toward him, the middle one slightly out in front. They would strike and sunder *Enterprise* amidships.

Hardison studied the wakes intently. Everything—Guadalcanal even—depended on his judgment. For one long calculating second Hardison stared at those three long lines of bubbles . . .

"Right full rudder."

"Right full rudder, sir!"

Slowly, ponderously, *Enterprise's* stern swung left, while her rudder—a huge steel blade three stories high—swept tons of water to the right. Slowly, with fraught majesty, her great bow swung toward the torpedo tracks. Captain Hardison walked to the left wing of his bridge to watch.

Admiral Kinkaid came to stand silently beside him.

As though increasing speed, the wakes bubbled toward *Enterprise,* and then they were out of sight beneath the left overhang.

"Rudder amidships!"

The helmsman swung his wheel to left. *Big E* straightened, the enemy's terrible trio sped harmlessly past the ship's left side.

But now destroyer *Smith* was on fire. A wobbling, smoking Kate had flown straight into her forward gun mount. *Smith's* bow was a mass of flames.

Hardison turned left again, and *Smith* dropped back to come astern of *South Dakota;* and then, her guns still firing, she buried her flaming nose in the battleship's high foaming wake to put her fires out and return to station.

"Torpedo on the starboard bow!"

There was no chance to turn inside the wakes this time, the torpedo was too close. Hardison made no calculated delay before coming hard right again. He gave the order instantly, *Big E's* stern skidded left again, and this time the torpedo ran harmlessly down the ship's right side.

Plunging down its wake, *Enterprise* passed the drowning enemy aviators who had launched it. They gazed up at Hardison in frustrated malevolence, and then *Big E's* wake thundered over them and they were gone.

Now there were five more Kates attacking *Enterprise* from dead astern. They maneuvered for a shot at her left middle. Hardison kept turning right to give them his narrow stern, while his force's gunners spat out a storm of 20-mm shells. Three Kates went down in quick succession, the fourth made a bad drop and crashed, but the fifth launched with good aim from nearly dead astern.

Hardison swung his ship to parallel the torpedo track and watched the enemy missile pass along his left side.

Enterprise plunged along at twenty-seven knots, her men still battling fires, others trying to patch her riddled flight decks, and lookouts watching carefully for periscopes again. Overhead, returning planes from both her own and *Hornet's* decks pleaded for permission to land. At last, Commander Crommelin insisted that they must land, holes or no holes, or else run out of gas and crash.

They began coming in, and as they did, *South Dakota's* radar picked up a large formation of enemy aircraft to the west. Planes that had not landed pulled up their wheels and banked away with roaring motors. Without altitude, they were out of the fight, and it was up to Kinkaid's gunners.

Once again, they beat the enemy off. Although the Japanese planes had had the advantage of low cloud cover, they were also denied the opportunity of singling out *Enterprise* for concentrated assault. Twenty of them attacked in shallow dives that are the delight of antiaircraft gunners, and eight of them were shot down while scoring only one near-miss on *Enterprise*.

A few minutes later, a handful of stragglers pounced on *South Dakota* and the cruiser *San Juan*. A 500-pounder hit the battleship's Number One turret. Inside that thick steel cocoon no one was aware of the hit, but a bomb splinter struck Captain Gatch in the neck. For a single confused minute, *South Dakota* spun out of control and made straight for *Enterprise*.

Once again Hardison was swinging his ship, and then *San Juan*, also knocked out of control by an enemy bomb, went careening left with whistle blowing, guns shooting, and breakdown flag flying—while the American ships broke formation and went scrambling off in every direction to avoid her.

Finally, *San Juan* was brought under control. *Enterprise* sailed on, her forward elevator still jammed, but already beginning to take on planes and turning south at full speed—retiring hastily south to escape the big enemy surface force now rushing down to finish her off.

Northampton had *Hornet* in tow and was dragging her over the ocean at three knots.

But Admiral Kakuji Kakuta, now in command of the Japanese carriers, had been closing the distance between himself and the Americans, and he had more strikes in the air.

In late afternoon a half-dozen Kates caught the plodding carrier. They came at her in a fast weaving glide. They launched six torpedoes. Only one hit, but one was enough.

It rammed into the aviation store room with a sickly green flash and cracked *Hornet* open. A tide of fuel oil two feet deep went cascading through the third deck to knock Commander Creehan's men off their feet, nearly drowning them, forcing them to rescue each other by a hand chain leading to a ladder and escape scuttle. *Hornet* listed sharply. Gradually the tilt built up to 18 degrees.

"Prepare to abandon ship!"

Hornet's men stood by, her guns firing on while dive-bombers came at her again, and missed, and a V of high-flying Kates made a horizontal attack, and missed, and then *Hornet's* men went over the side.

They left their dying ship in splendid order, going hand over hand down lines hung over *Hornet's* sloping sides, or jumping into the water to swim to waiting life rafts. But to a sailor, to leave a ship is to leave home. Many of them had fond memories of the big ship, dying just six days after her first birthday. They left part of their personalities aboard her, part of themselves stuffed into seabags that would now go down with their ship. One man might mourn the loss of his favorite books or his Bible, while another would regret having to leave his wife's picture or a bundle of dog-eared letters-from-home; others thought ruefully of the candy bar they had been saving for the midnight watch or cursed the loss of a collection of pornographic pictures or a souvenir of Honolulu or a good-luck charm or even a pair of loaded dice. A Marine sergeant going over the side protested that he had no time to save two Alka-Seltzer bottles filled with quarters. Officers and men who had money or valuables in the ship's safe were also abandoning ship at cost. Commander Gus Widhelm had $600 in poker winnings in the safe, together with the titles to two automobiles, and he was losing a record-player and his fifty-two Bing Crosby records and a collection of Strauss waltzes. Commander Dodson had managed to destroy the ship's secret papers but he could not save his collection of Greek and Roman coins. They, along with Commander Smith's lithographs and wood cuts and collection of French literature, would ultimately sink to the bottom of the sea.

Pat Creehan all but refused to leave, working stubbornly at his engines, until, with the water above his shoulders, he cast a last fond look at his turbines, and climbed out the escape hatch.

Out in the water, destroyers which had already taken off *Hornet's* wounded, moved rapidly among the life rafts to take able survivors aboard. Three of the men so rescued—Richard McDonald, Frank Cox, and Russell Burke—vowed loudly that never again would they light three cigarettes on one match.

Captain Mason was the last to leave *Hornet*. Silent and impassive, he climbed down a cargo net into a waiting boat, and then destroyers *Mustin* and *Anderson* ran in to sink his ship with torpedoes.

Isoroku Yamamoto was elated to hear that *Enterprise* and *Hornet*—the two ships which had violated inviolable Tokyo—had been caught and crippled by his fliers. His orders to his fleet were brief:

"Chase and mop up the fleeing enemy."

All ships gave immediate pursuit. Vice-Admiral Nobutake Kondo sent battleships *Kongo* and *Haruna* and a dozen cruisers and destroyers plunging southeast at a furious thirty knots. Rear Admiral Hiroaki Abe with battleships *Hiei* and *Kirishima*, and another flock of cruisers and destroyers, also poured it on. After both surface forces came Kakuta with *Junyo* and *Zuikaku*, hoping to get off a finishing strike at dawn.

But Admiral Kinkaid had wisely taken his ships out of range. The best that the Japanese could do was to find *Hornet* and to scare off the American destroyers which had failed to sink her.

Mustin and *Anderson* had fired eight torpedoes each at *Hornet*.

Nine of them hit, yet *Hornet* remained afloat; proof, if more were ever needed, that America's shipbuilders were superior to her torpedo-makers.

Only four Japanese fish were needed to do what sixteen American torpedoes could not do. They were launched by destroyers *Akigumo* and *Makigumo* and they put U.S.S. *Hornet,* seventh American ship of that name, beneath the wave.

Only crippled *Enterprise* now stood between the enemy and Guadalcanal.

In Tokyo a great victory was proclaimed.

But once again, the Japanese failed to understand that if they had won a tactical victory—as they certainly had in the Battle of the Santa Cruz Islands—they had suffered strategic loss. Although *Hornet* was gone and *Enterprise* was damaged, the Americans had once again bought time with blood. *Enterprise* could be repaired while more ships and aircraft were rushed to the South Pacific.

But for Japan, Santa Cruz meant that *Hiyo, Zuiho,* and *Shokaku* were out of the fight for Guadalcanal, and a hundred aircraft, with their precious pilots and crews, had been lost. After Santa Cruz, Japan's carrier-based aircraft would no longer be a factor at Guadalcanal. Perhaps Emperor Hirohito, again more prescient than his admirals, was aware of the strategic loss; for the Imperial Rescript issued to celebrate the victory was the very model of a cautious vaunt.

"The Combined Fleet is at present striking heavy blows at the enemy Fleet in the South Pacific Ocean," Hirohito said. "We are deeply gratified. I charge each of you to exert yourselves to the utmost in all things toward the critical turning point in the war."

Even as the Rescript was announced to the people of Japan, on Guadalcanal itself the men of the Emperor's own division were passing through an ordeal duplicating the travail of the Kawaguchi Brigade before them. Retreating east and west, the Sendai also clawed at trees for bark, or drank from muddy puddles, or gnawed their rifle slings.

Behind them, Colonel Masajiro Furumiya had decided that suicide was the only resort. He and Captain Suzuki had not been able to escape on the night of October 26–27. American fire had forced them back to their hideout. They were alone, for the others had been killed. Weak with hunger, Furumiya and Suzuki had barely enough strength to tear the 29th Infantry's colors into bits of bright red and white silk and to grind them into the mud. Then Colonel Furumiya wrote a letter which Suzuki was to deliver to General Maruyama, if he survived.

". . . I do not know what excuse to give . . .

"I am sorry I have lost many troops uselessly and for this result which has come unexpectedly. We must not overlook firepower. When there is firepower the troops become active and full of spirit. But when firepower ceases they become inactive.

"Spirit exists eternally.

"I am going to return my borrowed life today with short interest."[3]

Colonel Furumiya paused. He wrote his last line:

"The mission of a Japanese warrior is to serve his Emperor!"[4]

Masajiro Furumiya tottered to his feet. He straightened. He bowed profoundly in the direction of the Emperor, and the captain put the pistol to the colonel's head and pulled the trigger.

Part 5

CRUX

Chapter 1

FOR NEARLY three months, now, both sides had been frustrated in a war of blacks and whites: black for the nights in which the Japanese attacked, landed troops and supplies or shelled the enemy; white for the day in which the Americans attacked, landed troops and supplies or flew off airplanes to intercept bombing raids preparing the way for the enemy's movement at night.

But now, now it was November—the crucial month, the fourth month of battle—and both sides entered it with redoubling arms and confidence in ultimate victory.

In Tokyo, Imperial General Headquarters prescribed, for the third time, a massive co-ordinated assault by the Army and Navy. Tactically, there would be a difference. Surprise night attacks were to be abandoned in favor of steady driving operations launched from the Japanese platform west of the Matanikau.

The remnant of the Sendai Division was to assemble on that platform while awaiting the arrival of the 38th Division, and, later, the 51st Division then in China, and a mixed brigade, also in the Far East. Once the Sendai had recovered from its mauling at the hands of the Americans, and all of these units were in place, the offensive would be renewed.

Despite three bloody and unmitigated defeats, the Army betrayed no doubts about its ability to recover Guadalcanal, and with it, the Japanese offensive in the Pacific. The Army felt this way because it continued to believe Navy reports of smashing victories at sea, particularly the last exaggeration: two American carriers and three battleships sunk in the Battle of the Santa Cruz Islands.

Many admirals were not nearly so sanguine. They were not because they knew the truth of their own frightful losses in both carrier and land-based air, and because they appreciated, better than the generals, the terrible risks involved in putting men and supplies ashore in the face of enemy land-based air.

Some admirals, among them Gunichi Mikawa and Raizo Tanaka, argued against reinforcing while Henderson Field remained operative. They wished to suspend operations until Rabaul could be expanded as a rear base and a forward base near Buin could be established. Then, with Henderson Field truly knocked out, then and only then, they would renew the attack.[1]

Tokyo could not agree. Reinforcement was to commence immediately, in the customary way: nightly runs of the Tokyo Express preceded by daylight bombing of Henderson Field and accompanied by night surface bombardment so furious as to make The Night of the Battleships seem, in comparison, a veritable rosy dawn. Already, at his base in Truk, Admiral Yamamoto was at work on a plan drawing heavily from his formidable array of battleships.

Reinforcement was also an American concern, but as much, if not more, with aerial as with ground strength. Land-based air, the Americans knew, with all respect and admiration for General Vandegrift's skill and the doggedness of his doughty troops, was holding Guadalcanal. Accordingly, aircraft and pilots were being gathered to replenish a Cactus Air Force which, on October 26, the day of Santa Cruz, was down to twenty-nine combat planes.

On October 19, five days before President Roosevelt had ordered the Joint Chiefs to rush all available weapons to Guadalcanal, General Marshall had alerted the U. S. Army's 25th Infantry Division under the command of Major General J. Lawton Collins for movement from Hawaii to the South Pacific. Moreover, Admiral Halsey had canceled the Ndeni operation which Richmond Kelly Turner had found so attractive, and which Alexander Archer Vandegrift had considered so inimical, and he had ordered the 147th Infantry Regiment, the Eighth Marine Regiment, the Second Marine Raider Battalion, long-range artillery, and a battalion of Seabees forward to Guadalcanal.

However, American reinforcement had encountered two setbacks: one, the sinking of *President Coolidge* with an Army regiment's equipment, and, two, Kelly Turner's penchant for playing general. Balked on Ndeni, Turner, a persuasive man, convinced Admiral Halsey that another airfield should be constructed at Aola Bay, about fifty miles to the east of Lunga Point. Turner approached Halsey aware that Vandegrift's engineers, and Martin Clemens, who had lived at Aola, considered the area impossible as an airfield site. Turner also made his proposal without Vandegrift's knowledge or acquiescence, and so, a battalion of the 147th Infantry, half of the Raiders, all of the Seabees, artillery from the Americal Division, as well as Marine coastal and antiaircraft guns, were to go into Aola rather than into Vandegrift's perimeter.

Vandegrift protested, and though his arguments would ultimately move Halsey to withdraw the Aola expedition, they did not prevent the immediate loss of men and guns upon which the general had been relying. To lose the Seabees was an especially stiff jolt, for all of their skills and heavy equipment were very badly needed at Henderson Field; while long-range artillery could have been turned against Pistol Pete, again shelling the runways, and the Raiders and another battalion of infantry would naturally make the ground defenses that much stronger.

After the defeat of the Sendai, Vandegrift had about 23,000 Marines and 3000 soldiers in his command. But of these, 4000 Marines were with Rupertus on Tulagi, and the others—particularly the men who had landed on August 7—were very close to exhaustion.

They were shadow troops. Three months of uninterrupted ordeal such as no American troops had ever sustained, before or since, such as few soldiers in history have experienced, had made them walking skeletons of parchment flesh and quivering nerve. They were the young ancients, the old-young, staring with a fixed thousand-yard stare out of eyes that were red-rimmed and sunken. Their bodies were taut rags of flesh stretched over sticks of bone. They had come to Guadalcanal muscular and high-spirited young men, but now each had lost at least twenty pounds, some had lost fifty, and their high fervor had ebbed and nearly flowed away. They were hanging on by habit only, fighting out of the rut of an old valor.

They were lonely. It was an utter, aching, yearning loneliness, it was a feeling of what has been called "expendability," a conviction that their country had set them down, alone, in the heart of an enemy camp and then forgotten them. They could not comprehend the contradiction of their own total commitment to the war and news of labor strikes at home or, worse, of ships lying unloaded in their own Bay because merchant seamen wanted extra pay to unload them.

And they were losing hope. Hope, which had nourished their spirits better than enemy rice had kept their bodies, was all but gone now. It had been eroded like an island in a stormy sea. Tide after tide of adversity had washed over it, each time it had emerged intact—but with shrunken shores. Now hope was a cluster of sea-washed rocks and scraggly palm trees standing in the path of a new tidal wave of calamity gathering in the north.

Without hope, these men turned in upon themselves. They rarely spoke except to close friends. Squad by squad, they kept apart; they became tribal or clannish. Some men who had spent as much as two months in the same foxhole along the same river or on top of the same ridge could not, except by dire threats from NCOs or direct orders from officers, be made to move as much as fifty yards away from their holes. It was as though they feared to displease the local deity. Much as they might explain that bombs and shells fell in showers and instantaneously on this dreadful island, and that a man was a fool to be caught very far from shelter, they acted, actually, from an atavistic dread; three months of modern war in the primitive jungle had stripped away the acquired vesture of civilization and left them naked and trembling again before a tutelary god. In this hole they had survived, and they would not leave it.

Such men would not even leave their holes to go to chow, and other men could not go because the galleys were generally located so far to the rear that they had not the strength to get there and back. Their comrades brought food to them, just as they brought food to hundreds of men who burned with malarial fires but who were not considered sick enough to be admitted to the hospitals in the rear. And malaria was now also a scourge. In the First Marine Division there had been 239 cases of malaria in September, there were 1941 in October, and before November ended there would be 3200 more.

Malaria and dengue fever, yellow jaundice and dysentery, tropical ulcers that ate into the outer covering of the bone and the rot of fungus festering and leaving flesh encrusted and oozing pus by the canteen-cup, these were also enemies; foes as real as the Japanese with all their troops and ships and airplanes; adversaries as authentic as the miasmic jungle and those formless fears of the imagination which trooped into a man's mind each night, as dusk deepened into darkness, and remained there until dawn.

Dawn sometimes found men out of their minds; most often men who, losing hope, had also lost their sense of humor. For humor was the last rampart. More than hope, even, it stood between a man and insanity; and with all else gone, or going, these Americans held onto their humor.

It was not a dainty mirth. Men moved by it could shout with laughter to hear that a Marine's collection of enemy ears, pinned on a clothesline of enemy rope, had been lost in a single dissolving cycle of rain-and-sun; they could chuckle while sawing enemy leg bones in sections with a bayonet, prying out the marrow and shaping a grisly ring to grace their true love's fingers; or they could smile to hear of the two Japanese soldiers who had been found sitting in serene confidence in the center of the beehive that was Henderson Field, waiting there, as they had been ordered, "to rendezvous with the main body."

Private Phil Chaffee also possessed this grim sense of humor. It sustained him on his numerous overnight patrols into the enemy positions around Grassy Knoll. Twice a week, accompanied by a taciturn red-bearded sergeant, Chaffee came down the ridge held by Lucky and Lew Juergens, bantering with them as he walked toward the jungle between the ridge and Grassy Knoll.

"Hey, Chaffee, got your pliers?"

"You know me, boy, I'd sooner forget m' rifle."

"How about it, Chaffee? I'll give you ten bucks for that Bull Durham sack around your neck."

"Yeah, I know what you mean. How about a pint of my blood, too, huh?"

"How many teeth you got in that sack?"

"That's my business."

"A hundred?"

"Guess again, boy. Guess up a storm."[2]

Chaffee would vanish into the rain forest, reappearing a few days later with a triumphant grin and a heavier Bull Durham sack, and one day he came back from Grassy Knoll wagging two fingers and bursting with pride.

"Two Japs!" Juergens snorted. "Who'n hell ain't shot two Japs?"

Chaffee feigned surprise. He twirled the ends of his handlebar mustache, and asked:

"With the one bullet?"[3]

Thus these Marines facing November, the month of decision which Archer Vandegrift began by attacking to the west once more.

General Vandegrift wanted to upset his temporarily beaten enemy before he could consolidate west of the Matanikau again. He also wanted to knock out Pistol Pete and to force General Hyakutake to use landing beaches much farther west, thus complicating his supply problems.

Vandegrift's objective was the Poha River, a mile and a half west of Hyakutake's 17th Army headquarters at Kukumbona. To take it, the Marine general collected a force of five thousand Marines—the Second Marines less a battalion under Colonel John Arthur, the Third Battalion, Seventh, reinforced by the Scout-Snipers, and the Fifth Marines—all to be commanded by Red Mike Edson.

The Fifth Marines were to cross the Matanikau at Nippon Bridge while the Third Battalion, Seventh, crossed farther inland and punched farther west.

At midnight of October 31 engineers began throwing three foot bridges across the Matanikau. Then Marine artillery and cruisers *San Francisco* and *Helena,* with destroyer *Sterett,* began pounding the enemy. At dawn, the warships came in close to shell Point Cruz, and the attack went forward.

General Hyakutake fought desperately to hold his position. He plugged his riddled front with service troops, walking wounded, sick, typists, clerks, and cooks, mustering every able-bodied man who could fight. But the Marines drove them back toward Point Cruz. The night of November 1, Edson halted just short of the Point. Behind him, engineers threw a ten-ton vehicular bridge over the Matanikau. In the morning, Edson called upon Silent Lew Walt to wheel his battalion north and drive to the sea on the other side of Point Cruz.

Walt's men drove quickly into place. The Japanese at Point Cruz were now hemmed in on three sides with their backs to the sea. Edson ordered his men to attack in one of the Pacific war's rare bayonet charges. The Marines swept forward with a yell to kill every one of the 350 enemy soldiers caught in the trap.

And then General Vandegrift's third attempt to clear his western flank was again interrupted by events in the east.

On November 2, Vandegrift was informed by Admiral Halsey's intelligence section that the Japanese would land near Koli Point to the east that night.

Vandegrift decided to intercept them. He would mark time in the west while clearing the east. Once that was done, he could throw all his strength into the Matanikau thrust.

So Red Mike Edson returned to the perimeter, leaving a blocking force west of Point Cruz under Colonel Arthur, and Herman Henry Hanneken's tired but trusty battalion was pulled out of the line and sent on a forced march toward Koli Point.

Hanneken's Marines reached Koli before dusk, fording the Nalimbiu River which debouches into the Bay there, and pushing on to the east bank of the Metapona River a few miles farther east.

Hanneken organized a coastal perimeter and tried to reach Vandegrift by radio. But he could not. The river crossings had soaked his radios. There was nothing to do but sit down to await the arrival of the Tokyo Express.

Vice-Admiral Chuichi Nagumo had been relieved of his command. He was going home, and Commander Tameichi Hara came to see him before he left Truk. Hara was surprised to see that the hero of Pearl Harbor looked so haggard.

"You don't look good, Admiral," he blurted.

Nagumo tried to make light of his appearance. "Just a touch of flu," he said. "Once back home, I'll be in good shape."

Hara nodded. "Sasebo's climate will cure you," he said. "And you deserve a rest. Compared to your duty, sir, I've been on a pleasure cruise."

"Well, you'll have a tougher time from now on," Nagumo said grimly, informing his visitor that all but two of Combined Fleet's carriers were going home for repairs. Hara was astounded, and then dumfounded to hear Nagumo admit that although Santa Cruz had been a Japanese tactical victory, it was "a shattering strategic loss for Japan." To offset American replacement capacity, Nagumo explained, Japan had to win every battle overwhelmingly.

"This last one," he said, "was not an overwhelming victory."[4]

Saddened, Commander Hara returned to *Amatsukaze*. He knew that he would soon be sailing his destroyer from Truk as part of the Guadalcanal bombardment fleet. And now, as Nagumo told him, Japan's precious warships were to be risked without aerial cover.

The next day, November 3, Commander Hara stood on his bridge to watch cruisers *Isuzu, Suzuya,* and *Maya* and eight destroyers sortie from Truk. Standing on *Isuzu's* flag bridge was Hara's old chief, Rear Admiral Raizo Tanaka. He was taking his squadron to the Shortlands. Tanaka the Tenacious was returning to the helm of the Tokyo Express, and even as he sailed, the Express's first run in the new reinforcement operation was making for Koli Point.

One cruiser, three destroyers and one transport were bringing more men and supplies to Colonel Toshinaro Shoji at Tetere. Shoji had arrived at this village east of Koli Point—the place where Mr. Ishimoto murdered the missionaries—after an agonizing march from the October battleground. He brought with him 2500 starving and exhausted men, the remnant of the Sendai Division's right wing. He expected his badly needed supplies to arrive early in the morning of November 3.

Or roughly at the same time Admiral Kelly Turner's airfield-building expedition would arrive farther east at Aola.

Martin Clemens was at Aola.

With him were a handful of Marines and his cook, Michael, who had just been discharged from the hospital, his dark face pocked with pink shrapnel scars as mementoes of The Night of the Battleships. Clemens had brought his party to his old headquarters to provide landing beacons for Kelly Turner's Aola expedition. Three pyramids of logs twelve feet high were built on the beach at intervals six hundred feet apart. At three o'clock in the morning of November 3, in a pouring rain, they were set ablaze.

Clemens and his men stood watching the fire. Firelight made grotesque silhouettes of their lumpy, poncho-swathed figures. The cold rain made their teeth chatter. Then, from the east, Clemens saw the swell of high-speed ships washing over the beach. The wash continued west toward Koli Point. Clemens gazed at the beacons in apprehension.

"I hope they don't draw crabs," he muttered.

The Japanese ships had sailed north of Florida Island. They rounded its eastern tip and entered the Bay. Landing beacons were noticed at Aola, but they were considered an enemy trap—a very clumsy one—and the ships pressed west to anchor and unload at Gavaga Creek, midway between Koli and Tetere.

Colonel Hanneken was chagrined. He could see the enemy putting men and supplies ashore, but they were too far away for immediate action. He decided to attack at dawn.

He did, and his Marines collided with Japanese soldiers marching west to Koli. Both sides recoiled, but the Japanese snapped back faster. They struck the Americans with light howitzers and mortars, while working a force around to their rear.

Hanneken withdrew. He pulled back across the Metapona to the west bank of the Nalimbiu, where he had communications wire connecting him with the perimeter. He notified Vandegrift of his predicament and was told to expect aerial assistance.

It came, and it hit Hanneken's men.

Hanneken called for an end to aerial "assistance," and it was canceled. And then Vandegrift ordered Hanneken to hold while General Rupertus came over from Tulagi to take command.

Martin Clemens watched his second set of signal pyramids lose its brilliance with the arrival of first light of November 4. Then he saw a quartet of old American four-stack destroyers entering the Bay. Farther out were transports guarded by destroyers. Soon landing boats swung out from the four-stackers and the Raiders of Lieutenant Colonel Evans Carlson went down into them. They came roaring ashore, and the Raiders leaped out to go racing up the beach with fixed bayonets.

They had been told to land as though opposed, and they fanned out quickly into the jungle.

Martin Clemens watched them in amusement, for he was, by then, one of the Old Breed of American Marine. He had been there "when the stuff hit the fan," and he had the right to say, as the first Marine in history is reputed to have said to the second

Marine, "Lissen, boot, you shoulda been here when it was *really* rough." And so he was prepared when a Raider racing toward him and Michael came to an astonished halt at the sight of the Englishman in his slouch hat and the native with the face full of scars.

"What kinda disease is that?" the Raider asked, pointing at Michael.

"Bomb disease!"[5] Clemens snorted, turning to watch, with tolerant disdain, the arrival of the rest of Admiral Turner's well-dressed and well-fed Johnny-come-latelies.

Not all of the American transports stopped at Aola. Some moved farther west to Lunga Point, bringing General Vandegrift a pair of welcome acquisitions: the Eighth Marine Regiment and two batteries of 155-mm "long Tom" rifles.

The long Toms meant that the days of Pistol Pete's unchallenged reign were numbered, for the 155 rifles could outshoot the Japanese 150-mm howitzers. The Eighth Marines meant that the attack in the west could be renewed, as soon as Rupertus could clear up the situation in the east.

Listening to reports from Hanneken and Clemens's scouts, General Rupertus wisely concluded that there were quite a few Japanese to the east. He decided to hold at the Nalimbiu until Chesty Puller's battalion could come downcoast by boat to take the enemy in his seaflank while Colonel Bryant Moore took the 164th Infantry south to turn north and take the Japanese on his landward flank.

Late that day—November 4—the operation began.

To the west that same day—November 4—soldiers of the 228th Infantry Regiment of the Japanese 38th Division were marching to General Hyakutake's rescue.

Seventeen destroyers had landed them at Kamimbo and Tassafaronga early that morning. As they came ashore, Major General Takeo Ito, the 38th's infantry commander, turned them east to Kukumbona.

Meanwhile, General Hyakutake radioed Colonel Shoji at Tetere and ordered him to join him in the west.

Shoji was dismayed at having to forego the chance to avenge the Sendai. Nevertheless, he left a rear guard of five hundred men at Gavaga Creek and began swinging around Henderson Field along the trail cut by the Kawaguchi Brigade.

Rupertus tried to cut him off with Colonel Moore's two battalions of the 164th Infantry. But these units, having blundered into each other at night and fought a bloodless battle between them, were unable to halt more than a handful of Shoji's men. The main body, perhaps three thousand men, had escaped.

Gung ho!

In Chinese it means "Work together," and Evans Carlson had learned it during his prewar service with the Chinese Eighth Route Army. After taking command of the Second Raiders—and weeding out the fainthearted with the question "Could you cut a Jap's throat without flinching?"—Carlson gave them *Gung ho!* as both slogan and battle cry. One day the phrase would come to mean a Marine *esprit* bordering on chauvinism, and that would be partially as a result of the fury with which Carlson's Raiders scourged the men of Colonel Shoji's column in a month-long private war of their own.

Guided through the jungle by native scouts under the command of Sergeant Major Vouza, depending upon native carriers to lug the ammunition and rations of rice, raisins, and bacon that were periodically parachuted to them along the way, they killed five hundred of Shoji's men at a loss of only seventeen of their own. And they did this with a single, simple tactic which Carlson had also learned in China.

His main body marched, unseen, in a column parallel with the Japanese. His patrols followed directly behind the enemy. Each time the patrols encountered large numbers of Japanese, they opened fire. As Colonel Shoji began to rush reinforcements to his rear, Carlson's men struck from the flank with all their firepower.

Then they vanished.

Twelve times Carlson's Raiders savaged the enemy in this fashion, and by the time Colonel Shoji's haggard and reeling column reached Kukumbona, Guadalcanal was known in their language not only as *Ga Shima,* or Hunger Island, but also as *Shih Shima.*

Death Island.

On November 5—the day the lean and passionate Carlson led his men in pursuit of Colonel Shoji—Admiral Tanaka arrived in the Shortlands. Two runs of the Tokyo Express had already made those landings at Gavaga Creek and in the west, and Tanaka immediately prepared another one.

On November 7, eleven destroyers were to take 1300 men of the 38th Division to Tassafaronga. Tanaka hoped to lead the sortie personally, but Admiral Mikawa insisted that he remain in the Shortlands. Tanaka was needed to plan additional runs of the Tokyo Express scheduled for November 8, 9, and 10. In all, two cruisers and sixty-five destroyers were to be involved in these shipments. Finally the biggest convoy of all, eleven big fast transports carrying half the 38th Division, was to leave on November 13, after Admiral Kondo's battleships and cruisers had made powder and hash of Henderson Field.

So the eleven destroyers set sail without him, taking the northern route above the Solomon chain.

They would arrive at Tassafaronga at midnight of November 7.

November 7 dawned bright and hot. Martin Clemens decided it was a good day to return to the perimeter from Aola. The Army battalion there had set up a defensive line and the Seabees were already at work building roads. Clemens decided there was nothing more that he could do, and he was anxious to resume his interrupted duties as chief recruiter and straw boss for a force of native stevedores. He had planned to bring back a prisoner or two with him, but "Wimpy" Wendling, an exuberant Marine marksman, had shot holes in that hope.

Wendling and four scouts had gone to Koilotumaria to round up a few of the Japanese missed in the last foray. They had found four, but instead of capturing them they had killed them. Wendling reported that he had attempted to persuade a wounded, English-speaking officer to surrender. The officer refused. Wendling advanced offering a chocolate bar. The Japanese whipped out his saber and swung.

Fortunately, Wimpy explained, his finger was still on the trigger.

So Clemens led his party into their landing boat and sailed west for Lunga.

A mile offshore the lookout called, "White water to starboard."

Clemens was surprised. He knew there were no reefs in the vicinity. He raised his glasses to look for the "white water" and saw a bubbling wake leading straight into the side of the supply ship *Majaba*. A huge column of water spouted into the sky followed by a roar. *Majaba* listed, holed by the Japanese submarine *I-20*. Sinking fast, she staggered ashore and beached herself, later to be salvaged and patched up.

Destroyers dashed about, their sterns digging deep into the water, depth-charges arching off their fantails and geysers of water marking the underwater explosions. Dive-bombers came hurtling down, too, and Wendling jumped up on the prow to wave a huge American flag—just in case some inexperienced Dauntless pilot should mistake a Higgins boat for an enemy barge.

They reached Lunga and found that they had beached right next to a Japanese torpedo. It lay on the beach, long, silvery, and wicked, still hot and steaming from its futile run at *Majaba*. A bomb-disposal officer was at work dismantling it. Clemens walked back to his tent wondering if it were possible to find a safe spot or pass a dull day on Guadalcanal.

November 7 had seemed like a dull day at Henderson Field. It seemed that the aerial doldrums, begun after the Battle of Santa Cruz, were going to continue—until coastwatchers radioed reports of eleven enemy destroyers slipping down the top of the Solomons.

Major Paul Fontana led his newly arrived squadron of Marine fighters aloft first, and after him came Captain Joe Foss with more Wildcats. About 150 miles to the north Foss saw the specks of the enemy ships crawling over the flat obsidian surface of the sea like a file of ants. Then he saw six float Zeros flying escort. The Zeros struck boldly at the American bombers, trying to ruin their aim as they screamed down on Admiral Tanaka's skillfully maneuvering ships.

Some of their bombs scored direct hits on destroyers *Takanami* and *Naganami,* inflicting major damage and killing troops, but no ships were sunk and the Tokyo Express sailed on toward Tassafaronga.

The Zeros were not so fortunate.

"Don't look now," Joe Foss yelled by radio to his pilots, "but I think we have something here."[6]

They went zooming down in attack, practically jostling each other, giving each other the aerial elbow in their eagerness not to be left out in the scramble of seven Wildcats for six Zeros. Foss shot the first one, blowing it into an aerial dust bag. And then they were all gone. Foss looked up. He could see five empty parachutes ballooning gently downward. He wondered where the pilots were. Then he saw a sixth chute with an enemy pilot dangling from the harness.

The pilot unbuckled himself and plummeted head-first into the sea, and there were six clouds of empty silk swaying gently in the sky.

Strange enemy indeed, Foss thought, and prepared to go down to strafe the destroyers. Grasping the stick, he made his customary quick survey of the clouds—and saw a pontoon protruding from a bit of fluff above him.

He went up after it and found a single-motored biplane scout. He came in close, missed, and was raked by the scout's rear-gunner. Wind came howling through a hole in his windscreen. Foss came back and shot the scout into the sea. He caught a second scout by surprise and sent it down like a torch.

And then his motor began to fade and spout smoke, and Foss realized that he was far from home and coming down into the sea near Malaita Island.

Two or three miles offshore, his tail hooked into the water, his plane skipped, bounced, came down hard, nosed over and began to sink like a stone.

Foss was trapped. Water poured into his cockpit with the force of a sledgehammer, knocking him groggy. The plane was plunging toward the bottom of the sea, but Foss could not get out. He had forgotten to unhook his parachute leg strap, and now water was underneath both his chute harness and his inflated life vest, making him so buoyant he could not reach the leg strap.

Still descending, he became frantic and caught his foot under the seat. He was going to drown if he did not calm himself. Holding off death with iron self-control, he straightened, pushed down with all his strength, freed the foot and strap—and shot upward through a crushing weight of water.

But the leg straps of the chute harness were still buckled. They brought Foss to the surface behind-up and face-down. He gulped mouthfuls of sea water. He swallowed more, unbuckling the straps. Then his preserver shot up over his mouth and he took in more.

Still thrashing about, Foss undid his shoes and felt himself become more buoyant. He tried to swim toward Malaita. But the current was too strong and he was barely staying in place. A big black tail fin cut the water a few feet to the side of him. Another slid past on the other side. Foss remembered the chlorine capsule in his pocket. It was supposed to keep the sharks away. He grasped it and broke it.

In another hour it was dark, and the sharks were back. They were all around him.

Within the darkening stadium in Washington, D.C., the floodlights were just coming on. They came on at about the time that Joe Foss and his fellow Marines roared aloft to intercept the Tokyo Express. And as the stadium blossomed with light and the uniforms of the football players became more brilliant and the thick carpet of grass beneath their feet turned a brighter green, the loudspeaker crackled and blared:

"The President of the United States announces the successful landing on the African Coast of an American Expeditionary Force. This is our second front!"[7]

A single great cry of national pride went reverberating around the arena. The football players went cartwheeling and handspringing down the middle of the field. America, agonizing over prospects of fresh disaster in the Pacific, was looking eagerly away to a new theater.

Then the whistle blew and the sobering players lined up for the kickoff.

Little splashes of phosphorescence indicated to Joe Foss the places where the sharks were. He barely moved, fearing that if he extended an arm to swim, he would withdraw a spouting stub. Other splashes became audible farther away. They sounded like paddles. Peering through the murk, Foss saw a canoe and a native gondola coming toward him.

Were they Japanese?

Foss stayed motionless among the sharks and his fears. The boats passed to either side. Foss saw a lantern. For nearly a half hour, the lantern swayed eerily about him as the canoe and the gondola continued their search.

A voice said, "Let's look over 'ere," and Joe Foss's heart leaped.

"Yeah!" he bellowed. "Right over here!"

The lantern winked out and on the gondola above him Foss thought he saw natives raising war clubs and he knew he heard them jabbering wildly.

"Friend!" Foss yelled. "Birdman! Aviator! American!"[8]

Suddenly there was the man with the lantern above him, and friendly arms were outstretched toward him. Foss grasped them. They were those of Tommy Robinson, an Australian sawmill operator, and he pulled Foss into the canoe. Another man, in clerical clothing, said, "I'm Father De Steinberg," just as a flying fish leaped from the sea and smashed the lantern.

Foss gaped at the fish. It was twenty inches in length with a long, sharp needle of a bill.

"I should have kept this thing down," Robinson said apologetically. "But I guess I got the wind up a bit. Many a bloke has lost his eyes at night because of holding lights."[9]

Foss shuddered and instinctively put his hand over his eyes, shivering again while Robinson cheerfully advised him that he had been wise to remain offshore with his friends, the sharks. If he had come ashore at the point he had been hoping to reach, he would have had to ford a stagnant stream full of crocodiles.

The boats made for Buma Mission. Foss was welcomed ashore by Bishop Aubin, and another bishop who was Russian, as well as a Norwegian planter, four priests from as many different countries, and two brothers—one from Emmetsburg, Iowa—and eight sisters, one from Boston.

They fed him and gave him dry clothes and a bed. It was not really a bed, rather the lumpy pad of an ascetic monk with a rocklike sack for a pillow, but Joe Foss slept well on it.

Except for a bad few minutes at midnight when he awoke sick and retching from the sea water he had swallowed.

"It smells of exhibitionism," Bull Halsey said. "To hell with it!"[10]

The admiral was on Guadalcanal. He had come there Sunday, November 8, and he was, with customary bluntness, rejecting his staff's suggestion that he stand up in his jeep and wave or do something to make his presence known to the island's ragged defenders.

Halsey would not, for he had seen their faces, and he would not insult them by crowing, in effect: "Give a cheer, Halsey's here." So he drove without fanfare to Vandegrift's headquarters. Vandegrift took him on tour of the battlegrounds, and treated him to a dinner which so impressed the admiral that he asked to see the cook.

Butch Morgan appeared. His red mustache was carefully brushed. He wore clean khaki trousers and his skivvy shirt was immaculate. He stood ramrod straight while Commander, South Pacific, praised his cooking, until, reddening and fidgeting apace with the admiral's encomiums, he finally burst out!

"Oh, bullshit, Admiral—you don't have to say that!"[11]

Joe Foss also enjoyed his dinner that Sunday.

He had been to the thatched chapel and he had also been put on display for the benefit of curious natives. The fathers had asked him to stand between two huts while the Malaitans passed by to examine him. Short, with powerful muscles rippling beneath purply black skin, they not only made a striking contrast to the tall fair American, they seemed very much amazed that there was a difference at all.

One of the priests explained that many years before the war an American schooner had stopped at Malaita with a crew of southern Negroes. They had told the Malaitans that they were Americans, and so, the islanders had expected Foss to be black.

Foss was not surprised. One of the sisters he had spoken to had never seen an automobile, and the first airplanes she saw were those that flew and fought overhead. Hardly any of the missionaries knew anything of the war going on across The Slot, to say nothing of what had happened in the world during the past few decades, and that was why, as Foss sat down to dinner, they pressed him to stay with them for two weeks.

Foss thought he might stay a week—he could fish and inspect the wrecked Japanese planes in the hills—until he heard the familiar roar of a Catalina's motors and he rushed down the steps of the dining hall built on stilts to find that his friend, Major Jack Cram, had come for him.

Joe Foss went back to the war. He left his silk parachute for the sisters to sew into clothing, he promised to bring his hosts some tobacco, and he went out to the Catalina in a native canoe —returning to that Henderson Field from which, during the weeks to come, he would rise to score his twenty-sixth aerial victory and tie the record set by Captain Eddie Rickenbacker in World War I.

Behind him the Malaitans had begun to chant vespers.

Across the Bay, Washing Machine Charley and the Tokyo Express bellowed a martial vespers to introduce Admiral Halsey to Guadalcanal at night.

The admiral sat out the performance in General Vandegrift's dugout, rising, during a lull, to strike a sandbag with a knuckly fist.

"Stout structure you have here, Archie," Halsey grunted, and then the All-Clear sounded, and both men left.

Behind them, staff officers stared in wonderment at the stout sandbag which had just burst and was pouring sand on the floor with a weary sigh.

The departure of Charley and the Express did not mean that Marines on the ridge directly behind Vandegrift's dugout could also go back to sleep, as had the admiral and the general. No, it meant, rather, that now they could emerge in dripping discontent from the watery pits in which they had taken shelter, to pass a few unharassed hours squatting on their haunches while hoping the customary but rarely fulfilled hope that the rain would stop and they might dry off.

Private Juergens began to swear. He swore at the enemy with an ardent fluency, making masterly use of that ugly four-letter word without which most Marines, like handcuffed orators, are speechless. Suddenly they were all on their feet howling foul epithets at the enemy, real or imagined, in the dark jungle below them. They called Emperor Hirohito a "bucktoothed bastard" and they suggested that Premier Tojo impale himself upon the Japanese caudal appendage, and then, up from the jungle a reedy high voice screeched back in outrage:

"F—— Babe Ruth!"[12]

Chesty Puller was being evacuated from Gavaga Creek.

The day before, he had led his battalion of Marines in the western push against Gavaga while Moore's soldiers attacked from the south and Hanneken hit from the west. The enemy had replied with an artillery barrage.

Fragments from an exploding shell tore into Puller's lower body and his legs. He was knocked flat. Bleeding freely, he called to a nearby Marine.

"Call headquarters, old man."

"I can't, sir. The line's been cut."[13]

Puller staggered erect to help repair the break, and a sniper shot him twice in the arm. Puller sank to the ground again. His men placed him on a poncho, dug a foxhole and lowered him gently into it. He spent the night there. In the morning a corpsman came to tie an evacuation tag to Puller's uniform. Puller snatched it away, snarling:

"Go label a bottle with that tag! I can go under my own power."[14]

Puller arose unsteadily and limped a thousand yards down the trail to the beach. He sank to the ground again. To his agonized dismay, he could not, in front of his men, go farther. His proud spirit could no longer goad his weakening flesh, and he had to crawl into the landing boat.

Sailing down the coast in a fog of pain, he could hear the firing signaling the beginning of the end for the enemy at Gavaga.

On November 9—while Chesty Puller was taken by jeep to the primitive hospital inside the perimeter—Admiral Halsey held a press conference. A newsman asked how long he thought the Japanese would continue to fight.

"How long can they take it?" Halsey snapped.[15]

Another reporter asked the admiral how he proposed to conquer.

"Kill Japs, kill Japs, and keep on killing Japs,"[16] he shot back.

Later, Halsey decorated some of Vandegrift's officers and men. He met the general's staff, and also Martin Clemens. Turning to drive to the runway, Halsey said: "Well, Clemens, you carry on. We've got to beat these goddamed little yellow bastards."[17]

"At the airfield, Halsey said farewell with twinkling eyes. "Vandegrift," he said, "don't you do a thing to that cook."[18]

Then he was gone, and a few hours later Archer Vandegrift had resumed the attack in the west.

The arrival of the Eighth Marines under Colonel Hall Jeschke had prompted Vandegrift to renew his push toward Kukumbona. He sent this force to join Arthur holding the blocking position with his own Second Marines and a battalion of the 164th.

But the attack, begun in the afternoon, bogged down in a furious rainfall.

Next day the sun was blazing, and the Eighth Marines, like all new arrivals on Guadalcanal, wilted in its heat.

On the following day the sun shone even more fiercely. Although it did not deter the veteran units at Gavaga Creek—who finally reduced the enemy pocket, killing 350 Japanese at a loss of forty Americans dead and 120 wounded—the heat again slowed Colonel Arthur's advance. So did General Hyakutake's well-entrenched, stubborn, and enlarged forces.

By mid-afternoon only four hundred yards had been gained. By that time also, General Vandegrift had been informed by Admiral Halsey that a great fleet had sailed from Truk. Presumably, it was going to join other large forces gathering at Rabaul and in the Shortlands.

Later that day, two furious air raids signaled the end of the aerial doldrums and underlined Halsey's warning.

Once again Archer Vandegrift was forced to shift from an offensive to a defensive stance. He recalled his troops from both fronts. He strengthened his lines. He tried to conceal his apprehension, but with little success. Anyone who had been on Guadalcanal long enough could read the signs. They knew—at Henderson Field, along the beaches and the riverbanks, atop the ridges and down in the gloom of the jungle—they knew as they had always known that the breaking point had to be reached some time.

And this was it.

Chapter 2

FOR THE first time since the Japanese garrison on Tulagi had sent its last, heartbreaking message, "Praying for everlasting victory," Japan's Army and Navy had drawn up a plan that was concentrated rather than dispersed, detailed rather than complicated.

Admiral Yamamoto had placed Vice-Admiral Nobutake Kondo in command of an armada of two aircraft carriers, four battleships, eleven cruisers, forty-nine destroyers, eleven transports, and 14,000 men.

The troops were to augment General Hyakutake's 17th Army, which, in mid-November, at last outnumbered Vandegrift's forces by 30,000 to 23,000. Some 3000 of the reinforcements comprised a Combined Naval Landing Force, while the remaining 11,000 formed the main body of the 38th Division.

They were to land on the morning of November 13, after Henderson Field had been bombarded night and day. The first barrage was to be delivered on the night of November 12–13 by Vice-Admiral Hiroaki Abe with battleships *Hiei* and *Kirishima,* cruiser *Nagara* and fourteen destroyers. Gunichi Mikawa, with six cruisers and six destroyers, would bombard during the daylight of November 13 while a convoy of eleven high-speed Army transports, escorted by twelve Tokyo Express destroyers under Tanaka the Tenacious, put the troops ashore at Tassafaronga.

Throughout this operation, Admiral Kondo with carriers *Hiyo* and *Junyo,* battleships *Haruna* and *Kongo* and other ships would sail in distant support about 150 miles north of Savo. *Hiyo's* and *Junyo's* airplanes would, of course, bomb Henderson Field in concert with the eagles from Rabaul.

Thus the major assault-and-landing plan, simplified at last, with the knockout blow to be delivered "all at once, in big ships," as Gunichi Mikawa had argued in that late August of long ago. And among its details, finally, was the destruction of the Allied coast-watching network on Bougainville.

Japan now knew to what disastrous degree her movements of ships and aircraft had been made known to the Americans. Because she did, aircraft from Rabaul or New Ireland rarely flew above The Slot, now, and ships sailed south on three different routes.

Nevertheless, coastwatchers continued to operate close to fields such as Buin and it was very difficult to conceal the gathering of a great armada from those numerous native scouts who, as the Japanese also now realized, were not harmless "civilians" in lap-laps but rather very dangerous enemy spies. Since trapping the scouts themselves was obviously impossible, or at least impractical, the Japanese decided to strike at the organizing brains behind them.

Jack Read in the north of Bougainville and Paul Mason in the south at Buin were to be caught and killed.

Hunting dogs were shipped into Buin and kept there in a wire cage while a patrol of a hundred soldiers was brought up from the island's southern tip at Kahili.

Mason's scouts quickly discovered the dogs, and Mason signaled their location to the Americans. A Catalina flew over Buin and dropped a bomb.

"Killed the lot," Mason signaled cheerfully, before departing Buin for the towering green-black mountains that ran down Bougainville's north-south spine. After him came the Japanese patrol. Between the two moved the ever-faithful scouts, reporting every enemy movement or sending the patrol panting up the wrong slopes. Exhausted, convinced that no effete westerner could survive in such horrible terrain, the Japanese withdrew.

Paul Mason returned to his hideout in Buin. He resumed broadcasting with a report of the enemy's failure. Then he sent this ominous message:

"At least 61 ships this area: 2 *Nati*-class cruisers, 1 *Aoba*, 1 *Mogami*, 1 *Kiso*, 1 *Tatuta*, 2 sloops, 33 destroyers, 17 cargo, 2 tankers, 1 passenger liner of 8,000 tons."[1]

It was this message, joined to the reports of tirelessly searching Flying Forts and Catalinas, which sent the last American carrier force in the Pacific tearing north again.

Big E was coming back to battle a cripple, but coming back because Bull Halsey was throwing even half-ships and cockleshells into America's desperate struggle to save Guadalcanal.

Since the day *Enterprise* had staggered from Santa Cruz into the hill-girdled harbor of Nouméa, a battalion of Seabees, all of repair-ship *Vulcan's* crew, and the carrier's own craftsmen had been working around the clock to put her back in shape. *Enterprise* had lain there beside the dozing little French colonial town with its dainty white replica of Notre Dame de Paris crowning the harbor, while her decks rattled to the incessant pounding of air-hammers, while even the nights winked and twinkled with the spark and sputter of welder's torches, and while other ships sped north with the last of Admiral Halsey's available troops.

Six thousand of them, Marines and soldiers of the 182nd Infantry Regiment, had been rushed to Guadalcanal to even the 30,000-to-23,000 numerical superiority now possessed by the enemy.

The first group, the Marines, had arrived on November 11 in a convoy commanded by Rear Admiral Norman Scott. Even as they hurried ashore, the enemy struck with the two air raids which ended the aerial doldrums and underlined Halsey's warning to Vandegrift. The only damage was in near-misses suffered by transport *Zeilin,* while eleven enemy aircraft were shot down against seven Wildcats lost.

The second group led by Admiral Turner and carrying the 182nd Infantry Regiment was due to arrive the following day, November 12.

So also, Admiral Halsey learned, would the aircraft and battleships of Admiral Kondo's huge fleet.

Only *Enterprise,* still needing ten days of repairs, battleships *South Dakota*—also crippled—and *Washington,* two cruisers and eight destroyers could offset this powerful enemy concentration.

Halsey ordered them back.

On November 11, Seabees and *Vulcan*-crew and all, *Enterprise* stood out of Nouméa. She made the open sea with her decks still shaking and echoing to air-hammers, with welder's arcs still sparking, with a big bulge in her right side forward, without watertight integrity and one oil tank still leaking, and with her forward elevator still jammed as it had been since the bomb at Santa Cruz broke in half.

Fortunately, the elevator was stuck at the flight-deck level. Or at least it was thought to be. No one, not even Bull Halsey, would have dared to press the "Down" button to find out. If the elevator went down and did not come up again, there would be a big square hole in the flight deck and *Enterprise* would be useless.

Thus, depending on her after elevators to bring planes to and from the hangars below, *Enterprise* sailed back to battle only half a carrier. With her, though, were screening ships powerful enough to take on Admiral Kondo's sluggers.

If they could get there in time.

If . . .

This time there would be no complicated Japanese Army timetable of attack to work in their favor. This time all depended on a favorable wind.

If it blew from the north *Enterprise* could launch her planes without having to turn around. But if it blew from the south, the big ship would have to turn into the wind to launch. Leaving Nouméa behind and entering radio silence, Admiral Kinkaid stood bareheaded on *Big E's* bridge and saw that the luck of Santa Cruz had forsaken him.

It was a south wind.

Far to the north, the weather favored the Japanese.

At three o'clock in the morning of November 12, Admiral Abe had detached his battleships and three destroyers from Admiral Kondo's main body. He had sailed south for the Shortlands, making rendezvous with *Nagara* and eleven more destroyers, among them *Amatsukaze* under Commander Hara.

They sped down The Slot to bombard Henderson Field, and they ran into a fortuitous rain squall.

Thick clouds clotted overhead. Rain fell in sheets. The sky darkened as though night had fallen, and Abe jubilantly ordered his ships to keep on course at a steady eighteen knots.

Some of Abe's staff officers aboard flagship *Hiei* objected. Although the squall certainly would protect the ships against surprise attack, it also made it dangerous to keep plowing ahead in complex formation.

Admiral Abe had formed his fleet into a tight double crescent. Half the destroyers formed a leading arc about five miles ahead of *Nagara* and the other destroyers, which formed a second arc.

Following in column were *Hiei* and *Kirishima* better than a mile apart. Some of Abe's officers thought the fleet should slow down, or else risk collision in the darkness, but Abe replied:

"We must maintain this speed to reach the target area in good time."[2]

Charging south almost blindly, his men sweating despite the drenching rain, Admiral Abe pressed ahead.

And the covering squall stayed with him at the same speed.

"Twenty-four torpedo bombers headed yours."

The message was from Paul Mason at Buin, and it was acted upon immediately by the second group of American ships in Iron Bottom Bay.

Kelly Turner had brought them in early that morning of November 12. They had begun unloading hurriedly, and the 182nd Infantry was already ashore by the time Mason's warning was received. A few minutes later the Wildcats were taking off and Turner had broken off unloading. He set his transports in two parallel columns of three ships each and sailed them toward Savo. Around them cruisers and destroyers bristled with antiaircraft barrels.

Shortly after two o'clock the Bettys were sighted circling over eastern Florida Island. They had formed two groups, north and south, to make the customary "anvil" attack from both sides. Turner deliberately baited the northern group by turning right to give them his ships' broadsides.

The Bettys came boring in.

A ferocious storm of steel swept among them. One by one they began to crash into the sea, but many of them still dropped their torpedoes.

Turner swung his ships left. Only his narrow sterns beckoned to the Bettys, and their torpedoes ran harmlessly by either side of the transports.

To the south, Wildcats from Henderson ripped through the second group. Eight minutes after the enemy attack began, it was over and only one of the twenty-four Bettys, and five of eight escorting Zeros, had survived.

Destroyer *Buchanan*, damaged during that storm of American antiaircraft fire, was put out of action and sent home, while the heavy cruiser *San Francisco* had been slightly damaged by an enemy suicider who had deliberately crashed into the after control station.

Satisfied, Kelly Turner turned his ships around and resumed unloading.

Hiroaki Abe was jubilant. He actually chortled his delight with, "This blessed squall."[3] His spirits rose higher upon receiving a report from the scout plane he had launched before entering the storm. It said: "More than a dozen warships seen off Lunga."[4]

Abe smiled, and said: "If Heaven continues to side with us like this, we may not even have to do business with them."[5]

Heaven, it seemed, had no intention of deserting him; for the storm still raged around his ships.

Rainfall on Guadalcanal muffled Carlson's Raiders in their approach to an unsuspecting company of Japanese. Guided by Sergeant Major Vouza, the Raiders had moved stealthily up narrow native trails to the tiny village of Asimana on the upper Metapona River. They saw, to their satisfaction, that many of the enemy were bathing in the river. Colonel Carlson waited patiently until his men were in position. Then, he spoke one word:

"Fire!"

There were only a few minutes of massacre. Not one of 120 Japanese soldiers survived. The Raiders left their unburied bodies there to rot in the jungle, quickly resuming their pursuit of the harried Colonel Shoji.

The prospect of foul weather as a cloak to conceal the movement of the Tokyo Express did little to cheer Rear Admiral Raizo Tanaka, sortying from the Shortlands that afternoon. Aboard flagship *Hayashio*, Tanaka led twelve destroyers, eleven transports and 14,000 men toward Tassafaronga. But he had no faith in the fickle Solomons weather, and he also still thought that it was foolhardy to attempt to reinforce Guadalcanal in the face of Henderson's air power. Tanaka did not think that Abe would be able to demolish the field any more than Kurita had done so a month ago, and he wondered how many of his ships were going to survive.[6]

As Tanaka's ships neared Bougainville the weather began clearing.

Jack Read was on the run.

Having been warned by his scouts that the Japanese at Buka Passage were coming after him, he had notified Australia and been advised to flee, maintaining radio silence.

Read moved confidently into the high mountains on northern Bougainville. On the second day of his flight, November 12, a hot hazy morning sun turned into an afternoon downpour. Read and his scouts and the carriers bearing the teleradio slipped and swore while climbing higher to elude the pursuing Japanese.

They reached a mountain peak just as the rain stopped. Sunlight poured through a hole in rapidly dissolving clouds. The mists parted and the horizon became clear. Sailing down it in orderly formation were eleven large Japanese transports protected by twelve destroyers.

They were heading southeast.

Jack Read ordered his radio set up immediately and began broadcasting.

Although the storm was staying with Hiroaki Abe he had no reason to be so confident.

An American Catalina had sighted and reported him early that morning, even as he made rendezvous with Commander Hara's column, and now, Jack Read had warned Kelly Turner of the Tokyo Express's approach.

Turner realized immediately that this was the enemy's big push.

Abe's big ships were either out to sink Turner's transports or bombard Henderson Field. Kelly Turner was confident that he could lead the transports, already ninety per cent unloaded, south to safety.

But what of Henderson Field?

It must not be bombarded. It must not because the planes of Cactus Air Force would then be unable to rise to intercept the enemy reinforcements—the heart of the entire Japanese operation —the planes from *Enterprise* would not be able to land on Guadalcanal to join them, and because one more day, at least, must be gained to allow Admiral Kinkaid's powerful battleships time enough to enter the battle.

But to save the airfield, to gain the day, to stop the powerful enemy on this ominous and onrushing night of Thursday the twelfth and Friday the thirteenth, Kelly Turner had only two heavy and three light cruisers and eight destroyers. Nevertheless, he ordered them to halt the enemy—to stop the bombardment at all costs.

Turner gave command of this force to Rear Admiral Daniel Callaghan.

Admiral Callaghan had been Vice-Admiral Ghormley's chief of staff. It was Callaghan who had sat in silence at the acrimonious conference in the Fijis during which Frank Jack Fletcher had curtly advised Turner and Vandegrift that they would receive minimum carrier support for the invasion of Guadalcanal. After Halsey had relieved Ghormley, bringing his own chief of staff with him, Callaghan had gone back to sea.

He belonged there. Handsome with his shock of thick white hair and his jet-black eyebrows, his large dreamy eyes and straight, strong features, he might have been an ancient Celtic wanderer sailing a tossing coracle toward some undiscovered shore. Even his men idolized him, as does not happen often in any navy, and they called him "Uncle Dan."

But he had neither the experience nor the training for the mission given to him by Turner.

Callaghan was chosen because he was senior to Norman Scott, the victor of Cape Esperance, who was also in the Bay aboard his flag cruiser *Atlanta*. Scott's very victory also seems to have had inordinate influence on Callaghan, for he formed his ships in the same sort of column which had crossed the T on Aritomo Goto a month before.

Americans had yet to learn that the column was not the best formation to employ against the night-fighting, torpedo-firing Japanese. But it was chosen because of Cape Esperance, because it made maneuvering in narrow waters less risky, and because, presumably, it made communication between ships easier. So Callaghan set his ships in column: destroyers *Cushing, Laffey, Sterett,* and *O'Bannon* in the lead, heavy cruisers *Atlanta, San Francisco,* and *Portland,* followed by lights *Helena* and *Juneau* in the center; and in the rear, destroyers *Aaron Ward, Barton, Monssen,* and *Fletcher.* Unfortunately, Callaghan did not make good use of his best radar ships. They were not in the lead; moreover, *Atlanta* with inferior radar was ahead of *San Francisco* with excellent radar. Finally, no plan of battle was issued.

Nevertheless, for all of these oversights and omissions, the Americans led by Callaghan and Scott did possess that single quality which, so often in this desperate struggle, had extricated the unwary or unwise from a defeat of their own devising.

And that was valor.

The Tokyo Express was turning around.

Shortly before midnight Admiral Tanaka received word from Combined Fleet that the landing at Tassafaronga had been delayed until the morning of November 14. Admiral Mikawa was going to follow up Admiral Abe's bombardment by shelling Henderson Field on the night of November 13, rather than on the morning of that day.

From flagship *Hayashio* came the signal to reverse course and retire to the Shortlands.

There was tension on Guadalcanal. It was almost a living quality, like the gases composing the atmosphere. It was a quivering electric dread attuned to the jagged flashes of lightning flitting over the island in the wake of the clearing rain. It was brittle, like the emergent bright stars overhead.

General Vandegrift felt it. He was aware of Abe's approach, and of the outgunned fleet which Admiral Callaghan had to oppose him. The general's staff also knew that this was the night. They went to bed not only fully clad, as was customary on Guadalcanal, but wearing pistol belts and clutching hand grenades. Some of them expected to use these in the morning. So did all of Vandegrift's men, crouching beside their guns or perched on the edge of their holes. They spoke in low voices, often pausing to glance fearfully at the sky or to look furtively over their shoulders. It was as though they expected the enemy from every quarter. Upon the sinking of the new moon beneath the dark mountains their voices became hushed and whispering.

Out on the Bay a nine-knot easterly breeze blew gently into the faces of Callaghan's lookouts. At ten o'clock, Callaghan saw Turner's transports safely out of the eastern entrance, and reversed course toward Savo. His ships were still in column. He would make no attempt to flank the approaching Abe to launch torpedoes.

It was to be a straight-ahead plunge aimed at the enemy battleships.

It was now Friday the thirteenth and Admiral Abe's divine squall had fallen behind.

Hiei and *Kirishima* and their fifteen sister furies had sailed away from the storm after the admiral had reformed his scattered formation. At half-past one, one of *Amatsukaze's* lookouts cried, "Small island, 60 degrees to left."

Commander Hara looked to his left and saw the black round silhouette of Savo Island.

"Prepare for gun and torpedo attack to starboard!" Hara shouted. "Gun range, three thousand meters. Torpedo firing angle, fifteen degrees."[7]

Aboard *Hiei*, Admiral Abe was studying reports. General Hyakutake's headquarters had radioed that the rain had cleared on Guadalcanal. Scout planes had taken off from Bougainville. There were still no reports of enemy ships. Confident and elated, Abe ordered *Hiei* and *Kirishima* to prepare for bombardment. Type-3 shells, thin-skinned 2000-pound projectiles each containing hundreds of incendiary bombs, were stacked on the decks around the 14-inch gun turrets.

A quarter hour later, from *Hiei's* own masthead lookout came the frantic shout: "Four black objects ahead . . . look like warships. Five degrees to starboard. Eight thousand meters . . . unsure yet."

From *Hiei's* bridge came the cry: "Is eight thousand correct? Confirm."

"It may be nine thousand, sir."[8]

Hiroaki Abe was stunned. He had thought to bombard Guadalcanal unchallenged. He had piled the decks of his precious battleships with huge shells that needed but a single enemy hit to detonate them and turn *Hiei* and *Kirishima* into floating holocausts.

"Replace all those incendiaries with armor piercing," he yelled. "Set turrets for firing forward."[9] Abe staggered to his chair and waited in agony. It would take at least ten minutes to change over.

And the range between forces was closing rapidly.

The Americans had sighted the Japanese and they had sighted them first.

Cushing at the head of the column had nearly collided with onrushing *Yudachi* and *Harusame*. Lieutenant Commander Edward Parker flashed the word and turned hard left to avoid collision. Behind him, his quick turn had piled up the American column.

"What are you doing?" Admiral Callaghan asked *Atlanta,* directly ahead of him.

"Avoiding our own destroyers," came the reply.[10]

It was then that *Hiei's* lookout sighted the Americans, then that the gunners and seamen aboard *Hiei* and *Kirishima* rushed from their battle stations to haul the vulnerable Type-3 shells below, stampeding the magazines, pushing and kicking each other to get at the armor-piercing shells lodged deep inside—and it was then that confusion in Admiral Callaghan's column became compounded.

Excited voices began crackling over the Talk Between Ships. Reports of target bearings multiplied, but no one could tell if they were true bearings or merely relative to the reporting ships. No one knew which target to take under fire or when. From little *Cushing* still out in the lead came the voice of the destroyer leader, Commander Thomas Stokes, pleading:

"Shall I let them have a couple of fish?"[11]

"Affirmative," came the reply, but it was too late. *Yudachi* and *Harusame* had raced off into the darkness.

Four minutes had passed before Callaghan gave the order: "Stand by to open fire!" Another precious four minutes were to slip by before he bellowed: "Commence firing! Give 'em hell, boys!"

And then, with surprise squandered and opportunity lost, the Americans called upon their last resource—their valor—and went plunging full tilt toward the mastodonic foe.

One of the most furious sea fights in all history had begun.

Ashore on Guadalcanal, veterans of the campaign—Japanese as well as American—looked at each other in open-mouthed, overawed incredulity. Never before had the iron tongues of midnight bayed with such a maniacal clanging. Out there giants clad in foot-thick steel were contending with one another, and never before had the thunder of their blows rolled so mightily over glistening black Bay water.

Scarlet star shells shot into the sky with the horrible beauty of hell. Searchlight beams licked out like great pale crisscrossing tongues. Ships in silhouette, big and small, plunged wildly toward each other, heeled away, dashed in and out of the smoke, blew up, blazed, vanished—or reappeared with spouts of white and orange gushing from their guns. The surface of Iron Bottom Bay was like polished black marble shot with the bubbles of torpedo wakes, swirled with the foaming trails of careening ships, splashed with the red or the yellow of burning vessels.

And above the roar and reverberation of the battle came the voice of Admiral Callaghan, crying:

"We want the big ones, boys, we want the big ones!"

A trio of American destroyers was charging the big ones. They had broken through Abe's screen and taken on great *Hiei*. *Cushing* in the van loosed a spread of torpedoes from a half-mile range, missing, but forcing *Hiei* to turn away. But then *Cushing* was illuminated in searchlight beams and enemy shells began to take her apart.

Laffey swept in so close that she narrowly avoided collision. *Hiei's* pagoda-like masts swayed over the little American as she dashed past, pouring a torrent of automatic shellfire into *Hiei's* decks. Fires broke out aboard the big Japanese. But then *Hiei* bellowed and little *Laffey* began to burn.

O'Bannon bored in last. She came in so close that *Hiei* could not depress her 14-inch guns to shoot at her. Great shells howled harmlessly over *O'Bannon's* masts while her gunners raked the Japanese with guns aimed in the light of her flames. Then *O'Bannon* was gone, sheering sharply left to avoid burning *Laffey*, tossing life jackets to sailors struggling in the water as she passed.

Now *San Francisco* was battering *Hiei*. But the enemy battleship thundered back. Fourteen-inchers tore into *San Francisco's* bridge to kill Admiral Callaghan and almost every American there.

Norman Scott was also dead. *Atlanta* had been the first to be caught in enemy searchlights. With her port bridge clearly illuminated, bracketing warships gave her her death blows and killed the hero of Cape Esperance.

Thereafter the fight became a melee. It was a free-for-all, ship-for-ship and shot for shot, with Japanese firing upon Japanese and American upon American. Every ship but *Fletcher* was hit. *Barton* blew up, *Monssen* sank, *Cushing* and *Laffey* were lost, and so were the cruisers *Atlanta* and *Juneau*—the latter finished off by a Japanese submarine as she tried to stagger home from battle.

But the Japanese were fleeing.

Mighty *Kirishima,* late to enter the battle, was already streaking north at the head of a general retirement.

Every one of Abe's ships had been staggered. *Yudachi* was sinking and so was *Akatsuki. Amatsukaze* had been battered. A cascade of shells had fallen flashing around Commander Hara on his bridge, cutting down his men, blowing his executive officer over the side but leaving his legs behind, and so crippling the ship that *Amatsukaze* had to be steered manually.

Slowly, in the dawn lighting that glassy metallic sea, dragging herself past survivors lying burned, wounded, and dazed on their life rafts, or struggling to keep afloat in oily, debris-laden, shark-infested waters, little *Amatsukaze* made her way home.

Off his port bow Hara saw *Hiei.* The great ship was dying. She was almost dead in the water, crawling, with jammed rudder, in a wide aimless circle. Marine bombers from Henderson Field were already slashing at her. They shot down the eight Zeros flying cover above the battleship while Major Joe Sailer knocked out *Hiei's* remaining antiaircraft turret with a well-planted bomb, after which they bombed and torpedoed her without interruption.

But she refused to go down.

"We've *got* to sink her!" Henderson's pilots cried, landing to rearm and refuel and to return to the attack. "If we don't the admirals will stop building carriers and start building battleships again."[12]

Again and again they struck at *Hiei,* but on and on she crawled, glowing like a great red gridiron, circling and circling while destroyers ministered to her like cubs caring for a wounded lioness, until, at nightfall, after survivors and Admiral Abe had been taken off, the Japanese scuttled her and she sank with a hiss and an oil slick two miles long.

But on that morning of Friday the thirteenth, the heart of Commander Hara was heavy with grief as he saw the Americans hurtling down from the skies. They came, he knew, from that Henderson Field which had not been bombarded.

Nevertheless, Gunichi Mikawa was already coming down The Slot determined to succeed where Hiroaki Abe had failed.

Admiral Halsey was aware of Mikawa's approach, and he planned to intercept him with the battleships from Admiral Kinkaid's *Enterprise* force. To send these capital ships into the narrow and treacherous waters of Iron Bottom Bay was not, as Halsey knew, consonant with accepted naval doctrine. But the safety of Henderson Field seemed to him well worth the risk of his heavies, and so, on November 13, confident that the winds favored Kinkaid, he broke radio silence to tell him to put *South Dakota* and *Washington* and four destroyers under Rear Admiral Willis Lee with instructions to lay an ambush east of Savo Island. Kinkaid replied:

FROM LEE'S PRESENT POSITION IMPOSSIBLE FOR HIM TO REACH SAVO BEFORE 0800 TOMORROW.

Halsey was stunned. Mikawa would have a clear path to Henderson Field.

In the early afternoon of Friday the thirteenth the Tokyo Express moved toward Guadalcanal again.

Tanaka's eleven transports were in a four-column formation sailing at eleven knots with a dozen destroyers deployed to the front and either side.

Tanaka was still in flagship *Hayashio*, which means "Fast running tide." The tide, it seemed to Tanaka, who had heard of the disaster which had overtaken Abe, was running fast against Japan.[13]

At eight o'clock that morning *Enterprise* was still 280 miles south of Henderson Field. But she launched planes, some of which reached Guadalcanal in time to join the attack on *Hiei*, and continued to steam north.

All day long *Big E* remained buttoned up with her men at battle stations while her scout planes fanned out in search of the Japanese carriers and her combat air patrol flew overhead. But no enemy ships or aircraft were sighted. At dusk her men were secured from General Quarters and went below. Mighty *South Dakota* and *Washington* and their destroyers slid away from the screen and vanished into the darkness ahead. They could not stop Mikawa tonight, but they would at least be in the battle zone by tomorrow.

Enterprise ran steadily north at twenty-five knots.

It was happening again. It was not supposed to happen, Callaghan and Scott were supposed to have ended it, but there it was: Louie the Louse, flares, the lethal thunder-and-lightning of the sea cannonade, and flames engulfing Henderson Field.

Admiral Mikawa had brought six cruisers and six destroyers down to Savo. With flagship *Chokai, Kinugasa, Isuzu,* and two destroyers, Mikawa guarded the western gate at Savo while heavy cruisers *Suzuya* and *Maya,* escorted by light cruiser *Tenryu* and four destroyers, entered the Bay to bombard.

They hurled about a thousand rounds of eight-inch shell into the airfield, until six little torpedo boats under Lieutenant Hugh Robinson crept from Tulagi Harbor to launch torpedoes at them and scare them off.

Mikawa sailed jubilantly north on that morning of November 14, delighted to see his success celebrated in the intercepted plain-language radio message which Vandegrift had sent to Halsey:

BEING HEAVILY SHELLED.

In Washington the news that the Japanese had once again penetrated American defenses to batter Henderson Field produced a pessimism and a tension unrivaled throughout the campaign. Upon receipt of reports that heavy Japanese reinforcements were sailing down The Slot unopposed, even President Roosevelt began to think that Guadalcanal might have to be evacuated.[14]

Mikawa's guns had wrecked eighteen American planes and had churned up the airstrips. But they had not knocked out the field entirely, nor had Admiral Kondo sent any aircraft from *Hiyo* or *Junyo* down to protect Mikawa from likely pursuit. At dawn of the fourteenth, while fires still raged and ammunition dumps exploded, pilots raced to their armed planes and took off.

They found Mikawa's ships. They put two torpedoes into big

Kinugasa, leaving her to be sunk by pilots from *Enterprise*, who also bombed *Chokai*, *Maya*, and *Isuzu*. Admiral Mikawa, who had intended to provide indirect cover for Admiral Tanaka's ships, was forced to retire to the Shortlands.

Tanaka sailed south all alone.

Since dawn, when a few Flying Fortresses had been driven off by covering Zeros, Tanaka the Tenacious had stood on *Hayashio's* bridge anxiously scanning the skies. He had seen flights of enemy planes but they did not attack him. He conjectured that they had gone after Mikawa. He was positive that they had not been frightened off by the handful of Zeros circling overhead; all, it seemed, that Admiral Kondo to the north could spare from the crowded decks of *Hiyo* and *Junyo*.

At noon Tanaka's ships were only 150 miles from Guadalcanal, and it was then that the American planes came hurtling out of the sun and the slaughter known as the Buzzard Patrol began.

They flew in from everywhere: from Espiritu Santo, from the Fijis, from Henderson Field, from the decks of *Enterprise* still closing Guadalcanal at high speed. They flew in to bomb or launch torpedoes or to strafe, banking to fly back to base again or to land at Henderson where cooks, clerks, typists, mechanics, Seabees, even riflemen, had formed a human chain to hand along the bombs and bullets that would shatter the Tokyo Express forever.

Wildcats and Airacobras and the newly arrived twin-tailed Lightnings went flashing and slashing among Kondo's pitifully few Zeros and the other eagles racing to the rescue from Rabaul. They shot them down while the Dauntlesses dove or the Forts unleashed their high-level patterns or the Avengers came in low with their fish, and then they, too, went after the transports, screaming in at masthead level to rake the decks of ships already slippery with blood.

They struck five times, from noon until sunset, these pilots of the Buzzard Patrol, and they put six transports on the bottom while sending a stricken seventh staggering back to the Shortlands. Admiral Tanaka's destroyers were powerless to protect their transports. They could only scurry among these burning, listing, sinking charges to take aboard survivors or to fish a weaponless, terrified soldiery from the reddening waters of The Slot.

They *were* red, and so were bunks and bulkheads glowing with heat and visible beneath decks torn open as though by a monster can opener. American pilots sickened in their cockpits to see the slaughter that they were spreading, but they did not remove their hands from gun-buttons or bomb releases. Every enemy soldier spared meant a Japanese alive to kill Americans on Guadalcanal. And the bullets continued to spurt among the bobbing heads, and bomb followed bomb into smoking, settling ships.

Tanaka the Tenacious plowed on.

He had only four of his original eleven transports, his destroyers were widely scattered by hours of evasive zigzagging, but he was nevertheless determined to make Tassafaronga. After nightfall relieved him of his ordeal, he withdrew to the north. He would wait there until morning, resuming course after Admiral Kondo had bombarded Henderson Field.

Nobutake Kondo was already rushing south with mighty *Kirishima* escorted by cruisers *Atago, Takao, Sendai,* and *Nagara* and nine destroyers. Kondo was infuriated by two days of disaster. He would brook no further delay, no additional losses of ships and men, and he would personally see to the obliteration of the enemy airfield. Kondo was not only spoiling for a fight, he expected one.

In this, Ching Chong China Lee would not disappoint him.

Rear Admiral Willis Lee received the first part of his alliterative nickname at the Naval Academy, and the next two parts during extensive service in China, a land in which his last name, although spelled Li, was far from rare, and where he had befriended a Marine major named Vandegrift.

On the night of November 14, Ching Lee came to Vandegrift's aid, leading the battleships and destroyers he had detached from Kinkaid's force the night before. Screened by destroyers *Walke, Benham, Preston,* and *Gwin,* Admiral Lee took *Washington* and *South Dakota* around Guadalcanal's western tip. He went sweeping west of Savo, but found nothing, only the glare of Tanaka's burning transports.

Lee's six-ship column turned north, and then east to put Savo on the right and enter Iron Bottom Bay.

The bay was calm. Its waters gleamed faintly in the light of a first-quarter moon setting behind the mountains of Cape Esperance. Lee's deep-water sailors could sniff a sweet land breeze redolent of honeysuckle. They could see very little, only the heights of land looming to either side. Needles on the magnetic compasses fluttered violently as they passed, in grim reminder of their purpose, over the hulks of the sunken vessels that gave the bay its name.

Ching Lee tried to raise Guadalcanal by radio. Back came the reply:

"We do not recognize you."[15]

The admiral thought of his friend from China, and countered:

"Cactus, this is Lee. Tell your big boss Ching Lee is here and wants the latest information."[16]

No answer. But then, out of nowhere, but over the Talk Between Ships:

"There go two big ones, but I don't know whose they are."[17]

Lee stiffened. The chatter was from a trio of torpedo boats to his left. He spoke quickly to Guadalcanal again: "Refer your big boss about Ching Lee; Chinese, catchee? Call off your boys!"[18] And then, more sharply to the torpedo boats themselves:

"This is Ching Chong China Lee. All PTs retire."[19]

Over the Talk Between Ships a skeptical voice murmured:

"It's a phony. Let's slip the bum a pickle."[20]

"I said this is Ching Chong China Lee," the admiral roared. "Get the hell out of the way! I'm coming through!"[21]

Startled, the tiny craft scuttled aside and the battleships went through.

Lee led them west again toward Savo, straight toward *Sendai* and a destroyer coming east as Kondo's vanguard. Shortly after eleven o'clock, *Washington* and *South Dakota's* 16-inch guns boomed, and the battle was joined.

As always it began badly for the Americans. Japanese crews quickly launched shoals of shark-shaped steel fish. *Preston, Benham,* and *Walke* took the full brunt of them, of enemy gunfire as well, and were given their death blows. *South Dakota* was caught in enemy searchlights and an entire Japanese bombardment force opened up on her. She shuddered under their blows. She fought back, shooting out the searchlights—but Japanese shells tore into her superstructure, sweeping away her search radars and all but one gunnery radar.

But then mighty *Washington* found *Kirishima.*

Again and again her 16-inch guns flashed and roared, again and again her five-inchers fired starshell to illuminate the enemy giant or to rip her decks. *Kirishima* was staggered repeatedly. Nine of those terrible 2700-pound armor-piercers tore into her vitals. Topside she was a mass of flames, she was drifting helplessly, she was done. *Kirishima* would join her sister-queen, *Hiei,* on the bottom of the sea. And like *Hiei's* ladies-in-waiting, all of *Kirishima's* escort, excepting sinking *Ayanami,* were turning to flee. *South Dakota* and *Washington* had trained their terrible guns against *Atago* and *Takao,* who were caught in friendly searchlights, and these battered cruisers led the flight to the north.

Washington gave pursuit alone, for *South Dakota* and *Gwin* had withdrawn, but she found nothing—not even the Japanese transports whom Admiral Lee was also hungrily hunting—and so Ching Chong China Lee swung south of Guadalcanal to sail back to Nouméa in triumph.

Behind him, Admiral Raizo Tanaka began shepherding his four remaining transports for a last-ditch run into Guadalcanal. He asked Admiral Mikawa for permission to beach the troopships, but Mikawa replied: "Negative." He appealed to the retiring Admiral Kondo aboard *Atago,* and received the answer: "Run aground and unload troops!"[22]

Full steam ahead, with only *Hayashio* to guard them, the four transports raced toward Tassafaronga. Before the sun was up they had reached it and driven themselves hard aground almost line abreast. Tanaka the Tenacious turned to collect his scattered destroyers—many of them low in the water with rescued troops—and lead them sadly north.

And then came the dawn of November 15.

Men of the First Marine Division who had passed another of so many apprehensive and thundering nights looked west once more, and saw, at Tassafaronga, the familiar sight of enemy ships aground. But these ships were burning. American aircraft were already bombing them from the air, an American destroyer, *Meade,* was shelling them from the sea, and American long-range artillery was battering them from the beaches.

Air, land, and sea, it was symbolic of this savage struggle to wrest this poisonous green hag of an island from the hands of the Japanese; and now it was ending that way, for the crucial, three-day naval battle of Guadalcanal was over. The Americans had won. They had lost two cruisers and five destroyers, but they had sunk two Japanese battleships, one cruiser and three destroyers, as well as eleven precious troop transports with almost all of a 3000-man Naval Landing Force and half of the 38th Division.

Up on the ridges of Guadalcanal the Marines looked down at the beached and burning transports, and they smiled. It was full of savage satisfaction, that smile, nourished by a merciless and gloating glee. One hundred long days ago these aching, old-young men had begun this battle, and at any moment, upon any instantaneous hour, the black and bloody defeat symbolized by those burning transports could have been theirs.

But they had held, these Marines, the Army had come in, the Navy had fought back, and now, on the morning of November 15, Guadalcanal was truly saved.

Chapter 3

ON THE morning of November 15, Major General Alexander Archer Vandegrift also knew that the Japanese were beaten, and he sent the following dispatch to Admiral Halsey:

"We believe the enemy has suffered a crushing defeat. We thank Lee for his sturdy effort of last night. We thank Kinkaid for his intervention of yesterday. Our own air has been grand in its relentless pounding of the foe. Those efforts we appreciate, but our greatest homage goes to Scott, Callaghan and their men who with magnificent courage against seemingly hopeless odds drove back the first hostile stroke and made success possible. To them the men of Cactus lift their battered helmets in deepest admiration."[1]

Halsey agreed with Vandegrift's jubilant estimate. Only minutes before he had showed his staff reports of destruction of the enemy transports, and told them: "We've got the bastards licked!"[2]

But the enemy thought otherwise.

Immediately after proclaiming a smashing Japanese victory in the naval battle of Guadalcanal, Imperial General Headquarters set about the actual destruction of those Americans whom they had just annihilated on paper. This time, the fifth, there was to be intelligent respect for enemy air power.

Before any reinforcements were sent to Guadalcanal, an airfield was to be constructed in the Shortlands, the one recently completed in New Georgia was to be expanded, and a third base sought farther down the Solomons ladder.

This plan, however, was quickly wrecked by the Americans.

Cactus Air Force, at a top strength of 150 planes and still expanding by early December, bombed the Japanese base at Munda on New Georgia into twisted futility, showering a similar interdiction upon Japanese attempts to construct supporting bases. Far to the north, American submarines, gnawing for months on

Japanese supply lines, had begun to bite through. Finally, Australian and American soldiers had pressed Japanese forces on New Guinea back toward Buna-Gona, where they were to suffer ultimate defeat and General MacArthur was to gain the springboard from which he would drive up the New Guinea coast.

At bay on New Guinea, barely hanging on on Guadalcanal, the Japanese were not able to send the 51st Division and an independent brigade to the aid of Lieutenant General Haruyoshi Hyakutake, as they had planned.

They could only struggle to supply him, and this too became a costly ordeal.

The first method of supply was by drums. They were filled with rice or other supplies, linked to each other by rope, lashed to the decks of destroyers for quick transit down The Slot, and then cast into the water off Tassafaronga where they would either be washed ashore or caught and pulled aground by waiting swimmers.

The first attempt at drum-supply produced the Battle of Tassafaronga. On the night of November 30 the Tokyo Express, with Raizo Tanaka still at the helm, collided with a superior American force of cruisers and destroyers under Rear Admiral Carleton Wright. The cargo of drummed-rice had to be abandoned, but Tanaka the Tenacious gave the Americans another bloody lesson in night torpedo-fighting. His ships sank *Northampton,* put a hole big enough to admit a bus in the side of *Honolulu,* and knocked *Pensacola, New Orleans,* and *Minneapolis* out of action for nearly a year. For this, Tanaka only suffered the loss of destroyer *Takanami.*

On December 7 a second drum-supply attempt was broken up by American aircraft and those torpedo boats, which, now arriving at Guadalcanal in numbers, were beginning to take over at night where Cactus Air Force left off by day. And while the American sea and air arms were blocking the Tokyo Express, the ground troops had gone over to the offensive.

On December 9, command on Guadalcanal passed from the Marine General Vandegrift to the Army General Patch. Patch wisely decided to wait until he had sufficient forces before attacking. Eventually he would have an entire corps—the XIV—consisting of the Americal Division, the 25th Infantry Division, the Second Marine Division, and, later on, but not committed to combat, the 43rd Infantry Division. With these troops, Patch went out after Hyakutake and his diseased and hungry 17th Army.

The Japanese resisted stubbornly, nevertheless a slow, grinding, overwhelming American assault—supported by air and artillery—eventually dislodged them from their positions west of the Matanikau. Meanwhile, in Tokyo, staff officers exchanged blows during bitter debates over whether Guadalcanal was to be reinforced or evacuated.[3] The evacuation party, led by Premier Tojo, gradually gained the upper hand. Finally, at a conference of Imperial General Headquarters convened in the Imperial Palace, Japan admitted defeat. It was decided to evacuate.

The date of that historic decision was December 31, 1942, and by that time, most of the men who had landed at Guadalcanal on August 7 had left the island.

They had begun going out to their ships in late December, these men of the First Marine Division, and their departure would continue through early January. Some of them had been on the lines more than four months without relief, and they came down to the beach at Lunga ragged, bearded, and bony. Some of them had hardly the strength to walk to the boats, and yet, before they left, all of them had visited their cemetery.

It was called "Flanders Field," and it was a neat cleared square cut into the Lunga coconut groves. Each grave was covered with a palm frond and marked with a rough cross onto which mess gear and identification tags were nailed. Departing Marines knelt or stood there in prayerful farewell, wondering, dazedly, how it was that there were so few graves.

In all, 774 Marines of this division had died, 1962 had been wounded, and another 5400 had been stricken with malaria. Ultimately, the Second Marine Division casualties would reach 268 dead and 932 wounded, so that all Marine ground losses would total 1042 dead and 2894 wounded. Army casualties would total 550 dead and 1289 wounded, making a grand total in American ground casualties of 1592 dead and 4183 wounded. American naval casualties, never to be compiled, would certainly equal, perhaps even surpass this, while the much smaller losses among the airmen would also never be known.

Yet, the Japanese would lose 28,800 soldiers on Guadalcanal itself, many thousands more would die at sea, 2362 pilots and airmen would be lost, and unknown thousands of sailors would also perish—in all, a probable 50,000 men lost in the unsuccessful struggle to recover "this insignificant island in the South Seas."

But victory, as these Marines knew, is not always measured by casualties, nor do casualties describe how victory is gained. Sacrifice and valor and doggedness and skill, these gain victory, and these, though unmeasurable, at least may be described. In their cemetery, these Marines found an epitaph describing this greatest of Pacific victories and most glorious of American stands. It was a poem. Its words had been painfully picked out on a mess gear with the point of a bayonet. It said:

> *And when he gets to Heaven*
> *To St. Peter he will tell:*
> *"One more Marine reporting, sir—*
> *I've served my time in Hell."*

So they went out to their ships, with "hell" etched on their faces and evident in their sticks of bones and ragged dungarees. They went out so weak that they could not climb the cargo nets and the sailors, weeping openly, had to haul them aboard or fish them from the Bay into which they had dropped. They lay on the grimy decks of these blessed ships, gasping, but happy. And then they heard the anchor chains clanking slowly up the hawse pipes and they struggled to their feet for a last look at Guadalcanal.

They could not see, below the eastern horizon, that Aola Bay where Martin Clemens had begun an ordeal that was to end, in early December, with evacuation and a furlough in Australia. But they could see Red Beach, where they had landed, and Koli Point, where so many enemy had landed. There, still to their left, was the Tenaru, that evil green lagoon and sandspit in which the Japanese myth of the superman had been buried, and for the loss of which Colonel Ichiki had killed himself. To the right lay Henderson Field and all around it those sister airfields busy with two-way aerial traffic. Beyond it was Bloody Ridge which Red Mike Edson and the Raiders had held against the Kawaguchi Brigade, but the fields of kunai fertilized by the blood of the Sendai Division were not visible. Grassy Knoll was, though, rearing its tan hillside above the jungle roof, still, as it had been since August 7, an unattainable first-day's objective. On the right, west of Lunga Lagoon and those rapidly rising piles of food and supplies, lay the broad mouth of the Matanikau, and west of that, the hook of Point Cruz, and then, stretching far away to the western horizon, Kukumbona and Tassafaronga, and the last of the Japanese landing places from which, on an early February night, the Tokyo Express would depart on its last run, taking with it the last men of the first Japanese army in history to submit to the disgrace of evacuation.

All of these landmarks these men could see in that last long searching look made half of hatred and half of a warrior's poignant love for the battlefield that made him. And they could see also, while motors throbbed beneath their feet, while the transports made the customary sunset departure for the covering darkness of the open sea, they could see a round red sun beginning to set behind Cape Esperance.

It was sinking, like the Rising Sun of Japan, into the dark Pacific.

NOTES

PART I—THE CHALLENGE

Chapter 1

1. Morison, Samuel Eliot, *The Two-Ocean War: A Short History of the United States Navy in the Second World War* (Boston: Little, Brown, 1963), p. 35.

2. Fuchida, Capt. Mitsuo, and Okumiya, Masatake, *Midway: The Battle That Doomed Japan* (Annapolis: United States Naval Institute, 1955), p. 48. (Imperial General Headquarters was composed of two sections or divisions. The Navy Section was presided over by the Chief of the Navy General Staff and the Army Section by the Chief of the Army General Staff. These two sections "consulted" on strategy, operations, and allocation of forces. After an agreement was reached, a "Central Agreement" was drawn up and signed by the section Chiefs. Each Chief issued orders to his subordinates and they, in turn, were to consult each other at the lower, implementing level. Thus, the Japanese military operated on the basis of "cooperation" rather than on the American basis of "control" or "unity of command," and this, as will be seen, was not always conducive to clarity.)

3. *Ibid*, p. 11.

4. Clear, Lt. Col. Warren J., *Close-up of a Jap Fighting Man* (*Infantry Journal*, November 1942), p. 16.

5. Sakai, Saburo, with Caidin, Martin, and Saito, Fred, *Samurai: Flying the Zero in WW II with Japan's Fighter Ace* (New York: Ballantine Books, 1963), p. 72.

6. Feldt, Cmdr. Eric A., R.A.N., *The Coastwatchers* (New York and Melbourne: Oxford University Press, 1946), p. 78.

7. Clemens, Martin, *A Coastwatcher's Diary* (Unpublished manuscript on file at Research & Records [R&R], Historical Branch, G-3, Headquarters, U. S. Marine Corps.), p. 4. (In this passage, and all other quotations in pidgin English, I have taken the liberty of altering Clemens's faithful presentation of that *lingua franca* as it is spoken by the Solomon Islanders to what I believe may be a more readable form of pidgin.)

8. Halsey, Fleet Adm. William F., and Bryan, Lt. Cmdr. J., III, *Admiral Halsey's Story* (New York: McGraw-Hill Book Co., 1947), p. 101.

9. Vandegrift, General Alexander A., and Asprey, Robert B., *Once a Marine: The Memoirs of General A. A. Vandegrift* (New York: Norton, 1964), p. 61.

10. Pierce, Lt. Col. P. N., *The Unsolved Mystery of Pete Ellis* (*Marine Corps Gazette,* February 1962), pp. 34, 40.

11. Smith, General Holland M., *Coral and Brass: Howlin' Mad Smith's Own Story of the Marines in the Pacific* (New York: Scribner's, 1949), p. 177; and Davis, Burke, *Marine!: The Life of Chesty Puller* (Boston: Little, Brown, 1962), pp. 71, 72.

12. Davis, *op. cit.,* pp. 71, 72.

13. Vandegrift and Asprey, *op. cit.,* p. 25.

14. Author's recollection.

15. *Ibid.*

Chapter 2

1. Ito, Masanori, *The End of the Imperial Japanese Navy* (New York: Norton, 1956), p. 18.

2. *Ibid,* p. 19.

3. *Ibid,* p. 36.

4. Fuchida and Okumiya, *op. cit.,* p. 57.

5. *Ibid,* p. 60.

6. Vandegrift and Asprey, *op. cit.,* p. 100.

7. Halsey and Bryan, *op. cit.,* p. 103.

8. Fuchida and Okumiya, *op. cit.,* p. 71.

Chapter 3

1. Clemens, *op. cit.,* p. 17.

2. *Ibid,* p. 34.

3. Hara, Cmdr. Tameichi, with Saito, Fred, and Pineau, Roger, *Japanese Destroyer Captain* (New York: Ballantine Books, 1961), p. 97.

4. *Ibid.*

5. *Ibid,* p. 99.

6. Morison, Samuel Eliot, *Coral Sea, Midway and Submarine Action,* Vol. IV. *"History of the United States Navy in the Second World War"* (Boston: Little, Brown, 1960), p. 98.

7. Clemens, *op. cit.,* p. 43.

8. *Ibid,* p. 50.

9. Butterfield, Roger, *Al Schmid: Marine* (New York: Farrar & Rinehart, 1944), p. 57.

10. *Ibid,* p. 58.

11. Vandegrift and Asprey, *op. cit.,* p. 102.

12. *Ibid,* p. 105.

13. *Ibid,* p. 111.

Chapter 4

1. Clemens, *op. cit.,* p. 52.

2. Fuchida and Okumiya, *op. cit.,* p. 75.

3. Ohmae, Capt. Toshikazu, *The Battle of Savo Island* (United States Naval Institute Proceedings, December 1957), p. 1264.

4. *Ibid*, p. 1266.
5. Newcomb, Richard, *Savo: The Incredible Naval Debacle off Guadalcanal* (New York: Holt, Rinehart & Winston, 1961), p. 53.
6. *Ibid*, p. 53.
7. Vandegrift and Asprey, *op. cit.*, p. 46.
8. Author's recollection.
9. Butterfield, *op. cit.*, pp. 64, 65.
10. Griffith, Brig. Gen. Samuel B., II, *The Battle for Guadalcanal* (Philadelphia and New York: Lippincott, 1963), p. 35.
11. Vandegrift and Asprey, *op. cit.*, p. 120.
12. *Ibid*, p. 120.
13. *Ibid*.
14. Griffith, *op. cit.*, p. 35.
15. Author's recollection.

Chapter 5

1. Shigemitsu, Premier Mamoru, *Japan and Her Destiny* (New York: Grosset & Dunlap, 1950), p. 271.
2. Intelligence Summary No. 22, Headquarters, U. S. Army Air Force, Southwest Pacific Area; *History of 28th Bombardment Squadron (19th Bombardment Group)*, 8 Dec. 1941–1 Feb. 1943, p. 16.
3. Clemens, *op. cit.*, p. 124.
4. Author's recollection.
5. Vandegrift and Asprey, *op. cit.*, p. 19.
6. Leckie, Robert, *Strong Men Armed* (New York: Random House, 1962), p. 18.
7. Clemens, *op. cit.*, p. 125.
8. Japanese Eighth Fleet War Diary, Office of Naval Records and Library (ONRL), Document No. 161259, p. 6; Newcomb, *op. cit.*, p. 23.

PART II—ALONE

Chapter 1

1. Griffith, *op. cit.*, p. 46. (General Griffith, then a lieutenant colonel, was Edson's executive officer.)
2. Newcomb, *op. cit.*, p. 23.
3. Sakai et al., *op. cit.*, p. 146.
4. *Ibid*, p. 147.
5. Griffith, *op. cit.*, p. 44.
6. Hara, *op. cit.*, p. 104.
7. *Ibid*, p. 104.
8. Tregaskis, Richard, *Guadalcanal Diary* (New York: Popular Library, 1959), p. 77.
9. Leckie, *op. cit.*, p. 23.
10. Sakai et al., *op. cit.*, p. 156.
11. Griffith, *op. cit.*, p. 47.

Chapter 2

1. Author's recollection.
2. Griffith, *op. cit.*, p. 42.
3. Ohmae, *op. cit.*, p. 1272.
4. Newcomb, *op. cit.*, p. 92.
5. Ohmae, *op. cit.*, p. 1273. (Note: All subsequent Japanese battle orders quoted at Savo are from the same source.)
6. Vandegrift and Asprey, *op. cit.*, p. 130.
7. *Ibid.*

Chapter 3

1. Roscoe, Theodore, *United States Destroyer Operations in World War II* (Annapolis: United States Naval Institute, 1953), p. 153.
2. All these and similar quotations are from monitored Japanese broadcasts on file in the National Archives, Washington, D.C.
3. Letter, Commanding General, South Pacific, to Chief of Staff, U. S. Army, August 11, 1942. OPD 381, PTO1. World War II Archives, Alexandria, Va.
4. Letter, Commanding General, South Pacific, to Chief of Staff, U. S. Army, August 11, 1942. OPD 381, PTO1. World War II Archives, Alexandria, Va.
5. The Americans had a biblical precedent for this ruse. In a dispute with the men of Ephraim, the Israelite leader Jephte set guards at the fords of the Jordan with orders to ask each passerby if he were an Ephraimite. Each man who said "No" was asked to pronounce *"shibboleth,"* the word for an ear of corn or a flood or stream. Inasmuch as the Ephraimites could not make the sound "sh" they always answered *"sibboleth,"* thus betraying their identity. That is how the word shibboleth came first to mean a password, then a party slogan, and, finally, the sham or hackneyed rallying cry of some fashionable or partisan cause.
6. Leckie, *op. cit.*, p. 38.
7. Halsey and Bryan, *op. cit.*, p. 108.
8. Tsuji, Masanobu, *Singapore: The Japanese Version* (New York: St. Martin's Press, 1960), p. 330.
9. *Ibid.*
10. Sherwood, Robert E., *Roosevelt and Hopkins: An Intimate History* (New York: Grosset & Dunlap, 1950), p. 622.

Chapter 4

1. Author's recollection.
2. *Ibid.*
3. Butterfield, *op. cit.*, p. 92.
4. Author's recollection.
5. *Ibid.*

6. McMillan, George, *The Old Breed: A History of the First Marine Division in World War Two* (Washington: Infantry Journal Press, 1949), p. 61.

7. Few historians agree on the exact time that the Battle of the Tenaru began. Therefore, I have relied on my own recollection and those of other participants.

8. McMillan, *op. cit.*, p. 62.

9. Vandegrift and Asprey, *op. cit.*, p. 142.

Chapter 5

1. Tanaka, Vice-Admiral Raizo, *Japan's Losing Struggle for Guadalcanal*, Part I (United States Naval Institute Proceedings, July 1956), p. 690.

2. *Ibid.*

3. Griffith, *op. cit.*, p. 90.

4. Hara, *op. cit.*, p. 109.

5. *Ibid.*

6. United States Strategic Bombing Survey, Interrogations of Japanese Officials (Washington: Naval Analysis Division, 1946), Vol. I, p. 31.

Chapter 6

1. Hara, *op. cit.*, p. 119.

2. Tanaka, *op. cit.*, p. 694d.

3. Griffith, *op. cit.*, p. 93.

4. Tanaka, *op. cit.*, p. 696.

5. *Ibid*, p. 697.

Chapter 7

1. Sherrod, Robert, *History of Marine Corps Aviation in World War II* (Washington: Combat Forces Press, 1952), p. 82.

2. Vandegrift and Asprey, *op. cit.*, p. 147.

PART III—AT BAY

Chapter 1

1. Vandegrift and Asprey, *op. cit.*, p. 149.

2. *Ibid.*

3. Author's recollection.

4. Tregaskis, *op. cit.*, p. 154.

5. Hara, *op. cit.*, p. 120.

6. Sherwood, *op. cit.*, p. 632.

Chapter 2

1. Unsigned article by Marine Combat Correspondent under dateline Avu-Avu, Guadalcanal, Nov. 27, 1942. Article quotes natives in vicinity of Tasimboko. On file in folder marked "Guadalcanal, Miscellaneous" at R&R, Arlington, Va.

2. Russell, Lord, of Liverpool, *The Knights of Bushido: The Shocking History of Japanese War Atrocities* (New York: Dutton, 1958), p. 269.

3. Griffith, *op. cit.*, p. 110.

4. *Ibid.*

5. Vandegrift and Asprey, *op. cit.*, p. 151.

6. Davis, *op. cit.*, p. 118.

7. *Ibid*, p. 119.

8. *Ibid*, p. 120.

9. Griffith, *op. cit.*, p. 112.

10. *Ibid*, p. 113.

11. Vandegrift and Asprey, *op. cit.*, p. 152.

12. *Ibid*, pp. 152, 153.

13. *Ibid*, p. 153.

14. *Ibid.*

15. *Ibid.*

16. Griffith, *op. cit.*, p. 115.

17. Vandegrift and Asprey, *op. cit.*, pp. 153, 154.

18. Griffith, *op. cit.*, pp. 116, 117.

19. *Ibid*, p. 118.

20. Undated and unsigned story filed by Marine Corps Combat Correspondent and included in "Guadalcanal, Miscellaneous" folder on file at R&R, Arlington, Va.

21. *Ibid*, quoted in interview with "Lt. Col. Reeder."

22. *Ibid.*

23. McMillan, *op. cit.*, p. 78.

24. *Ibid.*

25. Griffith, *op. cit.*, p. 119.

26. *Ibid.*

Chapter 3

1. *Jitsuroku Taiheiyo Senso* (Personal Records of the Pacific War). The Kawaguchi memoir: "Struggles of the Kawaguchi Detached Force." I am deeply indebted to Brig. Gen. Griffith for having provided me with a translation of this source.

2. Hara, *op. cit.*, p. 120.

3. Arnold, Gen. of the Army H. H., *Global Mission* (New York: Harper & Bros., 1949), p. 338.

4. *Ibid.*

5. Whyte, Capt. William H., Jr., *Hyakutake Meets the Marines,* Part I (*Marine Corps Gazette,* July 1945), p. 11. (Note: Captain Whyte was to become famous a decade later as author of *The Organization Man.*)

6. Author's conversations with pilots.
7. Clemens, *op. cit.,* p. 183.
8. Hanson Baldwin, *New York Times,* Nov. 3, 1942.

Chapter 4

1. Whyte, *op. cit.,* p. 9.
2. Sherrod, *op. cit.,* p. 91, fn.
3. Davis, *op. cit.,* pp. 135, 136.
4. Vandegrift and Asprey, *op. cit.,* p. 169.
5. *Ibid,* p. 170.
6. *Ibid.*
7. *Ibid,* p. 164.
8. *Ibid,* pp. 171, 172.
9. Griffith, *op. cit.,* p. 141.

PART IV—CRISIS

Chapter 1

1. Clear, *op. cit.,* p. 20.
2. *Ibid.*
3. Clemens, *op. cit.,* p. 193.
4. *Ibid.*
5. Pratt, Fletcher, *The Marines' War* (New York: William Sloane Associates, 1948), p. 76.
6. *Ibid,* pp. 76, 77.

Chapter 2

1. Quoted in full in Miller, John, Jr., *Guadalcanal: The First Offensive* (Washington: Office of the Chief of Military History, 1949), as Appendix A, pp. 357, 358.
2. Griffith, *op. cit.,* p. 147.
3. *Ibid.*
4. Hara, *op. cit.,* p. 137.

Chapter 3

1. Morison, Samuel Eliot, *The Struggle for Guadalcanal,* Vol. V, "History of the United States Naval Operations in World War II" (Boston: Little, Brown, 1959), p. 193.
2. Author's recollection.
3. Leckie, *op. cit.,* p. 82.
4. Tanaka, *Japan's Losing Struggle for Guadalcanal,* Part II (United States Naval Institute Proceedings, August 1956), p. 815.
5. *67th Fighter Squadron History Mar.–Oct. 1942,* quoted in Morison, *op. cit.,* p. 175.

6. Quoted in undated and unsigned Marine Combat Correspondent's report filed at R&R, Arlington, Va.

7. Morison, *op. cit.,* p. 176.

8. Sherrod, *op. cit.,* p. 102.

9. Griffith, *op. cit.,* p. 157.

Chapter 4

1. Leckie, *op. cit.,* p. 92.

2. Halsey and Bryan, *op. cit.,* p. 109.

Chapter 5

1. Monitored Japanese broadcasts, National Archives, Washington, D.C.

2. Simmons, Walter, *Joe Foss: Flying Marine* (New York: Dutton, 1943), p. 66.

3. Halsey and Bryan, *op. cit.,* p. 117.

Chapter 6

1. Hara, *op. cit.,* p. 125.

2. *Ibid,* p. 126.

3. *Ibid.*

4. *Ibid,* p. 127.

5. *Ibid.*

6. Seventeenth Army Operations, Office of the Chief of Military History (OCMH) File 8-51, AC 34.

7. Author's conversation with Puller.

8. Leckie, *op. cit.,* p. 99.

9. Davis, *op. cit.,* p. 155.

10. *Ibid.*

11. Davis, *op. cit.,* p. 156.

12. *Ibid,* p. 157.

13. *Ibid,* pp. 158, 159.

Chapter 7

1. Hara, *op. cit.,* p. 127.

2. *Ibid.*

3. Leckie, Robert, *Helmet for My Pillow* (New York: Random House, 1957), p. 118.

4. Sherwood, *op. cit.,* pp. 624, 625.

5. Seventeenth Army Operations.

6. Whyte, *Hyakutake Meets the Marines,* Part II (*Marine Corps Gazette,* August 1945), p. 41.

7. Hara, *op. cit.,* p. 128.

Chapter 8

1. Hara, *op. cit.*, p. 128.
2. Stafford, Cmdr. Edward P., *The Big E: The Story of the U.S.S. Enterprise* (New York: Random House, 1962), p. 165.
3. Pratt, *op. cit.*, p. 93.
4. Whyte, *op. cit.*, p. 42.

PART V—CRUX

Chapter 1

1. Tanaka, *op. cit.*, p. 818c.
2. Leckie, *op. cit.*, p. 119.
3. Author's recollection.
4. Hara, *op. cit.*, p. 135.
5. Clemens, *op. cit.*, pp. 241, 242.
6. Simmons, *op. cit.*, p. 96.
7. Arnold, *op. cit.*, p. 351.
8. Sims, Edward H., *Greatest Fighter Missions of the Top Navy and Marine Aces of World War II* (New York: Harper & Bros., 1962), p. 57.
9. Simmons, *op. cit.*, p. 102.
10. Halsey and Bryan, *op. cit.*, p. 123.
11. Boyington, Gregory ("Pappy"), *Baa Baa Black Sheep* (New York: Putnam, 1958), p. 128.
12. Leckie, *Strong Men Armed*, p. 119.
13. Davis, *op. cit.*, p. 166.
14. *Ibid.*
15. Halsey press interview on Guadalcanal, November 9, 1942.
16. *Ibid.*
17. Clemens, *op. cit.*, p. 249.
18. Vandegrift and Asprey, *op. cit.*, p. 196.

Chapter 2

1. Feldt, *op. cit.*, p. 101.
2. Hara, *op. cit.*, p. 138.
3. *Ibid.*
4. *Ibid.*
5. *Ibid.*
6. Tanaka, *op. cit.*, p. 821.
7. Hara, *op. cit.*, p. 140.
8. *Ibid*, pp. 140, 141.
9. *Ibid*, p. 141.
10. Morison, *op. cit.*, p. 242.
11. *Ibid.*
12. Author's conversations with pilots.
13. Tanaka, *op. cit.*, p. 821.

14. Morison, *op. cit.,* p. 263.
15. Morison, *op. cit.,* pp. 272, 273.
16. *Ibid,* p. 273.
17. *Ibid.*
18. *Ibid.*
19. Stern, Michael, *Into the Jaws of Death* (New York: McBride, 1944), p. 120.
20. *Ibid.*
21. *Ibid.*
22. Tanaka, *op. cit.,* p. 824a.

Chapter 3

1. *New York Times,* Wednesday, November 18, 1942.
2. Halsey and Bryan, *op. cit.,* p. 130.
3. Hayashi, Saburo, with Coox, Alvin D., *Kogun: The Japanese Army in the Pacific War* (Quantico: The Marine Corps Association, 1959), p. 62.

BIBLIOGRAPHY

Arnold, Gen. of the Army H. H., *Global Mission.* New York: Harper & Bros., 1949.

Blakeney, Jame, *Heroes: U.S.M.C.* Published by author, 1957.

Blankfort, Michael, *The Big Yankee: A Biography of Evans Carlson.* Boston: Little, Brown, 1947.

Boyington, Gregory, *Baa Baa Black Sheep.* New York: Putnam, 1958.

Bryant, Arthur, *The Turn of the Tide.* New York: Doubleday, 1957.

——, *Triumph in the West, A History of the War Years Based on the Diaries of Field-Marshal Lord Alanbrooke.* New York: Doubleday, 1959.

Bulkley, Capt. Robert J., Jr., *At Close Quarters: PT Boats in the United States Navy.* Washington: Naval History Division, 1962.

Butterfield, Roger, *Al Schmid: Marine.* New York: Farrar & Rinehart, 1944.

Carter, Rear Adm. Worral Reed, *Beans, Bullets and Black Oil; The Story of Fleet Logistics Afloat in the Pacific During World War II.* Washington: Naval History Division, 1952.

Churchill, Winston S., *Memoirs of the Second World War: An Abridgment of the Six Volumes of The Second World War.* Boston: Houghton Mifflin, 1959.

Clemens, Martin, *A Coastwatcher's Diary.* Unpublished manuscript.

Conn, Stetson, and Fairchild, Byron, *The Framework of Hemisphere Defense.* ("U. S. Army in World War II.") Washington: Office of the Chief of Military History, Dept. of the Army, 1960.

Craven, W. F., and Cate, J. L., (Eds.), *The Pacific: Guadalcanal to Saipan.* ("The Army Air Forces in World War II.") Chicago: Air Force Historical Division, 1961.

Cronin, Capt. Francis D., *Under the Southern Cross: The Saga of the Americal Division.* Washington: Combat Forces Press, 1951.

Davis, Burke, *Marine!: The Life of Chesty Puller.* Boston: Little, Brown, 1962.

DeChant, Capt. John A., *Devilbirds: The Story of United States Marine Corps Aviation in World War II.* New York: Harper & Bros., 1947.

Feldt, Cmdr. Eric A., R.A.N., *The Coastwatchers.* New York and Melbourne: Oxford University Press, 1946.

Fuchida, Capt. Mitsuo, and Okumiya, Cmdr. Masatake, *Midway: The Battle That Doomed Japan.* Annapolis: United States Naval Institute, 1955.

Greenfield, Kent Roberts (Ed.), *Command Decisions.* ("U. S. Army in World War II.") Washington: Office of the Chief of Military History, 1960.

Griffin, Alexander, *A Ship to Remember: The Saga of the Hornet.* New York: Howell, Soskin, 1943.

Griffith, Brig. Gen. Samuel B., II, *The Battle for Guadalcanal.* ("Great Battles Series.") Philadelphia and New York: Lippincott, 1963.

Halsey, Fleet Adm. William F., and Bryan, Lt. Cmdr. J., III, *Admiral Halsey's Story.* New York: McGraw-Hill Book Co., 1947.

Hara, Capt. Tameichi, with Saito, Fred, and Pineau, Roger, *Japanese Destroyer Captain.* New York: Ballantine Books, 1961.

Hayashi, Saburo, with Coox, Alvin D., *Kogun: The Japanese Army in the Pacific War.* Quantico: The Marine Corps Association, 1959.

Heinl, Col. Robert Debs, Jr., *Soldiers of the Sea: The U. S. Marine Corps, 1775–1962.* Annapolis: United States Naval Institute, 1962.

Hersey, John, *Into the Valley: A Skirmish of the Marines.* New York: Knopf, 1963.

Hough, Lt. Col. Frank O., *The Island War: The United States Marine Corps in the Pacific.* Philadelphia and New York: Lippincott, 1947.

Huie, William Bradford, *Can Do!: The Story of the Seabees.* New York: Dutton, 1944.

Isely, Jeter A., and Crowl, Philip A., *The U.S. Marines and Amphibious War.* Princeton: Princeton University Press, 1951.

Ito, Masanori, *The End of the Imperial Japanese Navy.* New York: Norton, 1956.

Johnston, Richard W., *Follow Me!: The Story of the Second Marine Division in World War II.* New York: Random House, 1948.

Kenney, Gen. George C., *General Kenney Reports.* New York: Duell, Sloan & Pearce, 1949.

King, Fleet Adm. Ernest J., and Whitehill, Cmdr. Walter M., *Fleet Admiral King: A Naval Record.* New York: Norton, 1952.

Leahy, Fleet Adm. William D., *I Was There.* New York: Whittlesley House, 1950.

Leckie, Robert, *Helmet for My Pillow.* New York: Random House, 1957.

———, *Strong Men Armed: The United States Marines Against Japan.* New York: Random House, 1962.

———, *The Story of World War II.* New York: Random House, 1964.

McMillan, George, *The Old Breed: A History of the First Marine Division in World War Two.* Washington: Infantry Journal Press, 1949.

———, et al., *Uncommon Valor: Marine Divisions in Action.* Washington: Infantry Journal Press, 1946.

Merillat, Capt. Herbert L., *The Island: A Personal Account of Guadalcanal.* Boston: Houghton Mifflin, 1944.

Miller, John, Jr., *Guadalcanal: The First Offensive.* ("U. S. Army in World War II.") Washington: Office of the Chief of Military History, 1949.

Milner, Samuel, *Victory in Papua: The Campaign in New Guinea.* ("U. S. Army in World War II.") Washington: Office of the Chief of Military History, 1957.

Morison,* Samuel Eliot, *The Rising Sun in the Pacific.* (*History of United States Naval Operations in World War II, Vol. III.*) Boston: Little, Brown, 1959.

———, *Coral Sea, Midway and Submarine Action.* (*History of United States Naval Operations in World War II, Vol. IV.*) Boston: Little, Brown, 1960.

* All Morison volumes cited are revised editions.

————, *The Struggle for Guadalcanal.* (*History of United States Naval Operations in World War II, Vol. V.*) Boston: Little, Brown, 1959.

————, *Breaking the Bismarcks Barrier.* (*History of United States Naval Operations in World War II, Vol. VI.*) Boston: Little, Brown, 1960.

————, *Aleutians, Gilberts and Marshalls.* (*History of United States Naval Operations in World War II, Vol. VII.*) Boston: Little, Brown, 1960.

————, *The Two-Ocean War: A Short History of the United States Navy in the Second World War.* Boston: Little, Brown, 1963.

Naval Chronology, World War II. Washington: Naval History Division, 1955.

Newcomb, Richard F., *Savo: The Incredible Naval Debacle off Guadalcanal.* New York: Holt, Rinehart & Winston, 1961.

Okumiya, Masatake, and Jiro, Horikoshi, with Caidin, Martin, *Zero: The Inside Story of Japan's Air War in the Pacific.* New York: Ballantine Books, 1956.

O'Sheel, Capt. Patrick, and Cook, Staff Sgt. Gene, *Semper Fidelis: The U. S. Marines in the Pacific.* New York: Hawthorn Books, 1960.

Pierce, Lt. Col. Philip N., and Hough, Lt. Col. Frank O., *The Compact History of the United States Marine Corp.* New York: Hawthorn Books, 1960.

Potter, E. B., and Nimitz, Fleet Adm. Chester W., *The Great Sea War: The Dramatic Story of Naval Action in World War II.* Englewood Cliffs: Prentice-Hall, 1960.

Pratt, Fletcher, *The Marines' War.* New York: William Sloane Associates, 1948.

Reischauer, Edwin O., *Japan: Past and Present.* New York: Knopf, 1964.

Robson, R. W., *The Pacific Islands Handbook, 1944.* New York: Macmillan, 1945.

Roscoe, Theodore, *United States Destroyer Operations in World War II.* Annapolis: United States Naval Institute, 1953.

————, *United States Submarine Operations in World War II.* Annapolis: United States Naval Institute, 1949.

Russell, Lord, of Liverpool, *The Knights of Bushido: The Shocking History of Japanese War Atrocities.* New York: Dutton, 1958.

Sakai, Saburo, with Caidin, Martin, and Saito, Fred, *Samurai: Flying the Zero in WW II with Japan's Fighter Ace.* New York: Ballantine Books, 1963.

Sherrod, Robert, *History of Marine Corps Aviation in World War II.* Washington: Combat Forces Press, 1952.

Sherwood, Robert E., *Roosevelt and Hopkins: An Intimate History.* New York: Grosset & Dunlap, 1950.

Shigemitsu, Premier Mamoru, *Japan and Her Destiny: My Struggle for Peace.* New York: Dutton, 1958.

Simmons, Walter, *Joe Foss: Flying Marine.* New York: Dutton, 1943.

Sims, Edward H., *Greatest Fighter Missions of the Top Navy and Marine Aces of World War II.* New York: Harper & Bros., 1962.

Smith, Gen. Holland M., *Coral and Brass: Howlin' Mad Smith's Own Story of the Marines in the Pacific.* New York: Scribner's, 1949.

Stafford, Cmdr. Edward P., *The Big E: The Story of the U.S.S. Enterprise.* New York: Random House, 1962.

Stern, Michael, *Into the Jaws of Death.* New York: McBride, 1944.

The War Reports of General of the Army George C. Marshall, General of the Army H. H. Arnold, and Fleet Admiral Ernest J. King. Philadelphia and New York: Lippincott, 1947.

Tregaskis, Richard, *Guadalcanal Diary.* New York: Popular Library, 1959.

Tsuji, Masanobu, *Singapore: The Japanese Version.* New York: St. Martin's Press, 1960.

United States Navy, *Medal of Honor, 1861–1949.* Washington: Naval History Division, 1950.

United States Strategic Bombing Survey (Pacific), *The Campaigns of the Pacific War.* Washington: Naval Analysis Division, 1946.

———, *Interrogations of Japanese Officials,* 2 vols. Washington: Naval Analysis Division, 1946.

Vandegrift, General Alexander A., and Asprey, Robert B., *Once a Marine: The Memoirs of General A. A. Vandegrift.* New York: Norton, 1964.

Williams, Mary H. (Compiler). *Chronology 1941–1945.* ("U. S. Army in World War II.") Washington: Office of the Chief of Military History, 1960.

Willoughby, Lt. Malcom F., *The U. S. Coast Guard in World War II.* Annapolis: United States Naval Institute, 1957.

Zimmerman, Maj. John L., *The Guadalcanal Campaign.* (Marine Corps Historical Monograph.) Washington: Historical Branch, U. S. Marine Corps, 1949.

PRIMARY SOURCES

Jitsuroku Taiheiyo Senso (Personal Records of the Pacific War). This work, as yet unpublished in English, includes the following seven memoirs, all bearing on Guadalcanal.

Gadarukanaru: Guadalcanal, by Col. Masanobu Tsuji, member of the General Staff of the Guadalcanal Expeditionary Forces of the Japanese Army.

Kawaguchi shitai no shito: Struggles of the Kawaguchi Detached Force, by Maj. Gen. Kiyotake Kawaguchi.

Tokyo kyuko: Tokyo Express, by Lt. Senzo Kabashima: His diary of bringing supplies to Guadalcanal aboard destroyer *Yudachi.*

Ue to shi no kiroku: Record of Hunger and Death, by Maj. Yasuhei Oneda: A personal account of Oneda's ordeal with the 230th Battalion of the 38th Regiment.

Ningen no genkai: Limit of Human Invulnerability, by Lt. Yasuo Obi, bearer of the colors of the 125th Infantry Regiment with the Kawaguchi Brigade.

Gadarukanaru-to sakusen keikaku: Military Strategy for the Guadalcanal Campaign, by Col. Takushiro Hattori, Chief of the Operations Section of the Imperial Headquarters of the Japanese Army.

Jigoku no mogura yuso: Mole Transportation in the Hell, by Cmdr. Teiji Yamaki, navigation officer of Submarine *I-41:* Description of attempts to supply the island by submarine.

First Marine Division Final Report. Research & Records (R&R) Historical Branch, U. S. Marine Corps.

Japanese Eighth Fleet War Diary. Office of Naval Records and Library (ONRL). Document No. 161259.

Seventeenth Army Operations. OCMH. File 8-51, AC 34.

The Imperial Japanese Navy in World War II. OCMH. File 8-5.1, AC 127.

Southeast Area Naval Operations. OCMH. File 8-5, AC 48.

Outline of Southeast Area Naval Air Operations, Parts II & III. OCMH. File 8-5.1, AC 121, 122.

Order of Battle of the Japanese Armed Forces. Unclassified document, R&R, File 045930.

PERIODICALS

Infantry Journal
Field Artillery Journal
Marine Corps Gazette
Leatherneck Magazine
United States Naval Institute Proceedings

INDEX

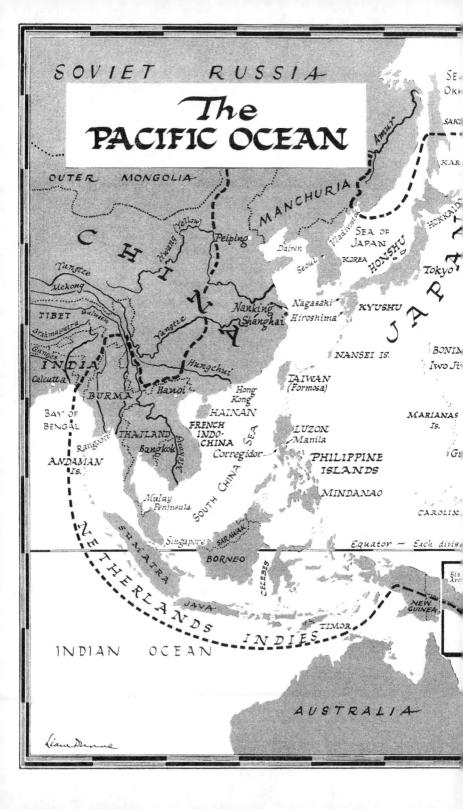

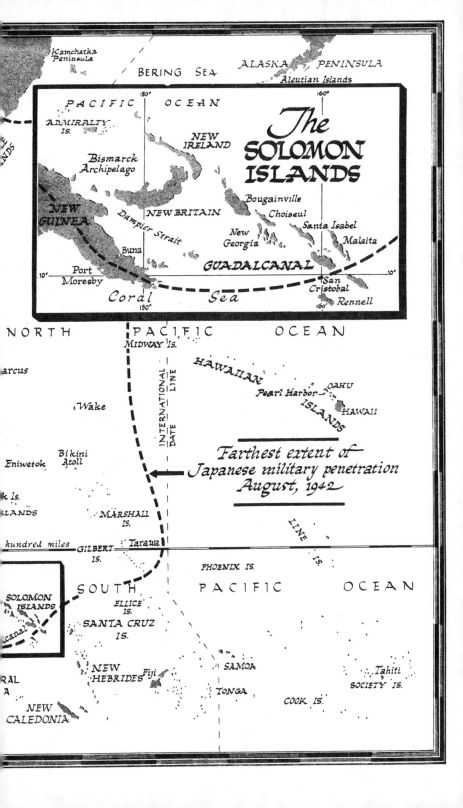

The Solomon Islands

Kamchatka Peninsula

BERING SEA — ALASKA PENINSULA
Aleutian Islands

PACIFIC OCEAN

ADMIRALTY IS.

Bismarck Archipelago

NEW IRELAND

NEW GUINEA

Dampier Strait

NEW BRITAIN

Buna

Port Moresby

Bougainville
Choiseul
Santa Isabel
New Georgia
Malaita

GUADALCANAL

San Cristobal

Coral Sea

Rennell

NORTH PACIFIC OCEAN

MIDWAY IS.

Marcus

Wake

INTERNATIONAL DATE LINE

HAWAIIAN ISLANDS

Pearl Harbor — OAHU

HAWAII

Eniwetok

Bikini Atoll

Farthest extent of Japanese military penetration August, 1942

MARSHALL IS.

LINE IS.

hundred miles

GILBERT IS. — Tarawa

PHOENIX IS.

SOUTH PACIFIC OCEAN

SOLOMON ISLANDS

Guadalcanal

ELLICE IS.

SANTA CRUZ IS.

NEW HEBRIDES

Fiji

SAMOA

TONGA

COOK IS.

Tahiti
SOCIETY IS.

NEW CALEDONIA